Leckie×Leckie

Scotland's leading educational publishers

N5 & CfE Higher
PSYCHOLOGY
STUDENT BOOK

Jonathan Firth

INTRODUCTION   **3**
Chapter 1: Introduction   **4**
What this book covers   4
What is psychology?   4
Structure of the course   5
The format of this textbook   6
Differences between units   7
Thinking psychologically   8

THE APPROACHES   **11**
Chapter 2: The approaches   **12**
Introduction to the approaches   12
The biological approach   18
The psychoanalytic approach   26
The cognitive approach   32
Approaches to psychology   39
The behaviourist approach   40
The evolutionary approach   48
Two further approaches: humanist and sociocultural   53

INDIVIDUAL BEHAVIOUR   **61**
Chapter 3: Sleep   **62**
The nature of sleep   62
Approaches to sleep and dreams   69
Theories of sleep and dreams   77
Real-world application: sleep disorders   81
Chapter 4: Psychopathology   **87**
What is psychopathology?   87
Common psychological disorders   94
Approaches to psychopathology   99
Theories of psychopathology   106
Real-world application: therapies   110
Chapter 5: Memory   **118**
The nature of memory   118
Approaches to memory   124
Theories of memory   131
Real-world application: eyewitness testimony   139
Chapter 6: Stress   **147**
What is stress?   147
Approaches to stress   155
Theories of stress   161
Real-world application: stress management   166
Chapter 7: Intelligence   **173**
Defining intelligence   173
Approaches to intelligence   180
Theories of intelligence   187
Testing intelligence   194

RESEARCH **201**

Chapter 8: Research **202**

The scientific method and the research process 202

Populations and samples 206

Experimental methods 211

Non-experimental methods 221

General research issues 231

Data and graphs 238

THE ASSIGNMENT **245**

Chapter 9: The Assignment **246**

Understanding the Assignment 246

Skills for the Assignment 247

National 5: planning and writing the Assignment 249

Higher: planning and writing the Assignment 257

Finalising the write-up 273

Appendix: Research materials for Assignment 275

SOCIAL BEHAVIOUR **277**

Chapter 10: Conformity **278**

The nature of conformity 278

Explanations of conformity 283

Obedience 289

Resisting social pressure 296

Chapter 11: Prejudice **305**

Prejudice, stereotypes and discrimination 305

Theories of stereotypes and prejudice 313

Reducing prejudice 321

Chapter 12: Non-verbal communication **328**

Aspects of NVC 328

Theories and debates in NVC: nature and nurture 334

Uses of NVC research 340

Chapter 13: Relationships **347**

The nature of relationships 347

Theories of relationships 357

Relationship conflict 364

KEY SKILLS **373**

Chapter 14: Key skills **374**

Tackling exam questions in psychology 375

Understanding research 381

Mnemonics 386

Added value 391

Practice questions on research (Higher only) 391

Answers **399**

Feedback **409**

References **410**

Index **425**

Introduction

1 Introduction

What this book covers

This textbook aims to help you develop the knowledge and skills needed to excel in your National 5 or Higher coursework and exam. Don't worry if you have never studied Psychology before – most people on this course are beginners, even at Higher level. If you are fortunate enough to be able to study National 5 one year followed by Higher the next year, then this textbook can be used for both years of study.

What is psychology?

A common and reasonable question is to ask what the study of Psychology is all about. In fact, you have asked psychological questions before – though perhaps you didn't realise it – whenever you have considered why someone behaves the way they do. If you have an idea about how people are affected by their parents or their friends, or why people get addicted to drugs, or what attracts one person to another, then you have the beginnings of a psychological theory or hypothesis. As a science, though, a theory is not enough in Psychology – we also need evidence. An important part of this subject is the research needed to find factual evidence about human behaviour.

It is worth dispelling a couple of myths before you start:

Myth: Psychology is all about mental illness. In fact, this is just one of a number of areas of study – and it is just as important to study what makes people happy and successful. In addition, only a small proportion of psychologists work as therapists. Some other psychology careers include sports psychology, forensic psychology, educational psychology, research and teaching.

Myth: Psychology is all about the brain. Studying the brain is not the same as studying the human mind. The study of the brain as an organ is known as neuroscience, and is a branch of biology. There are many important overlaps between the two, but the bulk of psychology does not involve looking at brains.

Myth: Psychology is all common sense. Psychology is based on the scientific method and regardless of what people *believe* to be true we need factual research evidence. Sometimes the evidence fits with what we consider common sense but sometimes it does not – many findings throughout the history of the subject have been highly unexpected.

Psychology involves the study of people's actions ('behaviour') and the thought processes in their minds, and is therefore often referred to as *the science of the mind and behaviour*. Have a look at the chapter headings in this book to get more of an idea about of the kind of areas that we study – though in fact, any type of behaviour can be (and probably is) studied by psychologists.

Structure of the course

In what order should the chapters be read? You may find that your school or college tackles the topics in a different order from the way they are presented in this textbook. Your teachers or lecturers will have chosen how to teach the course based on their knowledge and experience of the subject, and the chapters in this book can be used in more or less any order – though it may help to look at chapter 2 before tackling the topics in chapters 3 to 7.

Generally speaking, you will cover one of the optional topics in chapters 3 to 6, one of the optional topics in chapters 10 to 13; everything else is mandatory. Therefore, the following chapters, or at least part of them, should be studied by all learners at both National 5 and Higher:

- Approaches (chapter 2)
- Sleep (chapter 3)
- Research (chapter 8)
- The Assignment (chapter 9)
- Conformity (chapter 10)

All of these have differences depending on the level, and there is advice throughout the book to help you identify which part of the topics you need to focus on.

The National 5 and Higher Psychology courses include a free choice of two optional topics, and although this book covers the most popular options, it is possible that your school or college will choose a different topic. Refer to the Key Skills section at the end of the book to ensure that you understand how to tackle exam questions in any topic, and look out for further support materials on the Leckie and Leckie website.

There may be some topics that contain complex, philosophical issues that a teacher considers more appropriate to Higher than to National 5. However, all topics are presented in a way that is relevant to both National 5 and Higher, with guidance on differences between the two courses where appropriate, so the choice of topic for each course is left entirely up the learner and their school/college.

What's in the exam?

There is a single exam in this subject. For National 5, it asks about two to four topics:

- one to two of the topics from Individual Behaviour
- one to two of the topics from Social Behaviour

    (two to four topics in total – 90 minutes)

For Higher, there is also a section on the Research unit, so it is structured as follows:

- one section on Research
- one to two of the topics from Individual Behaviour
- one to two of the topics from Social Behaviour

    (three to five topics in total – 120 minutes)

Questions on approaches may be included within the sections on individual behaviour in both courses. At National 5, your understanding of research is integrated into the other topics and the Assignment, rather than forming a separate section in the exam.

The skills required to tackle exam questions successfully are explained in the final chapter of this book.

The format of this textbook

Each chapter on a topic area begins with a general description of the topic including key concepts, followed by an explanation of how approaches and/or theories are used in the topic, and a real-world application. Many research studies are integrated throughout the text, but certain studies that are especially important are highlighted in boxes and explained in more detail.

As the approaches to psychology relate to several different topics, a separate chapter has been devoted to them. In the subsequent chapters on Individual Behaviour topics, the most relevant approaches are highlighted, with an explanation of how they can be used to explain the topic.

Chapter 3 covers the mandatory topic, **sleep and dreams**. Chapters 4 to 7 cover four of the more popular optional topics from Individual Behaviour; you only need to study one of these for either National 5 or Higher. Check with your teacher/lecturer which topic you should focus on.

Chapters 8 and 9 cover the mandatory topic **research**, as well as the mandatory SQA coursework – the Assignment. These are linked together – research skills are assessed in the exam, but are also needed in order to conduct the Assignment (at National 5, an understanding of the research process is assessed in the Assignment, not in the exam).

Next comes the mandatory topic for social behaviour – **conformity**. Note that for Higher, this is referred to as 'conformity and obedience'. Everyone needs to study this topic, but National 5 students need to be careful to focus just on the elements that are relevant to that course, especially if you are learning in a mixed-level class, as the section on obedience is not required at N5.

The remaining chapters cover a selection of optional topics for Social Behaviour. Again, check with your teacher which one you should work on.

Each chapter also includes a number of short tasks or questions – so that you can continually test your own understanding as you progress – and provides an extended project to work on that will help you expand and consolidate your knowledge. These projects are not mandatory and will be smaller in scale than the Assignment, but will help you to develop research skills and add greater breadth and depth to the learning process. They also provide opportunities to develop research skills.

Differences between units

The 'Research' unit covers the skills and terminology of conducting scientific research in psychology. What you learn here will feed into the Assignment and to your learning of research in the other units, and it is therefore very important.

The other two units are very similar to each other in format: each contains two topics, one of which is mandatory. One is 'Individual Behaviour' which means aspects of psychology that are mainly studied by looking at one person in isolation. In contrast, 'Social Behaviour' covers areas of psychology where it is impossible to look at people in isolation and we instead study how people interact in pairs and groups.

Some key differences between the units include:

- Approaches are only specified as part of Individual Behaviour. They may also be relevant to some parts of the Social Behaviour unit – and you can get credit for making these links – but you are not required to explain them in assessments.

- Only Social Behaviour exam questions ask for **evaluation** of research evidence. However, evaluation of evidence is a useful skill throughout the course, and you should be aware of strengths/weaknesses of all major research studies.

- The Social Behaviour unit documents state that you can study 'theories and/or 'concepts'. What are concepts? Put simply, this just means an idea that you should be able to explain, but is not an entire theory or model. An example would be explaining what is meant by 'discrimination' when studying the topic of prejudice. This might seem a minor point but the implications are large – it means that concepts and theories can be seen as interchangeable in these topics (chapters 10 to 13), and in some cases it is sufficient to study just concepts and no full theories.

🔎 **Top tip**

SQA documents can be changed. ALWAYS check the most recent version of key course documents.

🔎 **Top tip**

Discuss exam format and assessment standards with your teacher or lecturer.

🔎 **Top tip**

Familiarise yourself with the format of SQA's specimen question paper.

Thinking psychologically

This course will help you to think psychologically and scientifically – a mindset that you can apply to your everyday life. Using psychological knowledge to improve your own life and other people's wellbeing in the real world is called **psychological literacy.** To get the most out of this course, don't just focus on preparing for your exam, but tackle the subject more widely – read current articles about psychology online, or in student magazines. Try to make connections between psychology and the real life situations that you are interested in.

You may feel confident enough to tackle some books related to psychology too. The following are very easy reads and ideal places to start. All are available as ebooks, or try asking your librarian:

- *What the Dog Saw* by Malcolm Gladwell
- *The Man who Mistook his Wife for a Hat* by Oliver Sacks
- *The Naked Ape* by Desmond Morris
- *Mindset* by Carol Dweck
- *Elephants on Acid: and Other Bizarre Experiments* by Alex Boese
- *Night School: Wake Up to the Power of Sleep* by Richard Wiseman
- *They F*** You Up: How to Survive Family Life* by Oliver James

If tackling these books seems daunting, remember that academic and popular science books are not novels, so you <u>don't</u> need to read them from cover to cover! Read the start, dip in to whichever chapters sound relevant, and skip bits that are of less interest.

> **🔍 Top tip**
>
> See chapter 7 for a discussion of Dweck's 'mindset' theory.

The approaches

2 The approaches

Some approaches are mandatory in Higher and National 5 Psychology and others are optional.

For **Higher**, you should know and understand:

- The key features of the biological and cognitive approaches to sleep, dreams and sleep disorders.
- The key features of one other approach to sleep, dreams and sleep disorders.
- The key features of any three approaches relating to an optional topic in individual behaviour.

For **National 5**, you should know and understand:

- The key features of the biological and psychoanalytic approaches to sleep and dreams.
- The key features of any two approaches relating to an optional topic in individual behaviour. (Note that at least one additional approach must be learned in the option topic, i.e. not the same two approaches as used for sleep and dreams.)

You also need to develop the following skills:

- Using approaches to explain topics within the course.
- Identifying links between approaches and research methods.
- Using research evidence to support statements of fact.

Eating and thinking are exmaples of behaviours

Introduction to the approaches

Why do we behave the way we do? Most issues in psychology are based on this fundamental question. Psychologists try to explain why we act the way we do and why we think the way we do. They try to explain all kinds of **behaviour**. In psychology, the word behaviour can be used very broadly and refer to all kinds of human actions. Shouting, eating, kissing, thinking or picking your nose – all of these are examples of behaviours.

Of course, behaviours usually don't happen for no reason, but are the reaction to something, such as when someone is rude to you and you get angry. Two other psychological terms are useful here – a **stimulus** is a very general word that means anything from the environment which impacts on an individual. This could be anything from a person smiling at you, to hearing music, to an uncomfortable seat. Essentially, a stimulus is anything that can be detected by your senses (Watson, 1913). It is a neutral word, which does not imply that anything good or bad is happening; the plural is 'stimuli'. For example, '…*the stimulus in this experiment was a serious of short noises played through* *headphones...'* A **response** is another general word meaning any action or biological reaction (i.e. any *behaviour*) that results from a stimulus. If someone tells you a joke and you laugh, the joke is a stimulus and the laughter is a response.

As well as actions, psychologists are of course interested in **the mind**. Psychology would like to explain why people have particular ideas, moods and attitudes, and how these things connect to behaviour. A general term for all of the activities of the mind is our **thought processes**.

Fundamentally, we are interested in thought processes, but the main thing we can observe is behaviour. The two things are linked and sometimes very hard to separate, and both are very much studied. Psychology is therefore often referred to as *the science of the mind and behaviour.*

Laughing is a reponse to the stimulus of a joke

Scientific explanations

In everyday life, people use many ways of trying to explain why behaviours occur, but most explanations are not very systematic. We might rely on assumptions, and our explanations are likely to be affected by prejudices and by the viewpoint of our particular culture. We may observe a stimulus and a response, and jump to a conclusion that the two must be directly connected.

For example, how would you explain it if someone commits a crime? Look at the following example:

? **Discussion point**
Do you understand what is meant by a stimulus and a response? Can you think of another example?

Rob's case

Rob was 14. His teacher shouted at him, and he was sent to stand outside the classroom. Instead of staying there, he ran out of school, picked up a stone, and smashed the window of a shop.

Our everyday explanations might look at the event at school that made Rob angry and prompted him to act that way. We might also think of Rob's parents and other role models, or say that he had something in his basic character that made him more at ease breaking rules than most people are. These explanations might have an element of truth, but they are not scientific explanations that have been tested or that rule out other variables.

In contrast, psychologists try to explain behaviour by studying it scientifically. They conduct experiments, often keeping conditions constant and changing just a single thing, to see what effect it has on behaviour. This is called an experiment and it is a key part of the scientific method. You will learn more about **research methods** in chapter 8.

Different approaches to psychology

The history of psychology has been dominated by conflicting explanations for behaviour and thought processes. These are called **approaches** to psychology. A key part of the Individual Behaviour unit in this course will be to understand these approaches and use them to explain human behaviour.

For any behaviour, there is more than one explanation for why it occurred. As the evidence we have may not be complete, there can be a scientific debate as to how best to explain the available evidence. Just as geologists might study rock samples and debate processes such as glaciation, so, too, psychologists try to make sense of the available evidence and draw conclusions.

The nature-nurture debate

A good example of different approaches is the well-known **nature-nurture debate**. In the previous section, a *nature* explanation would say that Rob is basically a bad person, perhaps with genes that made him more likely to commit an aggressive act. A *nurture* explanation would focus on Rob's upbringing, and look at the influence of his parents as well as social pressure from his friends in order to understand why he committed the act of vandalism.

Psychologists have been arguing both sides of the nature-nurture debate for years, but the choice is now seen as over-simplistic, as it has become clear that both nature and nurture can influence behaviour. Also, it is important to separate out different aspects of nature or nurture. For example, on the nurture side, what is more important – parental upbringing or the social group that we join?

What is more important – parental upbringing or the social group that we join?

> ### Make the link
>
> ...between the nature-nurture debate in Psychology and in other subjects such as Modern Studies.

What is an approach?

An approach is a particular way of looking at psychology and it involves certain key beliefs about human behaviour and the human mind. It can include:

- Particular types of theories: for example, some approaches prefer logical flow charts, some have highly mathematical theories and others prefer general concepts.
- Particular methods of study: whether researchers in the approach prefer experiments, surveys, case studies, etc.
- Particular areas of study: approaches tend to link to particular topics. However, as you will see during this course, topics can be explained using more than one approach, and psychologists do not often agree on which approach is the most useful.

Several approaches

The psychological approaches are more detailed and sophisticated explanations of behaviour. The short explanations that follow summarise eight major ways of explaining behaviour in a simplified form:

One viewpoint says that our brain is directly controlling what we do

- Due to the brain. One viewpoint says that our brain is directly controlling what we do and that our brain chemistry determines how we react to things.

- Due to upbringing. The person's personality and tendencies throughout life are shaped by our early experiences, for example, by strict/loving parents.

- Due to hidden emotions and thoughts that we are not even aware of (in the 'unconscious' parts of the mind).

- Conscious decision making and/or information processing. A person has a set of beliefs and knowledge that allows them to decide what to do. This perspective thinks our behaviour is based on rational choices.

- Due to learning, and the good or bad outcomes of interactions. The person has associated good outcomes with certain behaviours and now does those things more (and vice-versa for bad outcomes).

- As a product of our genes and evolution. Some psychologists think that behaviours are determined mainly by genetics, and that these genes evolved through natural selection because they helped our ancestors to survive.

- Human nature. Although people are basically good at heart, most people are not truly themselves because they have been treated badly in life and do not make the most of themselves.

- Culture and society. We learn how to behave from the people around us, and can be 'programmed' by our society. What we consider 'normal' depends strongly on our culture.

Some psychologists think that behaviours are determined mainly by genetics

Discuss how these explanations can apply to some human behaviours such as the following:

- why people get angry when they are insulted
- why some people work hard and others do not
- why many people are afraid of harmless animals like spiders
- why people have bad habits like biting their nails
- why someone dislikes a particular food

Feedback on discussion
In principle, any of the approaches can be used to explain any of the behaviours. The examples below show two fairly straightforward possibilities for each one, but well done if you considered other combinations.

- Getting angry when insulted
  Hidden emotions: threats to self-esteem may lead to a defensive reaction that we do not consciously understand. Genes and evolution: in our evolutionary past, it may have been advantageous to try to achieve higher status, and therefore to react aggressively to insults.

- Why some people work hard and others do not
  Upbringing: parental behaviour may play a role, with parents as role models. Human nature: some people may be fulfilling their

Top tip

Note how most of these approaches are based on either nature or nurture, but focus on a specific aspect.

How can nail biting be explained by the approaches?

full potential, while others have unfulfilled potential due to negative life circumstances.

- Why many people are afraid of harmless animals
  Genes and evolution: in our evolutionary past, these animals (or similar ones) might have presented much more of a threat than they do today. Learning: we may have had a bad experience with a particular animal in our early childhood, for example being barked at by a dog, or having seen someone else scream at a spider.

- Why people have habits
  The brain: certain brain areas give us a sense of reward/pleasure from our habits. Hidden emotions: habits such as nail biting may relate to unconscious emotions from childhood such as wanting to be fed as a baby.

- Why someone dislikes a particular food
  Culture and society: we tend to like what is normal to us, and foods that are unfamiliar for our culture may seem strange or unappealing. Conscious decision-making: we may have a belief that a particular food is dangerous or unhealthy, and have therefore decided not to eat it.

Which approaches should I learn?

Applying approaches to explain ideas in psychology is a challenging but very rewarding skill. The approaches are not a separate topic – you will use approaches to explain both of the topics in the Individual Behaviour unit. They are presented here as a separate chapter because the same approaches can be applied to several different topics.

For the purposes of assessments, the recommended and mandatory approaches vary depending on the course (National 5 or Higher) and the topic studied:

- Three approaches for each topic at Higher (can be the same approaches for both topics).
- Two approaches for each topic at National 5 (however, at least three must be learned overall, so it can't be the same ones for both topics).

The following table summarises which approaches you need to know for both mandatory and optional topics. As you can see, one possible way to simplify things is to use the biological, cognitive and psychoanalytic approaches for all topics in both courses, but you should listen to advice from your teacher or lecturer here. The choice of approach may depend on which option topic is selected – some topics have a more straightforward link with particular approaches. Several optional approaches are covered in this chapter.

🔍 Top tip

There is a degree of overlap between approaches and theories in this course. This is because most theories are based on a particular approach.

Course	Topic	Mandatory approaches	Optional approaches
Higher	Sleep, dreams and sleep disorders	Biological and Cognitive	Any one other
Higher	Individual behaviour – optional topic	none	Any three
National 5	Sleep and dreams	Biological and Psychoanalytic	None
National 5	Individual behaviour – optional topic	none	Any two (but at least one must be different from sleep and dreams topic)

GO! Activities

1. Look at the eight short explanations above again. Can you use them to explain a more complex behaviour, such as why Rob committed an act of violence? How about explaining why people fall in love or what job they choose to do? You may need to use a combination of approaches for this. Take some notes and report them back to fellow students or write a blog post with your ideas.

2. Discuss the optional approaches with classmates and your teacher/lecturer, and make sure you know which topics you will be studying, and which approaches you should apply to each topic.

⚷ Key concepts

- Behaviour
- Stimulus
- Response
- The mind
- Thought processes
- Research methods
- Approach
- Nature-nurture debate

Sample answer for Rob's case

Rob's parents may have been very strict

- Brain: some violent killers have been shown to have brain abnormalities – it is possible (though unlikely) that Rob has this kind of abnormality.
- Upbringing: Rob's parents may have encouraged aggression in some way such as by being aggressive role models, or alternatively they may have been very strict and he may be rebelling.
- Hidden emotions: Rob may be directing the anger he feels towards his teacher/peers/parents at an easier target by breaking the window.
- Decision making: Rob may have rationally decided it would be a waste of time to stand outside the classroom, and he would rather have some fun.
- Learning: perhaps Rob has done this in the past and been rewarded by attention and special treatment, or just by the fun of breaking things.
- Genes: humans, especially males, have a history of violence. Rob has inherited genes for anger and aggression.
- Human nature: Rob could be a good person but he is constantly getting a hard time from parents and teachers and perhaps being bullied too. Until he is in a warmer and more accepting environment, he can't be his true, creative self.
- Culture: Rob has grown up seeing violence all around him and on TV and he has learned that it is an appropriate response to dealing with problems. Also, he may be a member of an aggressive subculture such as a gang or be experiencing peer pressure that encourages him to appear as a rebel.

The biological approach explains aggressive behaviour in terms of hormones like testosterone

The biological approach

The **biological approach** tries to explain behaviour in terms of the biological processes within our bodies, especially the brain, our genes and chemicals such as hormones and neurotransmitters. For example, researchers into aggression who take a biological approach to psychology have tried to explain aggressive behaviour in terms of hormones such as testosterone, or in terms of parts of the brain that regulate emotion. This contrasts with researchers from other approaches who have tried to explain aggressive behaviour in terms of parenting and life experiences.

This approach uses an understanding of the human body to explain behaviour. There are four key biological processes that the approach focuses on:

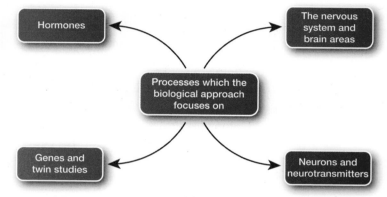

The nervous system and brain areas

A key aim of this approach is to understand the links between the **nervous system** and psychological processes. The nervous system is the network of nerve cells around your body, including the brain, the spinal cord, and all of the nerves that connect the brain and spinal cord to your organs, muscles and sense organs. In particular, the nervous system divides into two main branches – the central nervous system and the peripheral nervous system, each of which can be further divided up:

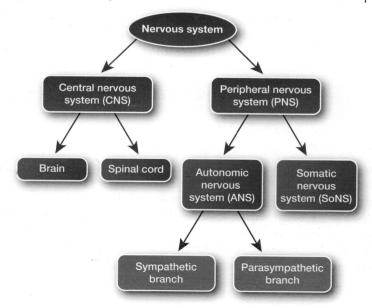

The central nervous system is comprised of **the brain** and spinal cord, and of particular interest to psychology is the brain – the largest and most complex part of the nervous system. Biological psychologists believe that all thoughts and behaviour ultimately depend on brain function. More complex thought processes are thought to take place in the outermost part of the brain, the cerebral cortex, and in particular, the outer layers of the cerebral cortex – the **neocortex**. This is the main part that you can see if you look at a picture of the outside of a human brain. The neocortex is proportionately smaller in other mammals and does not exist at all in fish or insects. It is often shown as comprising four main areas called lobes – the frontal, parietal, occipital and temporal lobes, though it is actually one continuous layer of cells:

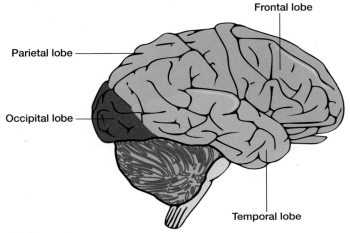

Frontal lobe

Parietal lobe

Occipital lobe

Temporal lobe

The brain

> ### 🔍 Top tip
>
> The neocortex is composed of the six outer layers of the cerebral cortex. There are other layers underneath it that are called the allocortex. However, psychologists tend to be more interested in the neocortex, as most of our advanced psychological abilities are processed there. *'Neo'* means 'new' – it is the most recently evolved part of the brain.

While biological psychologists believe that the brain and nervous system are responsible for our behaviour, it is difficult to know exactly what area(s) of the brain are involved in any particular behaviour or thought process. It has been a major aim of the biological approach to find out the functions of different areas of the brain. The idea that particular brain areas each have a specific function is called **localisation**.

In the early days of medical anatomy, the brain was a mystery; unlike other parts of the body, it is impossible to guess the function of a brain area simply by looking at it. A breakthrough came in the 1800s when surgeon Paul Broca studied a patient who had lost the ability of speech, but still understood language and had nothing physically wrong with his mouth or throat. Examining the patient's brain *post mortem*, Broca found that a small area of the frontal lobe was missing. Broca realised that this area must be vitally important for speech production; it became known as 'Broca's area'.

Since the 1800s, many further cases have been studied and researchers have found out about the function of many areas of the brain, and new techniques have been developed. Towards the back of the neocortex, for example, a huge area processes information from the eyes in order to perceive different shapes and textures. Also important is the frontal lobe, which is essential for planning and decision making, and the **limbic system**, where our emotions are processed. Loss of any of these

The brain studied by Broca, at the Dupuytren museum in Paris

key areas due to brain damage could have dramatic effects, making us lose key thought processes or emotions.

Through the 20th century, new techniques were developed that allowed researchers to study individuals who had suffered brain damage as well as healthy individuals. Two interesting techniques include:

Electrical stimulation

Researcher Wilder Penfield was an expert on the structure of the brain. He performed surgery on damaged brain areas of patients with severe epilepsy to try to stop electrical activity spreading from these areas throughout the cerebral cortex. Penfield's aim was to surgically remove this damaged area in order to stop the seizures from occurring. In order to do so with minimum harm to the patient, Penfield used an electrical probe that stimulated areas of the exposed brain on the operating table, while the patient was still conscious. Remarkably, patients reported vivid sensations and thoughts coming to mind when particular areas of their brain were electrically stimulated. One patient famously said, 'I smell burnt toast!' These medical investigations suggested that particular areas of the brain may be responsible for very specific psychological functions.

Another useful brain scan is called an electroencephalogram or **EEG**. This does not give an image of what the brain looks like, but instead measures the electrical activity of the brain, that is, the 'brain waves'.

Brain scans

Viewing the activity of a living brain is much easier nowadays due to the invention of brain scans. One of the most useful types, the **fMRI scan** (functional magnetic resonance imaging), involves measuring the activity of different brain areas by scanning for oxygen use using an electromagnet. Tiny changes in the brain's oxygen use can be detected and analysed using the scanner's computer. This is very useful to psychologists because it gives a picture of brain activity as someone is doing a task – if someone is reading, for example, visual and verbal areas would be 'lit up' on the scan because those areas are active and therefore using more oxygen.

Another useful brain scan is called an electroencephalogram or EEG. This doesn't give a image of what the brain looks like, but instead measures the electrical activity of the brain i.e. the 'brain waves'. This is an essential tool when studying sleep patterns.

With this new technology, biological psychologists are starting to find out more about how the brain controls behaviour and which brain areas are responsible for cognitive functions such as language, memory and intelligence.

A Canadian stamp celebrating Wilder Penfield

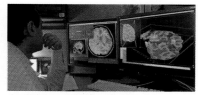

An fMRI scan of the the brain

EEG electrodes

📖 Key study: Raine *et al.* (1997): study of brain abnormalities in murderers

Aim: The study aimed to find out whether there are differences in the brains of people who commit violent crimes.

Method: This was a quasi-experiment. One group of participants consisted of 41 people (39 male, two female) who had been charged with murder and had pled not guilty on the grounds of insanity, then been referred for brain scans. They were compared with a control group of 41 people with no convictions.

Findings: The scans showed a lower level of activity in the prefrontal cortex, as well as in the corpus callosum – the area of fibres that connects the two sides of the brain. They also found that the murderers had more asymmetric brain function, with one side more active than the other in several areas.

Evaluation: This study provided an interesting perspective on how serious crimes may be linked to reduced brain function. However, we cannot be sure why these brain differences existed, and it is certainly not possible to determine a cause and effect relationship between brain abnormalities and murder – for example, we can't scan everyone's brain and determine who is going to commit a murder! Brain scans are useful but it is not always clear what a lower level of brain activity actually means. Also, murder is a varied crime, and it is hard to generalise to all murderers, or to people who commit other crimes.

Dr Adrian Raine showing a 3D MRI scan of a murderer's brain

Neurons and neurotransmitters

The human brain is composed of billions of individual brain cells and biological psychologists have become aware of the importance of the way these cells communicate with each other and interact. The most important cells are called neurons – these are the cells that process information and control behaviour.

> 🔍 **Top tip**
>
> The Raine *et al.* (1997) study could also be used as research evidence in the psychopathology topic.

In the late 1940s, Donald Hebb proposed the first major theory of the biological approach. He suggested that when we learn things, neurons in our brains are changed, with synapses between these cells being strengthened or new ones forming (Hebb, 1949). At the time, microscopes were not advanced enough to study the connections between neurons, and so nobody could check whether Hebb was correct. However, since that time, the electron microscope has been invented, and the general principle of Hebb's idea has been supported by later research – neurons do change their structure through experience (Kandel & Hawkins, 1992).

Neurotransmitters are messenger chemicals that are released into the gap between two neurons, called the **synapse**. Drugs can interfere with this process, as can be easily observed any time someone you know consumes a psychoactive drug such as alcohol – alcohol and other drugs work by interfering with or mimicking neurotransmitters in the synapses of a person's brain.

It is really important to have a basic understanding of how brain cells communicate. It will help you to understand medical treatments and the effects of drugs in the other topics. Also, this is an efficient thing to learn – all neurons work in essentially the same way – so learn about one, and you will understand billions.

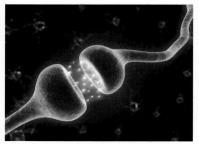

An artist's impression of a synapse

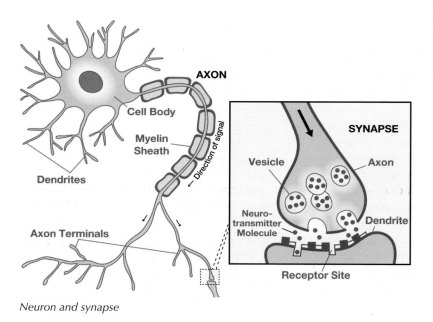

Neuron and synapse

Hormones

A **hormone** is a chemical that is released by a gland in the body that can affect our organs, including the brain. We have often heard moody behaviour of friends and family members, particularly adolescents, described in terms of 'hormones'. Is this idea based in reality – do hormones affect our behaviour and moods?

Some hormone levels change as we enter puberty, and several major mental illnesses also first appear at this stage of life – for example, the eating disorder *anorexia nervosa* tends to be diagnosed at around age 14. Depression is found in children, but from puberty onwards, it is more common in females. Angold *et al.* (1999) concluded that this difference was best explained in terms of hormonal changes (see chapter 4 for more information on these psychological disorders).

Hormones can affect our behaviour throughout life, usually in a helpful way – in fact, they play an essential role in governing mood, sleep, sexual arousal and many other functions. The hormone melatonin is released at night to help us start to feel sleepy as it gets darker, while stress hormones are an important part of how we react to threats.

One hormone has an especially positive effect – **oxytocin**, sometimes called the 'love hormone' is essential for bonding. It is released in large amounts when a woman gives birth, promoting an immediate strong emotional bond to be formed with the new baby (Gordon *et al.*, 2010). The same hormone also plays a large role in romantic relationships later in life, being released during attraction and helping to maintain fidelity (Scheele *et al.*, 2012; see chapter 13). The biological approach, therefore, tries to explain a range of processes from mental illness to falling in love in terms of hormones.

Oxytocin is released in large amounts when a women gives birth, promoting an immediate strong emotional bond

Genes and twin studies

In every human cell, there is a set of **chromosomes**, made of DNA, which control the development and behaviour of that cell. Each chromosome is made up of a number of functional units called **genes**. Each gene can control the development of proteins, and therefore, has an effect on how that cell works. Just as your genes can influence your physical appearance, for example, by making your skin and eyes a particular colour, it appears that the genes that control the development of the nervous system can have an effect on psychological processes too. Numerous psychological disorders are associated with genetic factors – both depression and schizophrenia are more likely to occur if a parent or identical twin has the disorder (e.g. McGuffin *et al.*, 1996 – see chapter 4).

One way of studying the effect of genes on behaviour is the **twin study**, where the researcher looks at one or more sets of identical twins. If one twin has a psychological disorder or an exceptional talent, what are the chances that the other twin has it as well? Of course, twins may have had a very similar upbringing to each other, and therefore, it is not just their genes that are similar – their environment is too. One way around this is to compare identical twins (who share 100% of their genes) with fraternal twins (who share approximately 50%, the same as any brother or sister). Numerous research studies have suggested that identical twins tend to share more characteristics, as evidenced by a greater level of similarity between identical than non-identical twins in areas such as intelligence, personality and the chance of having a mental illness.

Twin studies are used to examine the effects of genes on behaviour

? Discussion point

What is meant by 'et al.' in research? Why is it used? (See p.409 for feedback.)

Evaluation of the biological approach

It is usually an oversimplification to link a psychological process to a single brain area. Researchers are increasingly linking psychological functions to pathways involving several brain areas and the connections between them. In addition, there are individual differences in brain structure, and the brain can reprogramme itself through experience (Doidge, 2007).

Although Kandel and Hawkins (1992) found support for Hebbian learning, they also found it to be oversimplified, as there are other mechanisms by which brain cells strengthen their connections, not just the strengthening of a synapse. More recent research by Sheffield and Dombeck (2015) suggested that dendrites and cell body might be active at different times, which goes against the traditional biological theory of how cells communicate and form memories.

Stress in childhood could determine whether a gene is expressed

The biological approach explains disorders such as depression and attention deficit hyperactivity disorder (ADHD) in terms of genes and disordered brain chemistry. However, Brown and Harris (1978) researched social factors in depression (e.g. unemployment) and found that working class women were five times as likely to be depressed as middle-class women, while prevalence of depression is much higher in the USA (17%) compared to Japan (3%). ADHD is rarely diagnosed in France. These findings suggest that biological factors cannot explain psychological disorders and that culture and society must play a role too.

Genes can be influenced by our surroundings and upbringing – they can be 'switched on and off'. Whether they are **expressed** or not can depend on what happens in our environment. It is therefore impossible to predict how a person will act just by studying their genes. Stress in childhood is one possible environmental influence that could determine whether a gene is expressed (Raj & van Oudenaarden, 2008). The study of gene expression is known as epigenetics.

✔ Questions

1. What is the technical name for a brain cell?

2. What is the name for the part of the nervous system that includes the brain and spinal cord?

3. What area of the frontal lobe plays a key role in speech?

4. What particular psychological process is associated with the limbic system?

5. Which hormone plays an important role in love, trust and bonding?

6. Name two psychological disorders that show considerable changes after puberty.

7. What is the name for the type of body part that releases hormones?

8. What is the name for the functional part of a chromosome?

9. What does it mean if a gene is not 'expressed'?

10. What does 'et al' stand for in a research citation?

●━ Key concepts

- Biological approach
- Nervous system
- The brain
- Neocortex
- Localisation
- Limbic system
- fMRI scan
- EEG
- Synapse
- Hormone
- Oxytocin
- Chromosomes
- Twin study
- Expression (of genes)

GO! Activities

1. Draw a labelled diagram of both the brain and a neuron. Label all parts of the neuron. Label as many brain areas as you can and write a short description of what each one does. It doesn't need to be a work of art – just try to make it clear.

2. Make your labelled diagram of the brain into a mini-poster. You could focus on a particular part of the brain or certain parts e.g. the lobes, or brain parts related to language. Put your mini-poster up in your study space or classroom.

The psychoanalytic approach

The **psychoanalytic approach** (also called 'psychodynamic') emphasises the role of the **unconscious** mind in human behaviour, and states that childhood and interactions with our parents can shape personality. It was founded by Sigmund Freud, an Austrian doctor who came to believe that many physical illnesses had psychological causes. He thought that a large part of the mind was hidden to us, and that it would require his talking therapy - **psychoanalysis** - for people to uncover and deal with the hidden conflicts in their minds. Freud made extensive use of case studies of individuals rather than experiments, and made a huge contribution to the development of psychotherapy.

'…we come to the conclusion, from working with hysterical patients and other neurotics, that they have not fully succeeded in repressing the idea to which the incompatible wish is attached. They have, indeed, driven it out of consciousness and out of memory, and apparently saved themselves a great amount of psychic pain, but in the unconscious the suppressed wish still exists…'

Source: Freud (1910, p.189)

Sigmund Freud

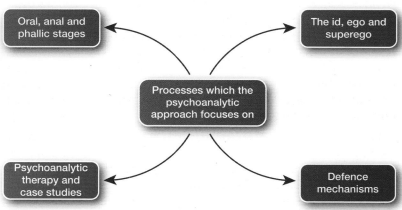

The id, ego and superego

Freud initially thought that the mind was divided into two parts – the conscious and unconscious. However, in his later writings, he explained that there are three main parts to the mind: the **id**, the **ego** and the **superego** (Freud, 1933):

- The id is the unconscious mind. It is the first to develop during childhood. Its motivations are simple and it desires pleasure and gratification. Like a very young child, the id does not understand rules or consequences. Nevertheless, it provides energy for the other parts of the mind, via the libido.

- The ego is the conscious mind – the part you are aware of and that controls all of our rational thoughts.

- The superego is partly conscious and partly unconscious. It is our awareness of society's rules, and therefore provides us with a moral sense of right and wrong. If we do things that our superego does not approve of, then we get a feeling of guilt.

Freud thought that the id (unconscious) was the source of energy and drives. One of the most important of these was the drive to obtain pleasure, and he called this the **libido**. Libido can be thought of as our sex drive, but is perhaps better seen more generally as 'desire'. Freud thought that even in childhood the libido motivates behaviour, although not in the same way as for adults (Freud, 1910).

Psychological problems can arise from **conflicts** between the conscious and unconscious. The rational ego may be urging a person to do one thing, but the irrational id is prompting them to do something different. Like an iceberg, the largest and most powerful part of the mind – the unconscious – was thought to be beneath the surface. The term **preconscious** is used to mean things that are not consciousness at the time – that is, we are not thinking about them – but they could become conscious (Freud, 1933). Our memories fall into this category.

The ego / superego / id iceberg

Oral, anal and phallic stages

Freud developed a controversial theory of how people's minds develop through childhood. He thought that just as adults get physical pleasure from sex, so children get pleasure from their bodies too, but from different body parts. He thought that a baby derives pleasure from its mouth (being fed) and called the associated period of development the **oral stage**. He also thought that toddlers get pleasure from controlling bladder and bowel movements when going to the toilet/potty. This was called the **anal stage**.

This theory was not just about explaining behaviour during breast-feeding or toilet training – Freud though that these stages had an important influence on later personality, too. He explained that some people develop a **fixation** in these stages, leading to effects on their personality later in life. Fixation might result from getting too little stimulation during these stages, or from being harshly punished, such as a child being strictly told off for having an accident during toilet training. The idea of people having an 'anal personality' derives from this idea – an *anally retentive* personality is fussy and strict, with an obsession with neatness. Someone with an 'oral personality' may habitually bite their nails, smoke or overeat.

Perhaps more important still was Freud's view of what happened next. Inspired by a dream that he had about his own mother, Freud stated that boys at around the age of five move into the **phallic stage**, and develop the **Oedipus complex**, where they become romantically attached to their mother as an idealised role model of the opposite sex (Freud, 1910, see box). The boy then feels guilt and fears being punished by his father. Freud's case study of **Little Hans** (see chapter 3) is a key example of this stage from his research – Hans was afraid of horses, but Freud though that in fact, he was afraid of his father. Therefore, Hans was seen as an example of the Oedipus complex.

? Discussion point

Do you agree that people are sometimes motivated by thoughts, feelings or memories that they are unaware of? Have you ever done something and been unsure why you did it?

Someone with an 'oral personality' may be a smoker

The Oedipus and Electra complexes

The Oedipus complex is named after a legend from Ancient Greece – Oedipus was the son of the king and queen of the ancient Greek city of Thebes. It was prophesied that he would kill his father and marry his mother, but instead, shepherds abandoned him on a hillside and he grew up to be a young man, unaware that he was really a prince. When he returned to Thebes, he fought and killed the king, and married the widowed queen, thus fulfilling the prophecy.

The Electra complex is named after Electra, daughter of the legendary King Agamemnon. According to Homer's Iliad, Agamemnon was the king who led an alliance of Greek armies to attack and besiege the city of Troy, after a Trojan prince abducted his brother's wife Helen. After he returned from the 10-year war, his own wife had remarried, and she and her new husband plotted to kill him. However, his daughter Electra plotted to murder her mother in revenge.

A painting of Oedipus with his daughter, Antigone

It may be obvious that this part of Freud's theory cannot be applied directly to girls; psychoanalyst, C.G. Jung (1961), later developed the idea of the **Electra complex** to suggest that a similar process of falling in love with the father happens to girls (see box above).

Freud said that this stage is resolved when the child appeases the same-sex parent by copying their behaviour, and therefore, at this stage, the boy starts to behave in a more traditionally masculine way and girls adopt traditionally feminine behaviours, such as the clothes that they choose to wear and the activities they are interested in (Freud, 1933).

Defence mechanisms

Freud believed that the ego tries to defend itself by distorting reality. According to this approach, a lot of problematic or disturbed behaviour may be caused by the **defence mechanisms** that the mind uses. Freud believed that some uncomfortable thoughts are a threat to the ego, so they are repressed – pushed out of the conscious mind and into the unconscious. This concept of **repression** is one of the most important defence mechanisms.

Sigmund and Anna Freud

In another famous case, Freud's patient, **Anna O**, suffered from paralysis on her right side, and felt nausea when eating or drinking. She also spoke in bizarre strings of apparently unconnected words, and at times seemed unable to understand people. Freud and his colleague Breuer believed that her discomfort with drinking stemmed from a repressed memory of a dog drinking from her water glass. Freud claimed that when the repressed memory was made conscious through therapy, the problem was solved (Freud, 1910). However, later researchers suggested that Anna suffered from a form of epilepsy worsened by drug dependence, making any attempt to generalise from her case problematic (Orr-Andrawes, 1987).

Sometimes thoughts and memories are thought to have been repressed, meaning that they have apparently been forgotten, but in reality have been pushed out of the ego and into the id because they are too painful or disturbing.

Sigmund Freud's daughter, Anna Freud, was also a prominent psychologist. She wrote a book entitled 'The Ego and the Mechanisms of Defence' that expended on her father's theories, such as repression, and established defence mechanisms as a key concept in the approach; some of the terms have become part of everyday speech. As well as repression, five major defence mechanisms you should be aware of are as follows:

Regression	Not to be confused with repression, regression means acting in a more childlike way. This links to Freud's theory of psychosexual development – comfort is found in a more childlike state rather than the threatening and conflict-filled present. Examples could include sucking your thumb/biting your nails or chewing on things when anxious, having a childish tantrum or just curling up in your bedroom like a young child might do.
Denial	This is when people distort reality, typically by stating that something is less of a problem than it is. They may ignore the risks of behaviour such as smoking or unprotected sex, or fool themselves into believing that their behaviour is normal or harmless.
Displacement	This is where it would cause anxiety or simply be impossible to direct our emotions towards their true target, so instead we begin to focus the same emotion on another, more accessible target. Examples could be feeling very angry with a strict parent but being too afraid to say so, and so bullying another child instead. Little Hans was thought to have displaced his fear of his father onto horses. Romantic attraction can also be displaced.
Projection	This is where we claim that our feelings belong to someone else. Have you ever heard someone say 'I think my friend is worried about her exams' or claiming that a friend is attracted to someone? Projection could include negative feelings about ourselves. 'You think I'm stupid, don't you?'
Reaction formation	This is when someone's behaviour is the opposite of their true feelings. For example, if someone is attracted to another person, they may be rude and hurtful instead of showing affection. Similarly, sexual desires may be warded off by exaggerated disgust towards sexuality. The behaviour is as far as possible from their true feelings, so that the ego does not have to consciously accept the true feelings that cause anxiety.

? Discussion point

What happens if two people simultaneously *project* their feelings onto each other?!

Psychoanalytic therapy and case studies

Arguably, this approach's most lasting influence has been on therapy. Sigmund Freud's approach of listening to patients and analysing what they say has had a lasting influence on how therapists work today. Many people still work as psychoanalytic therapists, and it is possible to receive psychoanalytic therapy for mental health problems either privately or on the NHS. What is more, even those who do not consider themselves psychoanalysts have been influenced, directly or indirectly, by Freud's methods and ideas.

In the early days of psychoanalysis, Freud used the technique of **dream analysis**, believing that dreams reveal unconscious thoughts and motivations (you will learn more about his theories of dreams in chapter 3). As time went on, Freud found **free association** to be a more reliable technique (Freud, 1910). This involves letting the patients speak in an uninterrupted stream of ideas, with one idea leading to the next. Freud felt that this allowed ideas from the unconscious to be revealed. Free association also aimed to strengthen the ego and help patients to develop a clearer idea of reality, and to make the pressure from the superego more humane and less focused on punishment and guilt (Nelson-Jones, 2000). During sessions, the therapist would stay relatively quiet and take notes while the client did most of the talking. Freud's preference was for patients to lie on a couch, not looking at the therapist.

This approach also became well known for using the **case study method**. A case study involves the in-depth study of one person, usually over many weeks or months (it is 'longitudinal'). It gathers a lot of data, and typically involves a range of techniques such as interviews, observations, personality tests and brain scans. It is an ideal technique for unique cases, such as people with unexplained mental illnesses or brain damage. You can read more about this research method in chapter 8.

Freud studied the dreams of his individual patients, for example in the case of Hans, mentioned above (see chapter 3 for more information).

Psychoanalytic therapy

Evaluation

Although it was once central to psychology, the influence of the psychoanalytic approach has decreased in recent years; many current university degrees in psychology now only teach it as a historical perspective. However, it is still an important approach to therapy (see chapter 4).

The concept of the unconscious mind and that idea that we may be unaware of the reasons behind some of our motivations has returned to popularity. However, many of Freud's theories of the mind are controversial and even 100 years on, there is a lack of research evidence to support them. Psychoanalytic theory as a whole is too vague and broad to be testable, and can therefore be called unscientific, though some of the mini-theories within it such as repression can and have been tested (Fisher and Greenberg, 1996).

Defence mechanisms are still a useful concept in therapy (Krauss Whitbourne, 2011), although there are various explanations for why people display these behaviours. Key terms such as 'denial' and 'projection' are still widely used.

🔍 **Top tip**

Summarise the main areas of this approach onto an index card. Write evaluation points on the back.

✔ Questions

1. Which part of the mind is entirely unconscious?

2. What object was used as an analogy for the fact that much of the mind is beneath the surface?

3. During which stage does an infant get pleasure from using the toilet, according to this approach?

4. What was the main psychological problem of 'Little Hans' that his father reported to Freud?

5. What is the name given to the complex experienced by little boys who love their mother and fear their father?

6. Which defence mechanism involves refusing to accept reality such as risky behaviour being a problem?

7. Which defence mechanism involves acting in the opposite way to your own feelings?

8. Which defence mechanism involves saying that someone else is feeling something, when you are actually feeling it yourself?

9. What became the main technique used in psychoanalytic therapy?

10. Give one feature of the case study method.

☐━ Key concepts

- Psychoanalytic approach
- Psychoanalysis
- Id
- Ego
- Superego
- Libido
- Conflicts
- Preconscious
- Oral stage
- Anal stage
- Fixation
- Phallic stage
- Oedipus complex
- Electra complex
- Little Hans
- Anna O
- Defence mechanisms
- Repression
- Regression
- Denial
- Displacement (psychoanalytic)
- Projection
- Reaction formation
- Dream analysis
- Free association
- Case study (research method)

🚦 Activities

1. Working with another student, write a short fictional dialogue that demonstrates one or more of the defence mechanisms. Then read it out to the class and see if they can figure out which mechanism is at work.

2. Look out for examples of defence mechanisms over the next few days, and report them back to class; for ethical reasons, you **must not** use real names if you are discussing the behaviour of friends or family during class.

The cognitive approach

The **cognitive approach** seeks to explain atypical behaviours in terms of knowledge, beliefs and thought processes. A key concept in the approach is that between every stimulus and response, there are a set of psychological processes, called **mediators**, that can affect the way an individual responds.

Two key examples of mediators are memory and perception:

> **Memory:** the process of taking in relevant information, storing it, and then recalling it when required.
>
> **Perception:** the process of using information from the senses in order to establish a coherent understanding of external events.

The Leeper's Lady illusion

Illusions are a great example of how perception relies on beliefs. When looking at the famous Leeper's Lady illusion, for example, some interpret the face as a young woman looking away, and some as an older woman looking downwards. Expectations and experience affect what we see. This demonstrates the importance of mental processes in making sense of our surroundings – our experience of the world is constructed in the brain according to our own unique set of cognitive processes.

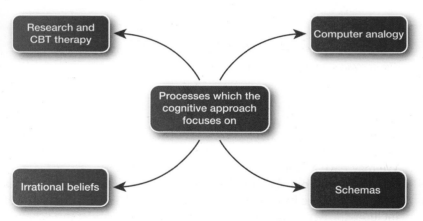

The computer analogy

The cognitive approach started to become the dominant viewpoint in psychology at around about the same time as computer science was taking off. Researchers inevitably began to make comparisons between human cognitive processes and the 'information processing' done by a computer. This **computer analogy** dominated the early days of cognitive psychology and researchers began to ask – would it be possible to develop a computer that could think like a person?

If you study the optional topic of memory, you will notice many similarities in the way human memory is described and terms that are used in computing. For example, researchers talk about:

- storage
- code/encoding
- processing

However, some researchers have rejected this comparison as over-simplistic. For example, Bruner (1992) stated that the mind and a computer are fundamentally different because a computer does not try to make sense of stimuli. It is important in his view that the cognitive approach focuses on *meaningful* processing.

The computer analogy dominated the early days of cognitive psychology

? Discussion point

What similarities are there between the human mind and a computer? What about differences?

Schemas

A **schema** means a set of ideas, or a pattern of thought about a particular concept or situation. The key idea is that information is not stored separately, but is linked together with other relevant information. We may have a schema for a school building for example, which will be drawn from our direct experience of school buildings, as well as buildings that we have seen or read about. The result is a concept that includes the typical or average features. A **script** is similar to a schema, but it concerns what to do or say in a social situation. Most situations involve scripted behaviour, for example, meeting someone for the first time, sitting down to do an exam or going into a job interview (Fayol & Monteil, 1988).

Schemas play a role when it comes to jokes or stories. If someone tells a joke which begins '*a man walked into a bar...*' this deliberately activates the schemas for a typical man and a typical bar. Of course, each person will have slightly different schemas for both of these things – because everyone has different experiences, everyone's schemas will be different. However, it is very likely that your schemas will be similar to those of other people with a similar upbringing, and someone from a different culture from yourself will have very different schemas (Bartlett, 1932 – see key study).

Sir Frederic Bartlett receives the Queen's Medal

...eric Bartlett, working
...ge University, was one
... British researchers to
...nemory and thought
...es. His approach was very
...nt to other early cognitive
...ologists in that he studied
...nory using meaningful
...terial such as folk stories and
...ctures.

Method: Bartlett showed participants images and stories that were from an unfamiliar culture. They then had to recall these items, sometimes over a series of recollections. His most famous task involved a Native American folk story called 'War of the Ghosts':

One night two young men from Egulac went down to the river to hunt seals and while they were there it became foggy and calm. Then they heard war-cries, and they thought: 'Maybe this is a war-party'. They escaped to the shore, and hid behind a log. Now canoes came up, and they heard the noise of paddles, and saw one canoe coming up to them. There were five men in the canoe, and they said:

'What do you think? We wish to take you along. We are going up the river to make war on the people.'

One of the young men said, 'I have no arrows.'

'Arrows are in the canoe,' they said.

'I will not go along. I might be killed. My relatives do not know where I have gone. But you,' he said, turning to the other, 'may go with them.'

So one of the young men went, but the other returned home. And the warriors went on up the river to a town on the other side of Kalama. The people came down to the water and they began to fight, and many were killed. But presently the young man heard one of the warriors say, 'Quick, let us go home: that Indian has been hit.' Now he thought: 'Oh, they are ghosts.' He did not feel sick, but they said he had been shot.

So the canoes went back to Egulac and the young man went ashore to his house and made a fire. And he told everybody and said: 'Behold I accompanied the ghosts, and we went to fight. Many of our fellows were killed, and many of those who attacked us were killed. They said I was hit, and I did not feel sick.'

He told it all, and then he became quiet. When the sun rose he fell down. Something black came out of his mouth. His face

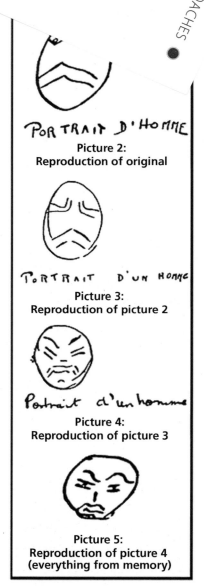

POR TRAIT D'HOMME

Picture 2:
Reproduction of original

TORTRAIT D'UN HOMME

Picture 3:
Reproduction of picture 2

Portrait d'un homme

Picture 4:
Reproduction of picture 3

Picture 5:
Reproduction of picture 4
(everything from memory)

Image from another of Barlett's studies, showing how drawings of faces changed as different people attempted to copy the previous version *became contorted. The people jumped up and cried. He was dead.*

Findings: *Bartlett reported that people change information as they try to recall it. The distortions that occurred when his participants recalled images could be dramatic.*

Bartlett observed several key distortions when participants recalled the 'War of the Ghosts' story:

- *Preservation of detached detail: remembering single unusual items out of context.*

- *Simplification: stories became more basic.*

- *Subtraction: removing elements that didn't fit the participants' culture.*

- *Transformation: things were changed to make them seem more familiar.*

He concluded that we refer to schemas if we are unsure about certain details, and memories are therefore a mixture of what has actually happened, and assumptions which fill in the gaps in our recollections. When doing his tasks, participants had tried to make sense of the story – but struggled because it came from a different culture. Bartlett called this attempt 'effort after meaning' – and considered it to be a key factor in memory distortions.

Evaluation: *This was one of the earliest demonstrations of the importance of schemas. A strength of the study is that it used real world stimuli such as stories, and it was therefore high in mundane realism. However, a weakness is that we very rarely come across information that is totally unfamiliar.*

> **🔍 Top tip**
>
> If you are studying the option topic of memory, Bartlett's (1932) study can be used as evidence for long-term memory.

Another early cognitive theorist who helped to develop the concept of schemas was Jean Piaget. Piaget was interested in cognitive development, which means how our cognitive abilities develop through childhood. In particular, he believed that a child's thinking is fundamentally different from that of adults.

Piaget studied his own children as they grew older and realised that their schemas became more complex and sophisticated over time. Piaget thought that schemas develop through two key processes.

- **Assimilation** means fitting new information to an existing schema, for example, seeing an unfamiliar type of dog and categorising it as a dog.

- **Accommodation** means changing the schema. For example, a young child at first may think that a zebra is a 'stripy horse', but then realise that it is a different animal. This results in two separate schemas – a horse schema and a zebra schema.

Piaget also realised that young children try to solve problems differently from adults, sometimes leading to errors. For example, a pre-school child will focus on just one element of a problem and ignore other equally important elements. Piaget called this **centration**. A classic demonstration

Jean Piaget

of centration involves showing a child two glasses of different shapes, one tall and thin and the other short and wide. Most children below the age of seven fail to realise that a tall glass of water contains the same amount as a shorter, wider glass, even if they see the water poured from one glass into the other. They reason that the taller glass is 'bigger' and therefore contains more. They centre just on one feature – the height of the glass – and therefore fail to judge its volume accurately.

Irrational beliefs

The traditional philosophical view of the human mind was that it was rational. Although Freud recognised that irrational thought processes can affect us, he considered these to be childlike unconscious forces, while the ego was seen as rational (see previous section). Piaget thought that errors were made by children and that we get gradually more rational – his theories didn't focus on errors made by adults.

However, later cognitive psychologists have identified several ways in which human thought processes are biased or **irrational**. One basis for this is that we are guided by **beliefs** about the world, and that these beliefs may at times be wrong and harmful. For example, Ellis (2003) states that a lot of anxiety can arise from distorted beliefs such as:

Personalisation: a tendency to relate all events to oneself. For example, if someone doesn't talk to you in the corridor, personalisation would be thinking *'she must be in a bad mood with me'* rather than, for example, *'she must be busy and distracted'*.

Overgeneralisation: taking one thing and applying it to many or all situations. For example, upon failing a test, a student may overgeneralise and think, *'I'm useless at everything'*.

Selective abstraction: tendency to focus on one small part of an event or series of events. For example, after a date that went well overall, the person may focus on one thing that went wrong (for example, maybe they tripped and felt clumsy) and ignore all the positive events, therefore remembering it as having been a really bad evening.

Humans don't actually work everything out like a computer, but instead rely on simplistic assumptions. These help the mind to save on limited mental resources such as attention. Tversky and Kahneman (1974) found that when shown the possible outcome of six coin tosses, people judged H-T-H-T-T-H as being more likely than H-H-H-T-T-T, even though each has exactly the same probability of happening. Essentially people's behaviour is not always rational, but is instead often guided by intuition.

Tversky and Kahneman argued that humans use simple rules to guide their behaviour, called **heuristics** (or 'rules of thumb'). One heuristic is called the **availability heuristic**, and it states that if asked how common something is, we judge it based on how easy it is to think of examples. This is often a good strategy – but also leads to major mistakes. Examples might come to mind more easily due to personal prejudices or obsessions, or simply because we have come across those examples more recently. On those occasions, the availability heuristic will bias us to give an inaccurate response.

Is there more water in the tall glass?

Top tip

See chapter 7 (Intelligence) for more about Piaget's theories.

The outcome of a coin toss is always 50:50!

Research and CBT therapy

The cognitive approach is known for its use of **experiments**. An experiment is a controlled study, where one thing is changed and everything else is kept constant. For example, researchers might conduct an experiment into the effects of noise on people's ability to solve problems – two groups of people might solve problems, one with background noise and one in silence. Everything else would be the same, for example, the amount of time allowed. Such experiments tend to be done in controlled conditions such as university laboratories. As the cognitive approach focuses on thought processes, experiments tend to be done on people rather than animals.

A lot of anxiety can arise from distorted beliefs

> **?** Discussion point
>
> Do these distortions seem more or less realistic/relevant to you than the defence mechanisms of the psychoanalytic approach? Are they similar? Should both be used to explain human behaviour?

Questionnaires are also widely used, for example, to ask people about their beliefs and attitudes (see chapter 8 for more on these methods).

According to this approach, if thinking can be changed then so can behaviour. The idea that irrational beliefs can influence feelings (rather than the other way round) is known as cognitive primacy. If a person's thinking about stress is changed, for example, then they will become less stressed. If their perceptions about eating and about their own weight change, then they may stop having an eating disorder. There have been various forms of cognitive therapy over the years, but currently the most popular and widespread form is **cognitive behavioural therapy (CBT)**. It is a very structured form of therapy, where the therapist will challenge beliefs that seem unjustified or irrational. There are also behavioural tasks that the patient should do in-between sessions, such as trying out new behaviours. CBT is explained in more detail in chapter 4.

CBT might be used to help someone with an eating disorder

Evaluation

The cognitive approach is hugely influential and its models of thought processes and decision making have influenced therapy and treatment methods. Ideas such as heuristics and schemas have influenced areas as diverse as memory, stress and prejudice, as you will see when you tackle the option topics in this course.

> 🔍 **Top tip**
>
> Summarise the main areas of this approach onto an index card. Write evaluation points on the back.

The approach is supported by a large body of experimental findings showing that thought processes are not always logical and can be distorted, such as the work of Tversky and Kahneman (1974). However, much of the research is based in the laboratory. In particular, research into the key cognitive areas of memory and perception has tended to be very artificial.

The approach assumes that thought processes cause people to have negative feelings and behaviours, but thoughts may sometimes be the result rather than the cause of conditions such as stress and depression (Schachter & Singer, 1962).

Research on cognitive processes has tended to ignore the underlying brain processes involved. This is changing, however, as brain scanning technology improves.

●━ Key concepts

- Cognitive approach
- Mediators
- Illusions
- Computer analogy
- Schema
- Script
- Assimilation
- Accommodation
- Centration
- Irrational beliefs
- Beliefs
- Personalisation
- Overgeneralisation
- Selective abstraction
- Heuristic
- Availability heuristic
- Experiment (research method)
- Questionnaires (research method)
- CBT – cognitive behavioural therapy

☑ Questions

1. What is meant by a mediator?

2. Complete: studying the mind as an information processor is part of the _____ analogy.

3. Why did Bruner criticise the emphasis on information processing?

4. What is a schema?

5. What is a script?

6. Which early researcher studied cognitive development in children?

7. What is meant by centration?

8. Which cognitive distortion concerns relating events to oneself?

9. What is selective abstraction?

10. What is the main form of cognitive therapy called?

GO! Activities

1. Find more illusions, in books or online. Choose one illusion and then make an A3-sized poster showing both the illusion and your explanation of how it works. These can then be used to decorate your classroom, corridor or study space. Alternatively, make a short PowerPoint of illusions and show it to your class.

2. Think of examples for each of the cognitive distortions from your own life experiences. (If you note them down, do not use real names.)

3. Divide an A4 page into four sections and in each section write a one paragraph summary of the following:
   - computer analogy
   - schemas
   - irrational beliefs
   - CBT

Approaches to psychology

The previous sections have described the biological, psychoanalytic and cognitive approaches. Focusing on just these three approaches would be sufficient to meet the mandatory requirement of either course (National 5 or Higher), as they cover the mandatory approaches specified, while both courses require a minimum of three approaches overall.

However, for the optional topics, the best choice of approach may depend on which topic is being studied and you should discuss this with your teacher or lecturer. For example, the behaviourist approach is a good fit with the topic of psychopathology (chapter 4), while the evolutionary approach is appropriate for stress (chapter 6).

In addition, you will ideally develop a basic understanding of all of the approaches, as they have all been so influential throughout the history of Psychology. The behaviourist approach, in particular, played a huge role in the 20th century. Although it is rare to find a researcher who agrees with the approach today in its more extreme form, the approach still has an influence on how psychology is studied, from the subject as a whole being based on objective experiments to the many ways in which theories of learning have been applied. Nowadays, the evolutionary approach is increasingly popular and current research often refers to the effect of evolution on behaviour.

Other approaches that are included here (although in less detail) are the humanist and socio-cultural approaches.

The behaviourist approach

The **behaviourist approach** was founded by American psychologist John Watson (1878–1958), through his article, *'Psychology as the Behaviourist Views it'* (Watson, 1913). Inspired by the work of Russian physiologist Ivan Pavlov and drawing on his own laboratory work at John Hopkins University in Baltimore, Watson proposed that the main aim of psychology should be to be able to predict and control behaviour. He argued that this could be achieved using carefully designed and controlled experiments and that psychology should be entirely an objective, scientific discipline.

Watson disliked a lot of the work being done in psychology at the time, considering it too subjective. In being more scientific, Watson said, it was necessary to study psychology in terms of learned behaviour and the formation of associations between stimuli and responses, and to avoid subjective mental terms: *'I believe we can write a psychology [and] never use the terms consciousness, mental states, mind, content, introspectively verifiable, imagery and the like'* (Watson 1913: 160).

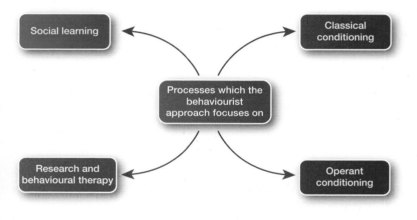

John Watson

Classical conditioning

The first major theory in the behaviourist approach is **classical conditioning**, which means learning an **association** between two stimuli. This occurs when one stimulus already produces a response, for example, a snake or a spider that causes us to feel fear, or a slice of cake that causes our mouths to water. Behaviourists call this the unconditioned stimulus. The other stimulus is neutral – it does not cause a reaction, for example, a light flashing on or a tone playing.

The key to classical conditioning is that the unconditioned and neutral stimulus are repeatedly paired together. In real life, this might happen by accident, but behaviourist psychologists generally test it under controlled conditions in a laboratory. After time, the neutral stimulus starts to cause the same response as the unconditioned stimulus. An association has therefore been learned – the individual has been *conditioned* to respond to a previously neutral event.

Russian biologist Ivan Pavlov was the first to experimentally describe classical conditioning – he observed it in his laboratory dogs and discovered it largely by accident. When studying the digestive systems of the dogs in his lab, Pavlov realised that the animals learned to react to hearing the lab assistant's footsteps before they were fed – they produced saliva in their mouths before they were given any food. The animals had learned to associate the food with the sound of the footsteps.

Pavlov then carried out an experiment to test this more systematically. A bell was sounded for a dog to hear. A few seconds later, food (meat powder) was presented so that the dog salivated and ate. This procedure, pairing together the bell and the food, was repeated several times. Finally, the bell was sounded but no food was produced. It was observed that the dog now salivated in response to the bell alone – a learned association. Pavlov had experimentally demonstrated classical conditioning.

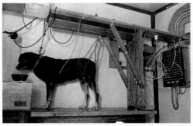

A dog taking part in one of Pavlov's experiments

Pavlov became famous for his discovery. Other psychologists such as Watson began to wonder if this basic form of learning might be the basis for all of our actions. Later researchers have confirmed that classical conditioning occurs in a huge range of organisms, from humans to sea slugs (Kandel & Hawkins, 1992).

The following abbreviations are used to describe stimuli and responses in classical conditioning:

US	Unconditioned stimulus
UR	Unconditioned response
CS	Conditioned stimulus
CR	Conditioned response

📖 Key study: Watson and Rayner (1920): the study of 'little Albert'

Aim: Watson and Rayner (1920) wanted to show that fear could be learned in a human child through classical conditioning, in just the same way that Pavlov's dogs had learned an association.

Method: The study was conducted on an 11-month-old child nicknamed 'little Albert'. They give the child animals such as a white rat to look at, and hit an iron bar behind his head with a hammer to make a loud unpleasant noise, causing him to become frightened and cry.

Now he fears even Santa Claus

Little Albert

Findings: The child soon learned to associate fear with the rat and he cried as soon as he saw it. This effect generalised to other small animals such as a rabbit. The way Albert was conditioned is similar in principle to Pavlov's research on dogs – learning occurred by an association being formed between two things.

Evaluation: This was an important demonstration of classical conditioning in humans, though highly unethical - an infant was deliberately made to cry and feel frightened.

Operant conditioning

A related theory of learning is **operant conditioning**. The key difference between this and classical conditioning is that rather than an association being formed between two stimuli, the person behaves in some way first, and this is then followed by a consequence. The individual then associates the behaviour with the consequence. If the consequence is pleasant, the person is more likely to repeat the behaviour.

Operant conditioning was first described by Jerzy Konorsky, but it was the American researcher B. F. Skinner who fully developed the concept. He used the term operant to apply to anything that modified the likelihood of a behaviour to be repeated. Skinner's early experiments were carried out with animals such as rats. The rat would be placed in a closed box – now known as a **Skinner box** (see image) – and its behaviour would be observed. Eventually, the rat's normal exploration would take it close to a bar, and when it placed its front paws on the bar, a pellet of food would be delivered. The rat would now be attracted to that part of the box and return there to repeat the process again. According to Skinner, the food is a reinforcer, and the bar pressing will continue as long as it is reinforced by food.

Operant conditioning can be a gradual process, with behaviours getting stronger or weaker over time. This strengthening of habits through rewards is known as **reinforcement**. According to Skinner, a reinforcer is an outcome which increases frequency of a behaviour - in other words, a reward, while a **punishment** reduces behaviour. Reinforcement could involve something good being given, such as a food pellet to the rat in a Skinner box, or something unpleasant being removed, such as loud noise being switched off. These are called **positive reinforcement** and **negative reinforcement** respectively:

B.F. Skinner with a rat in a 'Skinner box'

Positive reinforcement: something pleasant is given	Example: a food reward
Negative reinforcement: something unpleasant is removed	Example: a noise being switched off

Skinner (1938) stated that without a reinforcer, the behaviour would reduce in strength. However, a behaviour would reduce more quickly after a bad outcome, for instance, a punishment. Reinforcers and punishers are both types of **operants**, that is, outcomes. However, punishments cannot permanently stop a behaviour because the *lack* of a response cannot be reinforced (Catania, 1992).

? Discussion point

Think of examples of positive and negative reinforcements in the classroom or at home as you were growing up. Did teachers and parents always reward good behaviour? Could bad behaviour have been accidentally reinforced?

Social learning

People do not just learn things directly through their own experience – they can also learn from observing others. For example, if you see someone else try a trick on their bike and then fall off and injure themselves, you will probably avoid trying it yourself. In the behaviourist approach, **social learning** means learning from the experiences of others. We can learn from observation and from seeing others being rewarded and punished. In this sense, social learning can be like an indirect form of operant conditioning.

The most famous research study into social learning was conducted by Albert Bandura, who studied how aggression is learned. He believed that learning depends on its social context, and often takes place via **modelling** of a behaviour by another person, such as a parent or teacher. He conducted a study where children observed adults hitting a doll. After observing the aggression, the children observed the adult being rewarded, punished, or neither (no consequences). The children showed significantly more aggression after observing the adult being rewarded (Bandura, 1965). This work has been applied to the study of media violence (see also the optional topic of NVC – chapter 12).

Albert Bandura, with a photo from his study

> **Make the link**
>
> …to your knowledge of Media Studies.

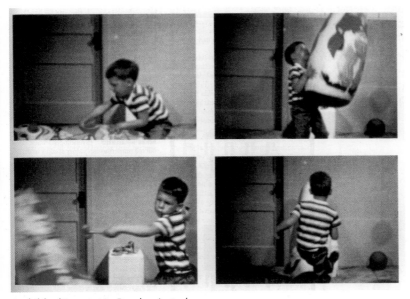

A child taking part in Bandura's study

Research and behavioural therapy

Research in the behaviourist approach is largely based on objective science. There is an emphasis on lab experiments, most of which involved direct observation of behaviour, because researchers in this approach do not focus on mental processes. In contrast to the cognitive approach, a lot of the research is done on animals rather than humans.

A lot of behavioural research is done using animals

Therapies based on the behaviourist approach rely on the theories of classical and operant conditioning. One such technique is **flooding** (also called *exposure therapy*), which suggests that a fearful stimulus should be presented at its worst, so that the person reacts very strongly to it, for example, taking a reptile-phobic person (herpetophobe) into the reptile house at a zoo. The person would of course react with extreme anxiety, but would use relaxation techniques to gradually replace the anxiety with a state of calm. Through classical conditioning, a new association between the stimulus and a feeling of calm would (hopefully) be learned.

A less traumatic version is **systematic desensitisation**. In this technique, a client works with their therapist to draw up a 'fear hierarchy' – a list of fearful situations from the least feared to the most feared. A classic demonstration of this was conducted by Lang and Lazovik (1963), who studied students who were phobic of snakes. One group of 12 were given systematic desensitisation and worked through numerous sessions with a therapist where first they developed a fear hierarchy, and then worked through it using relaxation techniques. Another 12 students formed a control group. Before and after the therapy sessions, researchers brought all participants one by one into a room containing a snake in a tank, and asked them to approach as close as they could, and touch or hold the snake if possible. They were ranked on how close they were willing to go, and results were therefore a direct test of their observable behaviour, rather than a subjective statement of their fear level. The researchers found that on average, the group who had experienced systematic desensitisation moved significantly closer on the second test, and seven out of twelve were willing to hold or touch the snake. The control group showed no change on the second test.

Systematic desensitisation can be used to treat a phobia of snakes

Operant conditioning-based techniques rely on reward and punishment. A person with an addiction could be given a reward for each hour that they manage to stay drug free. However, it's not always practical to reward behaviour every single time, so tokens are often presented instead, with a certain number of tokens adding up to the desired reward.

Nowadays pure behavioural therapy is rare, but the techniques are used as part of CBT therapy.

Evaluation

This approach has been criticised for relying on laboratory experiments with animals, as generalising the results of these studies to humans may not be valid. Although Watson viewed animal and human behaviour as being a continuous scale of complexity with humans at the upper end, many researchers feel that humans should be the main objects of study in psychology.

The two types of conditioning are useful in explaining many types of learning, but too simplistic to fully explain all human behaviour. According to Skinner (1957), babies learn language through conditioning. For example, if an infant sees a cup and hears an adult say the word 'cup', it forms an association between the two. Then, if the child tries to say the word, it will be rewarded by a *'well done'* from its carers, reinforcing the action (operant conditioning). However, linguist Noam Chomsky criticised Skinner's theory of language learning (Chomsky, 1959). He believed that babies develop mental rules of grammar, and use these to form sentences. For example, in English, the child learns that to make a verb past tense, it needs to add an '-*ed*' ending. Without having learned all the exceptions to this rule, it over-applies the rules, making mistakes such as '*I eated*' or '*I forgetted*'. These mistakes are significant, as the infant never hears them from adults, so it cannot be imitating them or learning their meaning through classical conditioning.

How does a baby learn what the word for 'cup' is?

It's not clear that animals always learn just through conditioning, either. When studying learning in an ape called Sultan, researcher Wolfgang Köhler (1925, cited in Glassman, 2000) observed that the ape appeared to think through a problem as a whole, and show insight. Sultan was inside a cage, and was given a stick that was too short to reach a banana that Köhler had placed outside the cage. Sultan then moved to the back of his cage and stared at the sticks for some time. Then, without any need for practice or reinforcement, he suddenly picked up the smaller stick, used it to pull the longer stick towards him, and then used the longer stick to reach the fruit. Sultan seemed to have had a moment of insight, unrelated to simple operant conditioning or trial and error.

Wolfgang Köhler

⚷ Key concepts

- Behaviourist approach
- Classical conditioning
- Association
- Operant conditioning
- Reinforcement
- Punishment
- Skinner box
- Positive reinforcement
- Negative reinforcement
- Social learning
- Modelling
- Operant
- Flooding
- Systematic desensitisation

✔ Questions

1. True or false: Pavlov's experiment with the dogs is an example of operant conditioning.

2. Which type of conditioning was demonstrated in the study of little Albert?

3. What is the name for the strengthening of a behaviour through repeated rewards?

4. Which leads to the weakening of a behaviour – negative reinforcement, or punishment?

5. Which type of conditioning is also called 'learning by association'?

6. True or false: behaviourists focus on thought processes that we cannot see or measure.

7. True or false: the behaviourist approach is also called 'stimulus-response' psychology?

8. What is the name of the apparatus that Skinner used to study rats and birds?

9. Which behaviourist therapy tries to treat phobias gradually?

10. What is meant by a token, in behaviourist therapy?

GO! Activities

1. Complete the gap-fill text:

   Behaviourism is based around two theories of learning – classical and _____ conditioning. Classical conditioning involves associations being formed between a response/behaviour and a stimulus that is initially _____ (has no effect on the animal). The process of classical conditioning involves an unconditioned stimulus (US) and an unconditioned response (___) being associated together, after which the stimulus is termed the conditioned stimulus (___) and the response is termed the _____ _____ (CR). Operant conditioning in behaviours increase or decrease in strength or frequency because they have a good or bad outcome. _____ conditioning is based around reinforcement and punishment. Actions increase if they are followed by positive or negative _____. Actions decrease if they are followed by positive or negative punishment. Positive means that something happens or it is given. Negative means that something does not happen or it is taken away. Classical and operant conditioning contribute a great deal to our understanding of human and animal behaviour. The behaviourist approach is very objective and uses the _____ method rigorously in order to support its conclusions. However, it is important to realise that not every behaviour is conditioned in behaviour. Behaviourism cannot explain all behaviours in humans (or even in animals). _____ development in humans, for example, and creative behaviour cannot be accounted for solely by behaviourist explanations.

2. Think of an example from your life of when an animal has learned a new behaviour. Now try to explain it in terms of classical and operant conditioning. Write some notes, and then try to explain it to a classmate. Do you think conditioning is enough, or has the animal shown intelligent thought?

3. Write the full terms beside the abbreviations below and give an example for each one, which could be drawn from the examples you have discussed.

   US: _____   UR: _____

   Example: Example:

   CS: _____   CR: _____

   Example: Example:

An illustration imagining Sultan riding a bicycle, from the Berliner Illustrirte Zeitung magazine

🔍 Top tip

Even if you don't use the behaviourist approach to explain the topics in the Individual Behaviour unit, it is still helpful to understand classical and operant conditioning – these ideas have had a major impact on all areas of psychology.

🔍 Top tip

Summarise the main areas of this approach onto an index card. Write evaluation points on the back.

! Syllabus note

At both National 5 and Higher, this is a suitable optional approach for any of the Individual Behaviour topics.

The evolutionary approach

The **evolutionary approach** to psychology states that human behaviour is best explained in terms of the **evolution** of our species over time. It has links to the biological approach, because it also emphasises the importance of genetics, but rather than explaining behaviour in terms of physical processes within the body, evolutionary psychologists are more interested in understanding what life was like for humans in the past, and how this affects our behaviour today. The way that genes and other structures affect our behaviour could be considered the '*how*' questions – how do genes affect behaviour? How do hormones affect mood? Whereas, evolutionary psychologists are more interested in the '*why*' questions - why do we have a stress response? Why do people typically form long-term romantic relationships? Why do people feel anxious if they are different from their peers? According to this approach, the answers to these questions come from understanding human evolution.

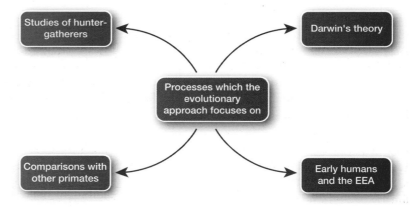

Darwin's theory

Darwin's key insight was that as successful characteristics were passed on from parents to offspring, then, over time, an entire species could change with characteristics that aided survival in their environment becoming more common. As the environment changes, so characteristics will change too. This principle of selection by the environment is called **natural selection**.

Humans, therefore, have evolved the way we have because – according to the principle of natural selection – certain characteristics made our ancestors more likely to survive. Why do we walk upright on two legs? Why are our brains much larger than those of other apes? These characteristics must have given our ancestors a survival advantage, according to the theory.

The same reasoning can be applied to behavioural and psychological characteristics, such as language, love and aggression. This is more controversial, as our behaviours are shaped not just by our genes but by learning, upbringing and culture.

Top tip

There are links between this approach and the biological approach, as both refer to genetics. If you are using both approaches, make sure you are completely clear about the differences between them.

Early humans and the EEA

As with other species, humans evolved gradually in response to changes in our environment. Groups of early monkeys and apes changed according to environmental conditions just as the finches Darwin studied on the Galapagos Islands did, with certain characteristics proving to be more successful. As early apes moved around and separated into different groups, they found different environmental conditions. Over a long period of time, the different conditions prompted different characteristics to evolve through natural selection, resulting in separate species of ape.

Of greatest interest is how early humans separated from chimpanzees and other apes. It is likely that a common ancestor of both humans and chimps lived around 7 million years ago. This does not mean that modern chimps are your ancestors! However, it appears that humans have changed a lot during this time, while chimpanzees – probably because their rainforest environment has not changed much – have remained fairly similar to our common ancestors.

Charles Darwin

The development of modern humans was gradual, and several species of **hominins** – that is, early humans – existed and then died out. **Australopithecus** was chimp-like in appearance but walked upright, and lived in Africa between 2 and 4 million years ago. **Homo erectus** was another major species that spread around the world and had a greater ability to build and use tools. The earliest fossil evidence dates from 1.9 million years ago, and the most recent specimens lived 143,000 years ago (Smithsonian, 2015).

Our own species of anatomically modern humans – technically called **Homo sapiens** – is thought to have evolved around 200,000 years ago in south-western Africa (Henn *et al.*, 2011), and eventually spread around the rest of the world via the Middle East (note that Homo erectus were still in existence when our Homo sapiens ancestors spread around the world).

A Darwin's Finch (also known as the Galapagos Finch or as Geospizinae)

Evolution is driven by the environment – characteristics that will help a species to survive depend on the environment that they are in. For example, characteristics that help animals to survive in an ocean are different from the characteristics that are useful in a desert. The **environment of evolutionary adaptiveness** (EEA) means the environment in which human ancestors are thought to have lived for most of our recent evolution. It is thought that modern humans evolved largely in a savannah (grassland) environment.

For most of this time, people lived in small tribal groups, hunting animals and gathering berries and roots, catching fish, etc. People made or used temporary shelters such as tents made out of animal skins, and moved around according to the seasons and the movement of animals that they hunted. These were the conditions in which we evolved. In comparison, it is only in the last 12,000 years or fewer that humans have developed agriculture and lived in settled villages and towns. Truly 'modern life' – with cars, computers,

A model of the face of an adult female Homo erectus on display at the Smithsonian Museum of Natural History in Washington, D.C.

Skulls of Homo Sapiens and Homo
Erectus

phones, modern houses, etc. – has existed for a tiny fraction of humans' time on earth.

As it formed by far the larger part of our evolutionary development, evolutionary psychologists attempt to explain psychological phenomena and problems with reference to the EEA. For example, stress and mental illness may be caused partly because we experience things that didn't exist in our EEA, such as money, exams, and junk food.

It appears that our early ancestors stopped living in rainforests. There is no way of knowing for certain why our ancestors stopped living in rainforest environments and began to live on the savannah – it may possibly relate to changes in climate, or gradual migration. Undoubtedly though, according to natural selection, the changed environment had an effect on the characteristics most useful for survival.

Frequently asked questions about evolution

Q: Isn't evolution just a theory?
A: It is a theory. As discussed in chapter 8, what this means is that it is the best explanation scientists have for the many factual observations that have been made. Scientific theories can never be proved – they are always our closest estimate and they are gradually improved and refined over time. There is a wealth of evidence that supports the general principles of Darwinian evolution, but some details are still a matter of debate.

Q: How does this explain the origin of life?
A: It doesn't. The theory of evolution is an explanation of how species change over time, and does not aim to explain how life originated on Earth. There are several other theories that attempt to explain how the first life forms appeared.

Q: I find it hard to believe that we evolved from monkeys.
A: Darwin's contemporaries also mocked him for suggesting that we evolved from primates (although he was not the first to suggest this – just the first to explain how it happened). The fact that a theory seems hard to believe at first glance is not a reason to reject it; for centuries, most humans refused to believe that the earth revolved around the sun.

Q: Does this mean that I shouldn't believe in God?
A: It's up to you what you believe. Scientific theories attempt to explain the physical world and the creatures in it, using natural rather than supernatural explanations. Many scientists do believe in god(s) and/or follow religions. However, it is fair to say that the theory of evolution does not fit with a *literal* interpretation of some religious texts.

Comparisons with other species

Another aspect of the evolutionary approach involves the study of other, closely related species such as the primates (apes and monkeys). The idea is to find out more about what our nearest relatives are capable of, and therefore draw conclusions about the earliest human ancestors. As chimpanzees and bonobos (pygmy chimps) are our nearest relatives, they tend to be the most studied.

It is thought that chimpanzees are our nearest relatives

One fundamental question is why humans and other primates have evolved relatively large brains compared to other mammals. In answering that question, it might be possible to explain why humans have exceptionally large brains and high intelligence. Two main possibilities are that:

1. A large brain is necessary to deal with a complex environment in terms of survival or feeding. For example, carnivores tend to have larger brains than herbivores.

OR

2. A large brain is necessary to deal with a large social group. With more individuals in the social group, each person requires more resources to deal with interaction, and maintaining relationships.

Dunbar concluded that the maximum functional group size for humans is approximately 150

Byrne and Corp (2004) found a correlation between levels of social deception in different primate species and the size of their brains – in particular, their neocortex – lending support to the second theory. Similarly, Dunbar (1992) studied the ratio of group size to neocortex size of various primates, and concluded a maximum functional group size for humans of approximately 150 (see page 360).

Comparisons with hunter-gatherers

Until around 12,000 years ago there was no agriculture at all, and all humans around the world lived as **hunter-gatherers**. As agricultural technology spread from one community to another, humans developed techniques for storing, planting and harvesting crops and for managing livestock and keeping them safe from predators. With the birth of agriculture, humans had regular surpluses of food for the first time, and began to trade.

> **? Discussion point**
>
> Can we figure out the ideal human group size from studying other primates? Do you believe that 150 is the ideal group size, and if so, what does that mean for the size of schools, companies, or of the neighbourhoods that we live in?

However, there are many groups of people around the world who still live as hunter-gatherers. Some move from one area to another in search of food and other resources, while others live in settled communities but forage and hunt for food rather than farming (Rowley-Conwy, 2001). Examples include the Inuit of the Arctic, the San people of the Kalahari, and the Pirahã people of the Amazon Rainforest. From the point of view of the evolutionary approach, studying hunter-gatherers provides an interesting demonstration of how people behave without modern technology. These societies may be the closest thing we have to being able to observe the conditions in which humans evolved.

The San people of the Kalahari

Dunbar's theory about group size (see previous section) has been compared to the size of groups in contemporary hunter-gatherers, and it was found that many modern hunter-gatherer tribes average around 150 individuals (Dunbar, 1993). This supports the idea that the social pressures of a larger group are too cognitively demanding, and that evolution has set an upper limit of group size beyond which the costs start to outweigh the benefits.

Evaluation of the evolutionary approach

This area of study is based on sparse fossil evidence, and theories about exactly how and when the various species of early hominids evolved are still being debated. For example, if a new Homo erectus fossil was discovered, it could change our understanding of exactly where and when these hominins lived. However, over time, a gradually clearer picture is emerging.

The evolutionary approach has been accused of justifying disparities between the sexes, such as men working and women looking after children. Similarly, there is an ethical debate over the study of how unethical behaviours such as murder and rape might have evolved. In response, evolutionary psychologists call such criticisms the **naturalistic fallacy**, stating that just because something *did* happen in evolution, doesn't mean that it *should* happen in contemporary society.

Pinker (1994) has criticised comparisons with other species, suggesting that little if anything can be concluded from comparing humans to other apes. Chimpanzees are our near relatives, sharing many physical characteristics, but humans have unique characteristics such as language which shows that some of our most important psychological characteristics have evolved very recently.

A Homo erectus fossil brow

🔍 Top tip

Summarise the main areas of this approach onto an index card. Write evaluation points on the back.

⚋ Key concepts

- Evolution
- Natural selection
- Hominins
- Australopithecus
- Homo erectus
- Homo sapiens
- Environment of evolutionary adaptiveness (EEA)
- Hunter-gatherer
- Naturalistic fallacy

✔ Questions

1. Who came up with the theory of evolution by natural selection?

2. How long have humans existed?

3. Are humans a type of ape?

4. Are apes and monkeys the same?

5. Did we evolve in the rainforest?

6. How long is it since agriculture was developed?

7. What does EEA stand for?

8. What is a hunter-gatherer?

9. How large is an ideal human group, according to Dunbar?

10. Give two evaluation points that relate to this approach.

GO! Activities

Australopithecus first evolve

Chimp-like hominins which walked upright and lived in Africa.

First cities

The earliest complex urban civilisations developed.

Modern humans first evolve

The first humans which were anatomically the same as ourselves.

Beginning of the most recent glacial period (or 'ice age')

The earth cooled and huge ice sheets spread across temperate areas, leading to a major drop in sea levels.

Neanderthals died out

Neanderthals were a species of hominin that lived alongside modern humans, but then became extinct.

Homo erectus first evolve

Early humans who spread around the world and were able to build and use tools.

Agriculture

Humans began to grow crops and keep livestock rather than hunting and gathering food.

The 'missing link'

The last common ancestor of both chimpanzees and humans.

1. Label the events marked on the cards on a timeline as to when they occurred. (See p.409 for feedback on this activity.)
2. Describe one human behaviour or problem, and think about how it may have been affected by evolution. Conduct some research to find out what scientists have said about this issue. Present this issue and your findings to your class.

Two further approaches: humanist and sociocultural

The five approaches described so far are not the only approaches in psychology, but they are the most well-known and influential, and the easiest to apply to the option topics covered in this book. The psychoanalytic and behaviourist approaches dominated psychology in the early-mid 20th century, while nowadays the cognitive, evolutionary and biological approaches are more popular.

The following two approaches are less prominent, but studying them will help you to understand psychology more fully. The humanist approach has made a major impact in therapy for psychopathology, and with some independent research, it could be used as an optional approach for that topic. The sociocultural approach is also relevant to psychopathology, and has influenced many of the ideas that you will study in the social behaviour unit.

The humanist approach

The **humanist approach** suggests that human nature is essentially positive and that people do bad things or are mentally ill because society stops them from fulfilling their potential. This approach, therefore, contrasts with the psychodynamic view of an irrational and violent human nature. The humanist approach is still very popular in therapy, but its key ideas do not feature strongly in other major areas of psychology research, perhaps because they are seen as rather vague and simplistic.

Hierarchy of needs

The **hierarchy of needs** is a humanist theory that humans have a series of needs, where more basic ones need to be satisfied before higher-level ones can. Abraham Maslow (1943) presented this in the form of a pyramid-shaped diagram:

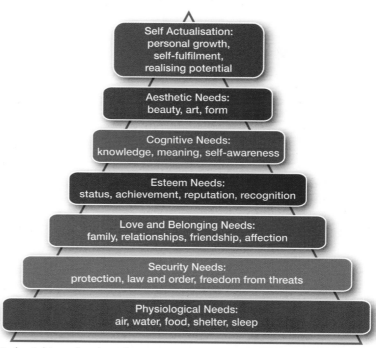

Maslow's hierarchy of needs

Albert Einstein – he may have been 'self actualised'

Notice that things like a love of learning (cognitive needs) and appreciation of art (aesthetic needs) are impossible to achieve unless the individual has first satisfied their safety, belonging and esteem needs. For example, a child is unlikely to care about learning if they are being rejected by their peers. At the top of the hierarchy is what humanist theorists saw as the pinnacle of human development – **self actualisation**. Maslow believed that only a few people ever achieve this, and cited Albert Einstein and Abraham Lincoln as examples of people who did.

Humanist therapy

On the surface, humanist therapy can resemble psychoanalysis – a discussion between the client and therapist, usually on a one-to-one basis. However, it is **client-centred**, which means that rather than being directed by the therapist, the client must make the main choices. Carl Rogers viewed counselling and therapy as a relationship between client and therapist, and stated that for it to be successful, the client must choose to improve. Meanwhile the therapist should provide a supportive environment, which involves showing **empathy** with the client's problems, and being honest about their own feelings.

Key traits of a successful humanist therapist	
Empathy	Showing concern for the client
Congruence	Being honest about their own feelings
Unconditional positive regard	Always being unconditionally positive and accepting

The socio-cultural approach

The **socio-cultural approach** suggests that all human behaviour is fundamentally programmed by society. According to this research, our behaviour cannot be understood separately from the social context in which it occurs. It is associated with the topics of social psychology, such as conformity and prejudice, but as an approach or perspective it applies to all areas of human behaviour. The fundamental assumption is that behaviour can be very strongly affected by the society and culture that we live in, and that we tend to adopt the beliefs and values of that culture. Most early 20th century psychology largely ignored culture, but as the study of **sociology** became more popular, researchers began to realise the important influence that society has on behaviour.

Individualistic versus collectivist cultures

A **culture** means a set of shared values. According to this approach, everyone is influenced in some way or other by the values of their culture. Inside any culture (e.g. Scottish) there can be many smaller cultures known as **subcultures**, some of which are easily identified – students, punks – and others that are less obvious.

One important cultural difference is the contrast between **individualist cultures** and **collectivist cultures**. Some human cultures including most Central American and Southeast Asian countries have been described as collectivist, meaning that they place great value on family success and group harmony. The wants of the individual are considered a lower priority than the needs of the group in these cultures. Other parts of the world – notably North America, most of Western Europe, and Australia – are described as individualist cultures. This means that the success of the individual is paramount. There is a lot of competitiveness in individualist cultures and family/community tend to be a lower priority.

Smith and Bond (1993) found higher **conformity** levels in collectivist societies in comparison to individualist societies, perhaps because an emphasis on group harmony makes people more inclined to conform to the behaviour of others around them.

Top tip

The socio-cultural approach does not tend to use lab experiments. According to this perspective, it is pointless to study behaviour away from its social context.

Features of individualistic cultures	Features of collectivist cultures
Personal success is important	Group or family success is important
Competition is prevalent	Cooperation is prevalent
People are encouraged to do things their own way	People are encouraged to do things according to traditions
People fear failure	People fear social rejection

Culturally biased research

A major issue in the socio-cultural approach is the level of **cultural bias** in mainstream research. Smith and Bond (1993) studied the references in the most popular North American social psychology textbook, and they found that 94% of the first-named authors cited were based in North America.

People are encouraged to do things their own way in individualistic cultures

A similar problem relates to the nature of the participants of much of this research. Out of convenience, many researchers test their own students. Sears (1986) found that in published social psychology research between 1980 and 1985, 54% used American psychology students as participants, and a further 21% used other American students. Additionally, only 29% of studies were conducted in a natural social habitat. This situation has resulted in a huge number of major studies and theories being based on a group of people that are different from the broader population in important ways, according to Sears (1996):

Family success is important in collectivist cultures

- They are more egocentric.
- They have a stronger need for peer approval.
- They are more likely to be compliant to authority.

This is an especially important issue in the study of human social behaviour. The socio-cultural approach would argue that many major ideas and conclusions in Psychology are biased.

Summary and evaluation

American students are commonly used as participants for social psychology studies

- The **humanist approach** sees humans as essentially good and creative, but constrained by society.
- The hierarchy of needs is Maslow's theory of the progression people have to go through in order to reach the stage of self-actualisation.
- Rogers suggested that therapists must be congruent, empathic, and show unconditional positive regard for clients.

- The **socio-cultural** approach suggests that human behaviour can only be explained in its social context.
- The approach suggests that most research is culturally biased because of the over-use of American students as participants.
- There is major cultural distinction between individualist versus collectivist cultures which can affect many behaviours.

Key concepts

- Humanist approach
- Hierarchy of needs
- Self actualisation
- Client-centred therapy
- Empathy
- Socio-cultural approach
- Sociology
- Culture
- Subculture
- Individualist culture
- Collectivist culture
- Conformity
- Cultural bias

GO! Activities

1. Research one of these approaches in more depth. If you are up for the challenge, exploring one of the other approaches to psychology is a great exercise in independent learning. Each approach is a piece of the overall puzzle in terms of understanding human behaviour as a whole. Nowadays, it is rare for a psychologist to fully endorse one approach and dismiss all others; instead, they refer to several according to what is most appropriate. Especially as a student, it is premature to dismiss any particular approach to psychology until you have fully understood its strengths and weaknesses.

2. Check back to the task at the start of this chapter. Which approaches do the simple explanations there link to?

GO! End of topic project

Individually or in a group, your task is to find out more about one of the key researchers who influenced the approaches to psychology and make a presentation in some form.

You need to select:

- A researcher or theorist. A historical figure is the obvious choice, for example Hebb, Freud, Watson, Piaget, Ellis, Darwin or Rogers, but a modern researcher is also fine provided you can explain how they contributed to one of the approaches.
- A method of presentation. There are many suitable choices here – essay, poster, blog post, PowerPoint. The following shows how one of the many fun 'fake Facebook' sites could be used to present information about behaviourist researcher Ivan Pavlov:

If possible, find out if you can get together with other classes in your school or college, or even among several different schools/colleges to present your work. You may be both informed and inspired by what others produce! If this isn't practical, you could post your project responses as blog posts, and invite other Higher/National 5 students to write their reactions as comments.

Top tip

Each approach is a different way of tackling the study of psychology, and they represent different philosophical viewpoints about how human behaviour is best explained. You could be asked directly about the approaches, but it is more likely that you will need to demonstrate that you can **apply** approaches to the topics that you study in the individual behaviour unit.

☑ End of topic specimen exam questions

1. Describe one strength or one weakness of the psychoanalytic approach to studying dreams and dreaming.   2 marks

2. Explain how the biological approach can be used to explain a topic in individual behaviour.   10 marks

Individual behaviour

3 Sleep

Sleep is a mandatory topic in both Higher and National 5 Psychology. Within the context of sleep, you should know and understand:

- The nature of sleep, including sleep stages and factors that affect sleep.
- The research of Dement and Kleitman (1957) and:
  - **National 5:** Freud (1909).
  - **Higher:** Czeisler *et al.* (1990).
- Approaches to understanding sleep and dreams, including the biological approach, and:
  - **National 5:** psychoanalytic approach.
  - **Higher:** cognitive approach.
- Theories of sleep and dreams, including the restoration theory and the reorganisational theory.
- An application: how knowledge of sleep can be applied to understanding sleep disorders including circadian rhythm sleep disorders (Higher only).

You need to develop the following skills:

- Distinguishing different processes involved in sleep.
- Using different approaches to explain sleep and dreams.
- Evaluating theories of sleep and dreams.
- Using research evidence to back up factual statements and evaluative points.

! Syllabus note

This topic is mandatory at both N5 and Higher. At N5, this topic is called 'sleep and dreams'. At Higher, it is called 'sleep, dreams and sleep disorders'.

The nature of sleep

Sleep can be defined as a state of reduced conscious awareness during which the body is less active and less responsive to the outside world. We spend a quarter or more of our lives asleep. What is the purpose of this behaviour? And why do we have dreams? Do they mean something, or are they just a by-product of brain processes while we rest? These are the issues that will be covered in this chapter.

Circadian rhythms and homeostasis

Our body has a way of keeping track of time that we call our **body clock** (or 'circadian clock'). This controls **circadian rhythms** – the body's natural processes that vary over a 24-hour cycle. The most obvious examples of circadian rhythms are **the sleep/wake cycle** and our appetite for food. Other things also vary across 24 hours, such as body temperature and hormone levels.

There are variations in when people sleep. Most people sleep for around seven to eight hours per night but there are individual differences, and some people function well on six hours of sleep or less (Van Dongen *et al.*, 2005). You have probably heard people describe themselves as *'not a morning person'* – this has a genuine biological basis, with some people more prone to early waking and early bedtimes than others (Phillips, 2009). Sleep researchers sometimes call the early risers **larks** and the late risers **owls**!

Until the 1800s, it was considered common to get up mid-way through sleep, sometimes to do some work or visit neighbours, write letters, or to have sex – so the idea of having a single period of sleep that begins well after dusk may be very much a modern phenomenon (Ekirch, 2006). What's more, if people are not exposed to extended artificial light but instead to just 10 hours of light per day, they revert to having two, four hour blocks of sleep separated by one hour awake (Wehr, 1992). An eight-hour block of sleep may therefore reflect our bodies' adaptation to modern life – and to electric lighting.

Some people feel that they function well on six hours of sleep or less. While there are a few people who genuinely need less sleep, most are accumulating a **sleep debt** – a lack of sleep that they have to 'pay back' by oversleeping on other nights, such as at the weekend. In a study of over 3,000 teenagers, Wolfson and Carskadon (1998) found that school students who got a longer night's sleep on a regular basis obtained higher grades. The mean amount of sleep reported among their sample of 13 to 17 year olds was seven hours and 20 minutes, but they stated that: *'undoubtedly, most adolescents require more'* (p.885). A limitation of their study is that it did not follow participants longitudinally, to find the long-term effects of lower levels of sleep on each participant.

What is the purpose of sleep?

Are you a lark or an owl?

Polyphasic sleep

Most people in the UK sleep in a single block of time, for example eight hours every day. However many people elsewhere in the world – as well as most other great ape species – break their sleeping time up, with a main block and a shorter nap or siesta.

Some people have tried taking this further by breaking their sleep time into three or more naps. This can reduce the overall amount time spent sleeping, but is difficult to adjust to and doesn't fit well around conventional work or study schedules! This 'polyphasic sleep' could form the topic of an interesting essay or blog post.

A study found that pupils who sleep for longer regularly get higher grades

What happens when we sleep? (Or when we don't?)

As part of the scientific method (see chapter 8), researchers make controlled observations of behaviour. This is difficult to do when people are sleeping, but one way of gathering evidence is to use a **polysomnography** – a study of a sleeping individual that records physical changes in the brain and body. An important part of it is a

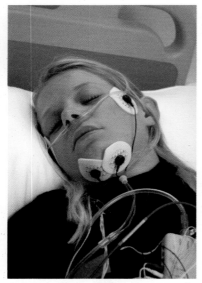

A woman being monitored as part of a sleep study

brain monitor called an electroencephalogram or **EEG**. This measures the brain's electrical activity, displaying it on a screen or printout. A polysomnography also measures other bodily activity such as eye movements and heart rate.

It is important to realise that the nature of sleep changes through the night. When we sleep, the brain goes through five **sleep stages**. In stages 1 to 4, we go gradually into a deeper sleep, becoming harder to wake. The change from one stage to the next can be observed using the size and speed of electrical brain waves that show up on the EEG in a polysomnography. Stages 3 to 4 have large slow waves called **delta waves**, and these two stages in particular are sometimes called **slow-wave sleep**.

In the fifth stage, **REM sleep**, the brain becomes much more active and we start to have dreams. The body is physically tense, but temporarily paralysed so that we cannot move. This type of sleep is found in all vertebrate animals, and it may well be the case that some other animals have dreams, too. REM stands for 'rapid eye movement' because the eyes show bursts of quick movements, even though the eyelids remain closed. Because this stage is so different from the others, the first four stages are often called **non-REM** (or nREM) sleep.

So what actually happens to you in the different stages? Each stage has its own features:

> **? Discussion point**
>
> Have you observed an animal such as a pet that appears to be dreaming?

Stage 1	This is the stage between wakefulness and sleep. You are easily woken in this stage and you can still hear noise around you such as talking or music playing. Your eyes are shut but occasionally flicker open. To put it in everyday language, you are 'drifting off'.
Stage 2	This stage begins after about 10 minutes. You now become less responsive to the environment and are sleeping soundly. However, if woken, you might not realise that you have been asleep. Sharp spikes of electrical activity called **sleep spindles** occur in the brain; some researchers think that these keep you from waking up at this stage (Halasz *et al.*, 1985).
Stage 3	After 25 minutes, you enter stages 3. The EEG begins to show some delta waves and the number of these gradually increases. You are now very unresponsive to the environment and would be hard to wake up.
Stage 4	There is no dramatic change to mark the start of stage 4. The sleep just gets gradually deeper, and delta waves become more common until they dominate the EEG recordings. Now only loud noise or shaking could wake you up, and you would be groggy and disorientated.
REM sleep	About 90 minutes on, a dramatic change occurs. The EEG pattern suddenly becomes very mixed in comparison to the slow regular delta waves of before. Your eyes will be rapidly moving from side to side beneath the eyelids. However, the rest of the body does not move – it is temporarily paralysed. If woken at this stage, you will be much less groggy – and will almost certainly report having been dreaming. All of us, therefore, dream every night, several times per night.

Sleep begins in stage 1 and progresses through stages 2 to 4 before entering REM sleep. Once REM sleep is over, the body usually returns to stage 2 sleep. This process is usually repeated four or five times per night (Carlson, 1998).

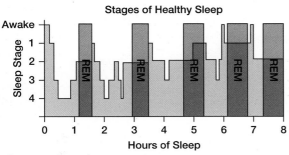

Sleep stages graph

📖 Key study: Dement and Kleitman's (1957) study of REM sleep

Aim: Dement and Kleitman aimed to find the link between dreams and sleep stages. In particular, they wanted to know the function of REM sleep and whether eye movements during REM sleep were connected to the content of dreams.

Method: In their study, they used nine adults (seven male, two female) who came to a sleep laboratory for a polysomnography. The participants had been told to avoid alcohol and caffeine during the day. The participants slept in the sleep laboratory and were woken several times during the night by the researchers. They were asked if they had been dreaming, and if so, what their dream had been about and how long it had lasted.

Findings: Dement and Kleitman found that participants were much more likely to say that they had been dreaming if woken during REM sleep, doing so on almost 80% of wakings, compared to around 9% if woken during nREM sleep. They also said that their dream had been shorter if they were woken five minutes after the start of the REM phase, compared to being woken 15 minutes after it started.

In terms of eye movements, these did appear to link to what participants had been dreaming about. A participant who had been making left-to-right movements of the eyes reported a dream about people throwing tomatoes at each other, for example. After each waking, participants generally got back to sleep inside five minutes.

Evaluation: This study used a small sample, and its artificial setting – including frequent wakings – may have affected the quality of their sleep or the content of their dreams. Nevertheless, this was strong evidence that REM sleep is dream sleep, which has been supported by subsequent research. It is harder to generalise the findings linking dream content to eye movements as each dream was different. Another limitation is that the study focused on adults, and the results can't be generalised to children.

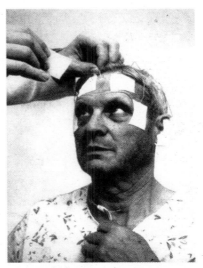

Nathaniel Kleitman taking part in one of his own sleep studies

🔍 Top tip

The Dement and Kleitman (1957) study is mandatory for both National 5 and Higher, meaning that you could be asked about it in the exam. Ensure that you know which studies are mandatory and which are optional.

Peter Tripp during the 'wakeathon'

❓ Discussion point

Do you think interrogation using sleep deprivation is immoral? Could it be pointless, given that people become delusional through sleep deprivation?

Sleep deprivation

We assume that sleep is essential – so what happens when you don't sleep at all? One famous case of **sleep deprivation** involved Peter Tripp, a New York DJ who stayed awake for 200 hours in aid of charity, while broadcasting from a booth in Times Square and being regularly tested by psychologists. His case shows how dramatic the effects of sleep deprivation can be:

He looked weary but no radio listener or casual onlooker could imagine the truth of his experience. It resembled a medieval torture… By 100 hours, only halfway, he had reached an inexorable turning point. Now he could only perform one or two of the daily battery of tests. Tests requiring attention or minimal mental agility had become unbearable to him and the psychologists testing him. As one later recalled, 'Here was a competent New York disc jockey trying vainly to find his way through the alphabet.' By 170 hours the tests were torture. A simple algebraic problem that Tripp had earlier solved with ease took such superhuman effort that he was frightened, and his agonised attempts to perform were painful to watch.

Loss of concentration and mental agility were not the worst, however. By 110 hours there were signs of delirium. As one of the doctors recalled, 'We didn't know much about it at the time because he couldn't tell us.' From his later statements, his curious utterances and behaviour at the time, it became clear. Tripp's visual world had grown grotesque. A doctor walked into the booth in a tweed suit that Tripp saw as a suit of furry worms. A nurse appeared to drip saliva. A scientist's tie kept jumping. This was frightening, hard to explain, and sometimes Tripp grew angry wondering if this were a bona fide experiment or a masquerade. Around 120 hours, he opened a bureau drawer in the hotel and rushed out calling for help. It appeared to be spurting flames. Tripp thought the blaze has been set deliberately to test him. In order to explain to himself these hallucinations – which appeared quite real – he concocted rationalisations resembling the delusions of psychotic patients.

Source: Lindzey et al. (1978: 172–173)

Clearly sleep deprivation can be harmful not just to our ability to function but to our mental health. It's so unpleasant that it is used as torture – the CIA's interrogation of terror suspects in recent years included keeping detainees awake for up to 180 hours at a time (Bulkeley, 2014).

Factors that affect sleep

On an everyday level, many people suffer from poor quality sleep or from not sleeping enough. This can be harmful to health; it has been linked to CHD, digestive illnesses and reproductive problems (Czeisler et al., 1990).

The quality of a person's sleep can be affected by a wide range of everyday factors:

Drugs

One factor that can affect sleep is the use of recreational or prescription **drugs**. **Stimulant** drugs have the effect of making people more alert or keeping them awake and can reduce the quality of sleep. One example of a stimulant is **caffeine**. This is the world's most popular psychoactive drug and it is present in food and drinks such as coffee, tea, chocolate and most energy drinks. It can also be taken in tablet form. People drink coffee to keep them alert, but taking it in the evening can make it harder to get to sleep. Many people don't realise that it can take over 5 hours for the level of caffeine in the blood just to drop to half of the level it was at after taking the caffeine (Statland & Demas, 1980). **Amphetamine** (often called 'speed') is another stimulant – although it is a class B illegal drug, it is widely used for socialising and by some workers on long overnight shifts.

Alcohol can also affect sleep – usually making people feel sleepier. Many people like to drink alcohol in the evenings to help them get to sleep, which changes the proportions of REM and non-REM sleep. However, tolerance to alcohol develops quickly, resulting in normal patterns of sleep for healthy people consuming moderate amounts of alcohol (Roehrs and Roth, 2001). Therefore, it is unlikely to be of any long-term use in treating insomnia.

Prescription drugs can interfere with sleep patterns as an undesired **side effect**, either by making it harder for us to sleep or by making us drowsy. Some drugs such as anti-histamines (taken for allergies) come in 'non-drowsy' versions.

Zeitgebers

Another factor that affects sleep is a group of environmental triggers called **zeitgebers**. The word is German for 'time-giver'; it refers to environmental signals that affect our circadian rhythms and make our brain think that it is time to sleep or wake up.

In our evolutionary past, we would start to feel sleepy as the day got late and it got darker. Light and darkness are both zeitgebers, telling our brain that it is time to sleep or wake up. Nowadays, of course, we use artificial lights and often stay awake (or get up) when it is dark outside.

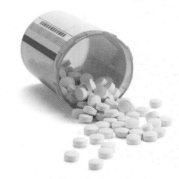

Recently, researchers have realised that artificial light can disturb our circadian rhythms and affect the quality of sleep. In particular, light from some low-energy lightbulbs and from screens contains a large proportion of blue wavelengths of light that can have a strong effect in suppressing sleep (Santhi *et al.*, 2012). In particular, they can suppress the production of sleep hormones such as melatonin.

Drugs can affect sleep

Noise and anxiety

Environmental factors can affect our ability to sleep. The most obvious one is **noise** – most people prefer peace and quiet to fall asleep. However, as noted above, once the deeper stages of sleep begin, people can easily sleep through noise and are hard to wake up.

If there is a lot of noise when we are trying to sleep, people feel anxious. **Anxiety** in itself can make it harder to sleep. People may

Artificial light can disturb our circadian rhythms

Top tip

You could also refer to jet lag and shift work as factors that affect the ability to sleep.

Make the link

...between the topic of sleep and your knowledge of RMPS/religious studies. Many religious texts refer to sleep, including when and where it should be done.

Key concepts

- Sleep
- Body clock
- Circadian rhythms
- Sleep/wake cycle
- Larks
- Owls
- Sleep debt
- Polysomnography
- Electroencephalogram (EEG)
- Sleep stages
- Delta waves
- Slow-wave sleep
- REM sleep
- Non-REM sleep
- Sleep spindles
- Sleep deprivation
- Peter Tripp
- Drugs
- Stimulant
- Caffeine
- Amphetamine
- Side effect
- Zeitgeber
- Noise
- Anxiety
- Sleep disorder

experience insomnia during times when they are worried or stressed. Common night time worries include:

- relationship problems
- family
- money
- job/studies

Such worries seem to be more common in women and to peak at age 35 to 55 (Breus, 2012). Such problems can be compounded when the inability to sleep becomes an additional worry!

Some of these factors are easy to control, while others are much more difficult. When any such factors disrupt sleep to the extent that the individual struggles to function, they may be considered to have a **sleep disorder**. Sleep disorders and possible treatments for them are explained in the final section of this chapter.

Questions

1. In what sleep stage do dreams mainly occur?

2. What term is given to the body's 24-hour rhythms such as the sleep/wake cycle?

3. What does an EEG measure during sleep?

4. How many sleep stages does the average person go through in total, in an entire night's sleep?

5. According to Dement and Kleitman, are eye movements relevant to dream content?

6. What three main factors affect a person's ability to sleep?

7. What does 'zeitgeber' literally mean?

8. Give two examples of drugs that make people less likely to get to sleep.

9. Give two examples of worries that can keep people awake.

10. Name two of the psychological changes Peter Tripp experienced during sleep deprivation.

GO! Activities

1. Delta waves are shown on an electroencephalogram during deep sleep. Find out about other brain waves – alpha, beta, theta and gamma. Print out a picture of how these look on an EEG recording.

2. Copy the following table into your notes and complete.

Factor in sleep	Effect	How it impacts on sleep

3. Find out about another case study of sleep deprivation. Explain the findings to a fellow student or to your class. Were any of the effects of sleep deprivation similar to those found in Peter Tripp? Are there any overlaps with the effects of drugs or illness?

Approaches to sleep and dreams

The biological approach to sleep and dreams

Revision points from chapter 2

The following points from the main section on the biological approach are especially relevant to this topic. Ensure that you can mention them in exam answers on approaches to sleep and/or dreams:

- the nervous system and brain areas
- hormones

The nervous system and brain areas

As in other areas of psychology, the biological approach explains sleep and dreams in terms of which brain areas control behaviour.

The brain in general is directly in control of sleep. During the day, a chemical called **adenosine** builds up in our brain's neurons as a natural by-product (Benington & Heller, 1995). When we sleep, this build-up is cleared, and the adenosine is replaced by energy in the form of glycogen. This is a homeostatic process – the body tries to maintain a balance. Evidence supporting this view is the fact that the stimulant drug caffeine blocks adenosine receptors, making the body less responsive to the build-up of adenosine, and reducing feelings of tiredness.

Biological psychologists have identified particular areas of the brain that control circadian rhythms: the **hypothalamus** is responsible for homeostasis and it contains an area called the **suprachiasmatic nucleus (SCN)** that controls our circadian rhythms. The SCN gets information from nerve cells in the eyes about whether it is light or dark, allowing light to function as a zeitgeber.

! Syllabus note

Higher students should learn all three approaches in this section. At National 5, only the biological and psychoanalytic approaches are required.

🔍 Top tip

You could remember the SCN as having the same abbreviation as 'Scottish Candidate Number'!

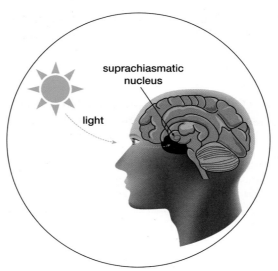

The SCN controls our circadian rhythms

This approach also explains **dreams** biologically. Rather than look for the meaning of dreams, the biological approach thinks that dreams largely result from random brain activity during sleep and are, therefore, meaningless. The **activation-synthesis** hypothesis devised by Hobson and McCarley (1977) states that dreams result from neurons in a brain area called the **pons** firing randomly, which then sends messages to the neocortex. The neocortex tries to make sense of the messages, creatively making up narratives that fit with the random signals that it is receiving, and these form dreams. The 'activation' refers to the firing of neurons in the pons, while 'synthesis' refers to the cortex putting this information together into a dream that makes sense.

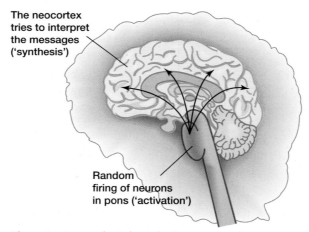

The activation-synthesis hypothesis

Hormones

One of the main functions of the SCN is to control the release of the sleep hormone **melatonin** – a hormone that makes us feel sleepy. In all animals, melatonin is released when it gets dark. Therefore, it is usually released into the bloodstream in the evening when the sun goes down and it gets dark. This makes us start to feel sleepy and eventually fall asleep. However, it doesn't act instantly – usually melatonin will start to be released in the early evening. Melatonin levels peak in the middle of the night and then start to fall back down towards daytime levels.

If the SCN is confused about what time it is due to zeitgebers, such as having bright lights on at night including screens (see previous section), it may release melatonin at the wrong time, or not release it when we do need sleep. Some people need to take melatonin supplements to help them sleep.

Evaluation

The explanation of sleep in terms of the SCN and melatonin is supported by studies of other animals. Even though sleep behaviour varies in different species, melatonin appears to play a key role, being released in darkness among all vertebrates.

However, the biological approach is limited in particular in its explanation of dreaming. Although the activation-synthesis hypothesis has been influential, most people do not find it satisfying to say that their dreams are entirely random, and it struggles to explain some major facts such as that 70% of dreams make sense and that experiences from the previous day tend to appear during dreams (Domhoff, 2005).

The psychoanalytic approach to sleep and dreams

Revision points from chapter 2

The following points from the main section on the psychoanalytic approach are especially relevant to this topic. You can mention them in exam answers on approaches to sleep and/or dreams:

- the id, ego and superego
- oral, anal and phallic stages

The id, ego and superego

The psychoanalyst, Sigmund Freud, saw the process of sleep as motivated – the mind desires to withdraw from the external world and go into a foetus-like state without troubles and worries. In this view, dreams are seen as a problematic interruption (Pines, 1976).

You will remember that the psychoanalytic approach is interested in the unconscious mind. It states that the id is the unconscious, while the ego is conscious. During sleep, the id becomes dominant, and the id's main motivation is pleasure; according to Freud's classic work '*On the Interpretation of Dreams*' (Freud, 1900), dreams reveal our unconscious wishes and fantasies. Freud believed that dreams involve **wish fulfilment**, that is, we dream about what we want – especially about wishes that have been thwarted in real life.

Psychoanalysts believe that only some thoughts are truly inaccessible. There are others that we may be unaware of at a particular moment but can become conscious if we make the effort under the right conditions – our **preconscious** thoughts. Most memories about ourselves and our lives are, therefore, preconscious, as are memories of our dreams.

The sleep hormone melatonin is released in all animals when it gets dark

🔍 Top tip

Don't forget the general evaluation points about each approach that were covered in the previous chapter.

🔍 Top tip

If a person has a fixation in an earlier stage of development, this could be reflected in the content of their dreams, according to the psychoanalytic approach.

Freud believed that dreams involve wish fulfilment

Freud believed that a dream about a storm was a sign that the person was experiencing emotional turmoil

A sleep study could involve a dream diary

Oral, anal and phallic stage

Freud also thought that dreams contain a series of **symbols**, with the true meaning of the dream hidden from the conscious mind. In particular, anything that is disturbing or embarrassing can be hidden by the unconscious mind using a symbolic image. These symbols may be based on the psychosexual obsessions of the person's psychological stage of development – for example, Little Hans dreamed about his penis during the phallic stage.

Two important terms to be aware of are the **manifest content** of the dream – what the dream appears to be about – and the **latent content** – what the dream is *really* about. For example:

Manifest content	Latent content
School	Learning or being judged
A storm	Emotional turmoil
Teeth falling out	Worries or lack of control
Pregnancy	A new aspect of the self

Understanding a dream involves a process of interpretation of the manifest content in order to understand the latent content, and therefore, the true meaning. In addition, Freud thought that several processes occur that distort the true meaning of the dream, making the content harder to understand. Two key processes include:

- **Condensation:** several ideas or symbols get merged together.
- **Secondary elaboration**: the dreamer's own interpretation or things that they add when telling the dream. This makes it harder for an analyst to recognise the latent content.

The psychoanalytic approach is known for the **case study method**, which for studies of sleep could involve interviews and dream diaries used to record individual patients' experiences (see chapter 8 for more on this method). One of the best examples of this is Freud's case study of Little Hans (see key study), in which the interpretation of Hans' dreams was crucial.

However, Jung (1964) disagreed with Freud's method of interpreting dreams. He said that dream symbols are unique to the individual and they cannot have a general meaning. He also stated that dreams should only be interpreted based on what actually appears in the dream, and not translated by the therapist – so, for example, he would not say that a dream about giraffes was actually a dream about your parents.

Carl Jung

📖 Key study: Freud's case study of 'little Hans'

Aim: *Freud wanted to provide evidence of his controversial Oedipus complex (see chapter 2). When he was approached by a friend, Herr Graf, whose son suffered from a severe phobia of horses, Freud decided to see if the boy's behaviour fitted his theory.*

Method: *Freud's study was a case study, although it was unusual compared to modern case studies in that he did not study the patient, 'little Hans', directly, but instead exchanged letters with Herr Graf, discussing the boy's behaviour, and in particular, his phobia of horses.*

Findings: *Hans had been frightened by seeing a horse collapsing in the street, and had developed a strong phobia of horses (horses were common on the streets of Vienna at this time). He was anxious about the birth of his baby sister Hanna, and, apparently, made a connection between her birth and a loaded cart pulled by a horse. Freud was very interested to hear about Hans's dreams and fantasies, because he thought that these were evidence of unconscious processes. Hans had three key dreams:*

In one, he dreamed that he was married to his mother and they had their own family. This was interpreted by Freud as showing Hans's romantic desire for his mother.

In another dream, a crumpled giraffe was being squashed by a large giraffe – Freud thought the giraffes represented Hans' parents, and that this dream showed Hans's fear and hostility towards his father.

In a third, a plumber came to the house and removed Hans's penis, replacing it with a larger one. Freud said that this showed Hans's desire to be a grown up man and marry his mother, as well as linking to the penis obsession of the phallic stage of development.

He also had certain fantasies and dreams about urinating. He was caught playing with his penis and his mother threatened to have the doctor cut it off! This provoked some anxiety.

Evaluation: *Freud saw the issues as being evidence for his Oedipus complex, but it is possible that he and Hans's father distorted the evidence to fit the theory. Hans, whose real name was Herbert, found out about the study in adulthood and claimed that he had no recollection of the dreams and fantasies described in Freud's research, or of fearing horses. It is hard to generalise from one patient in a case study – in this case, Hans's issues do not prove that all boys fear their fathers.*

❗ Syllabus note

Freud's (1909) study is only mandatory for National 5, but will also be useful evidence for any Higher students who are studying the psychoanalytic approach to sleep.

Freud with little Hans

❓ Discussion point

Do you think that our dreams have hidden meanings? Have you ever tried to analyse a dream or had someone else do it for you?

❓ Discussion point

Do you think, as Freud did, that Hans's behaviour and fantasies were relatively normal for his stage of development?

Evaluation

A strength of this approach is its impact in terms of popular understanding of dreams. It has had a major effect on society, in particular in terms of the idea that dreams have hidden meanings.

However, psychoanalysts do not all agree on how to interpret dreams – in particular, Freud and Jung took different approaches. Another obvious challenge for Freud's idea of wish fulfilment is that many dreams are unpleasant! The approach struggles to give a satisfactory explanation of nightmares.

In general, this approach to sleep and dreams relies too heavily on case studies such as the case of Hans. The findings of such studies are hard to generalise to other people.

The cognitive approach to sleep and dreams

Revision points from chapter 2

The following points from the main section on the cognitive approach are especially relevant to this topic. Ensure that you mention them in exam answers on approaches to sleep and/or dreams:

- computer analogy
- schemas

Computer analogy

The cognitive approach focuses on the role of sleep in memory and thinking. According to this viewpoint, the mind is a processor of information and sleep largely exists in order to facilitate this processing. During sleep, the mind can clean up the files, pruning out unnecessary items and strengthening links between memories.

Stickgold (2009) has investigated the processes by which memories develop during sleep. According to his research, sleep can be of benefit to every type of memory, but he suggests that those that have a medium (rather than strong or weak) memory trace gain the biggest benefit.

Sometimes a nap is just as good as an overnight sleep when it comes to consolidating learning through sleep. Mednick *et al.* (2003) found that for a perception task, the same benefit was found after a 90 minute nap (containing all sleep stages) as from a full night's sleep. This idea has been supported by research into infants – Seehagen *et al.* (2015) found that when babies were learning a new action, those who had taken a nap showed a better recall of the skill than those who had not.

Walker *et al.* (2003) used a finger-tapping task to study the role of sleep in memories. They found that sleep helps memories to be reliably encoded but that recalling an item the following day reactivates the memory, allowing a skill (such as playing a musical instrument) to be refined.

> **? Discussion point**
>
> Why do you think abbreviated names like 'Anna O' or fake names such as 'Hans' are sometimes used to describe patients in research?

> **🔍 Top tip**
>
> For Higher pupils, the psychoanalytic approach is not mandatory, so in this topic you can study the biological and cognitive approaches, plus one other approach of your choice (three in total).

A study showed that a nap helped babies to recall new skills

Sleep helps skills such as playing a musical instrument to be refined

Schemas

The cognitive approach look at the dreams in terms of normal thought processes such as schemas and scripts. According to Domhoff (2011), a dream is what happens when the mind does not have any other task. He draws comparisons between the dream and waking experiences, such as fantasies and daydreams, saying that they are very similar in content and that both occur when the mind is not set a particular task to do. From this point of view, the mind's usual processes of schemas, beliefs and emotions will play a large role in dream content. Therefore, this view studies dreams using knowledge of waking thought processes as a starting point.

The cognitive approach to dreaming would predict links between what we think about during the day and what appears in dreams, and is partly supported by evidence that dreams usually have a story that makes sense, rather than being a random mixture of memories. The idea that dream content is based on what we have been thinking about when awake is called the **continuity hypothesis of dreams**.

Evaluation

Stickgold's research is supported by a large body of research evidence. The cognitive approach provides a parsimonious explanation of the thought processes that happen during dreams. Rather than being explained as something completely different that has its own special processes, as Freud did, cognitive psychologists state that it is essentially similar to waking cognition.

The approach also has potential to be combined with the biological approach, in what is known as **cognitive neuroscience**.

However, there are some elements that are hard to explain in terms of continuity from daytime thought processes, such as the fact that so many dreams have bizarre elements that are totally unconnected with things we experience while awake, for example, flying or meeting famous people (McNamara, 2012).

? Discussion point

Why do you think babies sleep much more than adults do?

? Discussion point

Have you ever tried having a 'power nap' or otherwise napping during the day? Do you find it helpful?

Domhoff thinks dreams and daydreams are very similar

Many dreams are unconnected to our experiences while awake

⚷ Key concepts

- Adenosine
- Homeostasis
- Hypothalamus
- SCN – suprachiasmatic nucleus
- Activation-synthesis
- Dreams
- Pons
- Melatonin
- Wish fulfilment
- Preconscious
- Symbols
- Manifest content
- Latent content
- Condensation
- Secondary elaboration
- Continuity hypothesis of dreams
- Cognitive neuroscience

✔ Questions

1. What part of the brain contains the suprachiasmatic nucleus (SCN)?

2. What hormone triggers us to feel sleepy and fall asleep?

3. What chemical builds up in our brain cells during the day?

4. What is the term for the biological theory that dreams are due to random firing of neurons in the pons?

5. Which term means the true meaning of dreams according to Freud's theory – manifest content or latent content?

6. In Little Hans's dreams, which animal represented his parents, according to Freud?

7. What term means combining more than one idea or fantasy into a dream symbol?

8. What cognitive process is sleep essential for, according to Stickgold (2009)?

9. What problems are there with the continuity hypothesis?

10. What is the relevance of schemas to the cognitive explanation of dreams?

GO! Activities

1. Which of these approaches makes most sense to you? Discuss this question in a pair or group OR write a response to it in your notebook or blog.

2. Write down the events of one of your dreams. Underline any key events, people or objects. Now have a look at a dream dictionary (either a book, or an online version) and try to find out what this manifest content might actually mean (i.e. what latent content it represents). Does it make sense to you?

Theories of sleep and dreams

Why do we sleep, and what are dreams for? There are two main theories that try to answer this question.

Sleep theory 1: restoration theory of sleep

This theory of sleep, summarised by Oswald (1966), states that all animals sleep because it allows the body to carry out essential repair tasks.

Sleep appears to be universal among complex animals – it has been observed in species ranging from humans to fruit flies (Abel *et al.*, 2013). We know that for evolutionary reasons, sleep must fulfil an essential function, or at least have fulfilled an essential function in our evolutionary past – if it wasn't useful, animals would not do it, because any competing animal that did not sleep would have a survival advantage. One major possibility is that sleep is necessary for the body for **restoration**, that is, to rest and recover from exertions.

Possible restoration functions that the body might need to do during sleep include:

- repairing minor injuries
- removal of waste chemicals in the muscles
- replenishing neurotransmitters or energy in the nervous system

The rationale behind this theory is that a period of physical inactivity might be essential or at least very helpful for this restoration to happen. Sleep causes the body to be relatively inactive – repair functions may be more successful during inactivity as no further damage is being done to body tissues or because fewer toxins/waste products are being produced.

An alternative idea is that sleep helps animals to save energy by keeping them inactive when they are not gathering food or to keep them out of danger. This fits with the finding that carnivores sleep more than herbivores (Siegel, 2005), as carnivores generally have fewer enemies and spend less time gathering food. However, neither of these ideas can explain why animals completely lose conscious awareness during sleep, which is not a survival advantage.

Sleep may help injuries to heal

Horne found that sleep deprivation did not affect the participants' athletic ability

Evidence

The restoration theory found support from Shapiro *et al.* (1981), in a study of runners. After an ultramarathon, it was found that their sleep lasted on average 90 minutes longer than usual over the next two nights. In particular, non-REM sleep lengthened, rising from 25% to 45% of total sleep.

However, Horne (1978) reported that sleep deprivation did not interfere with participants' ability to play sport or make them ill. It seems that sleep is not essential for physical functioning, at least in the short-term.

Horne and Harley (1988) believed that a warming of the brain during exercise led to longer sleep in the Shapiro study, not wear and tear to the body. To test this, they heated people's faces and heads using a hairdryer! Four out of their six participants were then found to have a longer period of non-REM sleep. Their finding goes against the idea that sleep is needed to repair the body – but it could be repair of the brain that is the key function. Alternatively, perhaps some daytime activities such as exercise interfere with brain functions and the brain then needs to catch up on these during sleep.

Evaluation

Restoration is one of the main evolutionary explanations why all mammals sleep and is better able to explain the loss of conscious awareness compared to the alternative ideas that sleep evolved to help organisms save energy or stay out of danger. However, danger from predators could play a role in the variations seen in the amount of sleep.

Evidence seems to be growing that sleep is more important to restoration of the brain than the body, but this debate has not yet been fully resolved. It is clear that sleeping too little in humans seems to result in poorer performance (see the case of Peter Tripp in the previous section) and an increased chance of accidents. This supports the restoration theory (Coren, 1998).

Sleep probably has multiple functions, and REM sleep and non-REM sleep may have different functions (Siegel, 2005). Therefore, it is probably over-simplistic to suggest that sleep is just about restoration but this may well be one of the main functions of non-REM sleep.

Hobson (2005) disagrees with the restoration theory. He states that sleep is entirely for the brain, noting that bodily restoration could be achieved by simply resting.

Some researchers believe that the main function of dreams is the reorganisation of memories

Sleep theory 2: reorganisational theory of sleep

In 1983, researchers Francis Crick and Kenneth Mitchison famously wrote:

'We dream in order to forget'

Source: Crick and Mitchison (1983)

They devised a theory that stated that the main function of dreams is **reorganisation**, in order to improve memory storage. The theory is based on the concept of **reverse learning**, meaning that learning can be undone during REM sleep. They believed that dreams are just a side effect of a decluttering process that takes place in the brain – the cortex becomes overloaded with information during the day, and that during REM sleep, unwanted memories are deleted in order to improve organisation and make space.

Crick and Mitchison believed that there are two main categories of memories:

- **Adaptive memories**: things that will be useful for us to retain.
- **Parasitic memories**: useless or harmful memories that waste resources.

They feel that the brain benefits from reverse learning of parasitic memories and that this is the purpose of REM sleep. Therefore, the theory states that sleep is for cognitive reorganisation. As these unconnected memories and ideas are activated, a random selection of thoughts and memories form into a dream, as suggested by Hobson and McCarley (1977 – see p.70).

Research evidence

To support their theory, Crick and Mitchison refer to other species that lack REM sleep – the echidna and two species of dolphin. These animals also have larger brains than might be expected for their overall body size. The researchers conclude that the 'pruning' of memories during REM sleep allows the brain to be smaller and more efficient in other species.

The researchers have also run **neural network** computer models of learning. In these, they have found that memories are easily overloaded but that this can be reduced using reverse learning.

Evaluation

A strength of the reorganisational theory is that it gives a clear theory about why REM sleep could be important. By making memory more efficient, Crick and Mitchison (1983) argue that better use is made of the available space in the brain.

Top tip

This theory is only mandatory for Higher; however, National 5 students can also get credit for including it in their work/exam answers where appropriate.

? Discussion point

What did Crick and Mitchison mean by *'we dream in order to forget'*?

Francis Crick – who first became famous for his research into the structure of DNA

Certain species of dolphin do not dream; the large size of their brains could suggest that the 'pruning' of memories during REM sleep allows the brain to be smaller

🔍 Top tip

Running computer simulations of thought processes is a typical method used as part of the cognitive approach to psychology. This theory can be used as an example of the cognitive approach as it links to the computer analogy.

However, a major weakness of this theory is that it is based on computer models of memory, and lacks research support on human participants. Numerous studies have shown that rather than destroying memories, sleep is beneficial to memory (e.g. Rasch & Born, 2013).

This theory also does not explain why dreams have a narrative (i.e. a story) – our dreams appear to make sense the majority of the time (Domhoff *et al.*, 2006). This doesn't seem to fit well with the idea that random memories are being activated and destroyed.

⚷ Key concepts

- Restoration
- Reverse learning
- Reorganisation
- Parasitic memories
- Adaptive memories
- Neural network

✓ Questions

1. According to the restoration theory, why do organisms sleep – to repair their bodies or to hide from predators?

2. Give one example of a repair process that could occur during sleep.

3. Why would sleeping be a good time for the body to repair itself?

4. What type of sleep lasted longer in runners after a race, in the Shapiro *et al.* (1981) study?

5. What did Horne and Harley (1988) find when they heated participants' heads with a hairdryer?

6. Do all animals sleep for a similar length of time?

7. What can reverse learning do to a memory according to the reorganisational theory?

8. Why are parasitic memories deleted according to Crick and Mitchison?

9. What computer-based evidence was given in support of the reorganisational theory?

10. Do other researchers agree that sleep causes forgetting?

GO! Activities

1. Both of the above theories have used evidence from animals. Summarise this evidence. Now find out about how long some common animals sleep for and make a chart or a poster. You might be able to find out about species differences in both REM sleep and non-REM sleep, and about when species sleep. Are there any animals that particularly surprised you?

2. Find out more about the theory of sleep that suggests that sleep functions mainly to keep organisms out of danger. Do you find this a convincing theory of why we sleep? If not, could it be part of the explanation?

Real-world application: sleep disorders

Clearly, a lack of sleep can affect our mood and functioning. It can make it unsafe to drive, as well as cause severe health problems. As shown in the case study of Peter Tripp earlier in this chapter, extreme levels of sleep loss can cause people to hallucinate and can affect their mental health.

However, some people find it very hard to get a night's sleep and/or be fully rested. This could be a temporary situation or they may have a **sleep disorder** causing long-term sleep disruption due to lifestyle issues or an underlying neurological/medical condition.

Insomnia, hypersomnia and parasomnia

There are three general categories of sleep disorder. **Insomnia** means an inability to get to sleep or that the person cannot stay asleep. This is more common as people get older. **Hypersomnia** is the opposite – the person feels very sleepy a lot of the time, finding it hard to stay awake during the day. These problems can be cause by a wide range of factors. **Parasomnia** means sleep disorders that are not due to too much/too little sleep but abnormal behaviours or emotions while sleeping, for example, sleepwalking.

Insomnia is very common and it is often treated using drugs – in England there are over 10 million prescriptions per year for **sleeping pills** (NHS, 2014a). Essentially, these are sedative drugs that are often effective in making people feel sleepy but due to problems with side effects and addiction, they are not recommended for long-term use. Often they fail to tackle the cause, which may be environmental, for example stress, light or noise, as discussed earlier in this chapter.

Types of sleep disorders

Sleep apnoea
Sleep apnoea occurs when a person briefly stops breathing for a few seconds during sleep – sometimes tens or even hundreds of times over the course of a night. On each occasion, the body detects a build-up

! Syllabus note

This section is mandatory for Higher only.

A lack of sleep can make it unsafe to drive

In England there are over 10 million prescriptions per year for sleeping pills

? Discussion point
Have you ever suffered from insomnia or hypersomnia?

Ventilator treatment for sleep apnoea

7% of adolescents experience a delayed sleep phase

? Discussion point

Have you ever experienced a delayed sleep phase? What did you do about it?

🔍 Top tip

The explanation and treatment of CRSDs can be linked to the biological and cognitive approaches to psychology.

🔍 Top tip

Circadian rhythm sleep disorders are a mandatory part of the course and must be studied, while the other disorders are optional so you can choose which ones you wish to focus on.

of carbon dioxide in the bloodstream and prompts the person to wake up. These wakings are very short and they are characterised by sharp intakes of breath and spluttering, which can disturb other sleepers in the same household (Wilson & Nutt, 2013). Sleep apnoea results in a disturbed, shallow sleep and causes daytime hypersomnia – the resulting sleepiness reduces alertness and can massively increase the risk of the person having a driving accident.

Circadian rhythm sleep disorders

Our circadian rhythms prompt most of us to feel tired in the evening, even when we have not had an active day, and then go to sleep for a number of hours. However, some people's circadian rhythms do not function normally and this is known as a **circadian rhythm sleep disorder (CRSD)**. This is more likely among blind individuals who do not respond to light as a zeitgeber, but it also happens in sighted individuals. The problems can be made worse by a sudden change in schedule that requires an earlier or later waking time.

There are several types of CRSD:

- Delayed sleep phase: the person goes to sleep later every night.
- Advanced sleep phase: the person goes to sleep earlier every night.
- Irregular type: timing of sleep and wake are variable.
- Non-24 hour type: the person's circadian rhythm is regular but is not set to 24 hours (this may result in a delayed sleep phase).
- Shift work: here the CRSD is caused by work patterns such as night shifts.

A **delayed sleep phase** occurs when people go to bed progressively later each night due to insomnia. It is relatively uncommon in the general population but it can occur in over 7% of adolescents (American Psychiatric Association, 2013). This may be partly due to hormonal changes. It can cause major difficulties with work and education because an individual who goes to sleep later every night will feel increasingly tired by day. It can be made worse by anxiety over the situation.

To treat a delayed sleep phase CRSD, **melatonin supplements** are sometimes prescribed to mimic the natural release of this hormone and make the person feel sleepy at the desired time. In patients for whom lifestyle or anxiety are causing the problem, cognitive-behavioural therapy may be more appropriate.

Another problem with circadian rhythms is caused by **shift work** – when people work shifts rather than at the same time every day. The problem arises because during a night shift the individual's circadian rhythms are telling the body that it should be sleeping, but they have to stay awake. Then, when trying to catch up on sleep during the day, they may find it hard to fall asleep or to sleep soundly. In severe cases, a person with ongoing insomnia due to shift work can be diagnosed with a CRSD.

Shift workers are at risk of developing a CRSD

Jet lag can cause a similar problem in the short-term. This occurs when people travel to a different time zone by plane, for example, going from Scotland to North America on holiday or for work. The SCN takes time to adjust to a different time zone and the person may feel sleepy during the day and find it hard to get to sleep at night. This is because the SCN still causes melatonin to be released when it is evening in the old time zone. This can lead to insomnia at night and hypersomnia during the day. Melatonin supplements can help travellers adjust to a new time zone and avoid jet lag (Wagner, 1999).

After a long trip travellers may experience jet lag

As researched by Czeisler and colleagues (see key study), **light therapy** can be a very useful treatment for shift work. If scheduled effectively, the person's circadian rhythms can reset to the desired time schedule. The application of strong light acts as a zeitgeber, affecting the SCN. The idea is that by moving the person's circadian rhythms so that day and night are swapped over, the person will sleep more soundly during the day and function better when working at night.

Light therapy can also be an effective treatment for jet lag, helping the body to reset to a different time zone more quickly.

Light therapy can be an effective treatment for sleep disorders

📖 Key study: Czeisler *et al.*'s (1990) study of shift work

Aim: This study aimed to find a routine, including light exposure, which would help nightshift workers fully adapt to daytime sleeping. Nightshifts are associated with poor sleep and health problems but previous research had shown that the presence of light or darkness regulates the circadian rhythms and it can 'reset' the suprachiasmatic nucleus by up to 12 hours.

Method: The timing of exposure to light appears to be important, and therefore the researchers designed a schedule of light exposure to help nightshift workers. The study was carried out on eight healthy men in their 20s, none of whom had regularly worked a nightshift. Each came to the researchers' lab at 23:45 for six days of 'shifts' that involved staying awake, doing cognitive tests and reporting their own alertness and mood. Otherwise, they were free to do their own work. Men in the experimental group only were exposed to very bright light during the nightshift (12,000 'lumens' of brightness, compared to the approximately 150 lumens of normal artificial room lighting).

Charles Czeisler

Findings: Biological measures such as body temperature showed that the experimental group had had their circadian rhythms adjusted forward by over 9 hours, while the control group stayed roughly the same. Both subjective assessments of alertness and performance on cognitive tests were similarly shifted forwards. It appeared that their body clock had shifted from day to night due to the bright light exposure.

Evaluation: A strength of the study is that the light/dark schedule made allowances for the fact that night workers are typically exposed to natural light on their way home from work each morning – a problem of some other studies. In addition, the time difference between the mean low-point of body temperature of the control versus experimental group was huge, and statistically very unlikely to have occurred by chance. Conversely, the sample was very small, and contained only men, making it harder to generalise the results. Several extraneous variables were not fully controlled; for example, when they ate breakfast or how much time they slept for.

Top tip

The Czeisler *et al.* study is mandatory for Higher students.

Sleepwalkers may engage in everyday behaviour like eating

Night terrors

A particularly distressing sleep disorder is **night terrors**. During deep sleep, the individual sits up or screams and appears terrified. They may look awake but they are quite unaware of their surroundings and cannot be reasoned with. Their eyes may be open, but they show no sign of recognising people or their surroundings and they may lash out if people try to comfort them.

Night terrors are not the same thing as nightmares – they do not occur during REM sleep – but they are linked to sleepwalking (see below). Night terrors are much more common in children, typically aged 3 to 8, but can continue into adolescence or even adulthood. Although distressing, night terrors are usually brief – the individual may calm down and go back to sleep, or wake up and be disoriented. They typically have no memory of the incident the next day. It can be caused by being over-tired during the day, by stress or a traumatic incident, or by minor illnesses.

Sleepwalking

Similar to night terrors, an individual who is **sleepwalking** is unresponsive to their surroundings and cannot hear people who are talking to them. They may engage in common/routine everyday behaviour such as walking around the house, getting dressed, eating or going to the toilet. This can cause problems especially in unfamiliar environments, as the sleeper may urinate somewhere inappropriate or eat something harmful.

Sleepwalking is usually harmless, but steps may be taken to ensure the sleepwalker does not injure themselves; in some cases the person may leave the house and put themselves at considerable risk, for example a patient who woke up asleep on a high cliff, unable to remember how he got there (Wilson & Nutt, 2013).

✔ Questions

1. What kind of problems can result from poor sleep?

2. What bodily function is interrupted in sleep apnoea?

3. Why do some blind people suffer from CRSDs?

4. What is meant by jet lag?

5. What is the typical age range for suffering night terrors?

6. Does the sufferer of night terrors actually wake up?

7. For how long did Czeisler *et al.* study their participants?

8. What variables were changed for the experimental group in the Czeisler *et al.* study?

9. Do circadian rhythm sleep disorders only happen among blind individuals?

10. Explain how one sleep disorder is treated.

⚷ Key concepts

- Sleep disorder
- Insomnia
- Hypersomnia
- Parasomnia
- Sleeping pills
- Sleep apnoea
- Circadian rhythm sleep disorders (CRSDs)
- Delayed sleep phase
- Melatonin supplements
- Shift work
- Jet lag
- Light therapy
- Night terrors
- Sleepwalking

GO! Activities

1. Pick two areas from separate sections in this chapter – for example sleep stages and insomnia, or sleep deprivation and the cognitive approach to sleep – and create a poster explaining how the two are connected. You could include a box defining the key terminology.

2. Find out more about how CRSDs and one other sleep disorder of your choice can be explained and treated according to the 2 approaches you have studied in this topic. Prepare to give a short explanation during your next class.

🔴 End of topic project

- Working together with other students if possible, conduct a **survey** to find out the sleep habits of other learners. You could look at issues such as:
  - time of going to bed
  - time of getting up
  - whether people have a 'sleep debt' that they make up at weekends
  - how long it takes people to go to sleep
  - attitudes to being sleep deprived
- If you like, this could be conducted as a quasi- or natural experiment (see chapter 8) comparing, for example, larks versus owls or older versus younger students, on some aspect of their sleep habits or on the effect of sleep timing/duration on score in a memory task. Or you could simply survey sleep habits more widely and calculate percentages of responses to these questions.
- Discuss the details of your methodology with your teacher/lecturer before you begin.
- Write up your findings. Look up relevant research, and include at least one background study to support your conclusions.

✔ End of topic specimen exam questions

Remember that in the N5 exam, this topic will be called 'sleep and dreams', while at Higher, it will be titled 'sleep, dreams and sleep disorders'.

National 5

1. Describe REM sleep and non-REM sleep. 4 marks

2. Explain what the psychoanalytic approach means by 'latent content' and 'manifest content' of dreams. 4 marks

3. Describe and evaluate a key study into sleep and dreams. 8 marks

Higher

1. Explain three factors that affect brain function in relation to sleep/dreams/disorders. 9 marks

2. Discuss how the biological approach explains sleep and/or dreams. 12 marks

3. Explain two sleep disorders, referring to relevant approaches and/or theories. 20 marks

The total exam mark allocation for the Individual Behaviour unit will be 20 marks; however, there is no way of knowing in advance how this will be split between this topic and your chosen optional topic.

4 Psychopathology

What is psychopathology?

'Pathology' means the study of illness or suffering, so the term **psychopathology** literally means the study of psychological or **mental illness**. This topic is often referred to as 'atypical behaviour' or 'abnormal psychology' – you may see these titles on books in your school or college library. The kind of questions asked in this topic include:

- Why do people do things that harm themselves or others?
- Why do some people feel very unhappy?
- Why do people hear voices in their head?
- Why do some people obsessively harm themselves?

Explaining and treating mental illness has been one of the biggest concerns of psychologists throughout the history of the subject. As you know, there are different approaches to explaining human behaviour and they play a huge role in this topic. This chapter will explain how biological psychologists explain psychopathology in terms of brain chemistry, while cognitive psychologists consider that harmful beliefs and thoughts are the primary cause.

Psychopathology includes issues such as why some people feel very unhappy

Although this topic is the study of mental illness, in practice we cannot see and study the mind directly, so as with some other topics, much of the research and debate tends to focus on *behaviours* which are atypical/abnormal or problematic in some way.

Defining abnormality: social norms

The big problem with psychopathology is that it is very hard to define which behaviours are **normal** and which are **abnormal** or problematic. One way of doing this is to consider whether what a person is doing is socially acceptable. However, basing our understanding of mental illness on social acceptability involves a judgement, but our ideas of what is 'normal' are **subjective** – they depend on an individual's point of view.

Such judgements are also based on social and cultural values. The word 'normal' relates to the psychological concept of a **social norm**, meaning an unwritten rule for how to behave. Any behaviour that breaks these unwritten rules – even if it does no harm and is not against the law – tends to be considered abnormal by most others in the social group. However, these values are not fixed – in the past, British society told people that it was abnormal for women to want to leave their husbands or for people to have homosexual relationships. Each culture has its own norms and these vary over time. As social psychologist Solomon Asch pointed out:

'A member of a tribe of cannibals accepts cannibalism as altogether fitting and proper.'

Source: Asch (1955: 31)

Social norms vary over time – in the past it would have been considered abnormal for a woman to want to leave her husband

What this shows is that social norms can never be an absolute guide to what is normal, because they are **culturally relative** – they vary from one culture to another.

Defining abnormality: harm and distress

How can we be sure that we are not repeating the mistakes of the past and incorrectly labelling things as abnormal due to the prejudices of society? The short answer is that we can't be completely sure, but we can at least try to use **objective** ways of defining what is normal and what is not. Two in particular are based on **harm** and **distress**:

Abnormal behaviour can be defined as that which causes an individual harm or distress

- Is the behaviour causing the individual distress?
- Is the behaviour harming the individual and/or those around them?

Distress

Defining abnormality based on 'distress' means saying that something is psychologically abnormal if the person themselves is feeling stressed, unhappy or scared because of the behaviour. This is, after all, the basis on which someone is likely to seek medical or psychological help. It usefully applies to many disorders such as anxiety, sleep disorders and depression.

However, some disorders lack this aspect completely but are clearly abnormal and problematic – someone with antisocial personality disorder (commonly known as a 'psychopath') feels no guilt for their actions and does not accept responsibility. Such an individual tends not to feel distress and is a danger to other people.

Another issue with this way of viewing abnormality is that distress is subjective. Two people could experience the same thing, but one might be highly distressed and the other relatively unaffected (chapter 6, 'Stress', discusses individual differences in how we react to problems). Distress is an important consideration for a psychologist; however, they may wish to look at criteria that are more objective as well.

Harm and functioning

Harm could be direct. Sometimes individuals self-harm, abuse drugs, starve themselves to death or commit suicide. These behaviours are clearly causing harm – or the risk of harm – to the individual. The degree or frequency of a harmful behaviour is important in determining the severity of a behaviour – if someone gambles once per year this might be concerning but is unlikely to require any further action, while if it happens every day there is a clear need of intervention. One occurrence of a behaviour is called an **episode**.

One episode of gambling would probably not be cause for any action

A broader view of harm is that it includes anything that prevents a person from leading a normal life, that is, from functioning fully as a healthy human being. This could include being able to keep yourself clean and fed, having positive relationships, being able to concentrate on everyday tasks and being able to hold down a job. Things that stop an individual from functioning are called **maladaptive** behaviours. Literally, this means 'badly adapted' to living.

Unfortunately, this brings up the issue of social norms and subjectivity again. If someone wants to spend all of their time alone, is this a personal choice or should a psychologist try to change this behaviour on the basis that the individual is not fully functioning? What if the behaviour brings the individual comfort? These are difficult ethical choices that must be made by mental health professionals, usually working in teams and in collaboration with family members.

Defining abnormality: statistical extremes

One further aspect that psychologists consider is how frequently the behaviour occurs, and how extreme it is compared to other people. Judging these issues is more objective – they relate to **statistical norms**, rather than social norms. There are two aspects to this:

- **Rarity.** A behaviour that occurs in only 1% of the population is more statistically unusual than one that occurs in 20%.

- **Extremity.** Behaviours/traits that appear in most or all people can be rated on a scale as to how extreme they are, for example, a very high or low IQ, or an extremely introverted/extraverted personality. It is more common to be in the middle and rarer to be at the upper or lower end of such a scale. This can be easily seen on the normal distribution graph:

> **? Discussion point**
>
> Are we biased in what we consider harmful or risky behaviour? One researcher, David Nutt, stated that horse riding is statistically more dangerous than taking the drug ecstasy, but society considers it more socially acceptable. He also highlighted base jumping, hang gliding and motorcycling as risky but socially acceptable pastimes (Nutt, 2009). Should we ban behaviours based on their risk of harm or allow people to choose?

Base jumping is very risky, but is socially acceptable

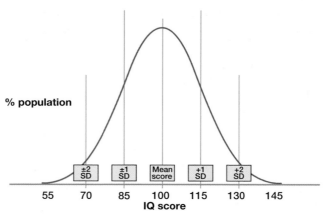

% population

±2 SD	±1 SD	Mean score	+1 SD	+2 SD	

55 70 85 100 115 130 145

IQ score

The normal distribution graph

Rarity is not a helpful way of deciding which behaviours are normal or abnormal. After all, problems such as anxiety are very common, while something may be rare but harmless/positive – such as being left handed or getting 'straight As' in your exams.

Extremity is more helpful in trying to define what is normal. For example, if most people take 15 minutes to get to sleep then it would be statistically extreme to lie awake for 2 hours. As the British Psychological Society (2011) put it, most mental distress is on a spectrum with 'normal' experience. The behaviour itself – for example, lying awake – may not be maladaptive, but the problem is the degree, frequency or duration.

Lying awake for several hours would be statistically extreme

This explanation is helpful when a patient's own view of their own distress is considered too subjective. Psychologists can use extremity compared to the general population as an objective way of determining whether there is a problem or not.

The DSM-5

The **DSM-5** is a manual for diagnosing psychological disorders. 'DSM' stands for 'diagnostic and statistical manual' and the current version is the fifth edition (the first one came out in 1952 and the most recent was published in 2013).

The DSM helps professionals to make objective diagnoses

This manual aims to help professionals such as psychiatrists and clinical psychologists make objective decisions when diagnosing people with disorders like depression and obsessive-compulsive disorder (OCD). It uses lists of behaviours – which in this context are often called **symptoms** – and defines whether someone has a disorder in terms of how many symptoms they show and for how long. The reason for having such criteria is that they help to make diagnoses **reliable** rather than being subjective and biased – in other words, different psychologists would give the same diagnosis to the same patient.

The DSM is the most popular manual for diagnosing psychological disorders in the USA and the UK. Elsewhere, a World Health Organisation manual called the International Statistical Classification of Diseases – or **ICD** for short – is widely used.

Drawing on debates over maladaptiveness and harm, the DSM states what it considers to be a psychological disorder (and what is not) as follows:

'A mental disorder is a syndrome characterized by clinically significant disturbance in an individual's cognition, emotion regulation, or behaviour ... Mental disorders are usually associated with significant distress in social, occupational, or other important activities. An expectable or culturally approved response to a common stressor or loss, such as the death of a loved one, is not a mental disorder...'

Source: American Psychiatric Association (2013, p.20)

The DSM-5

It may be clear from the above that even though it attempts to be objective, the DSM cannot avoid social norms having a role to play in whether professional psychologists consider a behaviour normal or not, as the quote above implies that:

- A disorder is a disturbance in functioning.
- Socially acceptable behaviours in response to life events are excluded, for example, grieving.

The DSM-5 lists 271 different psychological disorders categorised into groups such as mood disorders and eating disorders. Although earlier versions used an assessment of functioning/maladaptiveness, this was dropped from DSM-5 because of *'conceptual lack of clarity'* (American Psychiatric Association, 2013, p.16). Clinicians are instead recommended to use the World Health Organisation's Disability Assessment Schedule 'WHODAS' (World Health Organisation, 2010) which asks about daily difficulties in functioning such as:

- concentrating on doing something for 10 minutes
- getting dressed
- dealing with people you do not know
- maintaining a friendship

Problems on such everyday activities are rated on a scale of 1 (no difficulty) to 6 (extreme difficulty or cannot do it at all).

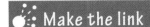

Being unable to concentrate is one of the measures used on the WHODAS

Make the link

Sleep disorders (see chapter 3) are often diagnosed using the DSM-5.

Evaluation of DSM-5

One general criticism is that DSM's lists of symptoms focuses too much on surface behaviours and not enough on causes. It lacks any explanation of why certain disorders can lead to particular symptoms/behaviours.

Another general criticism is that by relying on symptoms, people are 'pigeon holed' into categories. In reality, mental illness is not always so neat – a person may have some of the symptoms of one disorder and some of the symptoms of another and their symptoms may change in different surroundings (Dalal and Sivakumar, 2009).

Regarding the latest version of DSM, the DSM-5, there have been a number of further criticisms, including:

- It removed certain useful diagnoses including Asperger's syndrome.
- It has 'medicalised' normal experiences such as anxiety.

Some people believe that the organisation that produces the DSM is too closely linked to the drug companies

The Center Building at St. Elizabeths Hospital in Washington, D.C. where some of the participants were admitted

- The organisation that produces DSM is too closely linked to the drug companies that profit from diagnosis.

There are an increased number of disorders listed in DSM compared to previous versions. This has led to accusations that more normal behaviours are considered to be mental illness than before and continually changing the diagnostic criteria leads to confusion. However, there are positives to recognising new disorders – such changes generally result from research and can lead to better awareness and treatment that is more consistent. One example is **self-harm**; previously considered a symptom of numerous disorders, it is now treated as a separate disorder: 'non-suicidal self-injury'.

📖 Key study: Rosenhan (1973)

Aim: This study aimed to see how reliably the mental health profession could distinguish between the sane and the insane.

Method: Eight mentally healthy people (including the researcher) went to the admissions ward of large American psychiatric hospitals and stated that they heard a voice in their head. They were admitted, and once inside they acted normally. These pseudo-patients' sanity went undetected, and they spent an average of 19 days (range of seven to 52 days) on the ward, before being released. Normal behaviour was interpreted as abnormal. A pseudo-patient pacing up and down was asked if he was nervous, when really he was bored. Patients often queued outside the refectory before food was to be served and one psychiatrist described this behaviour as demonstrating the `oral-acquisitive nature of their syndromes'. An experiment was conducted to test for the level of student and staff interaction. The pseudo-patients asked staff simple questions, such as: 'Pardon me, Mr [or Dr or Mrs] X, could you tell me when I will be presented at the staff meeting?' or 'when am I likely to be discharged?' The vast majority of staff ignored the question, walking past without making eye contact. The doctors were the worst offenders!

Findings: The patients in general were powerless and not treated with human dignity. Some patients were physically beaten for initiating a conversation with an attendant, freedom of movement was restricted, and privacy was not respected – for example, there were no doors on the toilets. Rosenhan noted that labels are 'sticky' – once considered insane, your behaviour will be interpreted according to that label. He concluded that as a society, we are unsure what mental illness is and that psychiatric diagnosis in general was flawed and invalid.

Evaluation: The study was a participant observation and it is possible that the behaviour of patients and staff was affected by the participants' behaviour, which was noticeably different from other patients. In addition, the sample of participant-observers was small. Their presence was also a waste of staff time and of the medications they were given (which they flushed down the toilet). However, a major strength is that it raised awareness of the poor treatment and lack of dignity afforded to patients in psychiatric hospitals, and practices have improved as a result.

In an ideal world, with a clear idea of what disorders exist and an objective definition of 'abnormal', it would be easy to determine who is mentally ill. In practice, these issues continue to be controversial. The concept of social norms is unavoidable because our viewpoints are so influenced by culture and society; however, professionals generally try to use more objective definitions based on distress, functioning and how frequent/extreme the behaviour is. Psychologists use DSM-5 and similar manuals because it is better than not having any objective standard to work to, and because they limit the subjectivity and bias of the psychologist or psychiatrist who is making the diagnosis.

Psychologists use the DSM-5 to try to limit any bias or subjectivity they may have

✔ Questions

1. What is the topic psychopathology also called?

2. What is meant by a social norm?

3. What happens when people do not follow social norms?

4. What is meant by maladaptiveness?

5. Which definitions of 'normal' are seen as more objective?

6. What scale is sometimes used to assess maladaptiveness?

7. Give a conclusion of the Rosenhan (1973) study.

8. On what basis does DSM suggest that disorders should be diagnosed? Mention two main things.

9. Name three types of disorder described by the DSM-5.

10. Give a criticism of the DSM.

🔑 Key concepts

- Psychopathology
- Mental illness
- Normality
- Abnormality
- Subjective
- Social norm
- Cultural relativism
- Objective
- Harm
- Distress
- Episode
- Maladaptive
- Statistical norms
- DSM-5
- Symptoms
- Reliability
- ICD
- Self-harm

1. Take a little time to think of some of the social norms in your society. These should be things that are not required by law, but which you are expected to do by other people and/or it would it be considered strange not to. For example, wearing a coat on a cold day, being quiet during a speech or lecture. What would it be like if these 'normal' things were considered abnormal?

2. Take some time to investigate the system for describing disorders – the DSM-5. Find out at least one reason that it has been criticised. Report this back to your class or group.

3. Which definition(s) of abnormality can apply to these behaviours?
   - Overeating
   - Cruelty to animals
   - Hoarding

! Syllabus note

The following section includes several disorders, described briefly. It would be a useful and interesting project to investigate these in more detail, but the Higher/National 5 course does not specify which disorders you should know about, so it is really a matter for choice and interest.

A person with schizophrenia may show little or no emotion

Common psychological disorders

So far, the examples described in this chapter have included a range of behaviours, from bad manners to self-harm. In reality, behaviours don't tend to occur in isolation. Problem behaviours, moods or thoughts tend to be repeated by the same individuals and tend to occur as part of a general pattern. Psychologists use the term **syndrome** to mean a pattern of behaviours or symptoms. If the syndrome relates to significant distress or problems with functioning, then it is usually called a **disorder**.

Note that this section only illustrates the main signs and symptoms of some common disorders. Explanations/theories of psychopathology as well as treatments are covered in the subsequent sections.

Schizophrenia

Schizophrenia is a disorder of thinking that affects an individual's sense of who they are and leads to delusional behaviour. It affects as many as 1% of the population, and although some can control the symptoms with medication, others have to have long-term care in a psychiatric hospital.

There are two main types of symptoms in schizophrenia – **positive symptoms**, meaning abnormal behaviours and thoughts that are present, and **negative symptoms**, meaning normal behaviours that are absent. Some of the main examples include:

Positive symptoms	Negative symptoms
Hallucinations: the individual may hear voices in their head.	Lack of effect: the person may show little or no emotion.
Delusions: a person may show distorted thinking, such as believing themselves to be a god, or thinking that the CIA are hunting them down.	Mutism: the person may not speak at all.
Disordered speech: the person may speak in a bizarre way that is hard for others to understand.	Catalepsy: the person may stop moving entirely and stay in one position for hours.

Overall, schizophrenia is a severe disorder that often requires specialist care.

Depression

Depression is a very serious mood disorder that is characterised by a low, unhappy mood and a loss of interest in one's usual activities. In order to be diagnosed, individuals must show at least one of the two key symptoms – low mood or loss of interest in usual activities – for at least two weeks, as well as other symptoms from the following list:

A person with depression may experience a loss of energy

- difficulties in sleeping
- loss of energy/lethargic, or agitated
- change in body weight
- feelings of worthlessness and guilt
- difficulty in concentrating
- thoughts of death or suicide

The above description refers to **major depressive disorder** (also called 'unipolar depression'); a rarer diagnosis is **bipolar mood disorder** (formerly called 'manic-depression'), where individuals experience a cycle of extremely low and high moods. When the mood and activity is abnormally high, this is known as **manic state**, usually featuring an intense but unfounded excitement, hyperactivity, unrealistic plans and risky behaviour. Sometimes, behaviour in this state can be harmful to the self or others.

Major depressive disorder has a massive and increasing impact on public health and wellbeing. It is projected to become the second biggest cause of years lost to disability worldwide (Murray & Lopez, 1997). In a study of Dutch and Australian adults, Kruijshaar *et al.* (2005) suggest that when allowing for bias in reporting, such as people misremembering symptoms, 20% to 30% of people have at least one episode of major depression during their lifetime. Patel (2001) notes that culture, sex and income factors can all have a major impact on whether it affects people, with women more likely to be diagnosed than men.

One behaviour seen in anorexic people is food rituals

Anorexia nervosa

Anorexia nervosa means a 'nervous loss of appetite', though this is misleading as most sufferers retain a strong appetite for food, but attempt to control it. It typically starts in adolescence and it often follows a time of personal stress. To be diagnosed, sufferers must have an intense aversion to being overweight, a distorted body image, abnormally low body weight (85% or less of the average for their height), and in women, cessation of menstruation. Typical behaviours include food rituals (such as cutting food into tiny pieces). There are an estimated 70,000 sufferers of anorexia in Britain and the proportion of males is estimated at 10% and rising. It is one of the most life threating of all disorders – approximately 6% of cases are fatal.

Eating disorders are based on psychological insecurities, and there are many risk factors. One factor is the emphasis on being super slim in the media, but as this affects everybody, it can't be sufficient on its own to cause an eating disorder. Poor communication within the family can affect both the origins and recovery from anorexia (Humphrey, 1989).

Anxiety

Anxiety is the most common type of disorder, although it includes a huge number of individual disorders and syndromes. **Generalised anxiety disorder** (**GAD**) is when there is no particular focus or easily identified cause and the individual feels anxious a lot of the time with no way of resolving it.

The experience of generalised anxiety is similar to fear, but has important differences too – unlike a fear, it is not triggered by a specific situation or a thought. Fear may be rational, but anxiety has no rational basis and may be puzzling to the sufferer – they may not know why they feel so anxious (Rachman, 2004).

Other major anxiety disorders include phobias, OCD (see next sections), panic disorder and post-traumatic stress disorder.

Someone suffering from GAD may not know why they are feeling so anxious

Phobias

Phobia is an example of an anxiety disorder. It is a common and varied problem, as there are many different things that we can be phobic of. What they all have in common is that the phobia is a strong and irrational fear. Phobias fall into two main categories:

The fear of public speaking is a social phobia

- Specific simple phobias. These are phobias of a stimulus such as a fear of snakes, spiders, clowns, blood, etc.
- Social phobias. These are phobias of social situations such as public speaking, eating in public, parties, etc, or of social situations in general.

Phobia is one of the most common psychological disorders, with as many as 8% of the population suffering from a social phobia at any given time (Stein *et al.*, 1994). It also tends to appear early in life, and people who experience clinical levels of phobia are more likely to later be diagnosed with other anxiety disorders or depression (Wittchen *et al.*, 1999).

Experiencing the feared stimulus – or the immediate prospect of experiencing it – tends to result in an acute stress reaction or panic attack and the person may think about the stimulus excessively and try to avoid it.

OCD

Obsessive-compulsive disorder is another anxiety disorder. Here the anxiety focuses on a particular behaviour that the individual thinks must be done, for example, cleaning, tidying or hand washing.

The 'obsession' relates to the behaviour or fear that the person thinks about excessively and maladaptively. Rather like a phobia, the person's worries and fears are out of proportion to the risks posed. For example, someone who worries about the health risks of dust and vacuums their whole house twice a day despite having no particular health issues may be showing signs of OCD. However, if someone has a child with severe allergies, they may vacuum twice a day for a rational reason.

In OCD anxiety is focused on a particular behaviour such as hand washing

The 'compulsion' element refers to the behaviour that the person feels compelled to do, in order to relieve the anxiety (or to stop the anxiety getting worse). There are overlaps with addictions such as gambling that also involve obsessive thoughts and compulsive behaviour. The brain and behaviour of a person who is in love is very like that of an OCD sufferer (Marazziti & Canale, 2004) and they demonstrate irrational, compulsive behaviour and obsessive thoughts, but in the context of falling in love, it is considered normal! This is a good example of the role of context and social norms in this topic.

🔑 Key concepts

- Syndrome
- Disorder
- Schizophrenia
- Positive symptoms
- Negative symptoms
- Depression
- Major depressive disorder
- Bipolar mood disorder
- Manic state
- Anorexia nervosa
- Generalised anxiety disorder (GAD)
- Phobia
- Obsessive-compulsive disorder (OCD)

❓ Discussion point

Sometimes people describe behaviour as 'a bit OCD'. Is this offensive? Is it possible to have 'a bit' of a disorder, or should we look at it as all or nothing – you either have the disorder or you don't? Can people show the symptoms of OCD in terms of being obsessive with their studies or exam preparation, and if so, should it be seen as a problem?

As can be seen, major categories of disorder include mood disorders, anxiety disorders and eating disorders. Others that are not covered here include autism, disorders of childhood such as ADHD, disorders of ageing, for example, Alzheimer's disease, and many others.

✔ Questions

1. What type of disorder is a phobia?

2. Name one positive symptom of schizophrenia.

3. Name one negative symptom of schizophrenia.

4. What are the physical symptoms of anorexia nervosa?

5. Name the two key symptoms of depression.

6. How common is depression in the UK (and what is meant by 'lifetime prevalence')?

7. What does GAD stand for?

8. Are social phobias more common than anorexia nervosa, less common or around equal?

9. Give one example of a behaviour that has similarities to OCD.

10. What is meant by an obsession in OCD?

GO! Activities

1. Phobias: discuss with a group how much of a problem in terms of relationships, work/studies and everyday life these phobias would cause:
   - fear of air travel
   - fear of heights
   - fear of public speaking
   - fear of cats
2. Draw a 6×2 grid in your notes. On one side, write the names of the disorders described in this subsection, and the type of disorder that it is (e.g. mood disorder). On the other side, write up two to three major symptoms of each disorder.

Approaches to psychopathology

There are several approaches to psychopathology – in fact, any of the approaches mentioned in chapter 2 can be used to explain abnormal behaviour/disorders. Four examples are included here but other approaches are also very relevant and could form the focus of independent research. For example, it would be interesting to find out about evolutionary explanations of mental illness and consider how they differ from biological explanations.

Note that this section focuses on how the approaches *explain* disorders. Each approach is linked to a particular group of treatments/therapies, and these are covered in the final section of this chapter.

The biological approach to psychopathology

Revision points from chapter 2

The following points from the main section on the biological approach are especially relevant to this topic. Ensure that you can refer to them in exam answers on approaches to psychopathology:

- neurons and neurotransmitters
- genes and twin studies

Neurons and neurotransmitters

The biological approach to psychopathology tries to explain disorders in terms of the biological processes within the body described in chapter 2, and in particular, neurotransmitters and how they function. **Neurotransmitter imbalance theory** is the idea that the level of neurotransmitters in the brain is either too low or too high, and that this results in the symptoms of disorders. The theory makes an analogy with bodily illnesses such as diabetes, which have a biological cause. This idea is fundamental to mainstream psychiatry and clinical psychology today and it is the theory behind biological treatments in psychopathology, in particular drugs.

In unipolar depression, the approach looks at the role of the neurotransmitter **serotonin**, which is considered to be at a lower level in depressed patients. Serotonin is a neurotransmitter that is produced in the brain and plays a role in mood. It is hard to measure serotonin levels in the living brain but blood levels can be measured and they are generally lower in depressed individuals.

Other disorders are explained in a similar way – for example, schizophrenia has been linked to an increased level of the neurotransmitter dopamine.

! Syllabus note

For Higher, study any three approaches from this section. National 5 students should study two approaches, including at least one 'new' approach that you didn't study for the sleep topic. For example, you could cover the biological and behaviourist approaches. Check with your teacher/lecturer if you are unsure about which approaches to focus on.

The level of serotonin in the blood can be measured

Genes and twin studies

The biological approach also conducts twin studies, trying to find out the extent to which disorders are at least partly genetic. One such study was conducted by McGuffin *et al.* (1996; see key study), who found that for depressed patients who had a twin brother/sister, their sibling was much more likely to also have depression if they were an identical twin than if they were non-identical. Such research supports the idea of a strong genetic component in disorders.

Overall, the biological approach tries to look for physical explanations of disorders. It is also associated with the use of medical terminology for disorders – diagnosis, symptom, prognosis, illness, patient, etc. – and therefore, it is sometimes called the **bio-medical** approach.

Twin studies can be used to investigate the extent to which a disorder is genetic

Evaluation

The idea that a psychological disorder is a medical problem caused by neurotransmitters in the brain is prevalent in our culture. It removes blame from patients and it has been largely welcomed as a way of removing stigma by seeing a psychological disorder as 'just an illness'. However, there is very little direct evidence of chemical imbalances in the brain – and any such imbalances could be seen as the effect rather than the cause of psychological problems. Viewing depression and other disorders in entirely biological terms fails to take account of the important social processes that contribute (British Psychological Society, 2011). The emphasis on biology can lead to missed opportunities for intervening in social problems that affect an individual's mental health (Horwitz, 2007).

The genes related to being tall do not necessarily cause a person to be good at basketball!

Twin studies have reliably demonstrated that some genes correlate with disorders. However, it can't be concluded that they cause these disorders. By analogy, there is a correlation between having genes related to being tall and being successful at basketball. That does not mean that these genes cause you to have better basketball skills. Joseph (2012, p.65) notes that the genes that supposedly cause disorders have not been found and he criticises '*the failure to seriously consider the possibility that presumed genes do not exist*'.

📖 Key study: McGuffin *et al.* (1996): twin study of depression

Peter McGuffin

Aim: The researchers wanted to find evidence for the idea that depression has a genetic component.

Method: This was a twin study. The researchers studied the UK hospital records of patients with depression and identified 177 patients who had twins. They then contacted their twins, and assessed them to see whether they met the diagnostic criteria for depression too. They also tested each pair to determine whether they were monozygotic (identical) or dizygotic (fraternal) twins.

Findings: In twin studies, concordance means the extent to which both twins have the same trait – in this case, depression. Using a statistical technique called probandwise concordance, researchers found a concordance rate of 46% for identical twins, compared to 20% for the dizygotic twins. These rates represent the estimated risk that an individual person in either of these groups would develop depression if they had a depressive twin.

Evaluation: This study provides evidence that genetic factors play a role in depression, but clearly, some environmental factors must play a role too, as there was not a 100% concordance even among the identical twins. Like other twin studies, the research is quasi-experimental and it is possible that any effect of genetics on depression is indirect. For example, identical twins are more likely to have similar personalities than non-identical twins, even when raised apart (Tellegen et al., 1988) and it is known that personality traits, such as neuroticism, can affect depression (Duggan et al., 1990). Therefore, it is possible that other variables are involved, rather than there being a gene that directly causes depression.

Cognitive approach to psychopathology

Revision points from chapter 2

The following points from the main section on the cognitive approach are especially relevant to this topic. Ensure that you can refer to them in exam answers on approaches to psychopathology:

- schemas
- irrational beliefs

Schemas

According to the cognitive approach to disorders, how you think affects the way you feel, and people's emotional reactions are often based more on their thought processes about events than on the events themselves.

Why, then, are some people depressed or anxious while others are not? Beck (1976) stated that depressed people have negative schemas about three key things – themselves, the world and the future. These negative beliefs need to be tackled in order to change a person's mood or behaviour. Beck called these beliefs the **negative cognitive triad**.

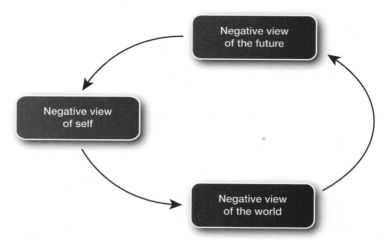

The negative cognitive triad

Later, Beck said that schemas could combine into a broader 'mode' that includes feelings, motivation and behaviour (Nelson-Jones, 2000). This is similar to the idea of a **mindset** (see chapter 7) but it also includes actions and habits, rather than just thoughts. For example, someone may have a failure mode, including a group of schemas and habits, overall leading to more negative outcomes and emotions.

In contrast, people who can be described as resilient have a positive set of schemas and habits, for example high expectations about the future. This helps them to adapt to changes and results in lower stress.

Resilient people have positive expectations helping them to deal with challenges

Irrational beliefs

Like Beck, Albert Ellis believed that it was necessary to tackle problematic cognitions through therapy. He argued that an activating event (A) is followed by a belief about that event (B), and then followed by emotional consequences (C). This became known as his **ABC model** (Ellis & Grieger, 1977):

Activating Event >> **B**elief >> Emotional **C**onsequence

He thought that beliefs fundamentally affect a person's emotional responses to life, but also that many of these beliefs are irrational. Many people have a tendency to overgeneralise pessimistically in their thought processes – leading to self-defeating core beliefs, each phrased as something we 'must' do; each has a range of emotional and behavioural consequences (Ellis, 2003):

Belief	Example of emotion/behaviour
I must do well and win approval or else I am a bad person.	Anxiety/unassertiveness
Other people must behave well or else they deserve to be punished.	Anger/intolerance
My life must be easy, without any discomfort or danger, or else I cannot enjoy life.	Fear/procrastination

Evaluation

The general idea that schemas can influence behaviour is well established in cognitive psychology. However, Zajonc (1980) stated that feelings arise independently from beliefs and the two involve different areas of the brain.

It is not difficult to find examples of distorted beliefs among people with psychological disorders. However, as discussed in chapter 2, irrational beliefs are found among the healthy population too. It is a lot harder to establish that beliefs *cause* disorders; if they are just symptoms of a broader problem then the focus on beliefs is a lot less helpful.

Together the work of Ellis and Beck has been applied in a widely used therapy, CBT. The popularity and success of this therapy supports the theoretical ideas in this approach.

Psychoanalytic approach to psychopathology

Revision points from chapter 2

The following points from the main section on the psychoanalytic approach are especially relevant to this topic. Ensure that you can refer to them in exam answers on approaches to psychopathology:

- oral, anal and phallic stages
- defence mechanisms

Oral, anal and phallic stages

Freud's patient Little Hans (Freud, 1909; see chapter 2) is a good example of how the psychoanalytic approach explains psychological disorders. Hans had a phobia of horses, and Freud believed that this had a hidden cause in his unconscious mind – a fear of his father. Therefore, Freud believed that surface behaviours – or symptoms – do not necessarily tell us the cause of a disorder. Similarly, this approach views depression as childhood grief, which the child cannot emotionally cope with, and so represses to the id. Anorexia is seen as being based on a teenager's unconscious fear of maturing sexuality (Bruch, 1979), while even things such as being the victim of abuse are seen in terms of the Oedipus/Electra complex.

As the approach believes that there is a deeper root cause of a disorder in the unconscious, it does not make sense to treat surface symptoms. For example, if someone has a phobia of animals, simply getting used to the animal (e.g. taking the child to a petting zoo) might make them less fearful of that particular animal, but this has not addressed the underlying problem. According to the approach, treating the symptom (e.g. fear of horses/snakes/birds) could result in the fear finding a new object – a process known as **symptom substitution**.

The psychoanalytic approach says that treating the symtom could result in the person finding something new to fear – symptom substitution

Defence mechanisms

Freud and the other psychoanalysts placed a huge emphasis on the role of defence mechanisms in psychopathology, and, in particular, repression. Freud thought that as we grow up, there are many things that cause anxiety but that we are too immature to deal with because the ego is not fully developed. These are therefore repressed to the unconscious mind as a defence, but as we become adults, many of these things return to consciousness, but only partially – in symptoms, dreams and Freudian slips of the tongue (Nelson-Jones, 2000). Therefore, the roots of many psychological disorders lie in childhood repression.

Other defence mechanisms can play a major role too. Addictions such as alcoholism can feature denial, while a person with OCD may be displacing an anxiety onto their compulsive behaviour to regain a feeling of control, according to the approach.

Evaluation

A strength of the psychoanalytic approach to psychopathology is that it attempts to find the root cause of disorders, while other approaches focus on the surface symptoms. If it is true that a phobia relates to an unconscious fear, then it makes sense to tackle that deeper fear.

However, the specific explanation of phobias regarding a repressed fear of one's parents is impossible to verify. Even if it were true in some cases, there is no evidence that it applies to everyone.

As a case study, the findings of Freud's research into 'little Hans' cannot be generalised to other people because Hans was a young boy and because the cultural context has changed considerably since Austria of the early 1900s. Freud also did not conduct a direct observation of the patient and relied on (possibly biased) correspondence with the father, making the findings suspect (see pp.70–71).

Behaviourist approach to psychopathology

Top tip

Studies described in chapter 2 that relate to disorders – such as Watson and Rayner (1920) – can be used as evidence in assessments for this topic.

Revision points from chapter 2
The following points from the main section on the behaviourist approach are especially relevant to this topic. Ensure that you can refer to them in exam answers on approaches to psychopathology: • classical conditioning   • operant conditioning

Classical conditioning

The behaviourist approach explains many fears and anxieties in terms of classical conditioning. This is where people learn to associate two stimuli together – one of which is neutral and one of which provokes a reaction, as with Pavlov's dog.

As discussed in chapter 2, Watson and Rayner (1920) demonstrated that an infant, 'Little Albert', could learn to fear a neutral stimulus through conditioning, by associating it with a feared stimulus. The researchers thought that fears were learned through experience – by associating a neutral stimulus with a fear-inducing noise.

Similarly, anxiety and panic could be learned through classical conditioning (Mowrer, 1939). If the individual repeatedly experiences anxiety-provoking situations in a situation (e.g. in a school classroom) then they may start to associate the initially neutral stimulus (the classroom) with fear. Then, simply entering that place could cause anxiety or even a panic attack.

If someone repeatedly experiences anxiety in a classroom the classroom itself could begin to be a cause of anxiety

Operant conditioning

The other main idea of the behaviourist approach is operant conditioning, which states that the frequency or strength of behaviour can be modified depending on its outcome. If actions have a pleasant outcome, the behaviour will increase. If they have an unpleasant outcome, the behaviour will decrease.

This idea can be used to help explain depression in terms of **learned helplessness**. Seligman (1975) restrained dogs in a harness and administered several electric shocks. The dogs were unable to escape these shocks and were therefore helpless. Then the dogs were placed in a shuttle-box where they could avoid the shock by jumping over a barrier. Most of the dogs in the experimental group failed to learn to avoid a shock. However, 95% of a control group of dogs learned to jump the barrier to avoid the shocks. Seligman argued that prior exposure to inescapable shock interfered with the ability to learn in a situation where avoidance or escape was possible. Seligman used the term learned helplessness to describe this phenomenon. He believed that in depression, humans are experiencing learned helplessness – their previous efforts to improve their situation have failed, so they give up trying.

Seligman (1975) restrained dogs in a harness and administered several electric shocks in his experiment.

Evaluation

A strength of this approach is that the key theories of conditioning have been demonstrated in controlled laboratory experiments of animals and these findings, in principle, can be applied to almost every type of human behaviour or disorder.

However, a major weakness is that the approach treats everyone as the same. It does not allow for genetic differences in behaviour or personality, and therefore cannot explain why some people are more susceptible than others to developing disorders.

The approach is also determinist. In explaining disorders as being the result of stimuli such as rewards and punishments in our environment, it does not allow any room for free will to play a role. In other words, disorders are seen as things that happen to us and we have very little involvement in the process! Many therapists would strongly disagree with this idea, as a client's desire to improve is often seen as highly important to recovery (see final section of this chapter).

Key concepts

- Neurotransmitter imbalance theory
- Seratonin
- Bio-medical approach
- Negative cognitive triad
- ABC model
- Symptom substitution
- Repression
- Denial
- Learned helplessness

Questions

1. Which approach tries to explain depression in terms of repressed memories of grief?

2. What is the name of the biological theory that states that disorders are due to neurotransmitter levels?

3. Which neurotransmitter is thought to play a role in depression?

4. Which neurotransmitter is thought to be important in schizophrenia?

5. How many pairs of twins were used in McGuffin's (1996) study?

6. Why did the British Psychological Society (2011) and Horwitz (2007) object to focusing entirely on biological processes in disorders?

7. Which approach to psychopathology makes use of twin studies?

8. What three negative beliefs are included in Beck's 'negative cognitive triad'?

9. What type of conditioning was shown by Pavlov's dog?

10. Name one of the distorted 'must' beliefs described by Ellis.

Activities

1. The biological approach also explains some disorders in terms of hormones. One example is postpartum (post-natal) depression, where women suffer a severe episode of depression after giving birth. Find out more about this condition – do you agree that it can be attributed to hormones or are there other possible explanations? Alternatively, find out about seasonal affective disorder (SAD).

2. Write two or more real-world examples in your notes of an activating event/belief/emotional consequence.

3. Find out how the psychoanalytic or the behaviourist approach explains OCD. Do you find this convincing?

Syllabus note

National 5 students can focus on Ellis's ABC model or on classical/operant conditioning as theories of psychopathology and skip this section.

Theories of psychopathology

The previous section on the approaches has already covered several theoretical ideas about why people have mental illnesses. These include Freud's early idea of repression and more modern cognitive and biological theories. The following two concepts are broader, more philosophical ideas about the nature of disorders and how they develop, which relate to more than one approach.

The diathesis-stress model

As you have seen, some approaches assume that psychopathology can be linked to biological differences between individuals, while others think that it is more to do with life events. The **diathesis-stress** model states that it is a combination of the two. Certain people are more prone to disorders than others but whether they actually develop them or not will depend on their life stressors.

An analogy is that in a hurricane, some houses are blown over and others are not. They all experience the same stress (the hurricane) but some succumb to that stress and others are able to stand up to it.

- Diathesis: a predisposition in someone's biology or thought processes that makes them more vulnerable to illness.
- Stress: life events involving suffering, injury or trauma that make the illness likely to develop.

During a hurricane some buildings are blown down whilst others stay standing

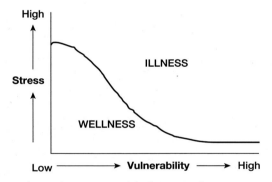

Zubin and Spring's model of stress / adversity vunerability

According to Zubin and Spring (1977), an individual's likelihood of developing schizophrenia cannot be explained entirely in terms of their life experiences, cognitions or biology. Instead, it is a combination of having a high vulnerability to the disorder and experiencing a high level of life stress.

The 'diathesis' could include several things – most obviously a genetic element, as described in the previous section. However, it could also mean that the person is mentally more vulnerable due to their personality, thought processes or a lack of social support.

Evaluation

The diathesis-stress model helps to combine elements of the different approaches. It recognises that some people may be more prone to a disorder than others due to genes or cognitive mindset, but also, like the behaviourist approach, recognises the important role of experiences.

? Discussion point

In the past 100 years, the number of disorders that could be diagnosed has risen from two to over 150, many of which have several subtypes. Have new 'illnesses' really been discovered? Do you think we have just found new ways of labelling people?

Psychopathology as a social construct

As you saw in the first section, social norms play a huge role in defining psychological abnormality and some believe that categorising people as disordered can never be truly objective and valid. It can even be argued that a 'disorder' doesn't actually exist at all, but is a **social construct** – something that is invented by society or culture. These constructs would have the purpose of explaining behaviour and/or controlling people who don't fit in.

The researcher Thomas Szasz was a major critic of mainstream psychopathology, as the title of his books such as *'Psychiatry: The Science of Lies'* and *'The Myth of Mental Illness'* might suggest! In Szasz (1962), he argues that there is no such thing as mental 'illness', as the mind is not a physical 'thing', so it cannot be physically ill. He is particularly critical of the mainstream approach to ADHD, stating:

'Labelling a child as mentally ill is stigmatization, not diagnosis. Giving a child a psychiatric drug is poisoning, not treatment.'

Source: Szasz (2004)

These ideas led to the **anti-psychiatry movement** which is fundamentally opposed to the way abnormality is defined and treated in the mainstream of psychopathology, including the DSM system of categorisation. A major researcher in this movement was the Scottish psychiatrist R. D. Laing, who said that certain major disorders do not exist but the terms are used to label people who do not fit in.

Together, these researchers see psychological problems as being issues of behaviour, not illnesses of the brain. They generally don't agree with the use of medication or of any forcible treatment (note that in the UK, under the **Mental Health Act of 2007**, individuals can be forcibly treated including being restrained or medicated if they are seen as being a danger to themselves or others).

Scottish psychiatrist R.D. Laing was a major researcher in the anti-psychiatry movement

Evaluation

Supporting evidence includes the fact that categories of mental illness have changed as society's norms have changed. If what is viewed as a mental illness is culturally relative and based on social norms, then it suggests that mental illness itself is a social construct.

On balance, this approach is too extreme – dismissing DSM categories entirely means ignoring the fact that some people do get helpful and arguably life-saving treatments – but its criticisms have helped to prompt more humane treatments, and to some extent, it continues to be influential.

✔ Questions

1. Which model states that developing a disorder is a combination of individual factors and life events?

2. What is meant by 'diathesis'?

3. Give two examples of possible diatheses.

4. What is meant by 'stress', in the context of psychopathology?

5. Which researchers developed the diathesis-stress model?

6. What is meant by a social construct?

7. Which researcher wrote *The Myth of Mental Illness*?

8. Which movement opposes mainstream psychiatry?

9. Which Scottish psychiatrist said that many disorders are used to label people who don't fit in?

10. Which law allows patients to be treated against their will?

●━ Key concepts

- Diathesis-stress model
- Diathesis
- Stress
- Social construct
- Anti-psychiatry movement
- Mental Health Act of 2007

GO! Activities

1. Organise a debate with two sides – one of which speaks in favour of contemporary psychiatric treatment and medication and one which opposes it.

! Syllabus note

This section is essential for Higher students, who may be asked for an 'application' of their chosen optional topic. At National 5, you will not be asked directly for an application, but a general understanding of therapy can provide helpful detail to include in answers on other questions, for example approaches.

Real-world application: therapies

The earlier sections discuss how to define what is considered a disorder and how best to understand why people have these disorders. This knowledge can help psychologists to devise effective ways of treating these problems, and perhaps even to identify people who are at risk of developing disorders before any symptoms appear. This is the main area where an understanding of this topic has been applied to help with well-being.

The word 'therapy' means treatment. You may come across the word **psychotherapy**, which means a psychological, talking-based therapy, such as counselling. **Chemotherapy** means a drug-based therapy, such as giving a depressed person anti-depressant medication. The ideas raised in the previous section should have made you aware that the theory or approach someone believes in will have a huge impact on the kind of treatment they would recommend.

This section focuses on three of the most common types of therapy – drug therapies, CBT and psychoanalysis. These three also link to the mandatory approaches for Higher/National 5.

Drug therapies

The use of drugs as a therapy for psychological disorders is called chemotherapy. It involves administering drugs to people who have been diagnosed with disorders. Drawing on the biological approach's idea of neurotransmitter imbalance, a huge range of psychiatric medicines have been developed. They all work in slightly different ways but the principles are similar – they are absorbed into the bloodstream and travel into the brain, where they influence the communication between brain cells at synapses. This could include mimicking or blocking a neurotransmitter.

Drugs may be used to treat psychological disorders

Two major examples of modern psychiatric drugs include:

Type	Example	Main action in brain	Target disorder	Side effect(s)
Anti-depressants	Fluoxetine (Prozac)	Boost serotonin by preventing re-uptake	Depression, anxiety disorders	Sexual dysfunctions, nausea, headaches, increased suicide risk
Anti-psychotics	Risperidone	Block dopamine receptors	Schizophrenia, bipolar disorder	Anxiety, nausea, weight gain, hormonal disruptions

Evaluation

For most patients, chemotherapy is a quick and easy method, and in the UK, it is usually cost-free to the patient. However, it is costly for the NHS, and some experts have criticised the pharmaceutical companies that develop the drugs for hiding the results of drug trials and promoting expensive new drugs that are little better than previous versions (Goldacre, 2012).

Drugs can provide relief but they do not work equally for all patients and tend to have negative side effects. Some have such severe side effects that people may prefer not take them at all. Drugs could also be viewed as a way of reducing the symptoms of a disorder, rather than tackling the cause.

Whitaker (2011) argues that some drug treatments have been marketed by drug companies even when they are known to be unhelpful, and suggests that over the long-term, drugs for schizophrenia lead to worse outcomes than no medication at all.

CBT

Cognitive behavioural therapy is a psychotherapy that aims to tackle irrational thought processes and to change what Beck saw as people's negative schemas of self, world and future.

CBT is currently a popular treatment for a range of psychological disorders. It was first developed for depression and then found to be effective for anxiety disorders. As discussed in chapter 3, it is also used for some sleep disorders. It focuses on dealing with the symptoms/behaviours in the here-and-now, rather than talking about parents and childhood.

CBT draws on both the behaviourist and the cognitive approach to psychology:

- Cognitive aspects focus on a rational discussion of the client's beliefs.
- Behaviourist techniques such as flooding can be incorporated.

According to Ellis's view, irrational beliefs mediate our response to situations. Therefore, the CBT therapist discusses the client's beliefs and tries to get them to see things more rationally. This process is called **cognitive restructuring**. In a CBT session, the therapist and client sit on chairs facing each other, rather like a meeting between a doctor and patient. Typically, the therapist runs through an agenda at the start. There is no free association or analysis of dreams – the conversation focuses on specific problem situations, for example, family or work conflicts. CBT therapists make use of numerical rating scales to get a quick assessment of how their client felt about specific situations or on specific days.

Many drugs have negative side effects

CBT aims to tackle irrational thought processes

Key study: The Treatment of Adolescents with Depression (TADS) study by the National Institute of Mental Health (March *et al.*, 2007)

Aim: *The aim of the study was to test the effectiveness of major treatments for depression for teenagers, in order to help tackle this harmful and common disorder.*

Method*: The study was a drug trial, involving a comparison of four groups:*

- *anti-depressant*
- *CBT*
- *both anti-depressant and CBT*
- *control group (placebo pill)*

The participants were 439 school pupils aged 12 to 17 from various parts of the USA. The anti-depressant used was fluoxetine, a generic form of Prozac.

Findings: *It was found that anti-depressants led to a bigger improvement than CBT after 12 weeks (61% versus 44% were 'much improved'), but after 18 weeks CBT had essentially caught up (65% for anti-depressants versus 62% for CBT). Both therapies were better than a placebo. The longer the treatment went on, the better the CBT group did. The best outcomes came from a combination of both anti-depressants and CBT, at least in the short to medium term. However, the drugs led to negative side effects, including new suicidal thoughts, which were not found in the CBT or control groups.*

Evaluation: *This study was longitudinal and conducted on a large scale with several hundred participants. It made a carefully controlled comparison of four main clinical interventions. In terms of location, it is a strength that it included students from many schools, but they were all based in the USA, which makes it harder to generalise the findings internationally. It was limited in that it did not include psychoanalysis or other major types of therapy/counselling.*

Evaluation

CBT is widely used because it is seen as fast and effective. It is the main choice of psychotherapy on the NHS nowadays, as well as in the USA.

The Treatment of Adolescents with Depression (TADS) study (see key study) compared CBT along with chemotherapy, a combination of both and a control condition. The best and fastest outcomes were found for people who had both CBT and drugs. However, CBT alone has the advantage that there are no risky side effects whatsoever.

As with any psychotherapy, there are costs in terms of both time and money when employing a therapist.

Psychoanalytic therapy

Psychoanalytic therapy is based on Freud's theory that psychological problems, such as depression and anxiety, have their roots in the unconscious mind, the 'id'. The main aim when treating psychological disorders is therefore to reveal conflicts that the patient was unconscious of, that is, to bring them into the conscious mind and address them.

The primary technique is **free association**, as discussed in chapter 2, but over the years a wide range of additional techniques have been used during psychoanalysis, including:

Dream analysis	Freud believed the symbols in dreams are transformed to make them less shocking, but ultimately represent 'wish fulfilment'. However, patients cannot always remember their dreams.
Hypnosis	The aim is to put the patient into a relaxed, suggestible state so that they will reveal unconscious thoughts. However, not everyone can be hypnotised and Freud came to regard it as unreliable.
Rorschach test	Swiss researcher Rorschach developed this technique, which involves asking patients what they see in ambiguous inkblot images. Because the images are unclear, the patient is thought to project their unconscious feelings onto it.
Word association	C.G. Jung developed the technique of giving prompt words and telling patients *'answer as quickly as possible the first word that occurs to your mind'* (Jung, 1910). The idea is that for stimulus words that provoke anxieties, patients take much longer to react. As with the content of dreams, conflicts that are uncovered can then be further discussed and analysed.

Evaluation

Psychoanalysis tends to be a long process and several sessions per week are recommended. This makes it a time-consuming and expensive process compared to CBT or drugs. However, psychoanalysts would argue that it is important to find the deeper, underlying causes of problems.

The therapy is based on Freud's controversial idea of the id, ego and superego – a theory that has not been scientifically verified. This makes the therapy potentially invalid. A randomised trial comparing two years of psychoanalysis versus five months of CBT in patients with the eating disorder bulimia nervosa found that CBT was considerably faster and more effective. Patients in the CBT group showed a 44% reduction in binge eating and purging, compared with 15% in the psychoanalysis group (Poulsen *et al.*, 2014).

General evaluation and comparisons

Both psychotherapies have the advantage over drugs that they do not cause any side effects but they take longer to have an effect, meaning that the patient has harmful symptoms for longer.

As psychoanalysis and CBT are both psychotherapies, it is easy to get them mixed up. The following table identifies some of the typical differences between the two styles – although it is worth remembering that each individual therapist does things slightly differently:

	Psychoanalysis	Cognitive-behavioural therapy
Focus	Underlying causes	Presenting symptoms
Tries to change	Personality/emotions	Beliefs/behaviours
Seating	Couch/facing away	Seated face-to-face
Structure	Unstructured	Structure with aims and agenda
Main topics	Childhood, parents, dreams	Recent problem situations

Rorschach tests may be used in psychoanalytic therapy

Although these are two of the best known, there are other approaches to therapy as well, such as person-centred therapy (based on the humanist approach). Although some trials such as Poulsen *et al.* (2014; see above) favour one technique over another, it is possible that the personality and skills of the therapist and how well they suit the patient will matter more than the type of therapy used (Sloane, 1975).

Some therapists use an **eclectic** approach to therapy, meaning that they use a mixture of techniques drawn from several approaches.

In CBT the patient and therapist are usually facing one another, whereas in psychoanalysis it is more common for them to face away

✔ Questions

1. What is meant by chemotherapy?

2. Besides depression, what disorders can fluoxetine be used to treat?

3. Name a drug used for schizophrenia and bipolar mood disorder.

4. What is a side effect of fluoxetine?

5. What does 'CBT' stand for?

6. What did the TADS study find?

7. Do psychoanalytic patients generally sit face to face with the therapist?

8. Which therapy works best in the long-term according to TADS?

9. Give a difference between psychoanalysis and CBT.

10. What is meant by 'eclectic' therapy?

●━ Key concepts

- Psychotherapy
- Chemotherapy
- Anti-depressants
- Anti-psychotics
- CBT
- Cognitive restructuring
- Free association
- Eclectic

GO! Activities

1. Find out about one of the more extreme medical treatments that have been used in therapy, for example, electro-convulsive therapy or frontal lobotomies. Find out:
   - Why was this treatment used?
   - When was it developed and is it still used today?
   - What disorders was it used for?
   - Did it work, and what side effects did it have?

2. Create two short descriptions of fictional characters with psychological problems – they could be based on famous people but not on fellow students! Now act out a therapy session in a pair. Take turns – one of you as a CBT therapist or psychoanalyst, and one as the patient. If possible, perhaps you can record the 'therapy session' and get feedback from your class.

GO! End of topic project

Make a poster or PowerPoint presentation about a psychological condition that interests you. Some possibilities could include:

- Schizophrenia
- OCD
- Bulimia nervosa
- Stockholm syndrome
- Sexual paraphilia
- Bipolar mood disorder
- Agoraphobia
- Dyslexia
- Post-traumatic stress disorder (PTSD)
- Another of your choice.

The aim will be to produce a poster or PowerPoint. Note that for psychology researchers and professionals, posters are often used to present research findings at conferences. Look out for poster competitions for psychology students, too!

Steps:

1. Check your choice with your teacher.

2. Find some sources to research the condition, for example, books on psychopathology or websites. There are some suggested sources in chapter 9, and the NHS website is also very useful.

3. Take notes. Include:
   - key features/symptoms
   - explanations of why people have the disorder
   - treatments

4. Compile your research into a suitable presentation format.

✔ End of topic specimen exam questions

As this is an optional topic, exam questions will be quite general and will not name the topic or its specific theories/research studies, for example:

National 5

1. Explain a topic from Individual Behaviour other than sleep and dreams.   4 marks

2. From your chosen optional topic in Individual Behaviour, name and describe one research study that has been carried out. Include the aim, method/procedure and results of the study.   6 marks

Higher

1. Choose a topic in Individual Behaviour other than sleep, dreams and sleep disorders. Explain how this topic can be applied in the real world.   10 marks

2. Explain a topic in Individual Behaviour other than sleep, dreams and sleep disorders, referring to at least two approaches.   16 marks

3. Discuss two theories relating to your chosen optional topic In individual Behaviour.   12 marks

The total exam mark allocation for the Individual Behaviour unit will be 20 marks; however, there is no way of knowing in advance how this will be split between this topic and the topic of sleep.

5 Memory

The nature of memory

Memory is part of what makes us human. Without our memories of years gone by, each of us would be unable to function and would have very little sense of who we are as a person. Without the ability to hold information in memory while we are working on it, we would be incapable of completing anything but the simplest of tasks.

It is important to understand the basic structure of human memory and to be familiar with certain widely discussed concepts. The first distinction to consider is the difference between **short-term memory (STM)** and **long-term memory (LTM)**. The idea that there are two different memory stores is a very old one in psychology. However, the terms are not used very consistently in everyday speech. Research into these two stores will be discussed throughout the chapter.

Regardless of which memory store is being studied, a logical set of processes must take place. First, information must enter the memory store. Then it must remain there for a period of time until it is needed or until it can be moved to another store. Finally, it must be retrieved from the store and used – or moved to another store. These three processes are usually called **encoding**, **storage** and **retrieval**. There are different ways that information can be encoded, as demonstrated by Baddeley (1966; see key study on page 122).

Storage of a memory may sound like a simple and passive process – like putting something in a drawer until needed – but it is not. In fact, researchers have increasingly found that new memories must be **consolidated** – strengthened and made permanent – in order to be

Our memories give us a sense of who we are

❓ Discussion point

What exactly do you mean by STM and LTM? How long do these stores last? Are they used for different things? And can you be good at one and not the other?

retained. Sleep appears to be important in this process; according to Rasch and Born (2013), slow-wave sleep (sleep stages 3–4) helps to consolidate new information into long-term memories, while REM sleep stabilises these memories. Walker *et al.* (2003) found that unbroken sleep is vital to the brain processes involved in procedural memories being consolidated.

The storage of a memory is not like putting something in drawer until it is needed!

Long-term memory versus short-term/working memory

If a person studies something and then forgets it a few days later, they may explain it as having only been in 'short-term memory'. However, in psychology, the term STM refers to much more immediate uses of memory, such as reading a phone number from a website and then holding it in mind for a few seconds before dialling it, or remembering a sentence for a moment before writing it down. It is often called working memory because it is used for current tasks.

Conversely, long-term memory (LTM) is a permanent memory store: information encoded to LTM can last a lifetime. It can also be encoded and used straight away, and there is no obvious limit to how much can be stored.

Typical tests of LTM involve meaningful, factual information, such as the name of a famous person or the capital city of a country. This type of information-based LTM is called **semantic LTM**, for example, remembering the name of the capital city of Germany. However, we can store other types of information too; remembering the events of your life, such as what you did yesterday evening, is known as **episodic LTM**.

Declarative memory versus procedural memory

Within LTM, a number of different things can be stored. One major type is **declarative** memory, meaning that we have learned information that we could describe in words. It includes not just the fact of having a memory but that we should also be aware that we know something!

However, there are also memories where the person is unaware of what they know or how they know it. For example, when learning a musical instrument, a player's skill improves but they might not be able to explain what the improvement is, or during which practice session they learned it.

Remembering things such as the capitals of countries is a test of semantic LTM

The most important type of non-declarative memory is called **procedural** memory. As with the example of learning an instrument, the person has learned a skill, task or procedure that they might not be able to describe in words.

Another type of non-declarative memory is called **implicit memory**. This means memories that someone is unaware of but that still have an effect on behaviour. For example, you may have no recall of hearing a song when you were five years old, but if you hear it again now, you are more likely to like it. This is known as priming. Classical conditioning (see chapter 2) is another example of implicit memory because it involves learning something (a response) without necessarily having a conscious awareness of it. Each of these types of LTM involves a different area of the brain (Squire, 2004).

When you learn to play a musical instrument you might not be able to explain how or why you are improving

If you hear a song when you are young you are more likely to like it now, even if you don't remember hearing it the first time!

Marsh's study suggested that using a daily planner does not help people to remember their appointments

The tip of the tongue phenomenon has been widely studied

Implicit memory is unlike other memory processes in that age does not seem to play a role – by age 3, a child's level of implicit memory is already as good as that of an adult (Tulving and Schacter, 1990).

Retrospective memory versus prospective memory

The memory stores discussed so far involve retaining information from the past. Often though, when people discuss having a 'bad memory', they mean remembering to do things in the future, such as go to an appointment or meet a friend. This is called **prospective memory**. For example, if you arranged to go and see a teacher/lecturer at lunchtime, how likely is it that you would forget?

Think about how often you:

- forget to bring things to school/college or do your homework
- forget to send an email or text that you intended to send
- miss hair/doctor/dental appointments

Research into prospective memory suggests that it is generally more accurate than we might assume. Marsh *et al.* (1998) asked participants to complete planning sheets for the next seven days. One week later, participants were asked to report whether they had actually done the planned tasks. Only 13% of tasks had been forgotten. Interestingly, students who used a daily planner were no better than those who didn't!

Recognition versus free recall

There are different ways of retrieving information, both in everyday life and in memory experiments.

Recognition involves seeing an item and comparing it with what we have in memory, whereas **free recall** involves doing a task or being asked a question and having to retrieve the information without a prompt or cue.

As an example of this, imagine an experiment where you have to name famous people. In one condition of the experiment, you are given photos and names of famous people, and asked if the names are correct. This uses recognition memory. In the second condition of the experiment, you are given photos with no names on them, and you have to name the people. Which do you think would be easier?

In cases of free recall, participants sometimes find that something is on the tip of their tongue (called the **tip of the tongue phenomenon**). This means that they feel they know the item, but cannot quite recall it. It has been widely studied; researchers Brown and McNeill (1966, p.326) reported that a typical participant '*would appear to be in mild torment, something like on the brink of a sneeze, and if he found the word his relief was considerable*'.

A **cue** is a hint or trigger that helps retrieval, such as the letter a word starts with. Recognition is generally considered easier than free recall because there is always a cue present. However, recognition can be hard when items are out of context (Tulving & Thomson, 1973) – have you ever seen a teacher or neighbour in an unfamiliar context, for example out shopping or on holiday – and struggled to recognise them at first?

Long-term *vs* short-term/ working	Declarative *vs* procedural
Retrospective *vs* prospective	Recognition *vs* free recall

Four key contrasts in human memory

Limitations of STM

As the name suggests, STM can only remember items for a short period. But how short? It appears to be limited to under half a minute unless information is **rehearsed.** Peterson and Peterson (1959) showed 'trigrams' – sets of three random letters (e.g. TBX) to participants, who then had to count backwards from a number in threes (e.g. '567, 564, 561…') to distract them. Results showed a high level of accurate recall after three to six seconds, but by 18 seconds, the recall level was very poor.

STM appears to be limited to under half a minute unless information is rehearsed

STM can also hold a very limited amount – a few words or numbers at time. Miller (1956) studied its **capacity**, and found that no matter what type of item is stored, STM could only hold between five and nine items. This became known as the *'magic number, seven plus or minus two'*. This observation can be easily tested, although more recent researchers have found that the limitation is not the number of items but how long they take to say: the capacity of STM is a phrase or group of items that can be spoken in around two seconds (Baddeley *et al.*, 1975, see key study p.135).

There is some debate about why information is lost from STM. One theory is that it simply fades away over time. This is known as decay theory. The other main idea is that because of the STM's limited capacity, new information that comes in has the effect of pushing old information out. This is known as displacement theory. Waugh and Norman (1965) used lists of items presented at different speeds to put these theories to the test. Presenting a list faster only made a slight difference to recall – what was most important was how late in the list an item appeared, later items being less affected by displacement. The researchers concluded that STM forgetting is mainly due to displacement but decay does have a slight effect too.

STM mainly uses **acoustically encoded** information – items in the basis of sound (Baddeley, 1966 – see key study). If a person is given visual information such as a set of pictures to remember they will typically transform them to verbal information and then hold the words in STM based on their sound. However, when people are prevented from using acoustic encoding they can take in items visually (Murray, 1968), so the store must include a visual element too. LTM, in contrast, encodes meaningful information. This is known as **semantic encoding**.

📖 Key study: Baddeley (1966): types of encoding in memory

Alan Baddeley

Aim: The study aimed to demonstrate an important difference between STM and LTM by showing that they encode words in different ways. Baddeley had done some research into people muddling up words over the phone and had noticed that mistakes tended to occur with words that sounded similar. However, in long-term memory we can easily retain words with similar sounds (or even the same sound, such as 'hair' and 'hare') without confusing their meaning. He believed that STM encodes words based on their sound – 'acoustic encoding' – while LTM uses the meaning of the word – 'semantic encoding' – and set up the experiment to test this idea.

Method: Baddeley provided participants with lists of five words, some of which were acoustically similar (they sounded alike) such as 'can, man, cap, mat, map' and some were semantically similar (similar in meaning) such as 'large, big, huge, giant, broad'. Other word lists contained five random words. Participants were either tested immediately, to test STM, or given a short training session with the lists and then asked to recall them after 20 minutes (i.e. testing LTM).

Findings: In the immediate test, retrieval of the acoustically similar lists was poorest. People appeared to mix up similar sounding words such as 'can' and 'cap'. This shows that STM encodes the sound of words. However, in the LTM test it was the items with similar meanings that people recalled poorly. Items from the lists with similar meanings such as 'large' and 'huge' were mixed up. This showed that LTM encodes the meanings of words – semantic encoding.

Evaluation: As a laboratory experiment, this study was well controlled but artificial. It can't necessarily be generalised to the broad range of real-world contexts in which we take in new words. It is also limited in just using words and it is now known that STM can also use visual encoding. Nevertheless, it provided strong experimental evidence that STM and LTM are separate and encode new information differently.

✅ Questions

1. Name the memory store that holds the required information while you are doing a task.

2. Complete: in any memory store, information must be encoded, then stored and finally _____ from memory.

3. What term do psychologists use to mean permanent memory storage?

4. What is another name for STM?

5. Which type of memory involves remembering to do things in the future?

6. Which type of retrieval is being used if you are asked whether a name is correct or not?

7. What are the three processes of memory?

8. Which process fails when something is on the 'tip of your tongue'?

9. What is the difference between free recall and recognition?

10. What type of encoding is used in LTM, according to Baddeley (1966)?

🗝 Key concepts

- STM - short-term memory
- LTM - long-term memory
- Encoding
- Storage
- Retrieval
- Consolidation
- Working memory
- Semantic LTM
- Episodic LTM
- Declarative memory
- Procedural memory
- Implicit memory
- Prospective memory
- Recognition
- Free recall
- Tip of the tongue phenomenon
- Cue
- Rehearsal
- Capacity
- Acoustic encoding
- Semantic encoding

GO! Activities

1. Prepare a version of the naming famous people experiment discussed under the section on 'recognition versus free recall'. You could use a PowerPoint presentation – the first 10 pictures have a name, and the participants have to say if it is the correct name or not (yes/no). The next 10 pictures of famous people have no name and the participant has to provide it. Which one do people find harder? Is this a fair comparison, or are there uncontrolled extraneous variables?

2. Find out more about the links between sleep and memory. Prepare a set of summary notes or a blog post on this issue. Now compare your summary with that of another student and give feedback/comments.

Approaches to memory

Biological approach to memory

Revision points from chapter 2

The following points from the main section on the biological approach are especially relevant to this topic. Ensure that you can refer to them in exam answers on approaches to memory:

- the nervous system and brain areas
- neurons and neurotransmitters

The nervous system and brain areas

The biological approach tries to link psychological functions to brain areas. The neocortex in the frontal lobe appears to be the location where STM processing occurs.

One brain area in particular has been repeatedly linked to declarative LTM – the **hippocampus**. This seahorse-shaped area of the limbic system is essential for new long-term memories to be formed. While the number of neurons we have is apparently fixed in most brain areas – new neurons are 'born' in the hippocampus throughout life (Eriksson *et al.*, 1998). This structure can be larger in some people than others and it has been found to be larger in taxi drivers, perhaps because their job places an exceptionally great demand on them to learn spatial information (Maguire *et al.*, 2000). However, cells in the hippocampus can also get smaller due to the effects of stress (McEwen & Sapolsky, 1995).

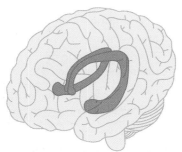

The hippocampus

Henry Molaison in 1986, aged 60, enjoying an unmemorable memory experiment at Massachusetts Institute of Technology

📖 Key study: Scoville and Milner (1957): the case of 'H.M.'

Aim: Some of the most dramatic cases of memory loss come from individuals who have been brain damaged – accidentally or through surgery. One such case was Henry Molaison (often referred to as 'H.M.'), a young man who suffered from very severe epilepsy in the 1950s. It was not possible to improve his condition using medication, and so his doctor, William Scoville, decided to try an experimental surgical procedure – removing a large area from his temporal lobe, the hippocampus. This case study aimed to find out the nature of his memory loss, and therefore deduce the role of the hippocampus in memory.

Method: The researchers conducted interviews with the patient and his family, and administered a range of tests including an IQ test and a memory test – the 'Wechsler Memory Scale'.

Findings: *In the opinion of his family, Henry's personality was unchanged and his IQ was undiminished. However, he suffered from dramatic loss of memory function after the operation. He was still able to recall his early life but could no longer remember anything from around the time of the operation. More importantly still, he could not encode any new information to LTM. This left him in a permanent state of amnesia, unable to hold a sustained conversation or take in anything new. His score on the Wechsler memory test was zero in some areas and he 'failed to improve with repeated practice' (p.17). Curiously, however, HM was still able to learn new skills – Milner (1970) later reported that he was still able to learn a mirror-drawing task, even though he had no recollection of his repeated attempts at the task. This suggested that non-declarative memory might have been unharmed by the damage to his hippocampus.*

Evaluation: *It is important to realise that this research is a case study, not an experiment, and the study of HM should not be considered unethical – his memory loss was an accidental side effect of earlier surgery. The precise nature of the damage has made him an especially useful case to science. It was a tragic case for Henry Molaison himself, but he became the most studied man in the history of psychology.*

🔍 Top tip

When describing the methodology of the Scoville and Milner study, remember that it was a case study involving tests and interviews. HM's operation was not part of the study itself.

Neurons and neurotransmitters

As discussed in chapter 2, biological psychologists see learning as being based on changes within the brain. In the biological approach, learning – and therefore LTM storage – is explained in terms of synapses between neurons being strengthened or new ones forming (Hebb, 1949). This process is called **long-term potentiation (LTP)** and it is thought to be one of the main ways that learning of new memories is represented in the brain on a cellular level. Interestingly, LTP was first demonstrated in the cells of the hippocampus – in rabbits (Lømo, 2003). Improved communication between cells after they 'fired' together has been found to last for several hours – after which time the process of sleep may play a role in consolidating these changes (Rasch & Born, 2013).

From this point of view, any limits to LTM capacity would be based on the number of neurons in the brain, and the number of synapses between them. There are thought to be around 86 billion neurons in a typical human brain (Herculano-Houzel, 2012), and each can have a large number of connections of varying strength – perhaps over 100 trillion connections in total (Williams & Herrup, 1988). Therefore, the biological approach can explain why healthy people do not appear to suffer from their LTM getting 'full' – the brain has a vast amount of storage potential.

LTP was first demonstrated in the cells of the hippocampus in rabbits!

Make the link

...between the biological approach to memory, and the topic of sleep and dreams

Evaluation

Studying how memory works at a neuronal level is beginning to have an effect on our understanding of learning. It is becoming increasingly clear that sleep plays an important role in consolidating the neuronal changes that occur when we form a new memory.

Through studying brain-injured patients, localisation of brain areas crucial to memory stores such as STM and LTM has allowed us to predict the effects of damage to the brain and avoid harmful memory loss, for example during surgical procedures.

However, critics would argue that although general areas involved in memory stores can be seen on brain scans, no clear biological links to specific cognitive processes (e.g. rehearsal) have yet been established, and it is therefore not clear that things such as the capacity of STM can be easily explained via the biology of the brain.

Another weakness is that the approach relies on case studies of brain damaged/injured individuals who have unique damage and it is hard to generalise this research to the whole population.

The cognitive approach to memory

Revision points from chapter 2

The following points from the main section on the cognitive approach are especially relevant to this topic. Ensure that you can refer to them in exam answers on approaches to memory:

- computer analogy
- schemas

Computer analogy

Cognitive psychologists compare human memory to the processing of information in a computer; LTM could be compared to a hard drive – the permanent storage of the system. Like a computer, we process new information, and store it until needed. Using this analogy, the STM is more like your computer's processing power.

Models of memory often focus on processing and storage too. In the next section, you will study two models – the multi-store and working memory models – which both emphasise the way that information can be processed and moved from one store to another, very like information being processed and saved on a computer.

In the computer analogy LTM can be compared to a hard drive

Schemas

Another useful concept from this approach is the schema, that is, a set of ideas and beliefs about something that you have experienced. Cognitive psychologists think that long-term memories are based on schemas, meaning that similar memories are stored together. As you have seen in chapter 2, Bartlett showed that memories could be distorted to make them more like our cultural expectations, subtracting elements that don't fit.

As our schemas are influenced by culture and expectations, people should remember things better if they are consistent with a schema. This is exactly what was found by memory researchers Brewer and Treyens (1981) who studied recall of objects in an office scene (see below). However, in a similar study, Pezdek *et al.* (1989) directly compared schema-consistent and schema inconsistent items, and found that the *inconsistent* items were better recalled. They concluded that this is due to more attention being given to items that seem surprising or unusual during the process of encoding. Either way, it is apparent that memory for objects is influenced by expectations from our schemas.

📖 Key study: Brewer and Treyens (1981): study of schemas in memory

Aim: *The researchers conducted an experiment to determine what effect it had on memory if items were consistent with a schema or not (i.e. they did or did not fit the context).*

Method: *This was a lab experiment, but quite an unusual one, as the 'lab' had been set up to look like an office. This small room was arranged with 63 carefully selected objects clearly on view. Some had been chosen to fit the office schema (e.g. a phone) while others did not fit the schema – you would typically not see them in an office (e.g. a brick, a picnic basket). Participants were told to wait in the room until the experiment began and they did not realise that their recall of the objects was part of the experiment. After 90 seconds, they were taken to another room and told to write down all of the objects that they remembered seeing.*

Findings: *Brewer and Treyens found that the level to which items fitted the schema – that is, the extent to which people would expect to see items such as a telephone, a notepad or a skull in a typical office – strongly correlated with level of successful recall. The researchers concluded that the office schema was acting as a retrieval cue. When people try to recall items, they mentally generate an image of a typical office from their schema and this process reminds them of items that were at the scene.*

Evaluation: *This study was unusual in that it used a real-world context rather than pictures or objects on a screen, and therefore, had higher ecological validity than other studies of its time. However, it is limited in that the use of correlation cannot determine cause and effect. There is no control over what the participants were doing while waiting in the room and it may be that they remembered some items better than others just because they were easier to see or because they paid more attention to them. Other research such as Pezdek et al. (1989) has contradicted the study, finding that schema-inconsistent items were better recalled.*

The lab used in the experiment

Human memory recalls things by association

Evaluation of cognitive approach

There are considerable problems with the computer analogy. Unlike a hard-drive, the LTM does not seem to have a limited capacity and memories can interfere with each other in a way that is very unlike computer storage. In addition, memories are not recalled in a similar way to a computer – a computer searches for files with no regard for meaning.

The concept of the schema seems to fit the evidence better, as human memory recalls things by association, and successful retrieval can depend on context, as seen in the Brewer and Treyens study. However, there is some contradictory evidence in the research into schemas, and the term 'schema' is not always used consistently in research. Fiske and Linville (1980) argue that overall, despite some truth in the accusation that the term is imprecise, the benefits of schema theory outweigh its flaws. It has also been applied to improve the understanding of eyewitness memory, as described in the final section of this chapter.

The psychoanalytic approach to memory

Revision points from chapter 2

The following points from the main section on the psychoanalytic approach are especially relevant to this topic. Ensure that you can refer to them in exam answers on approaches to Memory:

- the id, ego and superego
- defence mechanisms

Levinger and Clark used galvanic skin response as part of their study

Id, ego and superego

The psychoanalytic approach explains memory in terms of the interaction between the conscious and unconscious parts of the mind. Things that are in conscious awareness can be explicitly remembered. However, as you may remember from chapter 2, things that cause distress and anxiety can be distorted via defence mechanisms or repressed to the unconscious - the *id*.

When it comes to memory, most of what we think about is the work of our conscious mind or ego, according to this approach. An important implication of this view is that memory is largely rational and conscious, and therefore likely to be accurate. The concept of the ego has some overlap with 'working memory'.

As most things that are in the id cannot be remembered, what role do these things play in memory? Things that people remember from dreams and as a result of therapy are not truly unconscious but are actually in the preconscious. This consists of ideas in both the id and superego that can be brought to mind if we make an effort to remember them. Therefore, the preconscious can be loosely linked to the modern concept of LTM.

Defence mechanisms

According to Freud, repressed memories are pushed into the id, but not successfully forgotten, so they continue to have an influence on behaviour. Psychoanalysis believes that memories that are repressed in childhood can resurface when the individual reaches puberty (Glassman, 2000).

So what is the evidence that repression actually occurs? Some researchers have tried to test it experimentally. The best-known work was done by Levinger and Clark (1961) who compared memory for emotional versus non-emotional words. They used words of equal frequency, and tested not just perceptions of emotional level of words, but also galvanic skin response (GSR; one of the measures used in lie detector tests – GSR increases when a person becomes more emotionally aroused). Participants were first asked to make a word association with each item on the list and later to recall which word they had associated when prompted with the original word. Results showed that words such as *'fight'* that link to negative emotions were forgotten more - however, this was not the only factor, as there was also considerable random variation between participants and from one session to the next.

Parkin *et al.* (1982) replicated the basic results of Levinger and Clark, but pointed out that over a longer period of time, emotional items are remembered better than neutral items. The findings, they argue, can easily be explained in terms of existing theories of arousal and memory recall, and they do not demonstrate repression.

Other studies have looked at **suppression** – a deliberate form of repression where adults intentionally try to drive upsetting memories out of their mind. It is easier to study in the laboratory than true repression. Anderson and Green (2001) found that participants could be instructed to think of some word associations and try to forget others (sometimes called the 'think/no think' task), and when tested later, they had a poorer response on the latter. However, Bulevich *et al.* (2006) failed to replicate this finding. Both studies used just 32 participants, and it is possible that some people may just be better than others at suppressing a memory to the unconscious.

Freud believed memories of certain events are repressed

Evaluation

Given the influence of psychoanalysis in psychology over the past century and the many attempts to find evidence for its theories, it is surprising that so little hard evidence has been established.

However, these laboratory experiments are arguably not comparable to the kind of experiences that Freud believed would be repressed, such as existential childhood guilt over sexual or aggressive feelings. It is unlikely that such emotions could ever be fully replicated in a laboratory setting for ethical reasons.

At the present moment, it is fair to say that repression is not considered to be a major process in human memory by most memory researchers.

Key concepts

- Hippocampus
- Long-term potentiation
- Suppression

Questions

1. Which part of the brain controls STM?

2. What is the term for the changes in brain cell structure when we learn things?

3. What type of memory is the hippocampus important for?

4. Who conducted the study into schemas in an office room?

5. Name one area where distorted beliefs may affect memory.

6. Which study showed that schema-inconstant items are better remembered?

7. What part of the mind can unpleasant memories be pushed into, according to the psychoanalytic approach?

8. What is suppression?

9. What problem is there with the laboratory studies of repression and suppression?

10. True or false: repression is still considered a major explanation for all aspects of forgetting?

Activities

1. Each of the approaches in this section has something to say about forgetting. Summarise these explanations in your notes for each of the approaches that you have studied. Take at least half a page of A4 on each one and ensure that you use the correct terminology. Write at least one evaluation point as well – which could come from supporting evidence

2. Draw a mind map on one of the approaches. In the centre, write 'the ___ approach to memory'. Use the paragraphs and research studies in this section as your key branches of the map. Then fill in details as smaller offshoots of each branch.

An example of a mind map

Theories of memory

In the 1950s, memory was largely seen as a single unitary process; that began to change in the 1960s, as the cognitive approach became popular and people started to compare memory to the information processing of a computer (Baddeley, 2012). One model – the **multi-store model (MSM)** became popular during that decade. However, it became clear that while useful as a general overview, MSM could not explain the details of how we process everyday tasks such as writing, answering questions and following directions. The **working memory model (WMM)** of Baddeley and Hitch (1974) tried to tackle this problem.

The multi-store model

Atkinson and Shiffrin (1968) provided the best-known theory of how STM and LTM work together. They said that memory stores function in a linear (one-way) process, with each store acting as the gateway to the next store.

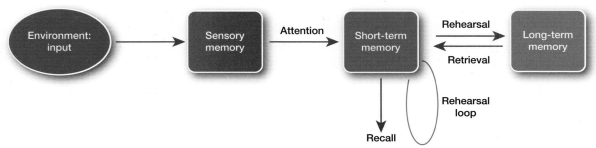

The multi-store model

Sensory memory

As discussed in the first section of this chapter, our memory has a temporary store known as STM or working memory, which has a very limited capacity. A lot of stimuli are picked up by our senses but most of them fade away rapidly and they are never encoded.

Sperling (1960) proposed that there is an even shorter store than STM that lasts for a couple of seconds or less. He called this **sensory memory (SM)**. It holds information for that brief period of time before you are able to focus your attention on it. Sperling showed that visual SM has a large capacity but fades after around half a second.

A good example of using SM is when a person speaks to you and you are not paying attention. If you switch your attention within a couple of seconds and try to focus on what they are saying, you still retain a sensory trace of what was said (allowing you to pretend you were listening!)

Sensory memory is thought to comprise a set of stores, one for each sense – sight, hearing, touch, etc.

Even if you are not listening you will retain a sensory trace of what someone said for a couple of seconds

? Discussion point

Can you think of any other examples of sensory memory in action?

You can hold information in the STM for longer by rehearsing it – for example repeatedly saying a phone number aloud

Structure of MSM

The model presents memory as a series of stores connected by one-way processes from SM through to LTM. Information coming in through the senses is placed briefly in a sensory store. If **attention** is paid to information, it travels from SM into STM. There, up to approximately seven items can be maintained in STM for a period of time – the longer an item is held there, the better chance it has of being encoded to LTM. However, things tend to be rapidly forgotten from STM within a few seconds due to decay. People can hold information in STM for longer using a process called **maintenance rehearsal** – essentially, this means saying things repeatedly to yourself in your mind (also called 'rote rehearsal'). This process also results in encoding the information to LTM. A major prediction of the model is that information will be better remembered in the long-term if it is maintained for as long as possible in the STM.

Research evidence for MSM

The **primacy effect** is a reliable finding from the recall of lists, where items from the start of a list are better remembered in comparison to the items in the middle. The **recency effect** is where later items are better remembered. This supports the idea of two separate memory stores, STM and LTM. According to this view, the primacy effect occurs because early items are rehearsed in STM and then encoded into LTM, while the recency effect occurs due to the final few items still being in STM when the list is recalled (Glanzer & Cunitz, 1966). These two effects together are also called the serial position effect.

> **? Discussion point**
>
> Do you agree that holding/ rehearsing things in your STM is a good way of encoding things to LTM? Think of your own experience of trying to memorise things, such as words in a foreign language, lines for a play, a shopping list or instructions for a task at work. How did you manage to do it?

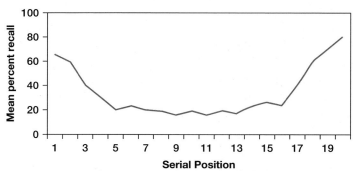

The serial position effect

Evaluation

Supporting the model, there is good evidence of separate STM and LTM stores. The serial position effect supports this idea, and neurological evidence from brain scans suggests that these two stores involve different brain areas. Case studies of patients with brain damage to one of the stores but not both such as HM (see previous section) have supported the idea that there are two separate systems in different parts of the brain.

However, brain-damaged patients also present problems for the model. Some patients with damaged STM rehearsal are able to function in everyday jobs (Baddeley, 2012). This suggests that STM must be more complex and have more than one part to it. STM capacity is also better viewed in terms of a two-second duration than in terms of holding seven items (Baddeley *et al.*, 1975, see key study).

The model is inaccurate in suggesting that memory is linear, because LTM can affect STM. Morris *et al.* (1985) showed that people with prior knowledge of football performed better on an STM recall test of football scores. If LTM can affect STM, then the one-way transfer of information as proposed by the multi-store model must be incorrect and the relationship between the two stores needs a rethink.

Holding/rehearsing info in STM does not guarantee that it is permanently stored in LTM – as every revising student knows! What is done with the information is more important than how long it spends in STM – Craik and Tulving (1975) showed that information was better recalled if questions were asked about its meaning (e.g. 'is it a type of animal?'), rather than about its appearance (e.g. 'is it in capital letters?'), showing that meaningless maintenance rehearsal is not the best way of encoding information to LTM. They developed a theory around the idea that meaningful information is processed more deeply, and called it 'levels of processing' (see activity 3, on p.138).

Overall, MSM is a useful general overview of the structure of memory; however, it lacks detail and there are several more recent research findings that it cannot account for.

The working memory model

In the early 1970s, researchers Alan Baddeley and Graham Hitch tried to combine key facts about STM into a new model. They wanted to replace the MSM and other older theories, which they saw as limited and inaccurate.

In particular, they focused on the way that STM is used as a flexible, active store with which we carry out numerous tasks on a day-to-day basis, such as holding a conversation, playing a game or following a map. They felt that it is not just a memory store but also a system that can process information and solve problems. Because of the active nature of the store, they prefer the term working memory (WM) rather than STM, and so their theory is known as the working memory model.

What is the best way to memorise lines for a play?

Items at the top of a list are usally better remembered than things further down

🔍 Top tip

Note that that several key elements in memory come in threes – three processes, types of long-term memory, three stores in MSM. Can you find any more?

STM is used as a flexible, active store for everyday tasks such as following a map

Structure of WM

Baddeley and Hitch (1974) proposed a model with a central component called the **central executive (CE)**, which controls the other parts of the model. It is based on the attention we are able to allocate to a task, to different parts of the same task or to several tasks simultaneously.

The original working memory model

? **Discussion point**

Can you imagine using these different parts of working memory as you try out a task? Baddeley suggests that you can experience working memory in action if you mentally walk around your flat or house and count how many windows it has. Take a moment to try this. Can you do it? Most people generate an image in their mind, and imagine moving from room to room.

The other major parts of the model were known as **slave systems**, because they were controlled by the CE. The original version of the model, shown above, included two slave systems processing different types of information. The **visuospatial sketchpad** processes visual tasks, and the **phonological loop** processes verbal information. In the windows task (see sidebar), the central executive forms a plan to tackle the problem, the visuospatial sketchpad allows you to picture the rooms in your mind and the phonological loop maintains and adds to the numbers. The CE also oversees the whole process to check that all the processes are running correctly.

Multi-tasking

The existence of two slave systems allowed for two different tasks to be completed at once, if enough attention is available. Of course, our attention is limited. Dividing attention between more than one task is called **multi-tasking** and it tends to result in both tasks being done poorly, especially if either task is complicated.

Inspired by research that had been done into brain-damaged individuals, Baddeley and colleagues gave ordinary participants tasks designed to use elements of WM, and told them to perform other tasks at the same time. These became known as **dual-task studies**. In one such study, Baddeley *et al.* (1973) asked participants to trace a 'hollow letter F' with a pointer at the same time as doing a verbal task. The two tasks could be done simultaneously without any deficit to either task. However, when participants tried to do two visual tasks at the same time, performance dropped significantly. The researchers concluded that a verbal and a spatial task can be done at the same time without much interference, as they involve separate slave systems.

Multi-tasking tends to result in each task being done poorly

Key features of the model

The WMM takes a very different view of short-term memory to the MSM – it sees it as an active processor rather than a store, that is, a system that is used to carry out day-to-day tasks rather than just hold information for a short time.

Just as MSM makes certain assumptions about how the memory stores work, there are key features of working memory according to this model. These are open to being tested and debated. They include:

- Processing time is based on real time to do tasks. For example, how long it takes to say a sentence in your head is equal to the time it would take to say it aloud. Doing a join-the-dots task in your head takes as long as it would take to do it with a pen.

- Attention is limited. Two tasks can be done simultaneously if they rely on different slave systems. However, complex and novel tasks will use up more attention from the CE, causing everything to run slower.

? Discussion point

Think of an activity that involves doing more than one thing at once, such as driving while having a conversation. What happens if one of the tasks suddenly becomes more difficult, for example, having to deal with an accident or diversion on the road ahead of you? (See p.409 for feedback.)

📖 Key study: Baddeley *et al.* (1975): the word length effect

Aim: In this study, Baddeley et al. *looked for evidence of one of the key principles of the WM model – that processing something in your head (e.g. rehearsing a word) is done in real-time, that is, it takes the same amount of time as it would to actually say the word.*

Method: The study tested short-term recall of lists of words by giving people groups of five words which were either short (e.g. 'book') or long (e.g. 'university'). Participants were asked to recall the first three letters each time.

Findings: The researchers found that rather than being simply limited to seven items, the number of words that could be held in STM depended on the length of the word – the longer the words, the fewer people could retain. They concluded that memory span is inversely related to word length; this became known as the **word length effect***. It was concluded that the phonological loop has a time-limited capacity based on around two seconds of pronunciation time. This fits the WMM assumption that tasks generally take the same amount of time to process in working memory as they would take to do in real life. In contrast, the findings go against the MSM, which states simply that short-term memory remembers approximately seven items.*

Evaluation: The research was useful in that it helped to distinguish between the two main models of memory, supporting the WMM over the MSM. As a lab experiment, it was well controlled, though rather artificial. The findings have been supported by several other studies, including research that found that bilingual speakers of English and Welsh had a shorter digit span in Welsh, in which it takes slightly longer to pronounce the numbers (Ellis and Hennelly, 1980).

🔍 Top tip

The word length effect is evidence *against* the MSM and evidence *for* the WMM. Therefore, it can be used as part of your evaluation of either model.

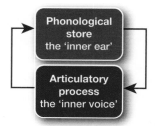

Phonological loop

The working memory has been continually changed and improved. One of the earliest changes came when Baddeley and colleagues realised that the ability to understand words must be separate from the ability to rehearse them. This was because some brain-damaged individuals could do one of these things but not the other. Therefore, they altered the theory to show the phonological loop as having two parts:

- The articulatory process. This is a rehearsal loop – the 'inner voice' when you say or rehearse words inside your head.
- The phonological store. This is responsible for brief storage/comprehension of sounds. It is nicknamed the 'inner ear'.

Another problem with the original version of the model was that it did not provide a clear explanation of how stimuli from different parts can be combined and linked with LTM. Baddeley therefore proposed a third slave system, the **episodic buffer** (Baddeley, 2000). This is seen as the mind's way of combining a mixture of sights and sounds into a coherent 'episode' that can then be encoded into episodic LTM.

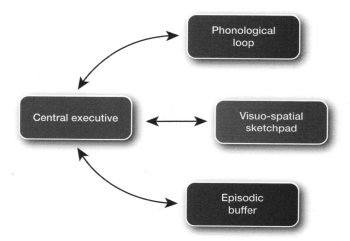

Current working memory model

Features of the WMM	• Proposed by Baddeley and Hitch in 1974. • Emphasises active processing– does not see STM as a passive store of information. • It is the part of our mind that we use for day-to-day tasks and problem solving. • States that we can do more than one task at once if attention from CE is sufficient. • Time to process tasks in the mind is equivalent to real time to do tasks.
Elements of the WMM	• Phonological loop: slave system that processes sounds and language. • Visuospatial sketchpad: slave system that processes images and spatial tasks. • Episodic buffer: slave system that combines stimuli into coherent events. • Articulatory process: part of phonological loop; rehearses words and sounds. Limited to 2 seconds pronunciation time. • Central executive: based on attention and controls all slave systems. • Phonological store: part of the phonological loop; allows us to comprehend the sounds of words.

Evaluation

The model explains certain key facts about STM, for example the word length effect, that were not explained by earlier theories. The word length effect supports the idea that processing of tasks is based on the real-world time to do the tasks, for example, to pronounce words.

Unlike other models, it can be used to explain prospective memory. According to this view, the CE, as the system for attention, would keep track of whether there are any tasks to be done at any given time. However not every researcher agrees with this view – some believe that prospective memories come to mind without us having to constantly pay a small amount of attention to them (Marsh *et al.*, 2005)

A weakness of the model is that the function and capacity of the CE is unclear: we don't know how much it can hold, how it manages to be modality-free or even if there is only one CE (Eysenck, 1986, argued that it might not be a unitary store). This is one area where a clearer understanding of the biology of working memory might be helpful in order to explain how our system for attention can link to slave systems based on vision, language, episodic memory and possibly others.

Theories need to change over time to take account of new evidence and this model has been able to integrate a large number of newer findings, mainly by making changes to the original model. It has also been used for real-world tasks – the phonological loop is thought to be essential for language acquisition (Baddeley, 2012) and a deficit in the phonological store has been linked to disorders of language development (Gathercole & Baddeley, 1990).

> **? Discussion point**
>
> Question: Why is this called a model? What is the difference between a theory and a model? (See p.409 for feedback.)

The phonological loop is thought to be essential for language acquisition

🔑 Key concepts

- Multi-store model (MSM)
- Working memory model (WMM)
- Sensory memory (SM)
- Attention
- Maintenance rehearsal
- Primacy effect
- Recency effect
- Serial-position effect
- Decay
- Central executive (CE)
- Slave system
- Visuospatial sketchpad
- Phonological loop
- Multi-tasking
- Dual-task studies
- Automaticity
- Word length effect
- Articulatory process
- Phonological store
- Episodic buffer

✓ Questions

1. What does SM stand for?

2. What factor affects whether information is transferred from STM to LTM, according the multi-store model?

3. What process affects whether a stimulus is transferred from SM to STM?

4. What is the name of the effect whereby items at the beginning and end of a list are better remembered?

5. Why do neurological case studies like HM help to support the MSM?

6. What effect did the study by Baddeley *et al.* (1975) show?

7. What term means doing more than one task at a time?

8. Which part of WM deals with verbal information?

9. What slave system was added to the model and explains how information can be combined into coherent episodes?

10. What part of the WMM is least well understood?

🔵 Activities

1. Would the following mainly require use of the central executive, phonological loop or visuospatial sketchpad? Would any of them require more than one of the systems to work together?

   - Counting to 100
   - Parking your car
   - Doing a maze
   - Singing
   - Composing a poem
   - Listening to speech

2. Take a moment to design an experiment on multi-tasking (you don't need to actually carry it out). Perhaps it could be a comparison of how well males and females multi-task. What two (or more) tasks would you use, and how would you measure success on the tasks? What things would you need to keep constant between your two groups?

3. Find out more about the idea of *levels of processing*. This is a separate theory of memory, which could be used in answers on this area of the topic. The concept of meaningful information being more reliably encoded to LTM could be useful for your studies as well – it suggests that re-reading your notes is a bad study strategy, and generating questions and summarising notes are much more effective.

Real-world application: eyewitness testimony

There are several real-world applications of memory research. After all, every area of human life involves memory, from parenting, to education, to care for the elderly. This section focuses on how psychology can help police and lawyers to gain more accurate testimony from eyewitnesses.

Memory of an eyewitness

Accurate **eyewitness testimony (EWT)** can be essential to the legal process. In many criminal cases, the identification of a suspect by an eyewitness and their memory of events is essential to gaining a conviction.

However, there is a problem. People like to think that their memory for events is accurate but there are many research studies that show that people's memory can be distorted in predictable ways. Criminal trials often take place many months after the crime itself but memory for unfamiliar faces is very poor, especially over a long period of time, resulting in people's testimony being unreliable.

Early studies into eyewitness testimony

A classic study of eyewitness testimony was reported by a German psychologist, Hugo Münsterberg. In his book '*On the Witness Stand*' (Münsterberg, 1908) he lists errors in his own recollection of a burglary. His report to the police turned out to be wrong in many respects, and he found it hard to know why – as a scientist, he had an excellent memory and he had delivered hundreds of lectures without relying on notes. In an early and rather unethical experiment on the issue, one of his colleagues staged an incident in which one student apparently shot another in a lecture theatre and the student witnesses were given a memory test afterwards. The smallest number of mistakes stood at 26% and the largest was 80%. Clearly human memory for a crime can be highly unreliable.

Another researcher Frederick Bartlett, discussed in chapter 2, used unfamiliar folk stories to study the effects of schemas on memory. Among other results, he found that people subtract elements that don't fit their cultural expectations and add/transform parts of the story to make them seem more familiar. These kind of distortions could play a role when witnesses are reporting a crime. However, it was not until the start of cognitive psychology that researchers like Elizabeth Loftus (see key study) began to fully investigate the processes that led to memory distortions.

! Syllabus note

This section is essential for Higher students, who may be asked for an 'application' of their chosen optional topic. At National 5, you will not be asked directly for an application but a general understanding of eyewitness memory can provide useful real-world examples in your answers on other questions.

🔍 Top tip

Use Bartlett's (1932) study as evidence in your work on this area.

Criminal trials often take place many months after the crime itself

Human memory for crime can be highly unreliable

Elizabeth Loftus

📖 Key study: Loftus and Palmer (1974): misleading questions to witnesses

Aim: *Loftus & Palmer wanted to test the 'misinformation effect' – the idea that memories can be corrupted by later information such as leading questions.*

Method: *The researchers showed video clips of car accidents to 45 student participants and then asked them several questions. The wording of one question was changed for each of five experimental conditions, as follows:*

- *'About how fast were the cars going when they* hit *each other?'*
- *'About how fast were the cars going when they* smashed *into each other?'*

Other key words used were 'collided', 'bumped' and 'contacted'. The highest estimates came in the 'smashed' condition with a mean of 40.8 mph; the lowest estimates came in the 'contacted' condition, with a mean estimate of 31.8 mph. This work showed that a witness's response could be distorted by a leading question. However, it was hard to know whether memory had truly been distorted or if the participants were simply responding to the wording of the question. After all, even people who hadn't watched the clip might have guessed a higher speed from the 'smashed' question. In order to settle this issue, the researchers showed another 150 participants a car accident clip. One group of 50 participants were asked 'how fast were the cars going when they hit each other?', the second group were asked the same question except with '…smashed into…' and the third (the control group) were not asked about speed at all. This time the researchers waited for one week, then brought the participants back and asked them 'did you see any broken glass?' In fact, there was no broken glass in the video.

Participants in the study were shown clips of car accidents

Findings: When asked about the broken glass, the participants were more than twice as likely to incorrectly say 'yes' in the 'smashed' condition than in the hit condition – 16 out of 50, compared to 7/50. Because the questioning about broken glass took place one week later, it can be assumed that participants did not remember the wording of the original question but that their memory of the original event had been distorted.

Group question about speed	Smashed	Hit	None (control group)
Number who remembered seeing broken glass	16/50	7/50	6/50

Evaluation: The study was a carefully controlled lab experiment, and although the groups were very small in the first study, the second (broken glass) study used a reasonably large sample. The sample were not very diverse as all were university students and the situation may have seemed very artificial – watching an accident on screen is not very similar to witnessing one in real life, reducing the ecological validity of the experiment. These issues make it harder to generalise the findings to real life accidents or crimes. Nevertheless, this study has implications for the criminal justice system – it raises a major concern that police questioning could distort a witness's memory. Since this time, more neutral ways of questioning, such as the 'cognitive interview' (see below) have been adopted.

Factors in EWT

Several factors affect how likely it is that witnesses will remember something accurately or make a mistake. Some of the main factors include:

Misinformation effect. As explained above, research has shown that memory is unreliable and easily corrupted. Information that we see or hear after an event can merge with, distort or replace our memory of the original event. Loftus and colleagues have since described the effect of subsequent misleading information to witnesses as the misinformation effect. For example, Loftus and Palmer found that people would misremember seeing broken glass at an accident scene (see key study).

Social pressure. Treatment of witnesses can pressure them into making errors, for example the way a witness line-up up is conducted. Wells and Loftus (2012) report how having a traditional six person physical line-up of suspects pressures the witness into choosing somebody and they find it very difficult to respond accurately if the true suspect is not present. Wright *et al.* (2000) found that memory can be distorted and reports changed when participants hear others giving a conflicting false story, demonstrating the effect of social pressure on EWT.

? Discussion point

What exactly is meant by a leading question? Can you think of an example? Why would it be a problem if the police asked leading questions to witnesses?

The way a line-up is conducted can distort a witness' memory

Emotion/anxiety. A crime or accident will cause a high level of stress and anxiety. The **Yerkes-Dodson law** suggests that we perform best at a medium level of anxiety, and therefore high levels of anxiety will harm memory. Loftus *et al*. (1987) found that the estimated duration of a crime could be as much as five times longer than the actual time taken.

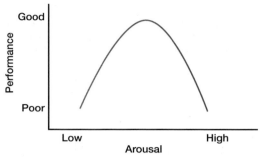

The Yerkes-Dodson Law suggests that performance in any ability is best at a medium level of anxiety/ arousal

Change blindness. Researcher Dan Simons has done a number of studies into how people fail to notice changes in their surroundings. The concerning thing for eyewitness memories is that people apparently do not focus much attention on a face unless it is unusual in some way and *may even fail to notice that they are looking at a different person* unless the actor changes a very obvious category such as race, sex or age. Demonstrating the relevance to EWT, Davies and Hine (2007) showed participants a film of a burglary where the actor changed mid-way through; 61% did not notice the change. You can watch an example of a change blindness experiment on YouTube here: https://www.youtube.com/watch?v=BZ0l9s8_Hmk.

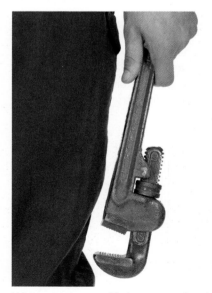

Witnesses are more likely to remember the face of a man holding a spanner than of a man holding a knife

Violence. Loftus *et al.* (1987) reported a cleverly designed study where participants waited in a corridor and heard a struggle in a neighbouring room. In one condition, a man emerged holding a knife with blood on the handle, whereas in the other condition he emerged holding a spanner with oil on the handle. Participants had a poorer memory for the man's face in the first condition. Loftus *et al.* (1987) believe that this is due to a process called **weapons focus** – the witness focuses on the weapon and fails to take in other details. However, it may link to the fact that a weapon is a very unusual object to see in most situations (Pickel, 1998) and does not fit our schema (see next point, below).

Expectations. Brewer and Treyens's (1981) study into schemas (see previous section) and related research shows that people's expectations can affect what they report seeing at a scene. Our culture and life experiences provide a set of expectations about social situations. In a crime, expectations and prejudice can affect what a witness perceives and what they later report. There is a tendency, according to schema theory, for witnesses to 'fill in the blanks' of anything they can't remember or didn't fully understand – a process known as **redintegration**.

> **⁜: Make the link**
>
> …with your studies of English, including autobiographical novels where authors try to remember their own life events many years later.

> **❓ Discussion point**
>
> Can you think of a mnemonic or another memory strategy to help you remember these factors in eyewitness testimony? Explaining three or four would be enough for a good exam answer.

Changes to the legal process

Research into EWT has prompted a number of changes to the legal system, although they have only been adopted by some police forces. Below are some of the key changes that have been proposed and/or implemented:

Using a cognitive interview. Many police forces now use a type of questioning called the **cognitive interview** that aims to avoid misleading witnesses by asking them to recall events more neutrally, often from different perspectives than their own (Geiselman *et al.*, 1985). It also avoids direct questions such as '*Did you see a green car?*' and instead asks more neutral questions such as '*Did anything else happen?*'	**Treat memory like a crime scene**. Just as detectives would avoid contaminating forensic evidence, they can now avoid contaminating a witness's memory by avoiding leading questions and by keeping witnesses apart so that they are not exposed to social pressure.
Witness line-ups. According to Wells and Loftus (2012), witnesses viewing a traditional line up may make incorrect judgements using a process of elimination ('*Well, I knew it wasn't two or three…*') rather than immediate recognition. The researchers advise showing photos of possible suspects one at a time, making a yes/no choice each time.	**Not relying on EWT alone**. The Devlin Report (1976) looked into the problems with EWT and concluded that despite its unreliabilities, it is essential to use it in the legal system. However, the report concluded that in order to convict a suspect there should be some other evidence as well – not just the word of a single eyewitness.

Many police forces now use cognitive interviews

The welfare of participants has to be consdiered when researching the witnesses of real crimes

Analysis of research into EWT

The idea of memories being distorted has become a key issue in the legal process. A huge amount of research has been conducted to find out the conditions under which items are best remembered. This research area has the potential to stop miscarriages of justice and to find ways of getting the most accurate evidence from witnesses.

Research in this area tends to include a lot of carefully controlled lab experiments. However, in such studies, the participants have little emotional involvement in what they are watching, and their reactions may not reflect real life. Yuille and Cutshall (1986) found that EWT is more accurate in the case of a real-world crime.

In addition, much of the laboratory research reported above has been done with student participants. As young adults, students have less life experience than an older witness would. As university students, they generally have good memory skills and in an artificial experimental situation they know that they need to pay attention to what they are watching. Real witnesses may have a lower IQ and memory ability than students and may miss key details because events are unexpected and they were not fully paying attention.

However, researching the witnesses of real crimes has a number of problems too. It requires the use of natural experiments, as participants cannot be pre-selected, and the welfare of participants has to be considered – asking them repeatedly about a crime that they witnessed may be distressing.

Overall, despite the methodological problems, the results of this research area have proved useful to the legal process. Many police forces now use the cognitive interview and a few have adopted Wells and Loftus's proposal of photo line-ups conducted by computer. Overall, the memory of a witness is increasingly seen as a fragile piece of evidence that must be treated carefully, and that can only be a good thing in terms of justice for both victims and crime suspects.

✔ Questions

1. Which two early researchers conducted studies relevant to EWT?

2. What was the aim of Loftus and Palmer (1974)?

3. What was the difference between the two Loftus and Palmer (1974) studies?

4. How many participants reported seeing broken glass in the second experiment?

5. Name three factors that affect EWT.

6. Which study showed that hearing incorrect testimony from others makes errors more likely?

7. What is 'change blindness'?

8. Why does the presence of a weapon make eyewitness statements less accurate?

9. What changes could be made to police practices to reduce errors from EWT?

10. What important difference(s) are there between lab experiments of EWT and real crimes?

🔍 Top tip

For an exam answer on an application of memory, eyewitness memory is a suitable topic. Structure an answer around the factors in EWT and support this with evaluated research by Loftus and others, and then explain how this knowledge has contributed to the development of the cognitive interview. For a top grade answer, make links with other aspects of the memory topic, such as the difference between LTM and STM, and use terminology such as *encoding* and *retrieval* accurately.

⁙ Make the link

...with social psychology topics, Modern Studies, Politics and Law.

🔵 Activities

1. Research a real-life case where eyewitness testimony led to mistaken imprisonment. For example, you could look at the CBS News '60 Minutes' documentary about the case of Ronald Cotton (see https://www.youtube.com/watch?v=nbARxiM0W_Q). Write a summary in your notes or as a blog post. Ensure that your summary explains some of the factors that affected the mistaken testimony.

2. Find out more about change blindness. There are many research studies on this area and some would be easy to adapt and conduct within the school to form a research project or perhaps for your Assignment (Higher students – choice of topic depends on SQA briefs for the year; see chapter 9). Consult with your teacher/lecturer before conducting any research in this area as there are potential ethical problems.

🔑 Key concepts

- Eyewitness testimony (EWT)
- Misinformation effect
- Social pressure
- Emotion
- Anxiety
- Yerkes-Dodson law
- Change blindness
- Weapons focus
- Expectation
- Redintegration
- Cognitive interview

End of topic project

You will conduct a case study into memory in the context of study strategies. Select a participant from your classes or outside school, ensuring that you get informed consent. The aim will be to find out how effectively the participant is studying and revising, and to make recommendations from your knowledge of memory to improve this effectiveness (see chapter 8 for general information on the case study method of research).

- Conduct a brief case history, using a semi-structured interview, to reveal the following points. Find out, up until now…

  - How often the participant typically studies outside class in general and for exams/tests.
  - Where, when and how thoroughly the participant completes his/her homework and revision.
  - What approach their peers and family members take/have taken to their studies.
  - The participant's views on learning and revision, and any changes that have taken place in these views.
  - Memory strategies the participant has adopted, for example, mnemonics, flash cards, etc.
  - How well the participant has performed academically, by their own estimation and by objective criteria (e.g. grades versus grade average).

- Now, follow up on this case history. Try using observation to find out how effectively the participant is studying – this could involve analysing a recording.

- Prepare recommendations based on your findings and your knowledge of human memory.

- If your participant consents, you could make a poster showing your results.

End of topic specimen exam questions

As this is an optional topic, exam questions will be quite general and will not name the topic or its specific theories/research studies, for example:

National 5

1. Explain a topic from Individual Behaviour other than sleep and dreams.   4 marks

2. From your chosen optional topic in Individual Behaviour, name and describe one research study that has been carried out. Include the aim, method/procedure and results of the study.   6 marks

Higher

1. Choose a topic in Individual Behaviour other than sleep, dreams and sleep disorders. Explain how this topic can be applied in the real world.   10 marks

2. Explain a topic in Individual Behaviour other than sleep, dreams and sleep disorders, referring to at least two approaches.   16 marks

3. Discuss two theories relating to your chosen optional topic in Individual Behaviour.   12 marks

The total exam mark allocation for the Individual Behaviour unit will be 20 marks; however, there is no way of knowing in advance how this will be split between this topic and the topic of sleep.

6 Stress

What is stress?

We use the term **stress** on a daily basis to describe our own feelings and behaviour, and those of other people. If we feel tense and can't sleep before an exam, we may recognise that we are feeling stressed. Stress is an interesting area partly because there is a clear interaction between the mind and the body.

We use the term stress on a daily basis

The fight-or-flight response

A short period of intense stress is known as **acute stress**. This could happen if you are in a fight, argue with your family or even if you have to give a speech.

When faced by an immediate severe threat, an animal or person reacts by releasing energy and preparing for action – either self-defence ('fight') or running away ('flight'). The outcome is a group of changes in our bodies called the **fight-or-flight response** (also called the 'acute stress response'). The effect on the body is the same no matter whether they fight or run – either way, the body is prepared for expending energy and using its muscles.

> ●: **Make the link**
>
> Your studies of Biology or Human Biology will help with this topic.

You may feel acute stress if you have to give a speech

The following chart summarises several major changes during fight-or-flight:

Raised heart rate	Increases blood pressure to pump glucose and oxygen to the muscles
Sweating	Helps cool the body in a fight or when running away
Tense muscles	A side effect of increased blood flow to the muscles in preparation for action
Increased blood clotting	Reduces bleeding in a fight situation
Glucose released into bloodstream	Stored energy is used to deal with the emergency
Slowed digestion	Side effect of reduced blood flow; causes nausea and loss of appetite
Heightened vision and awareness	All focus is on immediate threat and other things are ignored

? Discussion point

What kind of things make you feel stressed?

Your body will prepare itself if you need to run away from a threat

🔍 Top tip

If you are trying to describe fight-or-flight in the exam, think of a situation that you have experienced that made you very tense and when you experienced your heart beating faster. Use this as an example in your answer.

⠿ Make the link

...with homeostasis in the topic of sleep.

Notice how some of these changes – such as raised heart rate and reduced blood flow to the digestion – are part of the mechanism of improving survival chances, while others – such as tense muscles or nausea – are side effects of the same changes.

The changes in the fight-or-flight response are stimulated by the release of hormones in the body. Two hormones in particular are associated with stress – **adrenalin** and **cortisol**. Both of these hormones help our body to prepare for stress by releasing energy. Adrenalin also increases the heart rate, while cortisol suppresses digestion. The next section of this chapter explains more about the biological approach and why we experience stress.

Walter Cannon (1927) came up with the theory of 'fight-or-flight'. He believed that the body tries to maintain homeostasis, which means a steady state in things such as temperature and blood sugar. Cannon expanded this idea to include threats. It is now known that a part of the brain called the **hypothalamus** controls homeostasis – the same brain area that plays a key role in our circadian rhythms of sleep and waking.

Analysis of fight-or-flight

Acute stress is important but it is only part of the problem we face from stress. In practice, it is often the long-term effects of stress that cause more worry and harm. In addition, fight-or-flight is not shown in every species. Some animals such as snakes use a 'play dead' strategy in response to a threat; sometimes humans also 'freeze' in a threatening situation.

Causes of stress

Fight-or-flight situations are largely cases of acute stress. The minutes before a job interview or walking home on a dark night and hearing someone walking behind us – these are immediate situations that make people feel tense and the heart start to race.

However, as mentioned above, it is often the longer-term stressful situations that have the bigger impact in terms of our general wellbeing. Psychologists refer to prolonged or repeated stressful situations as **chronic stress**. There is no strict definition of how long the stress has to be shown to be termed 'chronic', but generally, it refers to situations that last for days, weeks or even months, whereas acute stress is a situation in the here-and-now.

There are a huge range of things that can cause people stress and this section will examine these in more detail. It would be illogical to use the same term 'stress' for both the cause, that is, a stressful situation, and the effect it has on the body (Selye, 1956). Therefore, researchers tend to use the term stress to refer to the physical and psychological *effects* of a stimulus, while the stimulus itself is called a **stressor**.

Snakes are one animal that 'play dead'

Stressors can be categorised into three main types:

Type of stressor	Examples
Environmental stressors	Noise, overcrowding
Occupational stressors	Workload, exams
Social stressors	Arguments, divorce

It is useful to know these terms as they often appear in books and research studies but they are not well-defined categories and they often overlap. For example, being bullied at work is both an occupational and a social stressor. Arguments with noisy neighbours would involve both a social and an environmental stressor.

Research into sources of stress

Environmental
Our surrounding environment can very stressful in many ways, with perhaps the most obvious stressor being noise. Every day, people are exposed to traffic noise, noise from machinery in the home and workplace, other people's music and dozens of other noises, much of it outwith our control. This can impact on healthy development; children in noisier homes show more frustration at school tasks (Cohen *et al.*, 1980) and higher levels of overnight cortisol (Evans *et al.*, 2001).

Hearing someone walking behind you at night may make you tense

The unpredictable nature of background noise increases its stressful effects. Glass *et al.* (1969) played noises to participants who were completing puzzles. Some heard regular, predictable noises, while others heard the same noises at random intervals. Those who heard the random noises experienced frustration and annoyance and became significantly poorer at solving puzzles, even after the noises had stopped. Those who heard regular noises did not do any worse than a control group who completed the puzzles in silence.

Another major environmental stressor is overcrowding. Anyone who has had to take a long journey on crowded public transport knows how tense this can make you feel. Calhoun (1962) conducted a longitudinal observational study into the effects of overcrowding on rats. He allowed

Overcrowding is an environmental stressor

Jobs which require focused attention for long periods can be very stressful

rats to breed in a 10′×14′ enclosure until it became overcrowded with 80 rats in the space for 48. Many rats became depressed and unresponsive, females failed to build nests or look after offspring, while others cannibalised or sexually assaulted other rats, sometimes attacking them in gangs. While it is hard to generalise from rats to humans, the findings suggest that the stress of brutally overcrowded conditions can dramatically impact on mental health and lead to antisocial behaviour.

Occupational

One of the clearest demonstrations of workplace stress was conducted by Marmot *et al.* (1997) in the British Civil Service. These government workers are ranked in a strict hierarchy and the researchers found that those at the top – the highest ranked managers – had the lowest level of illness. What's more, the illness level increased with each rank down the hierarchy. Interestingly, Sapolsky (1995) compared humans and baboons and found very similar health changes – lower ranked individuals in the baboon group being more stressed and less healthy. These findings suggest that having less power leads to stress, and consequently, to ill health.

Some jobs require focused attention for long periods. Johansson *et al.* (1978) studied workers in a Swedish sawmill and found that one group of workers had a high level of responsibility but a monotonous task (the stage of finishing/processing the timber that was monotonous but important). They also worked in social isolation. These workers were found to have raised levels of stress hormones and to take more days off sick than a control group.

Kiecolt-Glaser *et al.* (1984) conducted a study of medical students before and during their exams, and found that during exams, their immune system was weaker, with fewer virus fighting 'killer' cells in their bloodstream (see key study).

📖 Key study: Kiecolt-Glaser *et al.* (1984): study of stress in medical students

Aim: *The study aimed to assess the levels of 'natural killer' white blood cells in medical students at a time of low stress (midway through the year) compared with a time of high stress (exam time). These cells are responsible for fighting viruses and infections; therefore, they can have a major impact on our health.*

Method: *The researchers recruited 75 first-year medical students for this natural experiment. They collected blood samples twice – a month before exams and then at exam time, and measured levels of killer white blood cells. They also gave out a stress questionnaire.*

Findings: *The study found that during exam time, students showed a significantly lower level of killer cells compared to one month before. The biggest effect was found among students whose questionnaires showed that they were feeling socially isolated.*

Janice Kiecolt-Glaser

Evaluation: *This provides clear biological evidence that appears to link the stress of exams to ill health. The multi-method nature of the study was a strength, as questionnaire data were also gathered. The study had high ecological validity as it used a real-world stressor. However, this was a natural experiment, and it is therefore impossible to rule out other factors, such as a virus that was going round campus or the possibility that students' general lifestyle was less healthy at that time of year.*

The participants were 75 first-year medical students

Social

Humans are highly social animals. We suffer stress from being isolated (Cacioppo & Hawkley, 2009), yet a number of our stressors come from social interactions (Sapolsky, 1995). Our social group can also help us to cope with stress – in a natural experiment, Nuckolls *et al.* (1972) found that pregnant women under high stress had a much lower rate of health complications if they had good **social support** than if they did not.

A number of our stressors come from social interactions

Rahe *et al.* (1970) studied a range of major social stressors; they believed that the main factor in social stress was how much change 'readjustment' a stressor causes us to make in life. Their analysis included both negative items, such as being put in prison, and positive ones, such as a new job. They showed a positive correlation between two variables – the number of stressors a person experienced and their level of ill health. The correlation was weak, perhaps because there are so many other factors that affect health, but it was significant (see table on next page).

The work of Rahe and colleagues generated a huge amount of research and helped psychologists assess the impact of life events more accurately (Jones & Bright, 2001). However, it does not account for the differences in severity of the items on the list and makes no distinction between positive and negative life events. Also, later researchers have found that day-to-day minor hassles, while smaller in scale, have a larger cumulative effect on health (DeLongis *et al.*, 1982).

Life Event	Mean Value
Death of Spouse (Significant Other)	100
Divorce	73
Marital Separation	65
Jail Term	63
Death of Close Family Member	63
Personal Injury or Illness	53
Marriage	50
Fired at Work	47
Marital Reconciliation	45
Retirement	45
Change in the Health of Family Member	44
Pregnancy	40
Sex Difficulties	39
Gain new Family Member	39
Business Readjustment	39
Change in Financial State	38
Death of Close Friend	37
Change to Different Line of Work	36
Change in Number of Arguments with Spouse	35
Mortgage or Loan for Major Purchase (home. etc.)	31
Foreclosure of Mortgage Loan	30
Change in Responsibilities at Work	29
Son or Daughter Leaving Home	29
Trouble with in-Laws	29
Outstanding Personal Achievement	28
Spouse Begins or Stops Work	26
Begin or End School	26
Change in Living Conditions	25
Revision of Personal Habits	24
Trouble with Boss	23
Change in Work Hours or Conditions	20
Change in Residence	20
Change in Schools	20
Change in Recreation	19
Change in Church Activities	19
Change in Social Activities	18
Mortgage or Loan for Lesser Purchase (car, tv, etc)	17
Change in Sleeping Habits	16
Change in Number of Family Get-Togethers	15
Change in Eating Habits	15
Vacation	13
Christmas	12
Minor Violations of the Law	11

The Social Readjustment Rating Scale (SRRS)

Individual differences in stress

Does everyone respond to stressors in the same way? The short answer is 'no' – some people are better able to cope than others are, and this depends on several key individual traits.

Sex differences. There are certain biological differences in how our bodies react to stress. For example, women release less adrenaline than men do during fight-or-flight and it lasts for less time in the bloodstream (Frankenhauser *et al.*, 1976). There are also sex differences in the way the hormone oxytocin mediates stress. Oxytocin – sometimes called the love hormone – is associated with love, bonding, parenting and friendship. Large amounts are released when we fall in love and it is also released when we bond with other people. Taylor *et al.* (2000) explained that oxytocin could result in lowered levels of the stress hormone cortisol when we get social support during stress. However, oxytocin is affected by sex hormones: it is boosted by oestrogen, whereas testosterone makes it less effective. This means that women get more of a benefit from social support than men do.

Age differences. People of different ages often experience different stressors. As a teenager, typical stressors involve social interaction at school, conflicts with parents and exam stress. A young adult is more likely to be stressed by having young children to care for, while older adults may have to cope with issues such as retirement or age-related health issues. There is also some evidence that teenagers respond differently to stress than older adults. Colten and Gore (1991) studied the effects of stress on teenagers and found that they were more likely to show the symptoms of stress openly compared to older adults. As people go through life, they become more experienced at coping with stress and this may have an effect on how they react to a stressor.

Personality. Researchers Friedman and Rosenman were cardiologists who noticed that the patients with more severe heart problems were also more impatient and aggressive when they had to wait before an appointment. They hypothesised a connection between personality and the health effects of stress and ran a longitudinal study to test this (Friedman and Rosenman, 1974). First, they used interviews and questionnaires to put people into one of two categories – **type A personalities** were rushed and hostile, while **type B personalities** were relaxed and cooperative. Over 3,000 men were categorised into the two types – all participants were males aged 39 to 59; 8.5 years later, the researchers studied the health outcomes of these men. Even allowing for other risk factors such as diet, 70% of those who had contracted **coronary heart disease** (CHD) were type A. CHD is a major illness resulting from obstructed blood flow to the heart muscle and it can be fatal.

Thinking style. The way people think about themselves and about a stressor can have a major impact on how stressed they get. Our **locus of control** means how much we feel in control of the things that happen to us (Rotter, 1966). This is based on our beliefs about the world and ourselves. Folkman *et al.* (1986) interviewed married couples on a weekly basis about their main stressors for the previous week. They found that those who had a high internal locus of control had better health outcomes than those who did not.

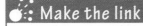

? Discussion point

Do you understand your own personality? Take a personality test at http://personality-testing.info/tests/BIG5.php.

Make the link

...with the individual differences that affect conformity.

Typical stressors for teenagers include conflict with adults

🔑 Key concepts

- Stress
- Acute stress
- Fight-or-flight response
- Adrenalin
- Cortisol
- Homeostasis
- Hypothalamus
- Chronic stress
- Stressor
- Social support
- Type A personalities
- Type B personalities
- Coronary heart disease
- Locus of control

✔ Questions

1. What is meant by 'acute stress'?

2. The heart rate rises during fight-or-flight. What else happens in the body? Name two things.

3. Name two hormones that are released when we are stressed.

4. Which term means the effects of a stimulus on the body and mind, 'stress' or 'stressor'?

5. Occupational and environmental are two types of stressor. What is the third major type?

6. What similarity was found between civil service workers and baboons?

7. Give an example of an occupational stressor.

8. Name two characteristics of Type A personalities.

9. Give an example of an age difference in stress.

10. Name one sex difference in stress.

GO! Activities

1. Draw a diagram of a person and label it with the changes that happen during fight-or-flight.

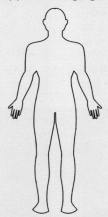

2. Find out more about one of the studies mentioned in this section, such as Friedman and Rosenman (1974), Calhoun (1962) or Sapolsky (1995). Write a blog post or make a poster explaining the findings. Don't forget to evaluate the study.

Approaches to stress

Biological approach to stress

Revision points from chapter 2

The following points from the main section on the biological approach to psychology are especially relevant to this topic. You can include them in exam answers on approaches to stress:

- the nervous system and brain areas
- hormones

As discussed in the previous section, there are certain key biological processes that occur when people are stressed. The biological approach focuses on these processes and tries to explain stress in terms of the body's reaction, as mediated by hormones and the nervous system.

The nervous system and brain areas

The biological approach states that behaviour is controlled by the brain, but also by other key parts of the nervous system including the spinal cord and other nerves around the body. Of particular importance to an understanding of stress are the nerves that control our organs and our glands, including the adrenal gland.

According to this approach, two key sets of biological processes control our stress response – one involving the **hypothalamus**, and the other involving the **autonomic nervous system** (see Chapter 2 for a diagram of nervous system):

- When the body is first aroused by a threat, the sympathetic branch of the ANS becomes active, sending a signal to the adrenal medulla (this is the sympathetic-adrenal medulla axis, or 'SAM'). When a threat has passed, the other branch of the ANS - the parasympathetic branch – triggers the body to go into a more relaxed state, which is sometimes referred to as 'rest and digest'.

- The second process that contributes to our stress response, is regulated by the hypothalamus, and leads to a set of reactions as shown in the diagram below. This system is known as the hypothalamic-pituitary-adrenal axis, or HPA for short.

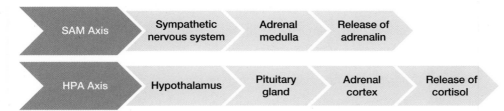

Hormones

In the SAM axis, the nervous system directly stimulates the adrenal medulla (the middle of each adrenal gland) to release the hormone adrenalin. This is a fast process, because nerve impulses travel very quickly. As mentioned in the previous section, adrenalin directly affects several bodily organs, increasing levels of glucose in the bloodstream and raising the heart rate.

The HPA axis also relies on hormones. Here, the hypothalamus instructs the pituitary gland to release a hormone called ACTH, which in turn triggers the release of the stress hormone cortisol from the adrenal cortex (the outer part of each adrenal gland). Cortisol helps the body to turn fats into energy, and high levels of cortisol are associated with longer-term stress.

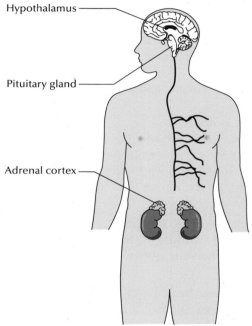

Hypothalamus

Pituitary gland

Adrenal cortex

The hypothalamic-pituitary-adrenal axis

Evaluation

The biological approach to stress can provide a detailed explanation of how the body responds to stress, in terms of the ANS and hormones. However, it does not really deal with the issue of why some situations cause stress and others don't, or with individual differences (although it does explain sex differences). Therefore, it is quite narrow and simplistic.

A lot of the research in this area has been conducted on animals. This has ethical problems and it can be hard to generalise from the stressors used on animals in a lab (such as forcing rodents to exercise) to experiences that cause stress in humans.

A major strength of the biological approach to stress is that it helps us to understand the health effects of stress. Increased levels of cortisol in the bloodstream are known to suppress the immune system and reduce wound healing (Kiecolt-Glaser *et al.*, 1995) and this helps us to understand why stress makes people more vulnerable to illness.

A lot of research in this area is conducted on animals

Evolutionary approach to stress

Early humans and the EEA

The second chapter of this book described human evolution and the 'EEA', where humans lived a hunter-gatherer existence. It is difficult to make sense of fight-or-flight without understanding this evolutionary past. In the modern world, the fight-or-flight response is often unhelpful – for example, nobody really wants to sweat and tremble when giving a speech or just before a job interview. Nobody wants to have clammy hands or feel sick at the start of an exam. Why, then, would our bodies make things so difficult for us?

The answer can be partly explained in that many of today's stressors didn't exist for the bulk of human evolution. There were no job interviews, exams, money worries or traffic jams for the vast majority of our species' history and these things have not been around for long enough to make a significant difference to the human gene pool. We still have hunter-gatherer responses to the stressors that we encounter!

According to this approach, therefore, the fight-or-flight response evolved to aid survival. It helped our ancestors to win fights or to run away from predators. Any individual who had a weaker fight-or-flight response would have been more vulnerable to being killed, and therefore, less likely to pass their genes on to future generations. This helps us to understand why our heart rate rises and we release energy when stressed – even when it is no longer useful in the modern world.

This approach also helps us to understand why we sometimes feel sick or nauseous when stressed. F-or-F is the response to an immediate threat and certain longer-term processes are 'switched off', for example, digestion – immediate survival is more important. It would have been a survival advantage to our ancestors for blood to leave the digestive system and go to the muscles during times of threat. Today, however, this may just result in tense shoulders and a queasy feeling when we have to do an exam!

Some groups still live hunter-gatherer existences where the fight-or-flight response is more useful

❓ Discussion point

What would be the stressors in a hunter-gatherer society?

? Discussion point

Do you agree with Taylor *et al.*? Are women today more likely to seek social support at times of stress? And if so, do you think this is due to genes or to culture?

As discussed in the previous section, there are sex differences in the stress response. Taylor *et al.* (2000) argue that these are due to our evolutionary past. Assuming that women in a hunter-gatherer society would have mainly been responsible for looking after children, the researchers argue that a **tend-and-befriend** response would have been more useful to them than fight-or-flight. This means that for women in particular, it would have been a survival advantage to group together and seek out stronger tribe members to protect them.

GO! Activities

1. Discuss the following questions in groups
   - What kind of events cause stress?
   - Stress is seen as a bad thing but does it have any benefits?
   - Why did the stress response evolve?
   - Are human beings a kind of ape?
   - Who were the first humans?
   - What did our early ancestors eat?
   - What differences are there between the lifestyle of our ancestors and that in the modern world?
   - How long ago did we split from monkeys?

2. Write a short explanation for what life would have been like for our ancestors 20,000 years ago – before the start of agriculture. Consider what kind of threats and problems people would have faced. You can do this as a piece of creative writing if you prefer.

Comparisons with other species

A number of research studies in this chapter have been conducted on non-humans, especially rats. This is partly because the nervous system of these animals is similar to that of humans and it is easier to study them experimentally. Some research, such as the work of Sapolsky (1995), takes a more evolutionary approach. It looks at baboons as a good model for what life would have been like for our human ancestors – living in tribes, foraging for food and having to deal with complex social interactions.

Evaluation

The evolutionary approach provides a powerful explanation of why apparently harmful effects might have evolved. It complements the biological approach and together they can provide a picture of why the body responds the way it does to modern stressors.

However, there are considerable unknowns about human evolution. Although most researchers agree about the theory of evolution and the idea that humans split from chimpanzees several million years ago, there is considerable debate about exactly how this happened, and about what our ancestors' lives were like after that. There are, of course, no historical documents from that long ago and the evidence is based on a relatively small number of fossils spread around different parts of the world. We may never have a precise picture of these events.

Cognitive approach to stress

Revision points from chapter 2

The following points from the main section on the cognitive approach to psychology are especially relevant to this topic. You can include them in exam answers on approaches to stress:

- irrational beliefs
- schemas

A third approach to stress is the cognitive approach. The above biological and evolutionary concepts do not say much about what we think about stress or why it is that people react to stress in different ways, despite having the same biological systems in our bodies and the same evolutionary past. This approach helps to explain the thought processes that lead to people seeing things as a threat or not.

Irrational beliefs

People often are stressed because they run short of time to complete essential tasks. This may not necessarily occur because the person doesn't have enough time but due to poor planning and time management. The **planning fallacy** is the tendency to underestimate task times and is one of a number of ways in which a person's view of reality is distorted and inaccurate (Tversky and Kahneman, 1974).

People tend to underestimate the time it will take them to complete a task

The planning fallacy was investigated by Buehler *et al.* (1994), who asked 37 university students to predict as accurately as possible when they would complete their final university project. They were also asked to predict completion dates if everything went as badly as possible, that is, the longest it was likely to take. Researchers then found out the actual task time. The results were that fewer than 30% of students were finished by their 'most accurate' estimate date and even by the more pessimistic estimate, fewer than half had actually completed. This is powerful evidence that stress can result from our cognitive biases – an essential inability to make accurate predictions about the future.

While useful, the above study is limited because the sample was small and an academic thesis was a one-off task that the participants had never tried before. To address these problems, the researchers asked a larger sample of 101 students to estimate completion times of non-academic tasks such as fixing a bike. They found that only 42.5% of students completed these projects when expected and the projects took on average almost twice as long as predicted. These findings support the idea that people systematically plan poorly and leave themselves insufficient time to do tasks.

The study asked 101 students to estimate how long it would take to fix a bike; on average it took twice as long as they predicted

In a study of teamwork, Lehner *et al.* (1992) trained pairs of participants on how to respond in a military simulation computer game. They trained the teams to follow a simple set of instructions. They found that teams performed well under low time pressure but when time pressure was high, they became vulnerable to bias. Instead of following the instructions in the time pressure condition, participants reverted to simplistic assumptions, resulting in getting the task wrong. This suggests that stress may lead to bad decision making – but that these bad decisions will also be the cause of further stressors!

We also make decisions about how to cope with stress that can be either productive, such as making an action plan, or harmful, for example, denying that there is a problem (see the next section of this chapter).

Schemas

According to the cognitive approach to stress, how you think affects the way you feel. People's emotional reactions are often based more on their thought processes about events than on the events themselves.

One of the main examples of the cognitive approach to stress is the **transactional model**, described in the following section. This model, devised by Lazarus and Folkman (1984), stated that our perceptions of ourselves and of a situation mediate whether we are stressed or not.

Beck (1976) stated that depression can link to schemas and it is known that stressful life events make mental illness more likely (see chapter 4). In a longitudinal study of children, Hammen and Goodman-Brown (1990) found that stressors that were linked to a child's schemas about themselves – their abilities or relationships – were particularly stressful, and more likely to lead to depression.

Panic disorder is a psychological disorder where people experience an acute stress response for no apparent reason. This can be connected to their beliefs or a sense of a lack of control. CBT is a highly effective treatment for panic disorder.

Evaluation

The cognitive approach is a modern approach to stress. It provides an insight into what is undeniably true – different people react to stressors in different ways.

Another strength of the approach is that it helps us to understand the role of stress in mental health and it clearly links to a successful method of treating stress disorders, based around CBT.

Just as the biological approach neglects thought processes, this approach neglects the biology of stress. It cannot provide a complete explanation of how stress makes us physically ill.

Lehner's study found that partipants had trouble playing a computer game well when under pressure

Stressors were found to be more harmful if they linked to a child's schemas about who they are

🔍 Top tip

The transactional model, described in the following section, can also be used as an example of the cognitive approach to stress.

✔ Questions

1. What are the two major biological systems that influence stress?

2. What does the hypothalamus do during stress?

3. Give a weakness of the biological approach to stress.

4. Why was the fight-or-flight response more useful in the EEA than it is today?

5. What is the name for the idea that women respond to stress differently from men and tend to look for social support?

6. Why is there not complete agreement about how humans evolved?

7. What is the planning fallacy?

8. What did the teams studied by Lehner *et al.* (1992) do when under time pressure?

9. What disorder results in an extreme and irrational level of anxiety?

10. Which therapy, based on the cognitive approach, can be used in stress?

⚷ Key concepts

- Autonomic nervous system
- Sympathetic branch
- SAM axis
- Parasympathetic branch
- Hypothalamus
- Tend-and-befriend
- Planning fallacy
- Transactional model
- HPA axis

Theories of stress

The general adaptation syndrome

Hungarian-Canadian researcher Hans Selye helped to popularise the modern day concept of stress, a term that had previously been used inconsistently and in a number of different contexts (Jones & Bright, 2001). While previous researchers had talked about fight-or-flight, Selye realised that the stress response had long-term effects and that a similar response could be triggered by a huge range of stimuli. He also suggested that the stress response to positive events could be the same as that for threats and that while stress could cause illness, some stress could be a positive thing.

Selye came up with one of the key biological theories of stress – the **general adaptation syndrome** theory. It states that stress is cumulative, just as physical stressors impact on a bridge or road. As such, it can be described as an 'engineering model' of stress.

A medical doctor by training, Selye believed that the changes his experimental rats experienced were an example of the way all animals, including humans, react to stressors such as illness. The exact nature of the stimulus wasn't important – all stressors impact on us in the same way, according to the theory, and it was therefore a 'general' response. The reaction to stress is called 'adaptation'; Selye believed that this is an important part of how the body adapts to environmental challenges. The response was called a 'syndrome' because it involves a set of biological symptoms that occur together (see key study).

📖 Key study: Selye's (1936) study of stress in rats

Aim: *Selye was trying to discover a new hormone that appeared to have an effect on the adrenal glands. He realised that his experimental rats were reacting to the stress of injections, not to the substance itself. He decided to test this out by subjecting rats to a range of different stressors and comparing the effects.*

Method: *He subjected rats to a number of different stressors, including surgical injury, extremes of temperature and injections of toxic substances such as formaldehyde. These stressors were repeated over many weeks so that the animals could not recover.*

Findings: *The animals showed a physiological triad: enlargement of adrenal glands, bleeding from ulcers in the digestive system and shrinking of lymph tissue (the body areas that produce white blood cells). After 6 to 48 hours of treatment, these systems returned to normal. However, after a further one to three months, symptoms returned, and the animal became vulnerable to disease. Because the response to all of the stressors was the same, Selye concluded that this was the body's general stress response to all threats.*

Evaluation: *Selye's study showed a systematic change over time, and being a lab experiment, it kept other variables constant. However, it is hard to reliably generalise the findings from rats to humans. The experiment was also highly cruel to the rats, and therefore, unethical.*

Hans Seyle carrying out the study

Stages of the syndrome

Because the symptoms occurred in three distinct stages, Selye included three main stages of stress in his theory:

1. **General alarm reaction**. The body's reactions are heightened and a 'fight or flight' reaction is experienced. Internally, the adrenal glands enlarge and stomach ulcers may be present. The immune system is damaged, with a shrinking of the lymph (white blood cell) system. This stage can last for several hours as the body reacts to a new stressor.

2. **Resistance**. If the stressor persists, the body starts to adapt to it. Cortisol is released and the body obtains energy by burning fats. Even though the stressor is still present, symptoms from the alarm stage disappear, as the body adapts. Selye (1956) compared this to a runner mid-way through a race – they are running at their peak and not yet significantly tired but they are using up energy fast.

In a race, a runner's body adapts to the stress

3. **Exhaustion**. If the stress is prolonged for weeks without being overcome, the body may become exhausted. After a month or more, symptoms from the first stage reappear. Ultimately, this can result in **diseases of adaptation**, such as CHD, and psychological problems, such as depression.

🔍 **Top tip**

Read Selye's (1936) short article online at http://bit.ly/1FziKxA.

Evaluation

The GAS is a detailed theory of stress, based on a large body of experimental evidence. The theory is based on sound knowledge of biological systems and detailed experiments looking at changes in the body. It links mainly to the biological approach to psychology.

However, a lot of the supporting research has been done on animals (especially rats and birds), making it harder to apply to humans, as well as the obvious ethical issues of harm to the participants. In addition, the use of extreme physical stressors such as injuries and injection of toxic substances in Selye's 1936 study makes it hard to generalise the findings to everyday life. It can't be assumed that the same physical reactions would occur due to ordinary human stressors such as having an argument or being late for class. In addition, Bell (2014) has reported that Selye was sponsored by tobacco companies who were keen to blame problems on stress rather than on smoking.

In recent years, the idea that all stressors produce the same physiological response has been challenged. Instead, it may be the case that it is only when the stressors are at an unusually high level that the body responds to them all similarly (Goldstein & Kopin, 2007).

A bear attack would cause stress in anyone!

The transactional model of stress

A problem with engineering models, such as GAS, is that they assume that everyone reacts the same way to stressors. It is the amount of stressors that matters according to this view, not the type of stressor, and they neglect the importance of individual differences. Certain things, such as being attacked by a bear, would lead to a fight-or-flight response in anyone, but most stressors are not so clear-cut – especially psychological stressors such as worries about the future. For example, some people find exam time overwhelmingly stressful but others do not. These different reactions could be based on factors such as confidence in their own ability to handle the stressor (if the student feels they could pass the exam with ease) or their perception of how much it matters (for example, if they need the qualification or not). The psychological processes where we weigh up the demands of a stressor are the focus of the transactional model of stress, based on work by Richard Lazarus and Susan Folkman.

Lazarus (1995) states that it is over-simplistic to look on a stimulus as something that stresses the individual. For example, in the workplace, the individual's behaviour affects the nature of the job, and stress (or lack of it) results from a combination of both the person and the situation (p.4). Lazarus calls this two way process a **transaction**. According to the model, being stressed or not stressed results from these everyday transactions that take place in three-stages:

Primary appraisal. This is where a stimulus/situation is assessed and the individual determines whether it is a threat or not. It is the process

Primary appraisal: a stimulus/situation is assessed

Seconday appraisal: the person assesses how well they are equipped to deal with the situation

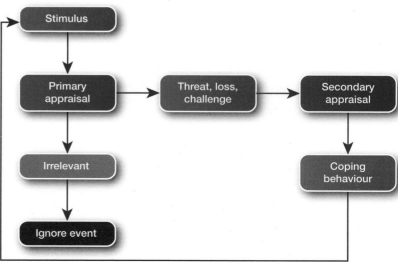
Transactional model

Top tip

The primary and secondary appraisal stages are fundamentally different. The first is about the stressor and how it relates to the individual's goals and needs. Whereas the secondary stage is all about the person's resources and the reality of the situation that might allow them to cope with or avoid the stressor. However, the appraisal stages have something in common – they both depend on perceptions, which can be inaccurate.

of determining whether a situation is relevant and potentially harmful. The transaction must be relevant to the individual's goals in some way in order for it to cause stress. Harmful situations that are not relevant to the individual can be ignored.

Secondary appraisal. This is where the person assesses their own resources to deal with the situation and makes a judgement about whether the demands involved will tax these resources or exceed them altogether. The appraisal is the process of assessing the options for dealing with potential threats or harm. For example, if a person is feeling tired, they may conclude that they are not in a good position to cope with an all-night party.

Coping. This is where strategies to deal with the stress are implemented. These can be taught or learned from experience – we can learn to cope better with the stressors that we have encountered before.

Health and coping

If the primary appraisal results in a person perceiving the stimulus as irrelevant then no stress will result. If it is relevant but the secondary appraisal shows that we can cope, then the stress level will be low. However, if the appraisal reveals a stressor that is important but difficult to deal with, then the stress level will be high. According to this model, the reason for being stressed is because of a mismatch between the perceived threat level and our perceived ability to cope (Lazarus & Folkman, 1984).

There are two main types of coping:

- **Problem-focused coping.** The person tries to tackle the problem, for example, by making an action plan or getting help from someone with experience.

- **Emotion-focused coping.** The person tries to feel better, for example, by going out with friends, staying in bed all day or using relaxation methods such as meditation. Substance abuse can be another form of emotion-focused coping.

Sometimes people do not attempt to cope with the threat at all, instead, they engage in what has sometimes been termed avoidance coping – this can include avoiding the threatening situation or trying not to think about it, or changing one's perceptions so that it is no longer seen as a problem.

Coping: Strategies to deal with the stress are implemented

Not thinking about it is one way people cope with a problem

Supporting research

Research studies such as Rahe *et al*. (1970) have tried to measure the effects of major life changes on stress and health. In contrast, researchers using the transactional model consider that stress is best conceptualised as minor annoyances or hassles rather than big life events (Lazarus, 1990).

A study that supports the model was conducted by Gaab *et al*. (2005). They used the **Trier social stress test** – a standard test of stress that simulates a job interview – and measured cortisol levels in the saliva of their 81 male participants. Cognitive processes involved in appraising and anticipating the stress test made a bigger difference to cortisol levels than the personality of the participants.

The Trier social stress test simulates a job interview

Evaluation

This is one of the most popular models of stress today and it was the first to emphasise cognitive aspects of stress – it states that our beliefs and the way we interpret a situation affect how we respond.

The model has led to a huge growth in interest in stress management strategies through the understanding that reducing stress lies not just in changing your environment but also in changing your thoughts. However, the role of cognition in managing stress is limited. Even if we feel that we can cope and even enjoy certain stressors, dangerous stimuli still produce the fight-or-flight response in the body. This can affect our health.

✔ Questions

1. When did the symptoms of the alarm stage disappear in Selye's rats?

2. What is the second stage of GAS called, alarm or resistance?

3. What are diseases of adaptation?

4. What over-simplistic assumption is made by 'engineering' models of stress?

5. Which researchers devised the transactional model of stress?

6. What happens in the secondary appraisal stage?

7. A student hears about a test at short notice but realises that she already has enough credit to pass the course, so doesn't worry. Which stage of the transactional model does this illustrate?

8. What type of coping means that a person tries to make themselves feel better about the stressor?

9. Place the three types of coping in order of best to worst in terms of how well they help people to deal with stressors.

10. Why has the transactional model had an influence on stress management?

🔑 Key concepts

- General adaptation syndrome
- Diseases of adaptation
- Transaction
- Primary appraisal
- Secondary appraisal
- Coping
- Problem-focused coping
- Emotion-focused coping
- Trier social stress test

GO! **Activities**

1. Draw three boxes in your notes, filling a whole page. Then try to explain the three stages of the GAS model, one in each box, without reading from the textbook or your notes. Include information from Selye's 1936 experiment. When you are stuck, check back and read the section again, then go back to the task. Do this until you have written a full explanation of each stage.

2. Draw a version of the transactional model diagram from page 164, completing each square with a real life example of a stressor that you have experienced.

! **Syllabus note**

This section is essential for Higher students, who may be asked for an 'application' of their chosen optional topic. At National 5, you will not be asked directly for an application but a general understanding of stress management can provide helpful detail to include in answers on other questions, for example, on the theories of stress.

Real-world application: stress management

Stress management is a term for a number of ways people use to reduce stress. There are several ways of tackling stress – some focus on the body's physical response by trying to reduce the symptoms of fight-or-flight, while others try to change their thoughts or emotions.

In order to fully understand stress management, first let's consider the many stress-related health problems, building on what you have already learned so far about the nature of stress.

Short-term health effects

Due to the physical nature of the fight-or-flight response, stress can result in health effects even in the short-term (i.e. anything from minutes up to a few days). Fight-or-flight can briefly boost our immune response but stress soon begins to have a negative effect on the immune system, leaving the body more susceptible to a range of infections. Cohen *et al.* (1991) found that high-stress individuals were more susceptible to the common cold. This may be because the GAS leads to shrinkage of the lymph system, the part of the body that produces white blood cells. The study of Kiecolt-Glaser *et al.* (1984) showing fewer white blood cells in students at exam time (see earlier section in this chapter) demonstrates in humans what Selye had shown in his rats – the body's immune system is compromised by stress.

Acute stress will also affect mental health – the person may anger easily, as well as being moody and irritable. This will be seen in behaviour such as emotional outbursts. They may dwell on the stressor, have difficulty concentrating on other tasks and find it hard to sleep (Cox, 1978).

Long-term health effects

As stress lasts longer, health effects tend to become more serious and it can cause permanent damage with diseases of adaptation such as CHD. Appearance can be affected, with skin conditions, such as psoriasis, likely to worsen when a person is stressed.

Psychologically, a person's mood is likely to suffer, leaving them prone to anxiety and even depression. Stress can be a triggering factor in a number of psychological disorders, including depression and eating disorders. Mumford *et al.* (1991) found that among Asian girls in the UK, those who were most traditional in their dress and outlook were more susceptible to eating disorders, perhaps because of a greater 'culture clash' making life more stressful.

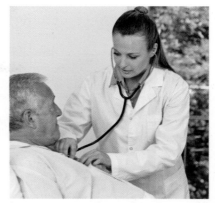

Stress can result in health effects even in the short-term

Long-term stress can result in diseases of adaptation such as CHD

Meditation

Meditation is a relaxation technique that anyone can try and it can prove helpful for dealing with day-to-day stress. Meditation involves focusing on a neutral or relaxing stimulus such as an object, a chant, or even on your own breathing. This focus is thought to help the person to clear their mind of hassles and distractions and to improve focus. The benefits can be boosted by deep breathing and by visualising a relaxing scene.

Many people do a **guided meditation** that involves listening to another person who instructs them in what to do and what to think about. You can find several such guided meditation tracks as YouTube videos or MP3 downloads. Typically, they ask the person to lie down in a quiet place, and encourage visualisation and deep breathing.

Meditation has become very popular in recent years and this has led to a large body of research evidence developing. One study by Slagter *et al.* (2007) found that participants were better able deal with a cognitive task that involved spotting numbers among series of letters (see key study). Meditation has also been shown to lead to physical changes in the structure of the cortex with potential long-term benefits (Wells *et al.*, 2013), although as with any comparatively new research area, results should be interpreted with caution. Meditation lacks unpleasant side effects but it requires comparative peace and quiet, and people whose stress relates to being busy may struggle to find the time to do it.

> **! Syllabus note**
>
> The following section describes five techniques. For an A-grade exam answer, you could cover two to three in greater depth or a larger number in less depth.

> **🔍 Top tip**
>
> Provide context to your answer on stress management by explaining why stress is a threat to health. However, the majority of your answer should focus on the techniques themselves.

Meditation can help relieve stress

📖 Key study: Slagter et al. (2007): study of meditation

Aim: *The study aimed to see whether a course of meditation had a measurable effect on people's cognitive abilities in order to see whether it might have long-term benefits for dealing with stressors.*

Method: *17 participants went on a three-month meditation retreat, during which they meditated for 10 to 12 hours per day. Before and after the retreat, they were tested on their ability to spot numbers on a screen among a series of both letters and numbers. Most items presented were letters and the task was to spot the numbers. If one number comes straight after another, participants tended not to notice it – this is known as the 'attentional-blink' deficit. As a control group, 23 participants received a 1-hour meditation class and they were asked to meditate for 20 minutes per day for a week prior to being tested on the attentional blink task.*

Findings: *All meditation participants improved on the task, compared to 16/23 of the control group. Overall, there was a reduction in the meditation group in terms of their attentional blink.*

Evaluation: *This is an impressive demonstration that meditation can have a real effect on the mind's ability to cope with incoming stimuli. However, their sample was small, and the task lacked mundane realism. The level of meditation is also extreme – most people would not be able to go on a meditation retreat for three months, making it hard to generalise the findings to people who meditate more occasionally.*

The participants went on a three-month meditation retreat

Stress inoculation

Sometimes people who are under a lot of stress may be referred to a therapist, especially if the stress is causing, or worsening, mental health problems or making the person unable to work. A specialised form of CBT designed for stress is Donald Meichenbaum's **stress inoculation** training. This teaches people to resist stressors (just as a disease can be resisted), using techniques such as role-playing, visualisation and practice. There are three phases:

- **Conceptualisation phase**. Clients are taught to break stressors down into smaller units, in order to tackle them.
- **Skills acquisition phase**. Coping skills are taught and practiced with the therapist.
- **Application phase**. Newly acquired skills are used in real-life stressful situations.

Essentially, the idea is that people learn to identify the component parts of stress and the situations that cause stress. They are then taught techniques for dealing with stress, and then they apply these to the real world outside of therapy, for example, in work, study or relationship situations.

There is good evidence that stress inoculation can be effective. A meta-analysis for the United States Army conducted by Saunders *et al.* (1996) found that it reduced performance anxiety and enhanced performance under stressful conditions. It can tackle both chronic and acute stressors and a complex mixture of both (Meichenbaum, 2007).

A positive aspect of stress inoculation is that it tries to deal with the causes of stress by making people less vulnerable and teaches strategies that can be applied in day-to-day situations. However, the therapy sessions themselves can be time-consuming and expensive; typically, a client would attend sessions once or twice per week for six to twelve weeks.

Time management

As discussed under the cognitive approach, people often are stressed because cognitive biases, such as the planning fallacy, lead them to underestimate how long it will take them to complete essential tasks. This can also happen because of procrastination, that is, failing to find enough willpower to get started.

Time management can help a person make better use of their time and avoid leaving essential tasks to the last minute, thereby affecting stress levels. One approach to time management in education or the workplace is the **ABC analysis**, which involves taking a task list and rating items A, B or C according to how important they are. Typically, the person starts with a **to-do list** in the morning, with the main tasks for the day. These do not generally include things that will happen at a fixed time, such as a meeting or an exam, but social/family duties might be included. Examples of things that might be on a psychology student's to-do list include:

People who are under a lot of stress may be referred to a therapist

Time management can help to reduce stress

- Email teacher about next week's homework.
- Finish first draft of Assignment.
- Practice for driving theory test.
- Write a personal statement for UCAS.
- Buy a birthday present for my brother.
- Play FIFA on the Xbox.

Each item on the list is then given a rating from A to C. The As are the items that are both important and urgent such as completing work for an imminent deadline. Bs are important but not urgent, while Cs (e.g. playing the Xbox) are things that you would like to do but are not essential.

Time management skills are quick to learn and can be of great benefit when dealing with a large number of relatively short tasks. They only really help us to deal with some stressors, however – we can't always do work in whatever order we want.

Exercise

As you have learned, the fight-or-flight response evolved to help early humans in the EEA to survive. For our early ancestors, this response would have been followed by immediate physical exertion such as running from danger. Nowadays however, stressors such as traffic jams and work deadlines do not lead to much physical activity.

One technique that can mimic the physical activity of the survival situations of our evolutionary past is **exercise**, for example going for a run or engaging in sport. In a study of laboratory rats, Fleshner (2000) found evidence that physical activity can reduce the negative effects of stress on the immune system. Exercise can also help us to use up glucose and metabolise stress hormones; clearly, it has a benefit at times of acute stress, provided it is possible.

However, it is unclear exactly how exercise affects chronic stress. De Geus and Van Doornen (1993) concluded that getting physically fit has no effect on the stress response itself. It may be that exercise benefits us simply by raising our mood; exercise causes the release of natural chemicals called **endorphins** that boost our mood. Long and Flood (1993) suggest that exercise can operate as an emotion-focused coping strategy.

There are many advantages of exercise as a strategy – it has other health benefits, most forms are relatively cheap to do and it can be more easily fitted in around a busy schedule than therapy sessions can. Depending on the type of exercise, it could have the additional benefits of social support and/or have meditative qualities.

Exercise can help relieve acute stress

Drugs

Another way to tackle the body's stress response is by giving a drug that directly tackles the stress response in the body. Such drugs are frequently prescribed by GPs both for stress and for stress-related problems such as insomnia or anxiety disorders.

One group of drugs is the **benzodiazepines**, including Valium, Restoril and Librium. These boost a neurotransmitter called GABA, making the person feel more relaxed and sleepy. The faster acting drugs make people fall asleep and they are used as sleeping pills; however, the slower acting versions relax the body and this makes people feel psychologically more relaxed.

Drugs may be prescribed for stress-related problems

Another commonly prescribed group of drugs are called **beta-blockers**. These act directly on the nervous system, reducing the effect of sympathetic activation by blocking the 'beta' receptors that respond to adrenalin. This leads to lower heart rate and reduced blood pressure.

A possible criticism of this strategy is that it provides short-term relief without helping to solve a person's underlying problems. In addition, all drugs can have side effects. Benzodiazepines can make you sleepy, which is potentially risky for driving and other activities. In some cases, they have more severe side effects, such as confusion, seizures or hallucinations. They are also addictive. They are only recommended for short-term use (Royal College of Psychiatrists, 2013).

Beta blockers are generally considered safe for longer term use, but can have some side effects such as dizziness and tiredness (NHS, 2014b).

Make the link

Benzodiazepines are also used as sleeping pills (see chapter 3).

✔ Questions

1. Which has the more serious effect on health – acute or chronic stress?

2. Name a short-term mental health effect of stress.

3. What does CHD stand for?

4. Name two psychological disorders where stress plays a role.

5. Which research study found that exercise reduced the harm of stress on the immune system?

6. Name two things that can be done while meditating to boost its relaxing effects.

7. What is the first phase of stress inoculation?

8. What does the application phase involve?

9. Which is the label given to the most important tasks when using the ABC technique?

10. Which group of drugs has the more severe side effects, benzodiazepines or beta-blockers?

🔑 Key concepts

- Meditation
- Meditation, guided
- Stress inoculation
- Time management
- ABC analysis
- To-do list
- Exercise
- Endorphins
- Benzodiazepines
- Beta-blockers

GO! Activities

1. Investigate one of the five stress management techniques above, including researching sources, and present your findings. You should:

- Read more about the technique and write a short summary of it.
- Use Google Scholar or another research website to find recent research studies (from the last 10 years or so). Find at least two such articles and summarise them in your own words.
- Briefly summarise how effective you think the technique is compared to other stress management techniques you have studied and how practical it is in everyday stressful situations.
- Present your findings of the previous three activities, for example on a PowerPoint or blog post.
- Share your findings with other students, for example by presenting your PowerPoint to the class or sharing a link to your blog post for others to comment.

GO! End of topic project

You will conduct a case study into stress at exam/prelim time. The aim will be to find out about a classmate's stressors related to studying and revising and to make recommendations based on your knowledge of stress management to help them relieve their stress at exam time (see chapter 8 for general information on the case study method).

- Draw up a plan showing how you will conduct the case study.
- Conduct a brief case history, using a semi-structured interview, to reveal the following points. Find out, up until now…
  - Where and when the participant studies for exams.
  - What environmental and social stressors have affected him/her.
  - What time management approaches he/she has taken, if any.
  - The participant's views on learning and revision.
  - Anything the participant does to relieve stress at present.
- Now, show how you would follow up on this case history. Try using observation to find out more about the participant's study techniques and what stress management works best for him or her – this could include video recordings.
- Prepare recommendations based on your findings and your knowledge of stress.
- If your participant consents, you could make a poster showing your results.

✔ End of topic specimen exam questions

As this is an optional topic, exam questions will be quite general and will not name the topic or its specific theories/research studies, for example:

National 5

1. Explain a topic from Individual Behaviour other than sleep and dreams. 4 marks

2. From your chosen optional topic in Individual Behaviour, name and describe one research study that has been carried out. Include the aim, method/procedure and results of the study. 6 marks

Higher

1. Choose a topic in Individual Behaviour other than sleep, dreams and sleep disorders. Explain how this topic can be applied in the real world. 10 marks

2. Explain a topic in Individual Behaviour other than sleep, dreams and sleep disorders, referring to at least two approaches. 16 marks

3. Discuss two theories relating to your chosen optional topic in Individual Behaviour. 12 marks

The total exam mark allocation for the Individual Behaviour unit will be 20 marks; however, there is no way of knowing in advance how this will be split between this topic and the topic of sleep.

7 Intelligence

Defining intelligence

You probably have a fairly clear concept of what an **ability** is – how good a person is at doing something. For example, people have a certain ability level in art, cooking, music, mathematics or dancing. **Intelligence** is a more abstract concept and it is very difficult to define in a way that most people would agree with. If it is an ability, then what is it the ability to do? It has sometimes been defined as one's ability at learning (Sternberg, 2005), but is more often assumed to mean a general ability to think and reason that affects all other mental abilities (Gottfredson, 1998).

Some define intelligence as one's ability at learning

Some researchers think that it is too narrow to see intelligence just as a single mental ability – it can be viewed as a large group of abilities (Guilford, 1967) and it should take account of how well we respond to problems in our surroundings, such as the everyday challenges in our work and lives (Sternberg, 2003).

Therefore, a good working definition could be 'the ability or set of abilities which help us to think and reason and respond to everyday challenges effectively'. Your view on whether this is an adequate definition may well change as you read the theories in this chapter. More than any other topic in psychology, the nature of the topic itself is a matter of debate and disagreement.

The remainder of this section focuses on two of the most important of these debates:

Your IQ or 'intelligence quotient' is just a score on an intelligence test

? Discussion point

Do you think that it is possible to measure a single intelligence factor that would tell us something about all of a person's abilities?

Fluid intelligence is used to solve novel tasks

- Is intelligence a single ability or are there separate types of intelligence?
- Are people born intelligent or is it a result of upbringing and education?

You will come across the term **IQ** during this topic. Although often used in everyday language to mean the same thing as intelligence, you should be aware that your IQ or 'intelligence quotient' is just a score on an intelligence test. IQ tests do aim to measure intelligence but they are not always considered a useful or fair way of doing so. The issue of IQ testing is discussed in the final part of this chapter.

Is intelligence a single ability?

A general 'g' factor

The concept of a single factor underlying all intelligent behaviour is commonly called **general intelligence**, or the **'g' factor**. It is based on work more than 100 years ago by Sir Charles Spearman, who found that grades of schoolchildren across seemingly unrelated subjects such as Classics, Maths and Music were strongly correlated and suggested that there is a basic general intelligence. This means that for anyone doing a task, their ability depends on two things:

- their general intelligence – their 'g' factor
- their specific ability in that task

Spearman argued that while general intelligence applies to all mental tasks, the specific abilities in those tasks are statistically unrelated to each other (Spearman, 1904). He later explained this general ability as being based on '*mental energy*' (Spearman, 1927, p.135), which he described in terms very similar to what modern cognitive psychologists call **attention**.

Gottfredson (2003) argued that 'g' exists in all cultures and it can be determined from any set of cognitive tests, regardless of their content or how they are administered. Many researchers who believe in a 'g' factor also consider that it is largely fixed and determined by genetics (see biological approach, next section).

Two factors

Later researchers have questioned Spearman's idea of a 'g' factor. Burt (1911) said that more than one factor was needed to fully explain intelligent behaviour – at least one verbal and one mathematical one. Cattell (1971) believed that there is a general intelligence but that it should be subdivided into two types: fluid intelligence (Gf) and crystallised intelligence (Gc):

- Fluid intelligence is the more basic of the two. It is seen as our flexible intelligence that is used to solve novel tasks, for example, problems that we have never attempted before. Some people are seen as having a faster and more effective general mental ability, and according to Cattell, this means that they have a higher level of fluid intelligence. Importantly, Cattell states that it is genetically controlled and it cannot increase after we reach adulthood.

- Crystallised intelligence is reasoning that is based on learned skills and strategies, which can develop separately for different types of tasks. As it depends on experience, crystallised intelligence can develop throughout life. According to Cattell, someone with an average level of fluid intelligence could still become very good at solving problems if they increased their crystallised intelligence through experience.

Multiple intelligences

More recent researchers have criticised the idea of a general intelligence. Sternberg (1999) notes that students who do well on one multiple choice test tend to do well on others, regardless of the subject matter – he suggests that these are measuring an *'ability at doing tests'* rather than intelligence! Similarly, Gardner (2006) argues that rather than being a fundamental ability, 'g' depends on how similar the tasks are to traditional school exercises: *'What seems clear to me is that one can manipulate 'g', depending on how "school like" the task is. The more the tasks/tests resemble the kinds of exercises undertaken in a Western secular school, the higher the 'g' will be.'* (Gardner, 2006, p.504)

Essentially these researchers are arguing that 'g' is a very narrow measure of mental ability related to solving logical puzzles. Gardner (1983) claims that this ability is just one type of intelligence and that there are several other 'intelligences' of equal importance. To put it another way, there is no reason to call our academic, test-passing abilities 'intelligence', and not allow the same term to be used for things such as interpersonal skills, ability to compose music or our judgement on a sports field.

Gardner proposed eight separate 'intelligences':

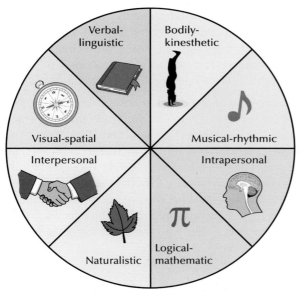

Multiple intelligences

Gardner sees each intelligence as a cognitive capacity that has evolved to process certain kinds of information in order to solve problems or create necessary products (Gardner, 2006). This theory has become

Sternberg found that students who do well on one multiple choice test tend to do well on others, regardless of the subject matter

? Discussion point

Are these two things, intelligence and ability at tests, really separate?

Can judgement on a sports field be called 'intelligence'?

very popular in education and it has the potential to benefit students who don't suit traditional teaching methods. However, the concept of multiple intelligences has been criticised for a lack of experimental research evidence (Sternberg & Grigorenko, 2004).

Are people born intelligent?

Perhaps more than any other area of psychology, the study of intelligence and abilities has led to a fierce debate over the roles of innate factors – 'nature' – versus learning and experience – 'nurture'. This is the so-called nature-nurture debate.

Nature arguments

Spearman (1904) and others felt that the 'g' factor was a fixed ability that couldn't be changed. Many other researchers have claimed that intelligence is innate and inherited – the reason successful people tend to have successful children, it is argued, is that they inherit the genes for high intelligence (see Gould, 1982). This is basis of the nature side of the argument.

Many researchers believe that intelligence is inherited from our parents

From this point of view, there is nothing that we can do to increase people's intelligence, and the job of an IQ test is just to measure it. What's more, this can be done early – some pupils in the USA are given an IQ test as early as kindergarten level, which then determines what school class or 'track' they go into for the coming years (Corbett Burris & Garrity, 2008).

? Discussion point

Consider yourself and the other people you know. Do you think that some people are more intelligent than others? And if so, could the less intelligent people become just as good or better with the right training?

The nature argument only makes sense if intelligence is an innate quality, determined by our genes. Therefore, what is the evidence that intelligence is innate? Some of the key evidence comes from twin studies – research into genetically identical twins who have been separated and raised in different environments. Some large-scale studies have found a strongly positive correlation in IQ between identical twins raised apart, but there are some problems with the methodology of these studies. This research is described in detail under the biological approach (see next section of this chapter).

A problem for the nature side of the debate comes from the fact that even though the human gene pool remains much the same, average IQ does not stand still. The **Flynn effect** is the observation that across the world, the average IQ score has gradually increased at an average rate of around three points per decade (Flynn, 1984). Though not fully understood, the Flynn effect could be due to better diet or to improved education. Another possibility is that people are becoming gradually more practiced at doing logic-type puzzles and that the effect is simply due to familiarity and practice. Either way, the effect suggests that IQ cannot depend just on our genes.

Some studies have found that twins raised apart have very similar IQ scores

Nurture arguments

In contrast to the idea that intelligence is innate, the nurture side of the debate sees intelligence as being dependent on experiences, particularly parenting and education. According to this view, intelligence level can be changed and improved through a stimulating environment and effective teaching. Therefore, if intelligent people have intelligent children, it is not because they have passed on 'smart genes' but because they have raised them in a way that promotes intelligent thought.

If a child experiences an especially bad environment, this can harm their intellectual development – this has been the clear conclusion of numerous studies of severe **deprivation** among infants; perhaps most notably among children who have been brought up in orphanages with little human interaction (Goldfarb, 1953; Rutter *et al.*, 2007). In addition, taking children out of an institution and putting them in an **enriched environment** – that is, one in which they are intellectually stimulated – can boost intelligence (Skeels & Dye, 1939). Animals can also benefit from an enriched environment – research on rats shows that their brains become more complex if they have a large amount of objects to interact with rather than a plain, featureless enclosure (Kempermann *et al.*, 1997).

Further evidence comes from studies of **birth order**, that is, what order a child is born in a family. This is found to affect IQ scores, with later-born children, on average, scoring lower – according to Zajonc *et al.* (1979), this is due to later children receiving less parental interaction, and being surrounded by, on average, simpler language and thought processes (as each additional baby in a family reduces the average level of spoken language).

Most of the ideas about intelligence see it as a **fixed entity** or 'thing', which people have in varying amounts and that could, in principle, be measured.

However, according to Sternberg (1999), intelligence shouldn't be seen as an entity that we either have or do not, but as **developing expertise**. He argues that just as you would expect a craft to develop over time, with an apprentice having a low level and a master craftsperson having a much higher level, so too our intelligence(s) can grow over time with the right experiences.

These researchers therefore see intelligence as **incremental** – it can grow and develop over time. Sternberg's theory of intelligence is explained in more detail later in this chapter.

Hart and Risely (1995) found evidence that positive parenting can boost verbal intelligence (a major part of IQ). Using tape recordings, they found wide variations in some aspects of parenting, such as parents using a wide vocabulary and asking their children open questions. Children who heard more complex language developed a broader vocabulary and scored higher in intelligence tests. This research benefited from using detailed observations and a longitudinal design, and strongly supports the nurture views.

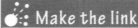

Make the link

See the discussion of the nature-nurture debate at the start of chapter 2. Consider how this concept applies to several different topics in your Psychology course.

Deprivation can harm a child's intellectual development

Studies have found that the youngest children have the lowest IQs within a family

Postitive parenting can boost verbal intelligence

? **Discussion point**

Do you consider intelligence to be fixed or do you think that it can grow and develop like a skill?

Top tip

Begin an exam answer with a definition of the term intelligence. Don't rush – it is worth taking some time to explain the term clearly. Give some thought to how it differs from IQ. IQ can be defined as 'a numerical measure of intelligence using a test, where scores are placed on a scale with the average set at 100'.

Education is another area where experience might have an effect on intelligence – usually a positive effect! Rosenthal and Jacobson (1968) demonstrated that when teachers have higher expectations of pupils, they subsequently score higher on IQ tests (see key study). Dweck links improvements to attitudes and the benefits of a growth mindset (see p.190 of this chapter).

Genetic elements could be seen as potential – a potential that might not be fulfilled without good education and upbringing. Someone with a genetic advantage could still do worse in IQ tests compared to other individuals if their upbringing and education was inferior or due to a failure to train their talents. An important question to ask, then, is how much can someone's intelligence improve and what conditions aid intelligence improvement?

Most researchers now recognise that both nature and nurture play a role in someone's intelligence. Even Spearman, who said that the 'g' factor was largely innate, felt that it was pointless to measure it at school, and instead emphasised the importance of education to improving someone's specific abilities – stating that everyone is a genius at something (Raven, 2011).

Many researchers have now moved away from the idea that either nature or nurture is responsible for our intelligence level; instead they think that nature and nurture can both have an effect and can interact with each other. For example, an individual might be born with a tendency to have a high level of intelligence but due to negative life circumstances and experiences, might not fulfil their potential. Likewise, genes for intelligence could theoretically influence someone's upbringing and improve their educational experiences. Therefore, genes and upbringing are not seen as two ingredients, but rather as things that can each have an effect, positive or negative, on the other as a child develops. This is known as an **interactionist** view.

✔ Questions

1. What is an ability?

2. Why is IQ different from intelligence?

3. Who first suggested there was a general intelligence or 'g' factor?

4. Which of the two types of intelligence in Cattell's model can develop throughout life?

5. What does 'g' mean in this topic?

6. What is the difference between intrapersonal intelligence and interpersonal intelligence?

7. What effect does birth order appear to have on intelligence?

8. What aspect of intelligence was studied by Hart and Risely (1995)?

9. What is the name of the gradual increase in IQ scores over the decades?

10. What is the name of the view that nature and nurture both affect each other?

●─ Key concepts

- Intelligence
- Ability
- IQ
- General intelligence
- 'G' factor
- Attention
- Fluid intelligence
- Crystallised intelligence
- Flynn effect
- Deprivation
- Enriched environment
- Birth order
- Fixed entity
- Developing expertise
- Incremental
- Interactionist view

GO! Activities

1. Try doing an IQ test – there are lots available for free online (although many are poor quality). What do you think of the questions? Are they fair? Would you do better with practice? Evaluate the test, and report back to your class (take screenshots of the test items).

2. Test yourself in the eight different 'multiple' intelligences at http://literacyworks.org/mi/assessment/findyourstrengths.html. Doing the test will help you remember them. Compare your scores with a classmate.

3. Find out more about the multiple intelligences. You could ask your teachers/lecturers if they consider this theory in their teaching. Most exams – including Higher Psychology – require a lot of writing but you can draw on your strengths in other areas in your revision, for example, using revision diagrams and mind maps if you are strong in visual-spatial intelligence.

Approaches to intelligence

Biological approach to intelligence

Revision points from chapter 2
The following points from the main section on the biological approach are especially relevant to this topic. Ensure that you can refer to them in exam answers on approaches to intelligence: • the nervous system and brain areas • genes

The nervous system and brain areas

As in the closely linked area of memory (see chapter 5), psychologists have identified several areas of the brain that are important in intelligence. In particular, the **frontal lobe** of the neocortex appears to be important in intelligent abilities. Shimamura (2000) found that metacognition – the ability to think about and monitor one's own thinking – is closely linked to the frontal lobe of the brain. Metacognition includes attention, error correction and monitoring one's own emotions. It is seen by Sternberg (1985) as a key part of intelligence.

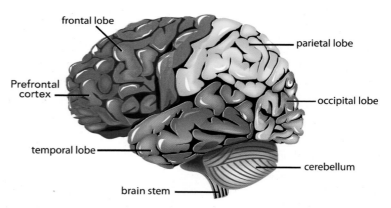

Parts of the human brain

Duncan *et al.* (2000) suggested a possible brain area for the 'g' factor. Using PET brain scans, the researchers found that the **lateral prefrontal cortex** in the brain became active on the tests that required problem solving but not on similar tests with no problem solving element ('lateral' means 'at the side', so this is the side area of the frontal lobe – roughly underneath the sides of your forehead).

Genetics

Many researchers, such as Spearman and Gottfredson have said that not only is there a 'g' factor but it is genetically fixed (and Cattell, 1971, said the same thing about the 'fluid intelligence' part of the 'g' factor).

Many researchers think 'g' is genetically fixed

Studies of identical twins that have been raised apart are potentially important evidence for this view. If such twins turn out to have a very similar level of intelligence despite their different upbringings, this would be powerful evidence that intelligence depends more on genes than on experiences.

A problem with such twin studies is that it is very uncommon to find twins that have been raised apart. In one of the first twin studies into intelligence, Shields (1962) placed adverts in the UK, and 44 pairs of identical twins came forward. The pairs showed a correlation in IQ of 0.77 – a strong correlation – and Shields reported personality similarities as well. Identical twins share the same genes, while ordinary siblings only share 50% on average – and the IQ correlation for siblings raised apart was found to be just 0.24.

However, Joseph (2001) noted that the Shields study might have been biased in several ways:

- Advertising for separated twins increased the chance that the twins were similar (dissimilar pairs might not have realised that they were identical twins!)

- Most of the pairs were raised in similar environments – often two branches of the same extended family.

- The standard for being 'raised apart' was that they had been in separate homes for just five years or more; therefore, many had shared the same home environment during a large part of their childhood.

A larger-scale study in the USA conducted by Bouchard and McGue (1981) came to a similar conclusion to Shields – identical twins raised apart had an overall IQ correlation of 0.72, despite the lack of a shared environment. However, the controversies over biases remain. In a study of adopted children, Horn (1983) found a 0.28 correlation between the children's IQ and the IQ of the natural mothers, compared with a 0.15 correlation with the adoptive mothers. Together, these research studies, despite their flaws, do seem to suggest that genetic factors can make a difference to someone's intelligence – or at least to how well they score on an IQ test.

Evaluation of the biological approach to intelligence

Overall, the biological approach has tended to make two main statements – first, that intelligence has a biological basis in terms of brain areas and genes. Second, that it is relatively fixed through life.

One problem is that as intelligence is a controversial issue without a universally agreed definition, it is difficult to establish which areas are important in a way that most psychologists can agree on. It does appear that the frontal lobe plays a key role in intelligent processes but there is still a lot of research to be done before the links between brain areas and intelligence processes are fully understood. The fact that a brain area is active when a process – such as solving a problem – is occurring does not mean that it is the 'problem solving area' – it could be one of several essential areas.

The brain itself changes through time and with experience, and as Dweck (2006) has pointed out, performance can change hugely with good teaching and a more positive mindset, suggesting that abilities are not biologically fixed – or that good education and a positive mindset helps people fulfil their biological potential.

If genes can programme people to be more or less intelligent then there could be racial differences in intelligence. Although some researchers have claimed to demonstrate such differences, the work is largely discredited nowadays (Colman, 1987). For example, IQ testing conducted on American soldiers during the First World War showed a statistical link with the recruit's ethnic origin. Gould (1982) noted several flaws and biases such as the fact that a lot of recruits were immigrants with a poor grasp of English and that many black recruits had only been educated until the age of nine.

Cognitive approach to intelligence

Revision points from chapter 2

The following points from the main section on the cognitive approach are especially relevant to this topic. Ensure that you can refer to them in exam answers on approaches to intelligence:

- computer analogy
- schemas

Programming a computer to think intelligently is known as artificial intelligence

Computer analogy

As with other topics, contemporary cognitive psychologists view intelligence in terms of computer processing. Solving a problem is viewed in terms of storage of the necessary information in memory, manipulating the information to perform an operation on it and then checking whether the operation has been carried out successfully.

You may have seen TV programmes or movies that portray a future situation where robots are intelligent. The idea of programming a computer to think intelligently is known as **artificial intelligence**.

A classic test of computer intelligence is known as **the Turing test**, as it was devised by the famous British researcher and Second World War codebreaker Alan Turing. Aware that the question of 'can machines think' was ambiguous and unscientific, Turing instead suggested a different question. It was very hard to define what was meant by 'artificial intelligence' and therefore, Turing (1950) set out a practical aim – could a computer be programmed to respond to questions in such a way that a person would be unable to tell whether it was a computer? For example, in modern terms, if you were engaging in an online text-only chat, how long would it take you to figure out whether you were talking to a person or to a computer that had been programmed to respond to common questions and statements?

Schemas

Piaget was hugely influential in the area of intelligence due to his theory of how cognitive processes develop though childhood. He believed that the schemas we have about the world start off quite simple but change and adapt to the world as we grow older. For example, a young child may consider all flying animals to be 'a bird', but an older child realises that there are different types of birds, developing his/her schemas through assimilation and accommodation (see chapter 2).

Piaget also thought that intelligence developed and grew in distinct **stages**, and that one stage must be completed before the child can move on to the next. The main four stages are:

- **Sensorimotor** (ages 0–2). The child's schemas are based on movements and learning how to manipulate objects. Babies are very interested in playing with new objects and discovering what they do.

- **Pre-operational** (ages 2–7). The child develops symbolic thought, that is, one object can represent another (e.g. two toys can represent a parent and child). However, the child's thinking is still not logical and it is highly egocentric – the child can't think about a problem from another person's point of view.

- **Concrete operational** (ages 8–11). The child can perform mental operations in a more logical way but only with things that they can see. Compared to the previous stage, they are less concerned with the appearance of an object, and realise, for example, that if something changes shape to be taller its volume/mass doesn't change (they can 'conserve' volume and mass – see chapter 2). This is because they can mentally reverse the operation.

- **Formal operational** (age 11+). The main difference to the previous stage is that the child is now easily able to think logically and scientifically about an object without the object being physically present. In other words, they can think abstractly. A child in this stage can determine whether a statement is logically correct or not regardless of whether it is true in real life, and can manipulate abstract mathematical symbols.

Alan Turing and his colleagues working on an early computer

●: Make the link

…between Turing's work on computers/code breaking and your study of History.

? Discussion point

Should we be trying to make computers more intelligent? Will it ever be possible for a machine to think as a person does?

Babies enjoy playing with new objects and discovering what they do

The theory sounds very rigid but Piaget recognised that some children develop through the stages faster than others (Piaget himself authored his first scientific paper at the age of 10!) Intelligence in childhood is not seen in terms of an absolute, biological ability, but in terms of how far a child has progressed; progress might be faster or slower than peers of the same age.

Evaluation of the cognitive approach

The cognitive approach has a long history of trying to explain intelligent behaviour in terms of logical processes and making a comparison to a computer. This has led to useful, objective models of thinking and controlled laboratory experiments.

However, as discussed in chapter 2, a limitation of this approach is that real human thinking tends to feature the use of heuristics and is prone to biases, rather than being strictly logical. This is not really taken account of in Piaget's model, which assumes that adults are generally logical and scientific in their thinking.

Some researchers have criticised the assumption in Piaget's model that children's thinking is flawed. Baron-Cohen *et al.* (1985) demonstrated that most children show an intuitive understanding of what adults know, even at pre-school age. Samuel and Bryant (1984) argue that Piaget's findings result partly from the confusing ways that questions were asked to children in his 'conservation' experiments – by asking the same question twice, they argue, children may have assumed that they were expected to change their answer.

A recreation of Piaget's liquid conservation experiment

The Turing test can be criticised on the basis that the computer may answer questions as it is programmed but does not consciously think or feel. However, Turing (1950) argues that although there is no way of knowing whether a computer can feel without 'being' that computer, neither can we know the same for sure about other people or animals, except by observing their behaviour. Therefore, a behavioural test is sufficient.

Evolutionary approach

Revision points from chapter 2

The following points from the main section on the evolutionary approach are especially relevant to this topic. Ensure that you can refer to them in exam answers on intelligence:

- Darwin's theory
- comparisons with other species

Darwin's theory

The evolutionary approach to human intelligence tries to understand how the path of human evolution has led us to have the brains we have today and how this might affect our abilities and issues such as IQ testing. We know that humans have a much larger brain and greater intelligence than our nearest relatives in the animal kingdom – chimpanzees, bonobos and gorillas. How did this happen and why? What pressures of natural selection caused our brains to grow so much larger than those of other apes?

Firstly, it is important to remember that large brains have a cost as well as a benefit. The human brain consumes around 25% of the energy from the food we eat – and the proportion is even larger for babies and children. Its large size also makes birth a riskier and more painful process than it is in other species. These costs must have been exceeded by a huge survival advantage.

One theory is that humans are specialised to deal with change. Primates remained in forested environments for many millions of years and most other primate species still live in rainforests today. However, at some point at around about the time that our ancestors separated from chimpanzees, we began to live on the grasslands of the African savannah and hunted rather than foraged for food. According to Morris (1967), this move put humans in direct competition with carnivores such as wolves and big cats – a competition we were not equipped to deal with due to our senses and speed being inferior. Instead, our ancestors had to rely on their only advantage over those species – their intelligence. One evolutionary change that resulted was a hugely prolonged childhood compared to other species, allowing offspring to learn more skills from their group.

Although there is some fossil evidence of early human skulls, the full picture of exactly why human brains grew so large remains unknown. Dunbar (1992) found no correlation between primate brain size and environmental complexity – but it does correlate with size of the social group. This suggests that our large brains may be an adaptation to social complexities rather than to hunting and survival.

The fossilised skull of Australopithecus boisei

Comparisons with other species

How intelligent are other animals? Some researchers trying to understand the evolution of human intelligence have tried to teach human language and skills to chimpanzees and other apes. Sign language is a complex language, equivalent to spoken language in its grammar and vocabulary and it should be made clear that no chimp or gorilla has ever learned anything close to the full language. However, some researchers did make some findings that suggest what early human ancestors might have been capable of before true language evolved.

The best-known study was the **ape sign language** project of Allen and Beatrix Gardner. The Gardners adopted a baby chimpanzee named 'Washoe' and raised her for several months, treating her like a human infant. They were able to teach her at least 175 recognisable signs, based on American Sign Language. She also spontaneously used signs paired together in short 'phrases' (Premack, 1971). These findings suggest that some of the building blocks of human intelligence were present in our early ancestors.

Dunbar found that primate brain size correlated to the size of the social group

Dr. Roger Fouts, a colleague of the Gardners, working on an ape language project

Evaluation of the evolutionary approach

This is an area where there is considerable scientific debate. It is clear that humans developed larger brains and greater intelligence than other species but the limited available fossil evidence means that people can only speculate about exactly how and why our greater intelligence evolved. Currently, ideas such as Dunbar (1992) that social factors drove the evolution of intelligence are becoming more popular.

In terms of language skills, Pinker (1994) argues that ape studies show very little because human language is fundamentally unique. However, to view it more positively, they do give us an insight into the cognitive starting point for language. Bonobos and chimps are undoubtedly very intelligent apes but they cannot learn true human language.

●━ Key concepts

- Frontal lobe
- Lateral prefrontal cortex
- Artificial intelligence
- Turing test
- Stages (Piagetian)
- Ape sign language

☑ Questions

1. What type of brain scans were used by Duncan *et al.* (2000)?

2. What area of the neocortex seems to be important in intelligent thought processes?

3. What IQ correlation did Shields (1962) find between identical twins raised apart?

4. How did Shields recruit his participants?

5. What is the difference between assimilation and accommodation in Piaget's cognitive theory?

6. Name one of the stages of Piaget's theory.

7. What term is used for intelligence in computers?

8. What does the Turing test involve?

9. What was the name of the Gardners' 'ape language project' chimp?

10. What did Dunbar consider the more important factor in the evolution of human intelligence – the environment or the social group?

1. In your notes, create a labelled sketch of brain areas that are involved in intelligence/problem solving.

2. Can you see any links between Piaget's theory and our education system? Speak to your teachers/lecturers and find out more about how Piaget has influenced education.

3. Research other ape language projects. You may be able to find some videos on YouTube. Prepare a short presentation for your class.

Theories of intelligence

The model of successful intelligence

Robert Sternberg's 'triarchic model of successful intelligence' or just **successful intelligence (SI)** aims to show that intelligence is not just about what happens in your head, but also how you react to situations in the real world (Sternberg, 1988). The theory is therefore broader than traditional views of intelligence. Sternberg also believes that intelligence can grow and develop through education – as mentioned earlier, he sees intelligence as something that can grow incrementally, like your skill at a craft.

There are three main 'sub-theories' in the model, relating to different types of intelligence that Sternberg says are statistically unrelated to each other:

Analytic

Analytic intelligence relates to the mental skills or 'components' used for solving problems. It includes the kind of reasoning and logic usually tested by IQ tests, as well as knowledge acquisition and metacognition (i.e. analysis of our own thought processes). This type of intelligence is therefore very similar to traditional views of 'g' or crystallised intelligence described earlier in this chapter (Gottfredson, 2003) and it is most closely related to what is taught and tested at school (Sternberg, 1997). An example of an analytic task would be to figure out the meaning of an unfamiliar word from its context in a sentence.

Analytic intelligence is most closely related to what is taught and tested at school

Creative

Creative intelligence describes the type of intelligence used for dealing with unfamiliar problems, especially ones that do not have a single solution. This includes drawing on experience and using creativity to deal with unfamiliar problems. It is also called the 'experiential' sub-theory. Sternberg feels that school learning often fails to encourage this important ability, a view that is supported by the British educationalist Ken Robinson (2001), who stated that schools 'kill' creativity by focusing too much on analytic ability. An example of a creative task would be to 'describe what the world would be like today if the Second World War had not taken place'.

Sternberg feels that school learning often fails to encourage creative intelligence

Practical

Practical intelligence describes a type of intelligence that is essential for practical success. The key idea here is that someone could have great analytic and creative skills but lack the common sense abilities to behave intelligently in their work and environment. Practical intelligence involves adapting to problems in the real world, rather than the abstract problems of an IQ test. An example task could be 'What can people do to slow down global warming?' (Sternberg, 2008).

According to Sternberg, there are three main ways in which people use practical intelligence:

- adapting an environment to suit you
- changing your own behaviour to suit the environment
- choosing a different environment

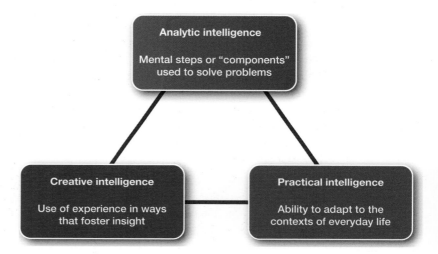

While recognising that different cultures use intelligence for different things – and may differ in their views about what is an intelligent response – the researchers behind SI believe that certain processes occur universally in all three intelligences. According to Stemler *et al.* (2006), these **metacomponents** or 'executive processes' include:

- defining problems
- planning what to do
- carrying out plans
- monitoring processes during problem solving
- evaluating solutions
- acquisition of knowledge
- learning new strategies

More recently, Sternberg has added a fourth component to the model – **wisdom**. He argues that developing intelligence alone is not sufficient for a good education. Wisdom can be defined as judging correctly and choosing the right course of action, based on experience (Sternberg, 2001), and in leadership positions, it involves using one's intelligence for the greater good (Sternberg, 2008). The model is sometimes now called the **WICS model**, an acronym for 'wisdom, intelligence, and creativity, synthesised' (Sternberg, 2008).

'Wisdom' has now been added to the model

Evaluation

The theory has many potential practical uses. Due to the focus on 'g' or analytic intelligence, students who are stronger in creativity and practical intelligence may get poorer results at school than they deserve, meaning they are denied opportunities for university courses where they might excel (Stemler *et al.*, 2006). Therefore, the model has the potential to improve education.

Sternberg and his colleagues have developed tests based on SI that have been used as entrance tests for university. These have resulted in better achievement at university level – that is, they have successfully chosen people who are better suited to university than the traditional SAT tests did (Sternberg, 1999; see p.195 for SAT tests).

Those who do well in SI tests have been proven to do well at university

The gradual changes to the theory, including the recent addition of wisdom as a fourth component, shows that the theory has been adapted to accommodate new ideas and research evidence.

Conversely, those who believe in a 'g' factor dispute the idea that all three sub-theories are types of intelligence. Gottfredson (2003) states that the practical sub-theory really represents life skills and argues that traditional 'g' is the best indicator of practical success.

Sternberg (1997) describes three research students who are each strong in one of the three types of intelligence in his theory. Alice is strong at analytic intelligence, understanding new research quickly, evaluating it and drawing conclusions. Barbara is good at thinking up new ideas for research. Celia understands how to deal with other people in the research team and how to successfully submit papers for publication. Each student has different strengths, unrelated to each other, but all three would be useful members of a research team.

Each student has different strengths but all three would be useful members of a research team

Mindsets

A **mindset** is a set of mental processes including attitudes and core beliefs. Rather than affecting just one type of behaviour, a mindset is broad enough to affect a range of different thoughts and behaviours. Mindsets can derive from our culture or from those in our immediate social group (Janis, 1972).

The researcher Carol Dweck agrees with Sternberg's view of intelligence as an incremental skill, rather than a fixed entity. What's more, she believes that a learner's own view of intelligence as either incremental or fixed can have a major effect on their academic achievement. According to Dweck, how people view intelligence depends on their mindset. There are two key mindsets, one of which leads to positive outcomes and the other to negative outcomes (Dweck, 2006):

- A fixed mindset is the belief that intelligence and abilities are fixed in an individual and cannot significantly change through effort.
- A growth mindset is the belief that intelligence and abilities only reflect an individual's current level and that anyone can improve their ability through effort.

Boys and girls did equally well in Maths after being taught about the incremental nature of intelligence

Mindsets can be seen to link to stereotypes about intelligence. As discussed in chapter 11, awareness of negative stereotypes leads to stereotype threat, harming performance. Good *et al.* (2003) found that teaching a growth mindset reduced gender and racial disadvantages in the classroom. The control group in their study, boys, outperformed girls at maths in accordance with the social stereotype, but when an experimental group were taught about the incremental nature of intelligence, the gender gap disappeared.

Which mindset do I have? Answer the following questions to determine your mindset. Overall, do you agree with these statements or not? (See p.409 for feedback.)

1. It's a very satisfying feeling when I finish something quickly and it's perfect.

2. People who are really good at drawing generally took a lot of time and effort to get to that level.

3. Tests at school don't tell you much about who will be successful later in life.

4. I'd rather not hear about the things that I am bad at.

5. Intelligence is something you are born with and there is not much you can do to change it.

6. The best sportspeople are the ones who trained the hardest.

The fixed mindset

Having a fixed mindset means that you see abilities, such as intelligence and skill, as basically fixed in each individual – they cannot be fundamentally changed through effort. Therefore, having a fixed mindset means that assessments and tests are seen by the individual as a measure of one's permanent ability. Getting an 'A' grade is seen by someone with a fixed mindset as revealing that they are clever, while failing is seen as revealing that they are stupid.

Those with a fixed mindset would belive that failing a test means that they are stupid

According to Dweck, this leads to the student fearing failure and trying their best to *appear* intelligent. A student with a fixed mindset would much rather do something easy and get an A than do something difficult and get a C – even though they may learn nothing from doing the easier task. Dweck argues that over the long term, this leads to the student with a fixed mindset failing to stretch themselves and suffering academically as a result. They would also be more inclined to cheat, because gaining a bad grade is seen as a threat.

The growth mindset

When someone has a growth mindset, they see problems as a challenge and they are motivated by finding things difficult. Getting questions wrong on a test is not seen as a disaster, but rather as useful feedback. The growth mindset individual realises that the score on the test does not reflect ability, so they do not see it as threatening. From the point of view of the growth mindset, getting full marks on an easy test is a waste of time – they haven't learned anything.

A growth mindset learner has a positive attitude to effort and wants to improve, so they see no benefit in getting a pat on the back for what they are already good at – they would rather get feedback on areas that they need to improve. Cheating is seen as pointless by these learners, as they have not learned or achieved anything.

Applications of the theory

One of the main applications of this theory is in education. Dweck (2007) notes that praise – often assumed to be a very healthy thing by teachers and parents – can actually be detrimental. By telling children that they are 'clever', we encourage them to try to look clever by repeating tasks that they have already mastered. Children may start to fear that if they try something new and fail at it, they will no longer be seen as clever.

Telling children they are clever can actually be detrimental to their development

Instead, Dweck argues, the child should be praised for **effort**. Trying hard at a new, challenging project and failing to complete it could be praised for effort, while doing something easy would not be. This way, parents and teachers can encourage the child to develop and improve.

In the theory, mindsets are not seen as permanent. By educating people about mindsets, they can start to identify areas where they can improve:

'Just by knowing about the two mindsets, you can start thinking and reacting in new ways. People tell me they start to catch themselves when they are in the throes of the fixed mindset - passing up a chance for learning, feeling labelled by failure, or getting discouraged when something requires a lot of effort. And then they switch themselves into a growth mindset - making sure that they take the challenge, learn from the failure, or continue their effort.'

Source: Dweck (2006: 46)

Evaluation

A strength of the theory is that it can be applied in many areas, not just in education, but also sports, art, business and personal relationships. For example, people with a fixed mindset think that sporting or artistic ability are fixed and there is no point in trying to improve. Dweck links successful business management to a growth mindset. In all of these cases, having a fixed mindset leads to thinking that ability is fixed, and therefore fearing any negative feedback rather than seeking it out and learning from it.

People with a fixed mindset think artistic ability cannot be changed

The idea of the importance of mindset is supported by Dweck's finding that putting people temporarily into a fixed or growth mindset (e.g. by getting them to read about someone with a growth mindset) changes their attitude towards effort (Dweck, 2006, p.10).

The theory does not sit well with the idea of a fixed, general intelligence that is supported by other researchers such as Gottfredson (1998). Dweck recognises that there are such things as natural talent – for example in sports or memory abilities, people don't always start at the same level – but she feels that effort makes more of a difference.

A limitation of the theory is that there is no universal test for being in a growth or a fixed mindset. Dweck recognises that people can show a mixture of the two mindsets or show a growth mindset in some areas of life and a fixed mindset in others. Therefore, it is difficult to determine objectively which mindset best describes an individual.

📖 Key study: Blackwell et al. (2007): longitudinal study of mindset

Aim: *The researchers wanted to test Dweck's theory that mindset can make a lasting impact on student attainment. They noted that the start of middle school is often a time when pupils who had been doing well start to struggle academically. They wanted to test whether mindset plays a role in this.*

Method: *This was a longitudinal study. The participants were 373 pupils at a New York middle school. Informed consent was obtained and participants were given questionnaires at the start of middle school (age 12 to 13) to assess their mindset. The questionnaire also tested effort and motivation. Pupils were then studied for the next two years, with maths grades being obtained twice per year. All students in the same year were taught by the same maths teacher, therefore controlling for teaching style.*

Results: *The study found no significant link between previous (elementary school) maths score and mindset. However, over the two years of the study a correlation was found, with higher levels of growth mindset correlating with better maths scores. What is more, the researchers found that the grades increased every time the students were tested (see graph).*

The participants were students at a New York middle school

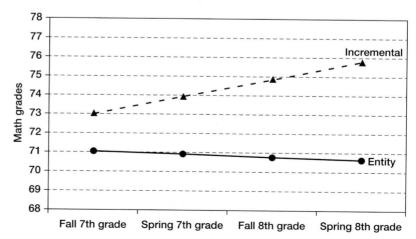

As can be seen, maths scores of participants who saw intelligence as an entity (fixed mindset) stayed static, while for those who saw intelligence as incremental (growth mindset), grades increased. Statistical analysis suggested that mindset had an effect on motivation and effort and that these things, in turn, had an impact on grades. It was concluded that having a growth mindset could cause pupils to be more motivated and put more effort into learning, resulting in better maths grades.

Evaluation: *Why did mindset apparently only began to have an effect in middle school, at the time of the study, rather than earlier life? Blackwell et al. argue that mindset only starts to have an effect when the level of challenge is higher and success is difficult. A strength of the study was its longitudinal design, allowing changes in maths performance to be determined. A limitation is that it was non-experimental; correlation studies cannot determine cause-and-effect between variables, as other factors are not controlled. The sample was large, but arguably not generalisable to other educational situations or to cultures outside the USA. Only maths achievement was studied, and other subjects may have shown different patterns.*

✔ Questions

1. Who devised the model of successful intelligences (SI)?

2. Is SI supposed to be more or less relevant to real world problems than traditional theories?

3. Which sub-theory is relevant to new or unusual problems?

4. What type of intelligence from the SI model would be used to answer a question like 'explain how knowledge of sleep and dreams could benefit society'?

5. Give an example of a metacomponent from Sternberg's theory.

6. Which mindset does Dweck think is more beneficial?

7. Does Dweck think it is a good idea to tell children that they are clever?

8. True or false: the idea of fixed and growth mindsets only applies to intelligence?

9. Who were the participants of Blackwell *et al.*'s (2007) study?

10. How long did Blackwell *et al.* study their participants for?

⚷ Key concepts

- Successful intelligence (SI)
- Analytic intelligence
- Creative intelligence
- Practical intelligence
- Metacomponents
- Wisdom
- WICS model
- Mindset
- Fixed mindset
- Growth mindset
- Effort

GO! Activities

1. Devise further questions to test growth and fixed mindsets. You could focus on another ability area, such as art or sports.

Testing intelligence

Intelligence tests are used to make an objective measurement of a person's intelligence. These tests typically have a mixture of short reasoning questions and results are then translated into an IQ score. Such tests have been used in a wide range of areas, including education and the workplace.

As will be clear from the earlier sections, intelligence is a controversial subject, hard to define, and there is disagreement about what IQ scores actually mean (if anything)! Intelligence tests also come in many different forms, each one influenced by a particular view of what intelligence is.

Origins of intelligence testing

The first intelligence tests were developed by a pair of psychologists called Alfred Binet and Théodor Simon. They had been instructed by the French government to find an objective way of finding out which children needed extra help at school. The aim of the first intelligence tests, therefore, was to help struggling children to improve (Binet & Simon, 1905/1916). Their test was translated into English at Stanford University, California and became known as the **Stanford Binet test** – an updated version is still used today.

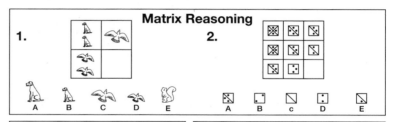

Matrix Reasoning

Number Series

3. 2, 4, 6, 8, _, _
4. 3, 6, 3, 6, _, _
5. 1, 5, 4, 2, 6, 5, _, _
6. 2, 4, 3, 9, 4, 16, _, _

Analogies

7. brother: sister ⟶ father:____
   A. child B. mother C. cousin
   D. friend

8. joke: humor ⟶ law:____
   A. lawyer B. mercy C. courts
   D. justice

Questions from an IQ test

Test materials for an early Stanford Binet test

There are many different intelligence tests nowadays, but most follow a similar pattern to the Stanford Binet, attempting to measure 'g' or fluid intelligence. They typically include a mixture or verbal reasoning, numerical reasoning, visuospatial tasks and working memory (see image example). One notable exception is **Raven's Progressive Matrices** – a test that is entirely visual. This allows it to be used by very young children or other people who have difficulty reading. It is also useful when people are not native speakers of English, as they will arguably not be disadvantaged on this test compared to regular tests such as the Stanford Binet.

Standard IQ scores and mental age

In the early days of intelligence testing, psychologists quickly realised that they needed a way to interpret a child's IQ scores – they needed a standard for comparison. This was done by testing several thousand children of each age and calculating a mean score for each age group. A child's score could then be compared to these averages. For example, if a child's score equals the typical score of a nine-year-old, (s)he was said to have a **mental age** of nine.

However, calculating mental age did not fulfil Binet's original aim – to see whether children's intelligence was behind the typical level for their age. By dividing the child's mental age by their actual age (or 'chronological age') in years, a comparison was made – children with a higher than expected mental age scored higher and those with a lower than expected mental age gained lower scores. To make the results easier to work with, the result was multiplied by 100 – resulting in the first **intelligence quotient** or 'IQ' scores.

If the child's mental age was equal to their actual age, then their mental development was typical and they scored an 'average' IQ of 100. A higher or lower score would result in an IQ below or above 100, as shown in the following examples:

Example 1	Example 2
Child's mental age: 10 Child's actual age: 8 10/8 = 1.25 IQ score = 125	Child's mental age: 9 Child's actual age: 10 9/10 = 0.9 IQ score = 90

Of course, these calculations can only apply to children – once we reach adulthood, our intelligence is no longer expected to increase as we get older. For adults, researchers calculate a mean score and standard deviation (see chapter 8) from previous scores and assess each score according to how far it is from the mean. However, the IQ scores that are used still relate to those originally devised to indicate children's mental age.

Practice exam papers for the 11-plus

Uses of IQ testing

Intelligence testing began in education with Binet and Simon's work and it continues to be widely used. One example is the use of intelligence tests as entrance exams for schools or universities. In Britain, the **11-plus** test was once administered to pupils at the end of primary school in order to allocate them to a particular type of secondary. Now it rarely used, and generally, entrance tests have become less popular here. Entrance exams are still widely used internationally – the **SAT test** for university entry in the USA is among the best known and comprises verbal and mathematical test items.

Another use for intelligence tests is **streaming** (also called tracking) – a system of dividing pupils into sets/classes based on IQ or ability (rather than having mixed ability classes). Streaming is thought to lead to better attainment for the brightest pupils (Kulik & Kulik, 1992). It might be assumed that it stigmatises pupils in lower streams, as they are put into a lower ability group, sometimes at a young age. However, Liu *et al.* (2005) found that pupils who were streamed into lower classes had lower academic self-esteem initially, but after three years showed higher levels than their peers. They suggested that this might be due to the reduced pressure and competition compared to top classes.

Streaming that uses tests based on general intelligence fails to take into account the different types of intelligence discussed earlier in this chapter, disadvantaging some able pupils. In addition, Rosenthal and Jacobson (1968) demonstrated that streaming by IQ could lead to a **self-fulfilling prophecy** where pupils improve *because* of positive expectations – or get worse because of negative expectations. In their study, teachers were told which children were the brightest and those ones went on to increase in IQ – even though they had actually been selected at random by the researchers (see key study).

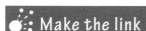

Discussion point

Is it a good idea to stream pupils into different classes, and if so, when should it be done? Do you have any personal experience of being streamed?

📖 Key study: Rosenthal and Jacobson (1968): the self-fulfilling prophecy in education

Aim: *The aim of the study was to determine the effect of teachers' predictions on pupils' IQ scores. Does a teacher's positive or negative expectation lead to a self-fulfilling prophecy?*

Method: *The researchers gave a non-verbal IQ test to all the children in an American elementary school (equivalent to a UK primary school) at the start of an academic year. They gave the teachers the names of 20% of pupils and told the teachers that these children had been identified as 'bloomers', meaning that they were likely to develop quickly over the coming session. In fact, the names had been picked randomly. The remaining 80% of children were the control group in the study. The researchers then administered a second IQ test eight months later, towards the end of the academic year.*

Findings: *The researchers measured IQ gains, that is, the amount by which their IQ scores increased between the first and the second test. Approximately 79% of children in the 'bloomers' experimental group had gained 10 IQ points or more, compared to around 49% of the control group. A few children had made very large gains of 30 IQ points or more – 21% of the experimental group had done so, compared to 5% of the control group. These differences were statistically significant.*

Make the link

…with the group expectations in Jane Elliott's classroom (see chapter 11).

The study found that high expectations caused children to perform better in IQ tests

Evaluation: This study helps to explain why students from poorer or stigmatised backgrounds do more poorly in education. It appears that if a teacher expects less of a pupil then they actually do worse, other things being equal, and that expectations of teachers, therefore, play a major role in outcomes. A weakness of the study is that we don't know how classroom processes interacted with teacher expectations. It would have been useful to include classroom observations to help identify what exactly the teachers did to encourage the 'bloomers'. In addition, performance on the second IQ test may have had more to do with motivation than intelligence. As the study looked just at IQ, it is hard to generalise the findings to attainment in specific subjects such as languages or sciences. It is also hard to generalise from elementary school children to older students.

Evaluation of IQ tests

IQ tests are thought to favour people from the same culture as the makers of the tests – that is, IQ testing is prone to **cultural bias**.

Any test can be evaluated in terms of **validity** and **reliability**:

- Validity means how well it measures what it sets out to measure.
- Reliability is the extent to which it gets consistent results.

IQ tests are often considered more reliable than tests of other factors that influence performance, such as interpersonal skills (Neisser *et al.*, 1996). People's IQ scores tend to stay roughly the same on repeated tests throughout childhood, when adjusted for age-based increases (Jones & Bayley, 1941).

However, the reliability of a test is less useful if the test does not measure what it aims to (i.e. if it lacks validity) – it can mean that a test is reliably wrong! There is disagreement about how valid IQ tests are, partly because there are disagreements as to what intelligence is. The correlation between IQ and performance in the workplace is low (Gladwell, 2010), supporting the idea that 'g' definitions of intelligence are narrow and neglect creative and practical intelligence. However, Sternberg (2003) does agree that IQ tests such as Raven's are a reasonable measure of the fluid intelligence component of 'g'.

? **Discussion point**

Why do you think Rosenthal and Jacobson used IQ tests for their study, rather than school tests of maths or spelling?

? **Discussion point**

Do you think that teacher expectations have affected your education at any point? And could students' expectations of teachers have a similar effect?

Make the link

...with the research by Ambady and Rosenthal (1992) in chapter 12. Find out more about the research careers of Robert Rosenthal and his colleagues.

⚷ Key concepts

- Intelligence tests
- Stanford Binet test
- Raven's progressive matrices
- Mental age
- Intelligence quotient
- 11-plus
- SAT test
- Streaming
- Self-fulfilling prophecy
- Cultural bias
- Validity
- Reliability

✔ Questions

1. Which two researchers worked on the first IQ test?

2. How is IQ calculated (in children)?

3. Name two IQ tests.

4. What is an advantage of Raven's progressive matrices?

5. What type(s) of intelligence do traditional intelligence tests fail to test for?

6. Name one type of question that is typically included in intelligence tests.

7. Name two educational uses for intelligence tests.

8. How long did Rosenthal and Jacobson's (1968) study last for?

9. What term is used to mean that tests give an advantage to some cultures and are unfair on others?

10. What term is used when tests consistently show the same results, time after time?

GO! Activities

1. Try to write your own intelligence items that are fair and unbiased. How can you be sure that you are really testing intelligence and not memory?

2. Find out about Sternberg and colleagues' 'WICS' model and how they propose it should be used for university entrance tests. What do you think of their example questions? Do you agree that this would be better than traditional tests such as the SAT?

GO! End of topic project

- As a group or with the whole class, run a study into the effects of growth and fixed mindsets on academic performance.
- One consideration is that classmates from psychology have an insight into mindsets due to studying the topic and this may bias your data. It would be best to use friends/family outside the class as your participants.
- Academic performance: decide on a way to measure this. You could use tests from the current academic year, or ask classmates what they achieved in their school exams or (for current students) in last year's exams, using a coding system (such as A grade = 3, B grade = 2 and C grade = 1), although this will only work for participants who were at school last year. Alternatively, devise your own test.
- Mindsets: decide on a way to measure this. You could use the examples in this book or on Dweck's website as a starting point and devise further questions on the same lines. You must be able to analyse the result so that people can be categorised into three groups: growth mindset/fixed mindset/mixed.
- You will need to get data from the same participants on both variables – academic performance and mindset. Once you have all of the data, calculate mean scores on the academic scores for each mindset group. These can then be plotted on a bar graph (see chapter 8).
- Make a poster showing your results!

✔ End of topic specimen exam questions

As this is an optional topic, exam questions will be quite general and will not name the topic or its specific theories/research studies, for example:

National 5

1. Explain a topic from Individual Behaviour other than sleep and dreams. 4 marks

2. From your chosen optional a topic in Individual Behaviour, name and describe one research study that has been carried out. Include the aim, method/procedure and results of the study. 6 marks

Higher

1. Choose a topic in Individual Behaviour other than sleep, dreams and sleep disorders. Explain how this topic can be applied in the real world. 10 marks

2. Explain a topic in Individual Behaviour other than sleep, dreams and sleep disorders, referring to at least two approaches. 16 marks

3. Discuss two theories relating to your chosen optional topic in Individual Behaviour. 12 marks

The total exam mark allocation for the Individual Behaviour unit will be 20 marks; however, there is no way of knowing in advance how this will be split between this topic and the topic of sleep.

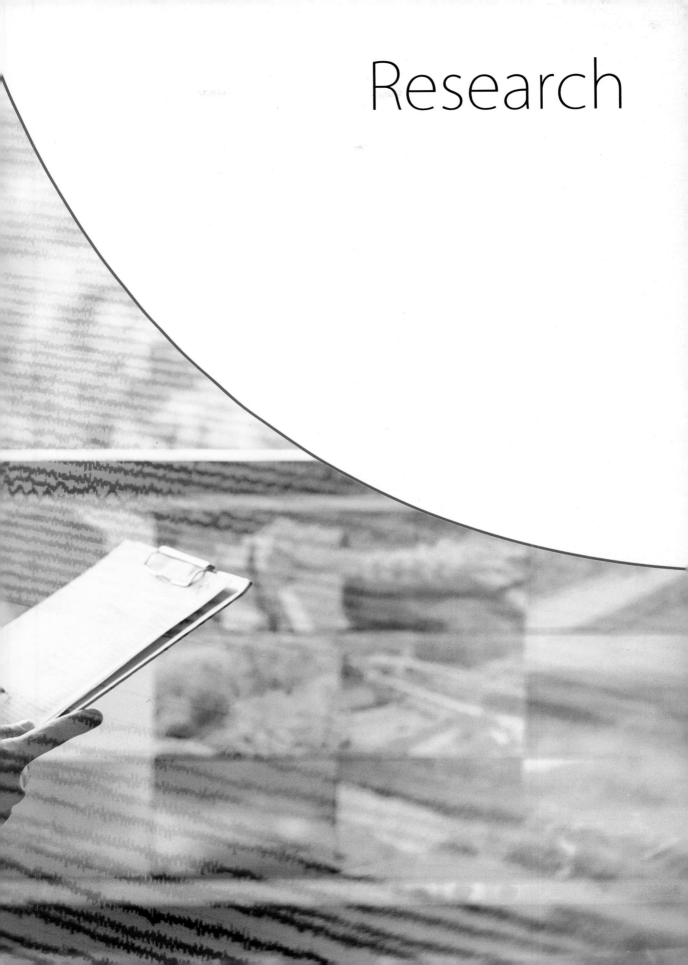

Research

8 Research

! Syllabus note

There is an important difference between Higher and National 5 in this topic. For National 5, you need to understand the following concepts in order to successfully conduct the Assignment. Use the following information to help you understand the research process and refer to it as you conduct and write up your Assignment. There is <u>not</u> a section on research in your exam.

However, at Higher, as well as using the knowledge and skills to conduct the Assignment, the topic of research methods <u>will</u> be in the exam. Therefore, you need to understand the key terminology in this chapter and use the practice questions to ensure that you have remembered the essential details. In addition, see the sample exam questions on research in the key skills section towards the end of this book.

The scientific method and the research process

The scientific method

The vast majority of academic psychology is based on the **scientific method**. This is the idea that theories must be backed up with valid, reliable evidence that has been gathered from practical research. This will be a theme throughout every topic in National 5 and Higher Psychology. Contrary to what you might hear from people outside the subject, psychology is not 'all common sense'! Even ideas that *seem* obvious need to be put to the test and confirmed with objective evidence.

The scientific method involves a cyclical **research process** of generating ideas, conducting practical research, analysing the findings of the research and then generating new ideas. This is the process by which we attempt to find out more about psychology and other subjects. We often take it for granted, but the scientific method is an incredibly powerful tool – Dartnell (2014) describes its *'knowledge-generating machinery'* as humanity's greatest invention. It has certainly contributed to our understanding of the world in all of the scientific subjects.

The scientific method involves practical research, such as experiments

Scientific standards

Although research in psychology is conducted on humans or animals, the same logical processes are followed as in the other sciences. This includes gaining empirical data and using statistics to analyse it. In addition, it must be possible to **replicate** studies (i.e. repeat them using the same methodology by other researchers, to test the findings).

Precise wording is important for researchers because we need to be clear about what we mean, and communicate ideas in such a way that others in the field will understand them. Even if you are new to the subject, you should try to use terminology accurately and consistently. It is worth bearing this in mind when people talk about scientific 'facts'. A fact in science is a piece of evidence that has been repeatedly confirmed. A theory is not the same is a fact. A **theory** is an idea that is supported by the current evidence – alternative ideas may have been rejected due to this evidence. Essentially, a theory is an explanation of how and why processes occur (Schmidt, 1992).

It is generally agreed that a theory should be stated in a way that can be tested. This means it must be possible to prove the theory wrong – it can't be so vague that no evidence could ever disprove it. If new evidence is found that the theory cannot explain, then one of two things can happen:

- The theory is changed to accommodate the new finding.
- The theory is abandoned in favour of a better theory.

Scientists also tend to avoid saying that theories have been 'proven', as it can only ever represent an explanation of the available facts. In the scientific method, a theory cannot be proven – although it can be disproven!

The research process

This leads to a research process of gathering data and developing/changing theories. The process goes through the following stages:

- **Generating a theory**. A statement is made about how a process in psychology (e.g. memory or prejudice) works.
- **Forming a research hypothesis**. From the theory, researchers make a prediction about what they will find in a particular situation.
- **Gathering data**. Researchers conduct experiments and gather data based on their prediction.
- **Analysing data**. The findings are analysed and compared to the hypothesis.
- **Publishing findings**. The data and analysis are published so that other scientists can comment on them.
- **Debating and amending theories**. If the evidence does not support the theory, it may need to be changed. However, usually findings must be replicated before anyone will accept the need to change a theory.

New hypotheses can be then generated from the (amended) theory, and so it goes on, in a cyclical process.

The process mentions the use of the experiment. This is in many ways the most useful research method, as it is highly controlled. However, there are four other major research methods described in this chapter that all contribute to our understanding of human behaviour – the observation, interview, case study and survey methods. These all have their limitations, but in combination can provide a range of evidence that contributes to the research process.

A key idea in research is that knowledge is **cumulative** – it builds up over time. No one research study is going to provide all of the answers but many individual studies each provide a piece of evidence that adds to our understanding.

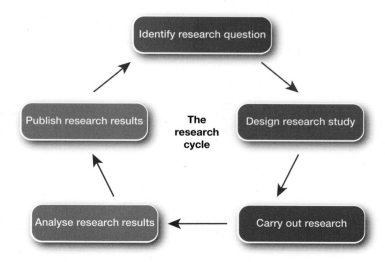

Revision of theories

Where does this research process end? Ideally, it ends with a full understanding of the particular issue – after major questions have been answered, researchers can move on to new questions and deal with those.

In practice, according to philosopher Karl Popper, the scientific method only leads to a progressively better understanding of an issue. This is in part because experiments cannot prove a theory to be true. They can only lead us to reject incorrect ideas. Therefore, the scientific community as a whole can move closer towards a better understanding of psychology (and other subjects) but never reach a perfect understanding of them.

Contemporary theories are, by definition, the best explanations that we have at present. We should just remember that every idea in science is open to being reconsidered, if new evidence becomes available.

Summary: the research process

In summary, psychology is based on the scientific method and research in the subject goes through a series of stages. These stages form a cycle, with theories being gradually improved over time. A theory represents the best available explanation of a psychological process, but there is always room for improvement, and any idea in science is open to evidence-based criticism.

☑ Questions

1. Can research studies prove a theory right or wrong?

2. Define a theory.

3. Why is psychology not confined to applying 'common sense'?

4. Which philosopher said that scientific understanding of an issue could never be perfect?

5. Is it ok to criticise theories?

6. What are the main research methods used in psychology?

7. What process comes after generating a hypothesis?

8. What is meant by knowledge being 'cumulative'?

9. Does it matter if research findings can be replicated or not?

10. What is the final stage of the research process?

☛ Key concepts

- Scientific method
- Research process
- Replication
- Theory
- Cumulative

Populations and samples

What is a sample?

The people that a psychology researcher studies are collectively known as a **sample.** They are drawn from a larger group known as a **population**.

A 'population' does not have to mean the entire population of the country (or the world) – the term can refer to any specific group such as workers, students, pensioners, the unemployed, etc. The population that a particular study is interested in is called the **target population**.

Sampling means selecting people to take part in your research. There are two logical steps:

- Define the target population that you want to study. Perhaps you live in Dundee and you want to do a survey on elderly people in your city.

- Unless the target population is very small, you can't study all of them. Therefore, you pick a smaller group from this population – the 'sample' – and conduct the research on them. A good sample will have three key features:

  - it should be **unbiased**

  - it should be **representative** of the population as a whole

  - it should be **large**

The people that a psychology researcher studies are collectively known as a sample

Being representative means that the sample should contain the same variety of people and behaviours as found in the target population.

This is less likely to happen if the sample is biased, that is, distorted by having too many/too few people from certain groups within the target population. For example, if your target population is people in their 20s, and you obtain your sample in a university library, the sample will be biased by including lots of students and very few people from other occupations.

A large sample is always better – it helps to even out random error and stop results being distorted by individual differences among participants. There is no perfect size for a sample but the larger the better.

? Discussion point

Think of how the term 'sample' is used in other areas such as geography, medicine, or just in everyday life. Does it have a similar meaning?

Generalising from a sample

If you have studied geography/geology and collected rock samples, the concept of sampling is logically similar. Rather than taking the whole rock/mountain, you collected a small piece and studied that. The problems are also similar. What if the area of the mountain that you collected the rock sample from just happened to have a different type of rock than 99% of the mountain? The problem is that the sample is not representative of the whole, and so, the results of the study on that rock sample can't be **generalised** to the whole mountain.

It is very similar in psychology. Imagine you want to conduct research into elderly people in the UK. If you selected a sample of elderly people by asking your grandmother's friends, they might not be representative of the whole population. Perhaps they are in better health or better educated than the average. Perhaps they are not as ethnically diverse as the whole population. If your sample is not representative of the population, then what you find out about the sample might not be true of the target population – making the research less valid (see 'external validity', page 233).

Top tip

People commonly mistake the words 'bias' and 'biased', perhaps because they sound very similar when spoken. Remember – bias is a noun and biased is an adjective. As discussed in the previous section, it is important for researchers to use language accurately!

How to select a sample

There are several sampling methods to choose from, each with strengths and weaknesses:

Opportunity sampling

An **opportunity sample** means a sample that is chosen based on convenience. This could be done by asking members of your class to take part in an experiment, or asking friends, or approaching strangers who walk past in the street and asking them to complete a survey. The sample may not be representative at all, because the researcher just uses whoever is easily available. This tends to lead to a biased sample but it is often used because it is quick and easy to do.

- Strength(s): usually the quickest and easiest sampling method – it is based on convenience.
- Weakness(es): suffers from bias – some members of the population will be under-represented. Researchers may be unconsciously biased when they choose people to ask.

Opportunity sampling could involve recruiting strangers in the street

? Discussion point

If you gather your sample by approaching people who walk past your classroom/lecture theatre, what kind of biases might there be in the sample?

Random sampling

A **random sample** means that everyone in the population studies has *an equal chance of being chosen*. This is a lot more difficult than it sounds! How do you ensure that everyone has exactly the same chance? Putting all the names into a hat might work, but it is not practical if there are thousands or even millions of names. Psychologists typically use **random number** software, together with a numbered list of every member of the population.

It may be that a random sample is not perfectly representative of the target population just by chance, but this method avoids any systematic bias and so it is generally considered the ideal method of sampling to use in most situations. However, the people who have been randomly selected may not want to take part in the study, leading to a high refusal/drop-out rate. In short, this is a very good method of sampling but it has many practical problems.

- Strengths: the best way of ensuring a representative sample.
- Weaknesses: time-consuming to carry out and people chosen may not be willing to take part.

Self-selecting sampling

A **self-selecting sample** (or 'volunteer sample') means that participants come forward of their own choice, responding to an advert or email request for participants. The key defining feature is that they come to you, rather than you selecting them. If you put up a sign asking for people to contact you/come to a lab at a particular time to be tested, then you are obtaining a self-selecting sample. Milgram's (1963) study of obedience (see chapter 10) used people who responded to a newspaper advert – a self-selecting sample.

Advertising for participants would result in a self-selecting sample

This type of sampling is simple to arrange but the sample may be biased because participants may differ from other members of the population in various ways, for example, by being more interested in helping scientific research, being more generally helpful ('pro-social') than others or just having more free time. They may also be more in need of the money paid to participants, resulting in a bias in the occupation/income level of the sample. Another cause of bias is that the sign/advert/email may not be seen by everyone – for example, the sample might contain an unrepresentative number of people who read newspapers.

- Strengths: a simple way to get a large number of participants. People want to take part, making it ethically sound.
- Weaknesses: people who come forward may not be representative of the population, for example by being more pro-social. In addition, the placement of the sign/advert asking for volunteers may lead to bias.

Systematic sampling

A **systematic sample** involves picking people at fixed intervals from a list of the whole population. For example, if you have a list of 1,000 students in your year and you pick every 20th name, you will obtain a systematic sample of 50 participants in total. Going through the telephone directory and picking the top person from each page would also be systematic. Another means of conducting systematic sampling would be to do it over a particular time and place, for example, asking every 10th person who walks past you in the street. The main reason for sampling this way is that it removes any choice from the experimenter, eliminating **researcher bias** – the tendency for researchers, often unintentionally, to distort research results through their actions.

Picking the the person at the top of each page of the phone book would be systematic sampling

- Strengths: it is generally a representative sample. Avoids researcher bias and avoids the biases of self-selecting samples.
- Weaknesses: The list chosen (e.g. phone book) may be incomplete, therefore, excluding some members of the population. If done in the real world (e.g. asking every 10th person) then it suffers from some of the drawbacks of opportunity sampling.

Make the link

Do you carry out research on people in your other subjects? If so, how are your samples obtained?

Stratified sampling

With a **stratified sample**, the researcher makes sure that key groups within the population are represented fairly within the sample, such as by selecting a 50:50 mix of males and females. The exact details of this may depend on what is important to the research. If religious belief is an important aspect of a study then researchers might ensure that their sample has the same proportions of religions as the population as a whole.

However, stratified sampling is not a complete sampling method and it must be combined with another method. For example, if you decided to pick 12 males and 12 females, you must then apply some other sampling method, for example opportunity sampling, to actually obtain these participants. It ensures a representative sample but only in the identified areas; in other areas, for example personality, they may not be representative.

Picking an equal number of men and women to take part in a study would be stratified sampling

- Strengths: helps to make a sample more representative in key variables, for example sex, religion, ethnic background.
- Weaknesses: the sample might be representative in terms of sex or religion but still unrepresentative in other ways, for example in occupation. It is not a complete sampling method – it must be combined with another method, and therefore, suffers from the drawbacks of whatever other method is used.

Quota sample

A **quota sample** is similar to stratified sampling, but here, the researchers specify numbers of participants from the key groups/ categories and then fill these 'quotas'. This helps to ensure representation of minority groups. Unlike stratified sampling, the researchers do not try to keep the proportions of each group the same as those in the population. For example, a quota sample may require a minimum of five people from every major religion; this would avoid missing out groups that have a very tiny population, and therefore,

Quota sampling might be used to ensure a numer of categories are represented by the sample

Top tip

For the Assignment, students often combine quota sampling with opportunity sampling. For example, if you aim to find 20 male participants and 20 female participants, then you could pick people leaving the school/college library until you have reached those numbers.

might not be included in a stratified sample at all because they make up less than 1% of the target population.

Again, quota sampling is not a complete sampling method – once the quotas have been set, some other method (e.g. opportunity sampling) must be used in order to fill the quotas.

- Strengths: helps to ensure small minority groups are represented within a sample.
- Weaknesses: does not always result in a representative sample as proportions of small groups are distorted. It is not a complete sampling method – it must be combined with another method, and therefore suffers from the drawbacks of whatever other method is used.

Key concepts

- Sample
- Population
- Target population
- Sampling
- Bias
- Researcher bias
- Representative
- Generalising
- Opportunity sample
- Random sample
- Random numbers
- Self-selecting sample
- Systematic sample
- Stratified sample
- Quota sample

Questions

1. What is meant by a 'sample' in psychology research?

2. Which is bigger – the target population or the sample?

3. How large should a sample be?

4. Why is it important for a sample to be representative?

5. Which methods of sampling are least likely to produce a biased sample?

6. Is a random sample always representative of the target population?

7. State three features of a good sample.

8. Why is random sampling often considered the best sampling method?

9. Why is quota sampling not a 'complete' method of sampling?

10. Which method of sampling is better at ensuring that the size of groups within the sample are proportionate to the size of groups within the target population – stratified or systematic?

Activities

1. Which, if any, of the following methods would guarantee you a random sample? Discuss them with your classmates:
   - Picking every 100th name out of the phone book.
   - Putting all target population names into a box and pulling 10 out.
   - Writing a list of names on a sheet of paper and putting a pin in with your eyes shut.
   - Picking people 'at random' from the street or corridor.
2. Find out about the sampling methods used in at least two research studies in different topics in psychology. What effect might the sampling method have had on their results? Are particular types of sampling more common and/or more suitable in particular topics? Write a short explanation.
3. Try out sampling in the classroom by picking coloured sweets from a bag. What can you do to ensure a representative sample in terms of different colours? Try experimenting with different proportions of sweets in your 'population', for example 5% red, 20% blue, 75% yellow sweets.

Experimental methods

What is an experiment?

Experiments are the main tool of the scientific method. Every experiment involves making a comparison between two or more things, in order to find out something about them and to uncover an objective piece of evidence.

The logic of an experiment is that if you change one thing and keep everything else the same, then any difference must have occurred because of the thing that you changed. In other words, you change one **variable**, and try to measure its effect on another variable, while keeping everything else constant. Therefore, experiments aim to study **cause and effect**.

A variable can be any aspect of behaviour, for example heart rate or any stimulus that affects behaviour (e.g. noise). The two key variables in any experiment are:

- The IV: **independent** variable (the variable that the experimenter changes).
- The DV: **dependent** variable (the variable that the experimenter measures).

Sometimes primary school children run a simple experiment where they put one plant in a dark place and another on a windowsill. The result? If everything else is kept the same, the one on the windowsill grows more and is greener. This result may seem obvious to us nowadays, but such experiments throughout history have allowed researchers to uncover previously unknown facts in science, such as the presence of chlorophyll in plant leaves.

? Discussion point

In the example experiment with the plants, what variables need to be kept constant? (Hint: things to do with the plant and environmental conditions...)

Conditions of the IV

Every experiment involves a comparison. In order to make a comparison, there must be two or more experimental **conditions** – parts of the experiment that are different. For example, if you want to study the effect of background noise on revision, you would have a low noise condition and a high noise condition, and compare the effect on people's exam scores. The IV in this example would be noise and the DV would be how well they perform in the test/exam.

Conditions are determined by the IV. Sometimes there is only one **experimental condition**, so the researchers use a **control condition** too. It establishes a baseline by measuring how things are under relatively normal circumstances.

Other variables

As you have seen, an experiment manipulates an IV to see what effect it has on the DV. In order to be sure that the IV is actually affecting the DV, everything else needs to be kept constant.

A well-designed study will keep the effect of other variables to a minimum or ideally eliminate them altogether. Outside variables that may cause random errors in results are called **extraneous variables**. These include environmental variables, such as background noise, and participant variables – differences between participants such as intelligence.

The independent variable is the noise level

Example experiment 1

A student research team are testing the effect of caffeine on short-term memory. In one condition, participants will be given a fairly high level of caffeine and in another condition they will be given no caffeine. To control for extraneous variables and demand characteristics, they decide to give the caffeine in the form of a mug of coffee and to give the control condition a mug of decaffeinated coffee without telling participants which one they are getting. An opportunity sample – students from a nearby class – are tested over two days. One day they get the normal coffee and then five minutes later do a memory test. The following day they are given the decaffeinated coffee and then five minutes later do a different memory test.

Does caffeine affect short-term memory?

Some variables cannot be eliminated. For example, a researcher cannot avoid the fact that participants have different personalities and life experiences or that they may be tired or in a bad mood. A researcher will try to keep the effects of such variables to a minimum by designing the experiment well but there will always be some **random error**.

However, if an extraneous variable influences one condition more than the other, it becomes a **confounding variable**. It then becomes difficult or impossible to know what causes a change in the results – the IV or the confounding variable.

In example experiment 1 (see p.212), participants may respond differently to caffeine. This is an extraneous variable but it is not a confounding variable, because the same participants are used in both conditions.

In example experiment 2 (see p.216), if the experimental group who used the memory strategy were also given more time to study the material, then *study time* would be a confounding variable. If the experimental group did better, it would be impossible to know whether this was due to the memory strategy or just because they had more time to learn the material.

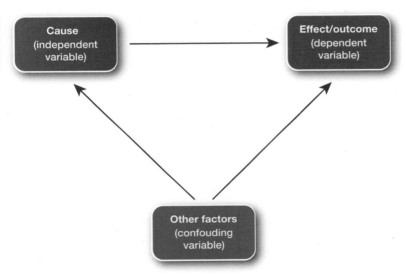

If there is a confounding variable, it is impossible to know which variable caused a change in results

Design

Design has a very specific meaning in the experimental method – it means the way in which participants are allocated to the different experimental conditions. There are two main options: either participants take part in every condition – a **repeated measures** design – or they are divided up into groups and each group completes one condition – an **independent groups** design.

Repeated measures

In a repeated measures design, every participant completes every condition. However, it is important to **counterbalance** the order in which participants complete the conditions. If there are two conditions, half will do condition 1 first and then condition 2, while the other half will do condition 2 first and then complete condition 1. Failure to counterbalance would lead to **order effects** – people will do better

In a repeated measures design, every participant completes every condition

An independent groups design uses two entirely separate groups of participants

(or worse) in later conditions than they did in the first condition, due to practice or fatigue/boredom. Counterbalancing helps to balance out order effects between conditions but does not eliminate them.

The main advantage of this design is that participants' scores in one condition are being compared with the same participants' scores in another condition, rather than comparing two separate groups of people. This reduces the effect of a particular type of extraneous variable – **participant variables**. These are things that vary from one participant to the next, such as personality and ability levels.

In repeated measures studies, order effects can be a problem, and **demand characteristics** are likely. This means that participants will alter their behaviour according to perceived requirements of the situation, in particular, to a researcher's wishes. According to Orne (1962), participants who do two or more conditions will find it easy to guess the study's aims and will modify their behaviour to fit expectations.

Independent groups

An independent groups design, as mentioned above, uses two entirely separate groups of participants. It is not ideal to compare two separate groups of individuals – the main reason for doing so is when a repeated measures study is not possible, for example, if there is an element of deception that would make the aims of the study obvious if participants did both conditions. This is the case in some conformity and obedience experiments – the same participants could not have been used in more than one condition of Milgram's experiment, as they would have realised the second time around that the electric shocks were fake (see chapter 10).

For an independent groups design, there needs to be one group for every condition, and therefore, the total number of participants in each condition is smaller with this design, especially if there are many conditions. For example, if you have selected a sample of 28 students and there are four conditions, then only seven would take part in each condition. In a repeated measures design on the other hand, all 28 complete every condition, resulting in more data overall.

Another limitation of the independent groups design is that with completely different individuals in each condition, the results can be strongly influenced by participant variables. It is possible that participants in one condition do better compared to those in the other, not because of the IV, but because they are different individuals and they just happen to be better at the task.

Matched participants

To minimise participant variables when a repeated measures design is not an option, a third experimental design is sometimes used – **matched participants**. This is essentially very similar to independent groups, except that each participant is matched up with one or more others and these matched (similar) participants are then allocated to separate conditions. For example, participants could be paired up with someone who is very close to them in age, and then from each pair, one person will be put into the first condition, and the other into the second condition.

There are many variables on which participants could be matched, for example age, sex, IQ and personality type. The choice of what to match will depend on what is being studied, and therefore, what extraneous variables especially need to be controlled. In a memory experiment it may be a good idea to match participants on their memory ability before they take part to ensure that participants in the different conditions have similar ability levels. However, to do so makes a study more time consuming and it might not be practical if participants are recruited gradually over a long period of time.

> **○ Top tip**
>
> Remember that if asked about 'design' in the exam, you should focus on repeated measures/independent groups/ matched participants and **not** on other aspects of the study such as variables.

In a matched participants design, each participant is matched with the participant from the sample that is most similar to themselves. In the following simplified example, six participants are given a memory test, with a maximum score of 50. They are then matched up – Lauren and Leah form one pair, Jim and Adil the second pair, and Roisin and Duncan the third pair:

Jim: 28

Adil: 34

Lauren: 18

Roisin: 41

Leah: 10

Duncan: 43

Pair 1: Lauren and Leah

Pair 2: Jim and Adil

Pair 3: Roisin and Duncan

In a matched participant design participants are grouped with others who are similar to them in a specific way

Types of experimental design			
Type	**Description**	**Advantage**	**Disadvantage**
Repeated measures design	The same participants do all conditions of an experiment	Participant variables kept to a minimum	Order effects and demand characteristics
Independent groups design	A separate group of participants in each condition	No order effects – participant only does one condition	Participant variables
Matched participants	Matching pairs/groups of participants, then dividing them between conditions	Avoids order effects and controls some participant variables	Time consuming and not always practical to conduct

Example experiment 2

A researcher wants to know whether a memory technique will improve students' grades. She recruits 40 volunteer 16-year-old school pupils during the summer holidays. She randomly picks 20 to be the experimental group and 20 to be the control group. Those in the experimental group are taught the memory strategy and then given 10 pages of information about satellites and space travel to learn. The control group are given the same material to learn but are not taught the memory strategy. Both groups are told that they will be tested on their memory for the information after two weeks.

Those in the experimental group are taught the memory strategy

Random allocation

In example experiment 2, the researcher randomly chose half of the participants to do condition one and the other half to do condition two. Any true experiment must **randomly allocate** participants to conditions. In an independent groups study, the researcher allocates every participant to one of the experimental conditions randomly, for example, by tossing a coin to see whether they go in condition one or condition two. In a matched design, each matched participant is randomly allocated to one of the available conditions (if there are just two conditions, then one member of the pair is randomly selected for condition one and the second is then assigned to condition two).

A repeated measures study is slightly different because everyone does all of the conditions. However, randomisation is still necessary. Here the researcher must decide randomly which condition each participant does *first*.

In *example experiment 2*, the researcher starts with 40 volunteers and then randomly puts 20 into each of the two groups. This could be done by putting the names into a hat and drawing them out or by tossing a coin. In practice, though, most researchers would prefer to use a computerised random number generator. The participants could be numbered 1 to 40, and then a computer programme could generate a list of the numbers 1 to 40 in a random order. The first 20 are put in one condition and the next 20 into the other.

Note that random allocation to conditions is <u>not</u> the same thing as random sampling. Experiments using other types of sample, such as opportunity, should still randomly allocate participants to conditions.

? Discussion point

Why is random allocation necessary in a true experiment? (See p.409 for feedback.)

○ Top tip

Try the website http://www.random.org/sequences to set a maximum number and then generate all of the numbers in a random order.

It might occur to you that random allocation does not guarantee that the participants in the two conditions are the same as each other, and you would be right – as mentioned above, there could be participant variables that affect the findings. It might happen just by random chance that the participants in an experimental condition are superior in some way to those in the control condition. In *example experiment 2*, the experimental group might have done better on the test anyway, regardless of whether they had used the memory technique or not. However, this chance is small (especially with a large group of participants) and a small amount of random error is accounted for in statistical tests. The important thing is that random allocation avoids systematic bias.

Lab or field?

Every experiment is conducted either in a controlled environment (laboratory) or in a natural environment (the 'field'). These are called **laboratory experiments** and **field experiments**:

- Laboratory ('lab') experiment: conducted in any controlled, artificial environment.
- Field experiment: conducted in the participants' natural environment, for example, home or the workplace.

There is no universally agreed standard for what a lab should look like; typically, it will be a plain room with no distractions – it is best if it does not have a window, as the researcher cannot control what might happen outside. A typical lab experiment would be conducted in a small room with a computer on a simple desk. Of course, some lab experiments might need more elaborate apparatus.

An advantage of lab experiments is that environmental variables are controlled. With no distractions, random error is reduced, allowing the researcher to conclude that any changes in their DV are due to the manipulation of the IV.

The disadvantage of any lab-based study (not just lab experiments) is that being in an artificial environment, they lack **ecological validity** – participants may not behave in the same way in the lab as they would in their everyday life.

Most research that you will conduct in your school, college or at home will involve field experiments. The field experiment has the opposite strengths and weaknesses of a lab experiment: ecological validity is higher, as participants behave more naturally in their usual surroundings, but environmental variables are not controlled. It is possible that noise or other distractions could affect the findings, reducing their reliability.

A lab where a psychology experiment could be carried out

? Discussion point

Should *example experiment 2* be conducted as a lab or a field experiment?

🔍 Top tip

All true experiments are artificial because the situation is set up by the researchers. However, they are more artificial if they use a controlled setting (lab) and/or an unrealistic task. Compare the observation method described in the following sections and consider why it might be preferred to an experiment in some circumstances.

It would be unethical to deliberately cause stress to pregnant women

Other types of experiment

A **quasi-experiment** (meaning 'partial experiment') is in most respects the same as a true experiment. It could take place either in a lab or in the field. However, there is something fundamental about the design that means that it lacks the control of a true experiment. The most common reason is that the IV is something that is fixed in a participant or otherwise cannot be controlled, and it is therefore impossible to randomly allocate participants to experimental or control conditions. Examples include:

- comparisons of males versus females
- comparison of extraverts versus introverts (or any other personality difference)
- comparison of vegetarians versus meat eaters

Because there is not full control over the IV, participants are in pre-existing groups rather than being randomly allocated. This means that there is no randomisation of extraneous participant variables either. There could be a confounding variable.

A **natural experiment** is not controlled by a researcher at all but the structure resembles an experiment – one variable changes and another is measured. However, the IV and DV occur naturally and all the researcher does is measure and analyse the DV. This might happen for ethical or practical reasons. For example, Nuckolls *et al.* (1972) studied the effect of high or low levels of social support on the health of women who were stressed during pregnancy (see chapter 6). They studied women who naturally experienced either a high or a low level of stress, because it would have been unethical to deliberately cause stress to pregnant women. The researchers also did not provide social support. These variables were naturally occurring.

In the Nuckolls study, it is possible to treat social support like an IV and health outcomes like a DV, but important to remember that with no control and no random allocation, this is not a true experiment – confounding variables cannot be ruled out and we cannot be certain that one variable caused a change in the other.

✔ Questions

1. What type of experiment uses controlled conditions?

2. Name the two variables that an experimenter manipulates and measures.

3. Which experimental design uses the same participants in every condition?

4. Which of the following is a key feature of all true experiments – being in a lab or control over variables?

5. Complete the following sentence: 'The most important feature of the experimental method is that it allows a researcher to establish…'.

6. Give a weakness of the experimental method.

7. What is the difference between a field experiment and a natural experiment?

8. What is the difference between a natural experiment and a quasi-experiment?

9. A researcher testing the effect of music on memory uses four different types of music. They also want to have a control group which does a memory test in silence. How many experimental conditions will they use in total?

10. Name three common examples of extraneous variables.

●━ Key concepts

- Variable
- Cause and effect
- Independent variable (IV)
- Dependent variable (DV)
- Conditions
- Experimental condition
- Control condition
- Extraneous variables
- Confounding variables
- Random error
- Experimental design
- Repeated measures
- Independent groups
- Counterbalance
- Participant variables
- Order effects
- Demand characteristics
- Matched participants
- Random allocation
- Laboratory experiment
- Field experiment
- Ecological validity
- Artificiality
- Quasi-experiment
- Natural experiment

GO! Activities

1. List all of the possible extraneous variables in the following study. How could they have been controlled?

   Abid, Gemma and Kirstie are 20-year-old students investigating gender differences in IQ estimates and each of them selects two participants – Gemma chooses her brother and sister. Abid selects his mother and father, as does Kirstie. Each asks these participants to estimate their own IQ. Abid asks this question at home; the others ask the question when out shopping. The group thus obtain six sets of data – three from male participants and three from female participants.

2. Briefly explain in your own words the difference between an extraneous variable and a confounding variable. Give examples.

3. Look at example experiment 2 in the section above. Identify the method (type of experiment) used, the design, the IV and DV. Are there any extraneous or confounding variables that the researcher has to consider?

4. Imagine you are going to conduct an experiment to see whether sleep affects memory for a skill. You will compare two groups of participants – one will train on the skill once before sleep and once after a night's sleep. The other will train on the same task twice in the same day, without sleeping in-between. Everyone will be tested after the second training session to see how well they have learned the skill.
   - What skill would you use and why?
   - What issues are there in terms of selecting a sample? Are there any people you would avoid using?
   - What extraneous variables would you have to control for? That is, what things would have to be kept constant for both groups? Think of as many as possible.

5. Look for examples of the four main types of experiments and the three experimental designs in other chapters of this book. Can you find at least one example of each? Take a note of your examples and compare them with a classmate.

Non-experimental methods

Experiments are arguably the best method to use in most situations, as they allow the researcher control over variables. However, sometimes behaviour in an experiment may differ from their real everyday behaviour because of the artificiality of experiments. In other cases, it is impractical or unethical to run an experiment. For example, it would be unethical to run an experiment into the effect of pollution on a person's behaviour by deliberately exposing an experimental group to high levels of pollution. Therefore, it is helpful to have the option of using other, **non-experimental methods** on occasion.

The main non-experimental methods you should be aware of include:

- survey
- interview
- case study
- observation

Surveys and interviews

A **survey** involves handing out a list of questions – a **questionnaire** – to participants, usually a very large sample of participants. An **interview** is conducted face-to-face, but otherwise has certain key similarities – in particular, both gather data by asking questions to participants.

You may have already come across versions of these methods outside of Psychology, for example in job interviews and marketing surveys. In scientific studies, such as psychological research, however, the design of interviews and questionnaires needs to be especially careful to avoid misleading participants or introducing bias.

A questionnaire is a non-experimental method

> ### 🔎 Top tip
>
> Often students use the terms 'experiment' and 'case study' to refer to any type of research study. Try to use terminology precisely – don't call something an experiment if it actually uses a non-experimental method and vice versa.

Writing the questions

For both surveys and interviews, questions will be carefully considered and written out in advance. Good question wording is essential in gathering valid and reliable data. There are various pitfalls that a researcher must avoid, as shown in the following table:

Issue	Explanation	Bad example question	Improved example question
Leading questions	This kind of question 'leads' participants to pick a particular response, often by using strongly emotional language.	'Do you think that buying a new car from a car dealer is a complete waste of money?'	'Do you think that buying a new car from a car dealer represents value for money?'
Loaded questions	A 'loaded' question includes an unwarranted assumption, perhaps reflecting bias on the part of the researcher. The following example includes an assumption that *some* immigrants should be prevented from accessing benefits and it is therefore not neutral.	'Do you think that all immigrants should be prevented from claiming housing benefit?'	'Do you think that any immigrants should be prevented from claiming housing benefit?'
Jargon	A question should use everyday language, avoiding technical terms that a participant might not understand.	'Do you struggle to focus your attention on brief cognitive tasks?'	'Do you sometimes lose concentration after revising for 10 to 15 minutes?'
Avoid vague/ambiguous language	The question should be as clear and specific as possible, avoiding statements that could be interpreted in different ways by different participants.	'Are some age laws of this country problematic?'	'Should the legal age for driving be raised from 17 to 18?'

Types of questions

Questions fall into two main categories: **open questions** (also called 'open-ended questions') and **closed questions**. Open questions allow the respondent to use their own words in response, whereas closed questions provide a selection of answers – yes/no, or a set of options. Some interviews/surveys use a mixture of both.

Generally closed questions are easier to analyse but don't allow people to express themselves as fully – this is a trade-off between detail and ease of analysis (see the following section, page 238, for a discussion of qualitative and quantitative data).

One of the most common type of closed question is the **Likert scale**. This is where a question is followed by a numerical scale, for example, 1–5 or 1–7, often labelled from 'strongly agree' to 'strongly disagree'.

Strongly Disagree	Disagree	Undecided	Agree	Strongly Agree
(1)	(2)	(3)	(4)	(5)

The Likert scale

Bias

Even if questions are carefully worded, there is the possibility that data gathered will be biased in some way. Two of the main reasons for this are as follows:

- **Acquiescence bias**: some participants tend to agree more than disagree, regardless of the question. For example, if asked 'do you have a good memory' a participant may say 'yes', but the same participant may also agree if asked, 'are you always forgetting things?' It is therefore important to have a balance of both positive and negative questions on the same issue.

- **Social desirability bias**: participants may distort the truth in order to look good. For example, if asked whether they are prejudiced, most participants will say 'no', even though their opinions and behaviour may indicate otherwise.

Distributing a survey

With a survey, the questionnaire is designed in advanced and then sent to participants. All potential problems must be thought of beforehand, as the researcher will not be there to guide participants when they fill in the questionnaire. It is important for questions to be clear and it helps if the questionnaire is fairly short – if it takes too long to complete, participants may give up and stop filling it in.

The questionnaire must then be distributed to participants. In the past, this would typically have been done by post, but it is now very common to use internet-based questionnaires.

> **🔍 Top tip**
> A Likert scale is a good way to gather numerical data for your Assignment if you are using a survey.

> **⚇ Make the link**
> …between research bias and bias in a sample.

> **🔍 Top tip**
> A popular tool for creating online surveys can be found at www.surveymonkey.com. There is a free version that is ideal for students.

A questionnaire

Types of interview

The key characteristic of the interview is that questions are asked face-to-face, making research more time consuming, but allowing misunderstandings to be clarified. Interviews can be divided into three main types:

- A **structured interview** uses a fixed list of questions that will have been carefully planned as described above. It is similar to a survey, except that it is conducted face-to-face; the interviewer will not to go beyond the questions on the list, except to make clarifications. They mainly use closed questions. Structured interviews are useful when interviewing a large number of participants.

- A **semi-structured interview** also uses a set list of questions but allows the interviewer some freedom to expand on these. The interviewer may ask the respondent to elaborate on some answers, prompting them with simple follow up questions, such as 'Can you tell me more about…?'

- An **unstructured interview** does not stick to a fixed list of questions, allowing the interviewer to vary the questioning depending on how a participant responds. It is more like a natural conversation. Many open questions will be used, providing rich, detailed data. However, responses are difficult to analyse and there is a danger of researcher bias.

As well as being used as the main method of research, interviews are also used in combination with other methods. For example, a participant may answer a short interview at the beginning or end of an experiment.

Observation

Observation is another major research method that can be used either on its own or in combination with other methods. Most experiments involve an element of observation but a typical observation study is less controlled than an experiment and it gathers data from watching behaviour as it happens. For example, you could observe a classmate as they are revising, and take notes on body language and how much time they spend looking at books/writing/looking at their phone, etc.

In an interview questions are asked face-to-face

There are certain key design considerations when conducting an observational study:

Naturalistic versus structured

A **naturalistic observation** involves simply watching and recording whatever unfolds in a natural, everyday situation. Naturalistic observation is the only method in psychology that gathers data on spontaneous behaviour as it happens. However, it lacks control over the many variables that could influence a person's behaviour. It is also impossible to replicate because the situation is natural and not set up by the researcher.

An alternative is to put participants into a lab and observe them doing a task – a **structured observation**. Here there is more control, and the situation could be replicated. One fairly common example is to set up a lab with particular toys/games and observe a child playing. A structured observation is more controlled but it may lack ecological validity – participants may not behave the same way in a lab as they would in an everyday situation.

Observation is another major research method

Disclosed versus undisclosed observation

Any observation can be either **disclosed** – participants know they are being observed – or **undisclosed** – kept secret. Disclosing the observation has the problem that if people know they are being watched, the presence of the observer may affect the results (would you behave the same way when revising if a classmate was observing you?) This is known as the **observer effect**.

Undisclosed observation provides more natural results. However, undisclosed observation may be unethical, as participants haven't consented to take part in the research. It is never ethically acceptable to make secret observations of people in private, although some ethical codes accept observation in public places, where people would expect to be observed by strangers (British Psychological Society, 2009). For example, a researcher might conduct an observation

Top tip

Ethics are highly important in research. Do **not** make undisclosed observations or recordings of other people for your Assignment. Discuss all research procedures with your teacher/lecturer before starting to gather data.

Top tip

Unless otherwise stated, descriptions of the observation method usually refer to naturalistic, non-participant observations.

? Discussion point

What could be included in an observation schedule to use on fellow students to find out what behaviours take place while eating? What about for observing behaviours in the corridor?

into the behaviour of sportspeople during a match/competition without disclosing the research beforehand (it would still be best to ask for consent retrospectively).

One way of reducing the observer effect while still disclosing the observation to participants is to use discretely placed video cameras. As cameras are less intrusive, behaviour may be more natural. Another way is to spend some time allowing participants to get used to the observer before starting to gather data.

Participant versus non-participant

In the example described at the start of this section, the researcher is on the outside and does not influence the situation, rather like watching birds or animals through a pair of binoculars. This is called **non-participant observation**. By staying out of the situation, the researcher tries to avoid directly influencing participants' behaviour. However, as described above, they may still affect results because of the observer effect, if the observation is disclosed.

In **participant observation**, however, researchers take part in the social situation and interact with the people that they are observing, resulting in a more natural situation. In a classic example of a participant observation, a researcher and his colleagues pretended to be hearing voices in their heads and they were admitted to a psychiatric hospital (Rosenhan, 1973; see chapter 4). They then took part in ordinary hospital activities, observing how psychiatric patients are treated by hospital staff.

Participant observation gives the observer a unique insight into a social situation and participants can more easily get used to their presence. However, it can lead to subjectivity, as the researcher becomes personally involved in the situation.

Participant observation can be either disclosed or undisclosed.

Observation schedules

Some observation studies use a list of key behaviours called an **observation schedule**. This may require the observer to tick key behaviours each time they occur or take note of what happens during a particular time period. By focusing the observer's attention on particular things, they help in gathering the data that the researchers are looking for and avoiding distractions. They may provide an objective timescale as well.

By providing an objective standard, observation schedules can also improve the reliability of recordings taken by more than one observer. Reliability means that results are consistent across different occasions and **inter-observer reliability** means the extent to which two observers produce the same results when looking at the same data. This is never perfect, but well-trained observers using observation schedules usually display high inter-observer reliability.

An observation schedule

Case studies

A case study is another example of a non-experimental research method. It is an **in-depth** study, which is usually based on one individual but could also be conducted on a small group such as a family or team. Case studies were famously used by Freud to build up his psychoanalytic theories (see chapter 2).

A case study is generally **longitudinal**, that is, it follows the individual or group over an extended period of time. Rich, detailed information is built up, including a range of historical information such as family details, education, relationships and employment. In this way, the researcher builds up a full picture of the participant(s). This would include any brain injury or psychological trauma, if relevant to the case. This background information in a case study is called a **case history**.

Case studies typically use a range of techniques to gather data. They may use interviews and observations as well as ability tests (e.g. IQ, personality and memory tests) and brain scans.

Research examples

Case studies are done for various reasons. Some of the most well-known case studies in psychology are of individuals with unique psychological problems. You can read more examples in the chapter on psychopathology. Other important examples include:

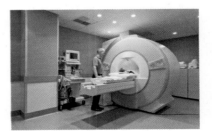

Brain scans may be used in case studies to gather data

- In cognitive psychology, several case studies have been conducted into the effects of brain damage on memory.

A still from the film of The three faces of Eve

• In developmental psychology, case studies of deprived children have been useful in understanding the psychological effect of neglect or abandonment.

In all of such studies, the case study method is particularly suitable because the individual involved was unique. Thigpen and Cleckley (1954) presented a famous case of dissociative identity disorder (also called 'multiple personality disorder'). In their interviews with a female patient, it became apparent that she had more than one personality. One, calling herself 'Eve White' was uptight and law abiding, while another who introduced herself as 'Eve Black' was flirtatious and shallow. Personality tests and IQ tests confirmed the differences between the two personalities, which could be brought out through hypnosis. A third, more reasonable personality emerged through therapy, and the case was made into a film, '*The three faces of Eve*'.

Evaluation of case studies

Case studies are an extremely useful, sometimes essential tool for studying unique cases, including rare brain damage that would be unethical to cause deliberately. However, as a researcher builds up a personal acquaintance with a participant and their case, (s)he may start to show researcher bias due to developing a relationship with the patient/client. It is also hard to generalise the results of a case study to the wider population. Because of these problems, case studies are limited and no area of psychology relies on them entirely.

Overlap between methods

When considering what method is being used in a study, consider first whether it is an experiment or not. Many experiments use observations or surveys, but they should still be described as experiments rather than surveys/observation studies.

In particular, many experiments use observations as part of their procedure. However, these are not observation studies, as they manipulate an IV and record one or more numerical DVs, instead of passively gathering observational data. It is useful to remember that there is a degree of overlap between research methods in psychology.

Some studies draw on several methods. A case study is not in itself a single method of gathering data; it typically involves one or more of the other methods described in this book. Typically, the participant will be interviewed and they may fill in some questionnaires as well. The researcher may decide to observe the participant, either in their own environment (naturalistic observation) or doing a structured task in a controlled environment.

Summary of strengths and weaknesses of non-experimental methods

Non-experimental methods	Strengths	Weaknesses
Survey	• Well-designed questionnaires with closed questions are relatively quick and easy to answer and can gather a lot of data. • Answers can be analysed easily, forming totals and percentages.	• As the answers to structured questionnaires are a fixed choice, they do not allow respondents to express opinions that are different from those offered. There may also be researcher bias in the selection of options. • Participants cannot usually ask for further explanation – risk of misunderstanding. • There is a low response rate for postal and Internet questionnaires.
Interview	• Face-to-face format allows questions to be explained if necessary. • Unstructured interviews can be personalised to each participant and provide rich data.	• Suffer more from social desirability bias than surveys do, due to being face to face. • Unstructured interviews are costly and time-consuming to run, and questions may be biased or leading. The data from open questions is harder to analyse.
Observation	• Detailed record of real-life behaviour as it happens. • Captures behaviour in its true social context.	• Lacks the control of an experiment, so cannot infer cause and effect relationships. • Hard to replicate the results of an observational study as social situation is unique.
Case study	• Allows the researcher to focus on a specific instance and identify processes and variables. • A source of very rich and meaningful data (qualitative). • Insights from participant(s) may reveal an unusual and highly relevant perspective.	• Results are specific to the individual – often impossible to replicate. • Time consuming and expensive to carry out. • Close relationship between researcher and participant(s) potentially interferes with objectivity.

⏺ Activities

1. What problems might there be with the data from an unstructured interview? Consider each of the following, and rank them in order of importance from 1 to 4 (in your opinion):
   - biased results
   - unreliability of answers
   - difficulty to analyse
   - too much/too little data

2. Draw a table showing the strengths and weaknesses of the different types of observation.

3. Design a survey to investigate an area of your choice relating to attitudes. Decide what type of questions to use, then design three or four questions. Get feedback and then complete a questionnaire with a total of 8–10 questions. Give copies of the questionnaire to other students for them to fill in and comment on.

4. In pairs, make an observation of a classmate volunteer for two minutes. Then compare your results with your co-observer to assess your 'inter-observer reliability'.

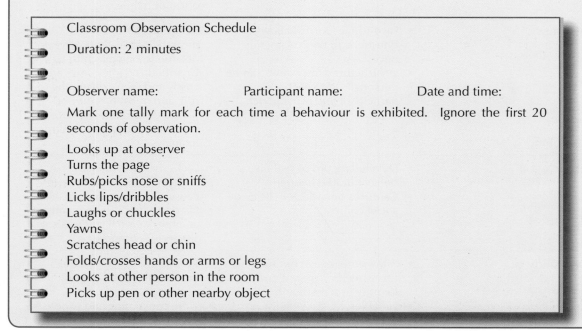

Classroom Observation Schedule

Duration: 2 minutes

Observer name: Participant name: Date and time:

Mark one tally mark for each time a behaviour is exhibited. Ignore the first 20 seconds of observation.

Looks up at observer
Turns the page
Rubs/picks nose or sniffs
Licks lips/dribbles
Laughs or chuckles
Yawns
Scratches head or chin
Folds/crosses hands or arms or legs
Looks at other person in the room
Picks up pen or other nearby object

✔ Questions

1. What is a closed question?

2. Give an example of an issue that needs to be avoided when writing survey questions.

3. Which type of interview mainly sticks to a list of questions but can include follow-up questions?

4. Why might you choose to use a structured interview instead of a survey?

5. Which type of observation involves watching participants in their everyday environment?

6. Being observed causes behaviour to change. What is this effect called?

7. Give a strength that is always true of observation.

8. Give three characteristics of the case-study method.

9. What techniques are used to gather data in a case study?

10. True or false: every study uses just one of the research methods?

🔑 Key concepts

- Non-experimental methods
- Survey (research method)
- Questionnaire
- Interview (research method)
- Open questions
- Closed questions
- Likert scale
- Acquiescence bias
- Social desirability bias
- Structured interview
- Semi-structured interview
- Unstructured interview
- Observation (research method)
- Naturalistic observation
- Structured observation
- Disclosed (observation)
- Undisclosed (observation)
- Observer effect
- Participant observation
- Non-participant observation
- Observation schedule
- Inter-observer reliability
- In-depth
- Longitudinal
- Case history

General research issues

There are certain issues that apply to every research method. All of these should be considered when planning and running your own research including the Assignment. Understanding them will also provide you with the tools to evaluate other studies. These issues include:

- hypotheses
- internal and external validity
- ethics
- data analysis

Hypotheses

Every study will include one or more hypotheses. A **hypothesis** is a statement of what a study expects to find. Regardless of the type of experiment, the researcher will have a prediction that they are looking to test. This should be stated clearly towards the start of a research write-up.

Experimental and null hypothesis

In an experiment, the **experimental hypothesis** is based on the prediction that the treatment applied to an experimental group will cause them to be different from the population – manipulating the IV will have an effect on the DV. For example:

People who take a vitamin pill once a day will do better in their exams than those who do not.

OR

The group who are taught a memory strategy will recall more foreign language words than the control group.

Note that the variables in hypotheses should be **operationalised**. This means that they are put into a specific, testable form. Rather than *'memory'*, for example, you could say *'number of items recalled from a list of words'*.

Another hypothesis is usually stated – the **null hypothesis**. This makes a baseline prediction, essentially stating that the experimental group will be no different from the rest of the population.

A good way to phrase the null hypothesis is to state that the IV will **not** affect the DV and any difference between conditions is due to chance (e.g. participant variables or background distractions). For example:

The null hypothesis is that there will be no difference between group 1 and group 2 other than random error as a result of chance factors.

Sometimes you may see these hypotheses termed H_1 (experimental) and H_0 (null).

Directional hypotheses

Compare these two hypotheses:

Stress will have an effect on scores on a memory test for celebrity names.

Stress will reduce scores on a memory test for celebrity names.

Here the IV is stress and the DV is memory for celebrity names. The researcher wants to find out whether stress will affect memory. There is good reason to think that stress will harm memory, rather than improve it. Therefore, it would be more logical to predict the direction of the effect, and use the second of these example hypotheses. This is called a **directional** or **one-tailed** hypothesis.

A hypothesis that just says the IV will have an effect and does not say whether it will increase or reduce DV scores is called a **non-directional** or **two-tailed** hypothesis. If the experimental hypothesis is directional, it would be logical to have a directional null hypothesis as well, for example:

*Stress will **not** reduce scores on a memory test for celebrity names and any changes found will be due to chance.*

? Discussion point

Why do you think the terms 'one-tailed' and 'two-tailed' are sometimes used to describe directional hypotheses?

Alternative hypotheses

Of course, not all studies are experiments, and as you might expect, the term 'experimental hypothesis' is only used in experiments. With a non-experimental study (e.g. a survey), the prediction is termed an **alternative hypothesis**. A null hypothesis is also used. For example, in a playground observation:

> *The alternative hypothesis is that younger children will play in larger groups than older children.*

Internal and external validity

Whether or not a study is valid relates to whether it is possible to draw a logical conclusion from its findings.

Internal validity

If an experiment has high **internal validity**, it means that it is well designed and research can draw a sound conclusion about whether the IV had an effect on the DV or not. Many of the design issues discussed so far in this chapter relate to internal validity – in particular, control of extraneous and confounding variables so that cause and effect can be determined.

External validity

Even if a study is high in internal validity, the results could be worthless if it tells us nothing about real life. Some studies are highly artificial. If it can be hard to generalise from the results in the study to a real life situation, then the study is said to lack **ecological validity**.

A study that takes place in a participant's natural environment is often considered to be more realistic. As discussed earlier in this chapter, lab experiments are seen as more controlled but less realistic, while field experiments are the opposite. Therefore, lab experiments usually have higher internal validity and lower external validity, while for field experiments the situation is reversed.

However, the level of artificiality depends a lot on the task that is done. Even in a field experiment, participants might be asked to do something quite unnatural. Experimental tasks that are not typical of everyday life are said to lack **mundane realism**.

These two issues both relate to a more general concept – can we generalise the results from a study to other situations? If not, the results are next to useless. The ability to generalise from a study is known as its **external validity** – its results/conclusions do not hold true outside of the experimental situation. A third type of external validity has also been raised earlier in this chapter – can results from a sample be generalised to the population as a whole? This is called **population validity**.

These three main types of external validity will be helpful when you evaluate research studies, as they are three of the most common criticisms made of experiments throughout psychology. In every study that you have to evaluate, consider whether these might be a problem.

Even if they are not a problem, for example, if mundane realism is high, you should be aware of this as a strength of the study!

Types of external validity

Ecological validity: can the results be generalised to another environment, for example from the lab to the workplace or the home?

Mundane realism: how closely does the experimental task resemble something that people do in the real world?

Population validity: can the results be generalised from the sample to the population as a whole?

Research ethics

Psychologists want to find out answers to their questions and that means carrying out research on people. However, people are very different from the objects of study in other scientific subjects – they have rights that must be respected and feelings that must be taken into account. Psychology researchers therefore must follow a set of moral principles known as a **code of ethics** that states what is and is not acceptable in research. Such codes are published by professional organisations such as the British Psychological Society (BPS). Some of the key ethical principles are as follows, based on the BPS code of ethics (British Psychological Society, 2009).

As well as following these guidelines in your own research, you should raise ethical issues when discussing research in the other topics of this course. In particular, ensure that you are aware of the ethical flaws of classic research studies. These issues don't necessarily invalidate the results of the studies, but in some cases they might make it impossible to replicate the research.

Consent and deception

At the outset of a study, participants should give their consent to take part, meaning that they agree to be part of the research. However, people should be in full knowledge of what they are agreeing to do, including how long it will take. This is called **informed consent**.

Deception is where participants have been deliberately misled about the nature of a research task. An example is Asch (1951) – a study of conformity, but participants were told it was a study of perception. Deception is unethical, and cases where it has been used in the past are controversial.

It is important that participants give informed consent

Getting informed consent does not mean that participants need to be told the aims or hypothesis of the study but they do need to be told what they will have to do. There are some areas of research where it is impossible to get fully informed consent because telling the participants about the experiment's procedure will distort the results and researchers must therefore use an element of deception. An example is the Mori and Arai (2010) study of conformity. BPS guidelines recognise this and state it is acceptable only when there is no other alternative and that consideration must be given to how participants will react when they are given the full information (British Psychological Society, 2009). Also, participants must be given as much information as possible at the earliest opportunity.

Briefing and debriefing

A **briefing** should be given, explaining what the study will entail. Usually this takes place after consent has been given. The researcher gives a summary of what the experiment involves and what to expect. The briefing is a general overview of the study in more details than was given during the consent process. The researcher will also provide specific task **instructions**, telling them what they have to do.

Participants must also be **debriefed**, meaning that after the study has taken place, all relevant aspects are explained to them. In particular, the aims of the study should be explained. If participants took part in only one condition of the IV, researchers may choose to tell them what the other condition involved. Participants are typically provided with the researchers' contact details, in case they want to withdraw their consent later. They may also be interested to find out the conclusions of the study once all of the data have been analysed.

Note that in relation to the previous section, the BPS code of conduct states that debriefing people afterwards does not excuse or justify unethical research (British Psychological Society, 2009).

Avoiding harm

Arguably, the most important and universal rule of research ethics is to avoid **harm** (or the risk of harm) during the research procedures or as a result of them. Of course, harm can happen accidentally (e.g. a participant falls off a chair and hurts themselves) but the principle set out by BPS and other research organisations is that the risk of physical or psychological harm should be no greater than in everyday life.

Psychological harm was shown in the Milgram (1963) study of obedience (see chapter 10). Participants later reported that they found it traumatic – but most reported that they were happy to have taken part (Milgram, 1974). Modern research guidelines ensure that such experiences could not happen nowadays.

Closely related to the risk of harm is that participants should not be exposed to any degrading or humiliating treatment.

Research on children

Some theoretical advances have been made through ethically dubious research on children, such as Watson and Rayner's (1920) study of 'little Albert' (see chapter 2). However, rules are much stricter nowadays: student researchers must not carry out experiments on children at all, and professional researchers take particular care to avoid any distress to child participants.

Children must be willing to take part and in addition to the child showing willingness, their parents must give written informed consent.

> **🔍 Top tip**
>
> When debriefing participants in a classroom experiment or as part of the Assignment, it is helpful to have a short written statement to read out. This ensures that you won't forget anything important. Don't forget to thank participants for taking part!

Parents must give written consent for a child to partipate in a study

This is because under-16s are vulnerable and may be too young to fully understand what they are consenting to.

Confidentiality

Confidentiality must be maintained. This means that data should be kept secure, and when results are published, no names or identifying information should be included. This ensures that participants are not embarrassed by their participation. In some cases, initials are used (e.g. 'the case of HM' in the famous case study of memory; Scoville & Milner, 1957). As well as being fair and respectful, this avoids unwelcome attention for the participants and also avoids putting people off from participating in the first place.

Right to withdraw

Participants also have the **right to withdraw** from any study at any time if they feel unhappy or uncomfortable or simply change their mind. They may also retrospectively withdraw consent when the study is over, in which case their data must be deleted/destroyed.

Example study: Piliavin's 'Good Samaritan' study

Irving Piliavin and colleagues were interested in diffusion of responsibility – the tendency for bystanders not to help a person in need if there are other people who could help. In a study that generated a considerable ethical debate, they conducted an observational study in a public place, where an actor faked a collapse on a subway train in New York. Researchers hid among the bystanders taking notes of who helped and how quickly they helped (Piliavin *et al.*, 1969).

Irving Piliavin conducted his 'Good Samaritan' study on the New York subway

Ironically, for a study into the unethical behaviour of strangers, there were several ethical problems in this methodology, including deception, a failure to gain informed consent from participants and psychological harm (stress).

For this study, it is vital to realise the historical context of ethical guidelines gradually tightening up. Such studies have helped to advance the ongoing process of deciding what is, and what is not, ethical in research.

✔ Questions

1. What is an experimental hypothesis and when is it used?

2. Is it necessary to operationalise the IV and DV for an experimental hypothesis?

3. Which type of validity means that the experiment is well designed/set up and controls extraneous variables?

4. What does ecological validity mean?

5. A researcher asks participants to count backwards in threes while clicking coloured squares on a screen. Does this task have mundane realism?

6. Which type of validity relates to the issue of whether results from a sample can be generalised to the wider population or not?

7. Do laboratory experiments always lack mundane realism?

8. What is meant by a 'code of ethics' for research?

9. What is the term for the ethical principle whereby research findings have to be kept secure and names of participants should not be disclosed or published?

10. Can children give consent to take part in a study?

⚷ Key concepts

- Hypothesis
- Experimental hypothesis
- Null hypothesis
- Operationalisation
- One-tailed/directional hypothesis
- Two-tailed/non-directional hypothesis
- Alternative hypothesis
- Internal validity
- External validity
- Ecological validity
- Mundane realism
- Population validity
- Code of ethics
- Informed consent
- Deception
- Briefing
- Instructions
- Debriefing
- Harm
- Parental consent
- Confidentiality
- Right to withdraw

Activities

1. To operationalise means to put variables in a testable/measurable form. How could you operationalise the following variables?
   - Noise level
   - Concentration
   - Popularity
   - Stress level
   - Success at school
   - Amount of caffeine
   - Long-term memory
   - Ability at sports

2. Write out possible experimental and null hypotheses for studies based on these three research questions:
   - Does smoking cannabis harm your short-term memory?
   - Does what a researcher is wearing affect participants' performance on a task?
   - Are men better than women at parking cars?

3. Summarise the three main types of external validity into a chart in your notes. Ask a classmate to test you on them. Now identify an example research study that lacks each of the three types.

4. Briefly describe the procedure of a famous study where unethical research has been conducted, and give your views on whether such research should be conducted in the future or not.

Data and graphs

Research aims to produce good quality, valid data. But what do researchers do with their data? Data analysis is a key part of any research process and a useful transferrable skill to learn. This builds on basic concepts that you will have come across in other subjects on the curriculum.

Qualitative versus quantitative data

Some types of studies, for example, unstructured interviews, produce **qualitative data**. These are non-numerical data, especially verbal data such as descriptions. Images and videos (e.g. made during an observation) are also qualitative.

Other studies, in particular experiments, produce **quantitative data** – data based on numbers. The data can be analysed, or displayed in graphs.

In some cases, such as with observation methods, it may be matter of choices – verbal descriptions could be written during an observation, or quantitative data could be recorded (e.g. a record of the number of times that a behaviour is observed), or the study could use a mixture of both.

Sometimes qualitative data is converted into quantitative data to make it easier to analyse. For example, a researcher could ask interviewees an open question about prejudice and then score their responses out of 10 based on how much prejudice they showed. This is quite subjective. A more objective way to convert the data is to use a software package to search for the frequency of key terms or phrases in people's answers.

Descriptive statistics

Descriptive statistics are ways of calculating numbers that describe the data in some way – that is, summarise a set of data in a single number. The most obvious example is to calculate an average.

Averages

People use the term **average** in everyday speech but there are three main ways of showing the average or most typical value of a set of data:

The mean	The **mean** is calculated by adding together all of the values and dividing by the number of scores. It is the most useful score statistically as it includes all of the scores in the calculation and is the basis of other calculations such as the standard deviation. However, it can be distorted by extreme high or low scores.
The mode	The **mode** is the most common score. This can be useful to avoid extreme values of the mean, and although less useful statistically, it may be of interest to know which score was actually the most common. However, some sets of data do not have a mode. Sometimes there are two modes ('bi-modal') or several (multi-modal), that is, two or more scores that are equally the most common.
The median	The **median** is the midpoint of the data, obtained by putting scores in order, low to high, and finding the one in the centre. If there is an even number of scores, the mean of the middle two scores is calculated.

Dispersion

The mean, mode and median are useful statistics but having the average alone gives us no indication of whether scores are generally close to or far away from this midpoint. **Dispersion** means how widely data are spread out and it is calculated using a different set of descriptive statistics:

Top tip

At National 5 and Higher, *descriptive statistics* are required but you do not have to calculate the *inferential statistics* that more experienced psychology researchers use. Inferential statistics are useful because they tell us whether the difference between two groups is likely to have occurred by chance or not. They are essential for published research. Although time-consuming, they are not especially difficult to calculate. Ask your teacher or lecturer for more information.

Top tip

Get plenty of practice to ensure that you can perform these simple calculations with ease – you may need to calculate the average of a simple set of data in the exam.

Make the link

When journalists talk about averages such as 'average income', ask yourself – and try to find out – which statistic they are using. Sometimes it can make a huge difference!

The range	The **range** is a very simple summary of the spread of data, based on the difference between the lowest and highest scores. It is easily calculated by subtracting the lowest score from the highest. However, it is limited in that it does not reflect the distribution of the other data. Worse still, the lowest and/or the highest score are extreme values, which may be abnormal in some way. For example, if the data were based on time to do a task, you may find that the highest values are very much out of line with the bulk of scores due to one or two people giving up or misunderstanding the instructions. This affects the value of the range as a summary of the data.
The interquartile range	An easy way to avoid the extreme scores used by the range and still get a simple-to-calculate figure is to use the **interquartile range**. This involves listing numerical data in order from lowest to highest and then finding the difference between the scores at the 25% and 75% points, that is, the difference between the score one quarter from the bottom of the distribution and the score one-quarter from the top.
The standard deviation	For a more reliable calculation of the spread of scores, the **standard deviation (SD)** shows the typical amount by which the scores in the distribution differ from the mean. The calculation is based on finding the difference between each score and the mean and then calculating the average of these differences. A large range could be the result of just two people failing to conform; however, the SD takes everyone's response into account.

? Discussion point

Note that Jenness (1932, see chapter 10) used the range rather than the SD. However, his groups only had three members. Why would this make a difference to his choice of statistic?

🔍 Top tip

Higher students may have to calculate the range in the exam but the other measures of dispersion are optional and will not be asked about directly. However, they are very useful for analysing your data in the Assignment.

! Syllabus note

Correlation is not mandatory in this course but a basic understanding of the concept will help you understand research evidence that uses correlation.

Correlation

A typical correlation study in psychology uses a non-experimental source such as a survey to obtain numerical values on two variables (e.g. IQ and extraversion). The researcher then uses a statistical technique to find the relationship between these variables, typically called the 'co-variables'. This technique gives the research a number which tells them if the relationship between the two variables is:

- strong (closely connected) or weak
- positive (rise and fall together) or negative (move in opposite directions)

The strength of a number is shown between 1 and 0, with the closer it is to 1, the stronger the correlation between the two variables. Negative correlations show strength in the same way, but they are shown using a negative number (i.e. between 0 and −1).

A scattergram is used to display the relationship: for each participant, a point or cross is marked at the point on the graph where their scores on the co-variables meet.

A correlational hypothesis should state that a relationship will be found, instead of saying that one variable will affect the other. For example: *'The correlational hypothesis is that there will be a strongly positive relationship between the number of hours of sleep a student gets and their grade average.'*

Graphs

Graphs are used to present results and to perform a basic visual analysis. You may have to interpret a graph in the exam or suggest a suitable graph for a set of data. It is also an essential skill for your Assignment. Some of the most common types include:

> **🔍 Top tip**
>
> A positive or negative correlation means that the variables do have a relationship but cause and effect cannot be assumed – just because two things seem linked, it doesn't mean that one is causing the other to change. A classic example is that the time your alarm clock goes off is correlated with the time the sun comes up but this doesn't mean that the sun is making your alarm clock go off or that your alarm clock is making the sun rise!

A **bar graph** shows scores as heights on two or more separated 'bars,' which often represent the different conditions of an experiment. It allows for an easy comparison of means. Note that the IV is shown along the x-axis, at the bottom of the graph.	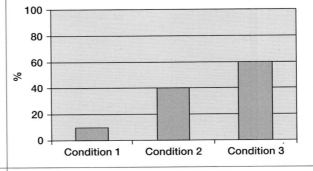
A **histogram** looks similar to a bar graph, except for the lack of gaps between the columns. This is because a histogram shows a range of values from the same category, e.g. scores on a test. The height of the columns shows frequency.	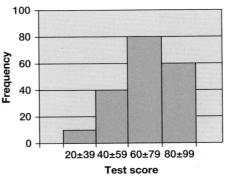
A **pie chart** is not commonly used in psychology but it can be helpful for showing the percentages of a population which engage in a behaviour. The size of each slice represents its proportion and the total should add up to 100%. Scores on a DV, such as memory test scores, should not be presented on a pie chart.	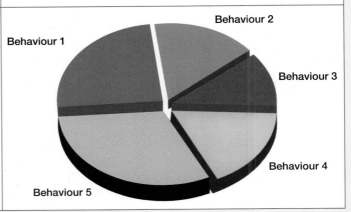

As mentioned above, scattergrams are widely used in psychology, but only for correlational studies. They should not be used to present experimental data.

Percentages

Finally, you should be aware of the use of **percentages**. As you will be aware from your studies of maths, percentages are easily calculated by dividing the score by the maximum and multiplying by 100.

(score/maximum) × 100

Percentages help to standardise scores, making them easier to compare. For example, if participants have done two tests, one out of a maximum of 80 and one with a maximum of 65, it can be hard to compare the results. Is 49/80 better than 38/65? A percentage makes it immediately clear – the first result converts to 61.2% and the second is 58.5%. Therefore, the first score is superior.

Key concepts

- Qualitative data
- Quantitative data
- Descriptive statistics
- Average
- Mean
- Mode
- Median
- Dispersion
- Range
- Inter-quartile range
- Standard deviation
- Bar graph
- Histogram
- Pie chart
- Scattergram
- Percentages

Questions

1. Name three ways of calculating the average.

2. Name three graphs.

3. Which descriptive statistic shows the midpoint of the data?

4. When is a mean not the best way of calculating the average of a set of data?

5. Name the statistic that is calculated by subtracting the lowest score from the highest.

6. Summarise verbally what the SD is.

7. What major disadvantage does the mode have?

8. Why is the SD considered the most 'powerful' way of calculating dispersion?

9. What is the difference in appearance between a bar graph and a histogram?

10. Why is it often useful to use percentages to summarise scores?

Activities

GO!

1. Calculate the mean, mode, median and range of ages in your classroom, <u>or</u> of members of your family. Does this task highlight weaknesses of any of the statistics?

2. Calculate descriptive statistics for the following scenario:

> The following data were obtained from an independent groups study in which two sets of participants (total n=26) studied a section of a psychology textbook and were then given a 20 question multiple-choice test. In condition 2 only, a memory strategy was used.
>
> Scores on condition 1:
>
> 3   7   10   8   14   2   9   8   7   13   7   5   11
>
> Scores on condition 2:
>
> 19   10   11   8   9   9   11   14   3   6   3   10   17

3. Fill in the following table:

Type of graph/chart	Appearance/key features	Example(s) of when to use
Bar graph		
Histogram		
Pie chart		

4. Draw examples of the three types of graph from the previous task. Find out about other kinds of graphs, and add them to your notes too.

The Assignment

9 The Assignment

! Syllabus note

For National 5, the Assignment is based around a research plan and gathering data is not compulsory. There is an open choice of topic for the plan.

At Higher, you must conduct a practical study and gather data, based on an SQA 'brief'. The write-up will be based on the data that you gather.

Planning, conducting research, and scientific writing are valuable skills to learn

Understanding the Assignment

Place in the course

The **Assignment** is a mandatory part of both the Higher and National 5 courses in Psychology. It is a research project that forms part of the research unit of your course and it is externally marked by the SQA. It forms over a third of your overall marks for the course – enough to bring a poor exam mark up to a pass, or turn a C into an A, so it is essential to complete it as well as possible. Chapter 8 has equipped you with the skills and knowledge needed to conduct research. In this part of the course, you will develop those skills and put them to use. You will complete a piece of scientific writing based on a practical research project. This will then be submitted to the SQA for marking.

Planning, conducting research, and scientific writing are valuable skills to learn, which will be of great use to your future studies, not just in psychology but in business, medicine or any scientific subject, and to careers such as working for local or national government, the police, management or a range of other areas. In this topic, you will learn how to write a report in a formal style, including in-line citations, references and appendices. You will also learn how to evaluate your own research activities.

Evidence and spot checks

Your school or college will put measures into place to ensure that your Assignment is your own work. This could include short interviews with you to ensure that you understand what is included. It is vitally important that you write it all yourself. Copying from any source (including this textbook!) is out of the question and could lead to you failing the whole course. Likewise, getting anyone else to help you write your Assignment is unethical as well as highly risky, while cheating is generally easy for teachers/lecturers and markers to spot.

Working as a group

You can plan and conduct the data gathering element of your Assignment in a small group, provided your teacher/lecturer agrees. There are some research situations where it is helpful to have more than one person available, for example to hand out materials or debrief participants. However, the analysis of data and all report writing should be your own work. Also, do not show the work you have done on your Assignment to a classmate, as to do so puts you at risk of being copied.

Deadlines and drafts

It is a good idea to get started with the Assignment early – perhaps after you have studied the first topic or two of your course. You will then work on it over a period of months, completing by the SQA deadline, which is usually in the spring. It is important to be organised and much easier to produce an excellent piece of work if you work at it regularly. Keep detailed notes and make sure you back up all saved files.

Your teacher will support you through the process and will look at drafts that you write, but ultimately, this is your work. You should not expect detailed corrections of your drafts, but more general feedback.

Skills for the Assignment

Background reading

In order to fully understand the topic area of your Assignment, you should conduct some independent background reading as you work on the Assignment. The background will feed into the introduction section of your plan/write-up.

It is important that you keep track of your sources. If you come across a useful website or book, make sure that you take a note of it (or bookmark the site or take a photo) to help you find it again later. This is good research practice and will save you wasting time later when you come to write your references section.

Copy-and-pasting text from the internet, even if you plan to re-word it, is strongly discouraged. In any case, you will get a much better end result if you read the material and then try to explain it in your own words without looking at the source.

Speak to your school/college library, as they will be able to direct you towards suitable books. Every textbook has different background research studies so look around. Most also have a section on writing research reports.

You can plan and conduct the data gathering element in a small group

As well as books, there are several useful online sources for you to look at:

Name	Source	Comments
The SQA Assignment research briefs for your year (Higher only)	www.sqa.org.uk or via search engine	Ensure that you have the most recent version. It may include background research studies to get you started.
This textbook and other suitable books	Library	Any psychology textbook can be useful for background – it doesn't need to be a book aimed at your course.
BPS research digest	digest.bps.org.uk	Summarises the best current research studies each week. Began in 2005, so it now contains a great database of studies from over 10 years of psychology.
Psyblog	spring.org.uk	A more populist blog, but it contains very interesting articles on a huge range of topics and has links to all research studies mentioned.
Google Scholar	scholar.google.co.uk	Don't forget to look for a link to a pdf version of the study – these links are sometimes out of date, but often you can read the full original article.

You should conduct some independent background reading as you work on the Assignment

Avoid using an ordinary Google search for your background reading. Wikipedia and other encyclopaedias are best used just as a starting point for your reading, if at all. The introduction section of your write-up will include a review of background research, in which you will outline the topic area and summarise the most relevant previous studies.

References

You will have noticed in your studies of psychology so far that there are many references to previous research, which often look like this:

Smith and Bond (1993)

or

Cohen *et al.* (1981)

You will include **references** in a standard format in your Assignment. In the main body of the text, put the author's name and year in brackets, each time you are referring to an idea or a research finding that came from their work. This is called an **in-line citation**. Then, at the end of the document, there should be a reference section, which will give full publication details of the sources that you refer to – what book, website or journal the findings were published in. This allows a reader to find and check these sources.

There is no single correct way of formatting the reference section, but it is important that it is well presented and consistent. They key is to pick an appropriate standard format and then stick to it. The following is suggested as it is based on British Psychological Society guidelines:

Books like this:

Baddeley, A.D. (1999). *Essentials of Human Memory*. East Sussex: Psychology Press.

Journal articles like this:

Craik, F. I. M. and R. S. Lockhart (1972). Levels of processing: A framework for memory research. *Journal of Verbal Learning and Verbal Behaviour, 11*, 671–684.

Websites like this:

Harkness, T. (2014). Does brain structure determine your political views? Retrieved 21 May 2014 from *http://www.bbc.co.uk/news/uk-politics-27437799*.

Writing style

It is important to present the Assignment clearly and to make it look like a professional piece of work. It would be a good idea if possible to word-process the Assignment, as it makes it much easier to edit and improve it as you go along. Present it with 1.5 or 2.0 line spacing, in a standard-looking font such as Times, Arial, Optima or Tahoma, and in 11 or 12 point text size.

It is also standard in scientific writing to use the **passive voice**, for example: '*questionnaires were handed out*' (instead of: '*I handed questionnaires out*'). There are many exceptions, but at this early stage, it would be best to stick to the passive voice as it sounds more formal.

Scientific writing is generally done in the **past tense**, and in the Higher, most of the write-up will be in the past tense as you are reporting on an experiment done in the past (remember this if you start writing before gathering your data). However, for National 5, the Assignment is based around a plan, so in some elements it will be more suitable to talk about what you are *going to* do in the future. See the sample Assignments in the following two sections for examples of this.

> **Key concepts**
> - Assignment
> - References
> - In-line citation
> - Passive voice
> - Past tense

National 5: planning and writing the Assignment

> **! Syllabus note**
> The details of planning and writing-up the Assignment are very different for Higher and National 5. The following sections focus on National 5 planning; for Higher, skip to page 257.

Skills for the National 5 Assignment:

- Developing a research outline/brief into a workable research plan.
- Identifying ethical issues that will affect your study.
- Writing up the plan in a standard scientific format and formal language.

At National 5, you have an open choice of topic. However, it will be easier to do something linked to one of the topics that you have studied so far, or will study soon, because material from the topic will help you to develop research ideas and conducting the Assignment will consolidate what you have learned so far.

Note that you have to consider ethical issues as part of the assessment. Do **not** plan a highly unethical study on the basis that it will give you more to talk about! Even if you don't actually run the study that you describe in the plan, it must be something that you could practically and ethically carry out. Showing ethical awareness is part of the task.

The suggestions in the following section might help you to decide on a topic. However, it is possible that your teacher/lecturer will want everyone in the class to do the same topic, so take advice on acceptable choices before you begin.

SQA's general assessment requirements for N5

A. Describe behaviour associated with a chosen psychological topic

B. Explain features of the topic with reference to psychological research evidence

C. Describe an aim for research on this topic

D. Give an experimental/alternative hypothesis for the proposed research study

E. Describe a suitable research plan, including method, sampling, variables and procedure

F. Describe ethical issues and ways of addressing these in the research plan

G. Use appropriate terminology and provide basic references

Source: www.sqa.org.uk

National 5: suggested studies

The following suggestions draw on the mandatory/optional topics that are described elsewhere in this textbook:

Conformity. A replication of Jenness's classic study of conformity (see chapter 10) could be planned. This would involve a stimulus of some kind, such as a jar of sweets. Measurements of estimates could be taken individually, and then further estimates taken after discussing the number of sweets as a group. The range and mean of estimates could be compared.

For a variation of the study a sheet of faked high or low answers could be prepared and shown to half of the participants. A control group are asked to estimate the number of sweets without being influenced, while others are shown the (fake) guesses of previous participants and then asked to give estimates. Variations of this idea could include using illusions, to see whether people conform to a crowd when stating what they see.

Sleep. A questionnaire study could be conducted to look at the relationship between hours of sleep and cognitive function. Questions could be asked about how late people go to bed and how many hours of sleep they get, as well as about ability to concentrate. Grades at school/college could also be studied or an IQ or memory test given to students.

Memory. A study could be conducted to look at the 'primacy/recency effect'. This is where items at the beginning and end of a list are better remembered compared to those in the middle. Typically, a list of words are read out or shown on screen, or a set of items/pictures shown. Items must be shown one at a time, not all together. Recall is then immediately tested by asking participants to name or write down the items. Usually people remember items at the beginning and end of the list, but not the ones in the middle.

Prejudice. The 'halo effect' is where our general impression of a person biases our judgement of their abilities. For example, if you like someone overall, you might overestimate how good a flatmate or research partner they might be. For this study, you could plan two versions of a short article, one with an attractive photo and one with a less attractive photo, and include a caption saying that the photo is a picture of the author of the article. Different participants of the experiment will see the same information but different photos and they will be asked to rate the quality of the article.

Intelligence/mindsets. Compare answers to a short questionnaire with or without 'activating' a growth mindset. As described by Dweck (2006), a growth mindset can be activated by giving people a passage suggesting that anyone is capable of changing and improving. According to the theory, this can then affect their motivation and how they deal with stereotypes – attitudes that can then be tested using a questionnaire.

Top tip

For more research ideas, have a look at the suggested studies for Higher in the following section – although these may involve more work in terms of background reading.

It is fine to choose a different idea to those mentioned above, but give some thought to practicalities and to research ethics – as mentioned previously, you should not plan a study that is impossible or highly unethical. If any deception is involved, consider how participants will feel after the deception is revealed to them during debriefing – if it is likely that they will be upset or annoyed then it is best to rethink the procedure.

National 5: sections of the write-up

The following describes a standardised structure for your write-up based on section headings used at other levels of psychology, including Higher, HN and degree level. Although SQA does not provide a mandatory structure, it is suggested that you follow this guide as the section headings fit the task well, and will be recognisable to your marker.

Each section is allocated a particular number of marks on the marking scheme. The table below explains what should be included:

Section	Must include	Marks
Introduction/ background (350–550 words)	Define topic with relevant behaviour described. Explain relevant previous research. Aim and hypothesis.	13 marks overall: 2 marks for definition/ explanation of topic 7 marks for previous research (1 per fully explained point) 2 marks for aim 2 marks for hypothesis
Research Plan (300–450 words)	Should cover: **Method:** state proposed method (e.g. lab experiment) and state its strengths and weaknesses. **Sampling:** proposed sampling method must be described and reasons given for the choice. **Variables:** key research variables (usually IV and DV). **Procedure (including materials):** description of procedure – steps to be followed and materials that will be used.	12 marks overall: Method: 4 Sampling: 3 Variables: 2 Procedure: 3
Ethics (100–200 words)	Must be specific to plan. Four or more ethical points must be made, including both the ethical principles and how they will be considered in the plan.	4 marks overall
References and terminology	Accurate terminology should be used throughout. References to previous research should be listed at the end (should be clear enough that a reader can identify the sources).	1 mark holistically for both Total: 30 marks

Bear in mind that marking guidelines can change and you should consult the most recent SQA documents.

The overall Assignment will be 800 to 1,200 words in length.

Title

You don't get marks for your title but you should include one – it is part of good presentation to do so. Something simple, such as 'the effect of ___ on ___' usually works best. Include this on a separate title page along with your name, school, Scottish Candidate Number and a picture if you wish.

For National 5 your Assignment should be 800 to 1,200 words in length

Contents

It is good style to include a **contents page** with page numbers matching the page number of each section.

Introduction

In the first main section, usually called the **introduction** section in published research, you describe the behaviour that your research aims to study. The section starts by stating the topic of study and general area of psychology (e.g. social psychology). It should then progress from general background (the topic/area, e.g. conformity) to more specific similar previous research studies (e.g. a study that you are replicating).

> 🔍 **Top tip**
>
> The introduction should simply describe the research area *without mentioning your own study*. In many ways, it is like a short essay on the topic.

- Define the topic.
- Discuss two to three real world examples of behaviour relevant to this topic, using relevant terminology.
- Describe one relevant theory/model.
- Briefly explain how one of the approaches has been used to study the topic.
- Explain the methodology and findings of the study that your Assignment is based on.
- Explain one other relevant study.

State the aim and hypothesis

Next, state your aim in general terms. This is what you say about what the study is trying to do. Perhaps it could say that the aim is to replicate a previous study, or to find out the effect of something, or to test/find support for a theory. Example:

The aim of this project is to test the primacy and recency effect in order to evaluate the multi-store model of memory.

Now, give the **hypothesis** – the predicted finding of the study. If it is an experiment, put this under the heading 'experimental hypothesis', otherwise it should be titled 'alternative hypothesis'. If it is a correlational study, use the heading 'correlational hypothesis' and remember that is should be described in terms of the relationship between two variables (see p.240 for more about correlation).

Explain the research plan

The **research plan** is where you explain what the proposed practical research will involve. Use the heading 'Methodology'. Include:

- Method to be used, for example field experiment.
- Sampling method, for example opportunity sampling, volunteer sampling.
- Variables: the IV and DV to be studied (or the two co-variables for a correlation).
- Materials or apparatus to be used, for example, questionnaires, experimental apparatus.
- A description of the procedure.

Where appropriate, explain why a choice was made, such as why you plan to use a field experiment instead of a laboratory experiment.

Sub-sections can be used here if it seems clearer, such as method/sample/variables/procedure. If the materials are especially complex (e.g. a long questionnaire) then it might be best to have a separate section under the subheading 'Materials', as well.

Ethical procedures

The **ethics** of your study must be carefully considered. Under a suitable heading such as 'Ethics', describe any ethical problems that will arise and procedures that should be used to avoid or minimise these. For example:

> *It is anticipated that participants may feel stressed and want to stop doing the experiment. To deal with this problem, they will be told at the start that they can withdraw at any time. A classmate will be available to debrief anyone who leaves early.*

Think of things about this study in particular that could upset, stress or harm participants. Also consider general ethical principles such as briefing/debriefing, consent (participants under the age of 16 are generally considered too young to consent on their own behalf) and confidentiality of results. If there is any deception involved, this should be considered and discussed.

References

It is essential that you provide basic references. These are the sources that you mentioned in your introduction/background section. Simply including the name, year and title of sources is acceptable (with a url if it is a website), although you are encouraged to start using a standard reference in the British Psychological Society format. See the previous section of this chapter for more information or just use the same format as the examples at the back of this book.

National 5: example plan

The following gives an example plan in the popular topic of memory. The same structure could be used for any topic. This example follows the structure suggested in the previous section and covers all of the essential points, although it is relatively short and there would be room to give more detail in places.

Top tip

In a real Assignment, a contents page would be included as well.

The effect of word length on working memory.

By Nadia Bachmann

Dundee Academy
SCN: 0900011991

Background

Memory can be defined as the ability to encode information and retain it for future use. Immediate uses of memory to deal with tasks like retaining a phone number while we are dialling it are called short-term memory (STM). Some researchers prefer the term working memory, because STM is not just a store but is used to do tasks.

The cognitive approach states that the mind is like a computer. It sees long-term memory as being similar to a computer hard drive. However working memory is like the computer's processor, that deals with tasks and coordinates the other systems.

One real-life example of working memory would be if someone is listening to a lecture, and trying to write down what the lecturer says. The words would go into their memory, and they would retain them for a few seconds while their hand wrote the same words into a notebook. However people can only retain a small number of words at a time in the working memory.

In the above example, it would be harder to remember long words such as the names of some brain areas, according to the working memory model (WMM). This model states that the real time to do a task is reflected by how long it takes within the mind. It takes more time to say a long word, so it takes longer to process it within working memory. This means that not so many words can be retained if they are long e.g. cerebellum compared to short words like house.

One study which showed this was done by Baddeley et al. (1975). They showed people either lists of long words like 'university, organisation' or short words like 'bun, house'. They found that people could not remember as many of the long words as the short words. People were able to remember as many words as they could say in two seconds.

Another study that did not agree with Baddeley was Miller (1956). He studied memory for items and said it does not matter what kind of item it is, we are limited to around about 7 'chunks' of information. This is sometimes called Miller's magic number, 7 plus or minus 2.

Aim

This project aims to test the idea of the word length effect. It will see whether Miller's idea of the magic number 7 is correct, or Baddeley's idea of the word length effect is more accurate.

Experimental Hypothesis

Participants will remember more items from the list of short words than from the list of long words.

Methodology – Plan

A laboratory experiment will be used, with a quiet tutorial room as a lab. It will be best to keep all distractions to a minimum and avoid errors creeping in, so a controlled lab is the best choice of location.

Opportunity sampling will be used – this is taking the most conveniently available participants i.e. friends from other courses, and this will be acceptable as everyone is thought to have a similar memory span so random sampling is not really necessary.

The IV of the proposed study is the length of words on the lists, and the DV is the number of items recalled. One thing to be kept constant is the time they are shown – this will be done by showing words on a PowerPoint, with each slide set to appear for the same number of seconds. Another thing to be kept constant is recall time, and this will be done by asking just for recall of the first three letters of the word.

Procedure

The procedure will be as follows: participants will be brought into the laboratory by a research assistant (classmate) and the main researcher will meet them there. They will be asked to sign a consent form (taken from page 391 of 'Psychology Student Book') and told that the experiment is on short-term memory and will only take a few minutes.

They will then watch a slide show which will be set up to show six lists of words. Each list contains six ordinary words – 3 lists of short words and 3 lists of long words. There is also going to be an instruction slide at the start. The word list slides will be set up to display for 5 seconds and after each one a blank slide will show for 30 seconds to give them time to write the words down (the slideshow is attached at the end).

At the end they will be debriefed, told the true aims of the study, and thanked.

Ethics

People may find the task very hard. If they are showing signs of a lot of stress the researchers will finish the test early and discard their data.

There is a level of deception necessary as the researchers cannot tell participants which list they think is harder. To avoid psychological harm, the researchers will debrief them and explain why this was necessary.

It may upset participants if the researchers laugh when they do badly. The researchers must conduct the research respectfully and professionally to avoid this.

Participants should not be children. To avoid choosing any participants who are under 16, friends from other college classes will be used, and all are school leavers. In addition the consent form will ask them to declare their age.

An ethical strength is that this kind of research is controlled, and does not put the participant into a dangerous situation or discriminate against them in any way.

WORD COUNT: 925 words.

Higher: planning and writing the Assignment

! Syllabus note

The following section applies to Higher – for National 5, refer to the previous section.

Skills for the Higher Assignment:

- Developing a research outline/brief into a workable research plan.
- Identifying ethical issues which will affect your study.
- Identifying variables which will affect your study and controlling these where possible.
- Creating clear materials relevant to your topic, for example, questionnaires.
- Identifying a sample of participants and gathering data.
- Writing up the study in a standard scientific format using formal language.

The topic for your Higher Assignment must stick to one of the general areas in a document called 'Psychology Assignment – Assessment task' supplied each year by the SQA. This provides a set of scenarios to choose from, with an associated **research brief** or instructions. Make sure you have the document for the current year's course, as previous years may have had different topics. The topics tend to be broad – giving you ideas, but still allowing for a large amount of personalisation and choice. Nevertheless, you must read them carefully and ensure that any ideas you have fit within their guidelines (*more on this in the following section*).

SQA's general assessment requirements for Higher

1. Choose a SQA Psychology research brief

2. Carry out background research on the topic outlined in the brief

3. Plan primary research according to the topic brief and following ethical guidelines

4. Carry out primary research according to the research plan and following ethical guidelines

5. Produce a report that conforms to the style and format of a psychology research report

Source: www.sqa.org.uk

Higher: suggested topics

The following will give you some ideas of how to develop your chosen Assignment research brief:

Line drawing task apparatus

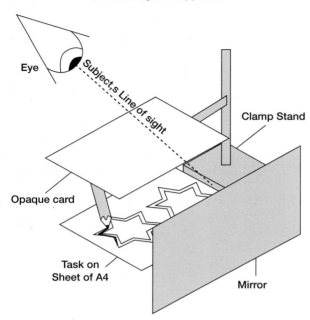

Mirror drawing is a classic way of testing improvement on a procedural (non-declarative) memory, as used with the memory patient HM (see page 124). This could be used for a number of studies, such as testing age differences, comparing skill/improvements on mirror drawing with other memory tasks or with IQ, or even looking for the effects of sleep on procedural memory – do people improve more after a night's sleep rather than in the same day, keeping the amount of practice the same?

Link to research briefs: this task could be connected to a scenario that asks you to investigate individual differences, learning and memory, or asks you to devise a test that could be used to assess children or brain injured patients.

Multitasking – give participants two things to do at once, such as completing a simple video game while answering questions. The wire game pictured is a good visuospatial task for such experiments and it could be used for other studies including stress and reaction times. Card sorting tasks or following a moving spot with a pointer could also work well. Stoet *et al.* (2013) found evidence that women are better than men at multi-tasking, but there are still many unanswered questions – does the gender difference depend on the type of task participants are trying to do?

Link to research briefs: this task could be connected to a scenario that asks you to investigate learning or education, individual differences or anything to do with the workplace.

The 'marshmallow test' is a classic test of willpower. Typically, a child has a sweet put in front of them and they are told that if they can resist eating if for 10 minutes, they can have a second sweet and eat both. Those who could resist were later found to score better on school tests and be less likely to commit crimes (Mischel *et al.*, 1972). Perhaps you could compare classmates' ability to resist this temptation with their school exam results? Mischel *et al.* also noted that people could successfully use strategies for resisting temptation (e.g. thinking of something else rather than looking at/sniffing the sweet). Perhaps you could try teaching these strategies to classmates (see http://bit.ly/1tZ08zi for a simple summary).

Link to research briefs: this task could be connected to a scenario that asks you to investigate individual differences, anything to do with children, or cultural differences. It could also be linked to some scenarios in political or environmental psychology.

Illusions are fun and interesting and they can be used in various studies. Visit http://www. michaelbach.de/ot/ for an excellent selection of illusions, most of which can be modified in various ways. Illusions can be used to investigate the nature-nurture debate, as things such as culture and experience can affect how we see them.

Link to research briefs: this task could be connected to a scenario that asks you to investigate individual differences, especially cultural differences. Although you probably won't be conducting brain scans, the role of visual areas of the brain could in principle be investigated using illusions as a stimulus. It could also be used as part of a memory or multi-tasking experiment.

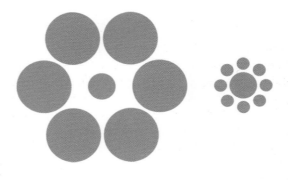

Adorno's (1950) F Scale, or the more modern version, Altemeyer's RWA scale, is a great way to conduct a practical study of prejudice. Versions are available online - see for example http://www. panojohnson.com/automatons/rwa-scale.xhtml. Another option would be to give people information to remember that either fits or goes against prejudiced schemas, and see how well these are remembered, similar to the study by Cohen (1981; see page 308).

Link to research briefs: this task could be connected to most research briefs that mention social psychology or culture, particularly scenarios where prejudice could play a role. It could also be linked to memory, upbringing, personality or individual differences.

There are a number of quick and simple ways of studying the body's response to stress, such as 'stress dots' that measure skin temperature, a heart-rate monitor or even just taking the participants' pulse rate by hand. Note that any study of stress **must** be ethical and it is not acceptable to stress people more than they would experience in everyday life, for example, during a typical class. Consult with your teacher/lecturer on the research ethics of this area.

Link to research briefs: this task would most obviously connect to a health-related scenario but it could be linked to any situation where stress plays a role, for example, the workplace or sport.

'Happiness' is a concept that has gained increasing attention in psychology, as researchers have realised that economic prosperity is not enough to make people feel happy. The 'Oxford Happiness Inventory' is a widely used survey to investigate happiness. This could be used on its own, for example to compare gender, age differences or some other naturally occurring variable such as quantity of sleep per night. Alternatively, it could be compared with the results of another survey such as the F-Scale (see above) or a personality test. It can easily be accessed online, http://happiness-survey.com/survey/.

Link to research briefs: this task would link to any scenario that asked about personal wellbeing or improving society as a whole. If there is a scenario relating to the mandatory topic of sleep, this could fit well. It could also be linked to cultural differences.

Bower (1972) looked at how linking two items (e.g. a cat and wall) into a single mental image led to better recall of both items. A version of this could be done in various ways, such as using objects, cards with words on them or a PowerPoint. Ensure extraneous variables, such as timings and familiarity of the objects, are controlled.

Link to research briefs: this task will link well to any scenario relating to education or memory. It could also be used for briefs that relate to choosing employees for a workplace.

PURPLE YELLOW RED
BLACK RED GREEN
RED YELLOW ORANGE
BLUE PURPLE BLACK
RED GREEN ORANGE

Stroop (1935) tested people's ability to state the colours of words, when the word said a different colour to the ink it was printed in, for example, 'green' or 'yellow'. Reading is so automatic for most people that we cannot 'switch off' the process. Even when asked to name the ink colour, we automatically read the word at the same time, resulting in two conflicting pieces of information, therefore slowing down the correct response. This is an easy experiment to run on classmates – ask others to read random coloured words as a comparison and time how long each list takes. There are good computerised versions available such as http://www.psytoolkit.org/experiment-library/stroop.html.

Link to research briefs: this task could be connected to a scenario that asks you to investigate learning or education, individual differences or anything to do with the workplace.

Note that the above are just examples of tasks that could potentially fit with some SQA briefs. A good research study will usually make some kind of comparison, between two different types of tasks (e.g. long words versus short words) or groups (e.g. ages, sexes, personality types).

You can get many other ideas from looking at the research studies described elsewhere in this book – although note that some of the 'classic' studies would nowadays be considered unethical.

Once you have selected a general area to work in and the aim of your study, you can work on planning your experiment at the same time as starting to read up on background research.

Higher: preparing materials

Once you have selected a topic from the SQA briefs and planned all aspects of your study carefully, you will need to prepare all of the materials required for data gathering. These will depend on the study, but as a general guideline, ensure that you have:

✓ Consent forms (see p.275 – Example consent form).

✓ Instructions. Should be standardised, that is, written/typed in advance to ensure that they are the same for all participants. Could appear on a PowerPoint slide or at the start of a questionnaire.

✓ Task materials. Any questionnaires or apparatus as described in the previous section. If you need to borrow apparatus, ensure that you do so in plenty of time.

✓ Clipboards/paper/spare pens. For example, you may need blank paper for responses in a memory test.

✓ Debriefing. Again, this should be standardised. Make sure that all aspects of the study are explained and that participants are thanked.

Higher: data gathering

Once all materials are ready, it is time to gather the data. As with all aspects of the Assignment, it is important to be organised and to communicate well. If you have arranged with a participant to test them at a particular time and place, ensure you are punctual and have everything you need. The experiment should be run smoothly and professionally.

If things don't seem to be going to plan, it is very important that you don't change the procedure mid-way through the experiment. To do so would invalidate all of your findings. Don't worry if the findings do not seem to be turning out the way you expect. In many ways, it can be more interesting to interpret and discuss unexpected findings. There are classics of psychology such as Milgram's (1963) obedience experiment that obtained unexpected findings.

Sample

You need participants to complete your task. For practical reasons, this will probably be an opportunity sample rather than a random sample. For ethical reasons, participants must be at least 16 years of age. If you are based in a school, then only fifth or sixth year pupils can be used (and make sure they actually are 16 or over, as some may not be). You may also use your friends and family.

Pilot study

It is advisable to test out the procedure/materials before you actually collect data. How this is done can range from running a full **pilot study**, which is similar to the actual experiment but with fewer participants, to researchers simply trying the tasks themselves. For things such as memory tests, you need to ensure that it is not too hard or too easy. For questionnaires, it will allow you to ensure that all of the questions are understandable. As well as checking for problems, a pilot study allows you to estimate how long data gathering will take.

Gathering data

When everything has been prepared and checked, you can begin to collect your data. In experiments, each participant in the study should be randomly allocated to an experimental condition – tossing a coin is an acceptable way to do it.

Take care to follow the same standardised procedure with all participants and to follow ethical guidelines, including obtaining written consent, and giving a debrief.

Higher: data analysis

If you have run an experimental study (or a quasi-experiment or natural experiment) for your Assignment, it should be a fairly simple matter to analyse the data. For each condition, you have a set of scores. Calculate the mean, mode and median (as described on p.239) to get an idea of the average/typical score on each condition. Calculate the range and (optionally) the inter-quartile range and standard deviation to get an idea of the spread of data. These findings will go into the results section of your write up.

With a survey or observation, it depends largely on the type of data that you have. Some observation studies will result in numerical data such as time taken to do a task.

Higher: how to structure a write-up

The write-up should use headings and sub-headings. There is a very standard structure in psychology research and it is best to stick to it as far as possible. If you go on to HNC or degree level, you will see that these courses use much the same format for write-ups, as do published research studies. Perhaps you will be publishing your own psychology research articles one day!

Each section is allocated a particular number of marks on the SQA marking scheme. The following table explains what should be included:

Section	Must include	Marks
Introduction (500–700 words)	Background research and theories Aim Hypothesis	10 marks overall: 1–2 per theory/study in background 1 for the aim 1 for the hypothesis
Method (400–600 words)	Four subsections: **Design:** states method (e.g. lab experiment), design (e.g. repeated measures), variables (e.g. IV and DV plus controlled variables). **Participants:** sampling method and group/participants must be described. **Materials:** should be described. **Procedure:** description of procedure; ethical procedure.	8 overall, 1 for each of the following provided it is clear and fully explained: • method • design • variables • sampling method • participants • materials • procedure • ethical procedures

(continued)

Section	Must include	Marks
Results (200–300 words)	Usually does not have subsections but should include: A description of how data were analysed (e.g. use of mean, standard deviation etc.) A table of statistical results. One or more appropriate graphs. A summary of the main findings and whether they support the hypothesis or not.	6 marks overall. Results should be fully explained, though some information can be in an appendix rather than the results section. Marks for: • explanation of analysis • good choice of statistics • accuracy of calculations • choice of presentation (e.g. tables/graphs) • clear use of presentation including labelling of graphs • statement of whether results support hypothesis
Discussion (300–800 words)	Structuring this section into subsections is optional – doing so may make it easier for you to organise your ideas. It is best not to think too much about the marking scheme here but to attempt a full and detailed explanation of your results, linking them to previous theories/studies, and critically evaluating your own study.	12 marks overall: 8 marks for analysis and 4 marks for evaluation; 1 mark for each relevant point. Usually these four things are covered: • links between your findings and previous research • evaluation of your methodology and ethics • discussion of real-world implications and future research that could be done • drawing an overall conclusion from the findings
Supporting information/ overall style and presentation	Must include references – cite sources in text and include a reference list at the end that allows a reader to locate these sources. Should include supporting materials such as questionnaires used as **appendices.** Should be well presented in an appropriate format with page numbers, contents page and correct headings. Overall should be in an appropriate style for a scientific write-up.	1 mark for references (must allow reader to locate the sources used). 1 mark for appendices. 1 mark for format (correct section headings). 1 mark for style (appropriate to scientific writing).

The overall Assignment will be 2,000 to 2,500 words in length.

Title
You don't get marks for your title but you should include one – it is part of good presentation to do so. Something simple, like 'the effect of ___ on ___' usually works best. Include this on a separate title page along with your name, school and Scottish Candidate Number and a picture if you wish.

Contents
It is good style to include a **contents page** with page numbers matching the page number of each section.

Introduction
In the first main section, 'Introduction', you describe the behaviour that your research aims to study. The section starts by stating the topic of study and general area of psychology (e.g. social psychology). It should then progress from general background (the topic/area e.g. conformity) to more specific similar previous research studies (e.g. a study that you are replicating).

- Define and explain the topic (in more detail than would be required at National 5 level).
- Discuss how this behaviour can relate to everyday life.
- Describe one or more relevant theories/models/approaches and explain how they link to the aims of the investigation.
- Explain the methodology and findings of a range of relevant previous studies (a small number in detail or a larger number in less detail).
- Use accurate terminology throughout.

The introduction sets the scene for your own study, describing the background in a 'funnel' shape – starting general and gradually narrowing in focus until you state the aim and hypothesis.

State the aim and hypothesis
First state the aim in general terms. This is where you say what the study is trying to do. Perhaps it could say that the aim is to replicate a previous study, or to find out the effect of something, or to test/find support for a theory. Example:

> The aim of this project is to test the primacy and recency effect in order to evaluate the multi-store model of memory.

Next, give the **hypothesis** – the predicted finding of the study. If it is an experiment, put this under the heading 'experimental hypothesis', otherwise it should be titled 'alternative hypothesis'. If it is a correlational study, use the heading 'correlational hypothesis' and remember that it should be described in terms of the relationship between two variables (see p.240 for more about correlation).

Overall, a good introduction is typically 500 to 650 words long, that is, around one quarter of the total word count.

Top tip

Bear in mind that marking guidelines can change and you should consult the most recent SQA documents.

Top tip

The introduction should simply describe the research area *without mentioning your own study*. In many ways, it is like a short essay on the topic.

Method

The method section is divided into four sub-sections as follows: design, participants, materials and procedure. Use **subheadings**.

- **Design**. This sub-section explains the design of your experiment – RMs or IGs or matched, and states IV, DV and controlled variables (things you kept constant).
- **Participants**. This subsection says who your participants were – how many there were, what sex and age, etc. The sampling method should be stated.
- **Materials**. Here you describe materials used such as sheets and apparatus – give precise details.
- **Procedure**. This subsection states what the participants actually did. Do not include things the researchers did, for example, analyse data. The level of detail should make it possible to replicate your study exactly. This is often the longest part of the Method – it can be in bullet points but is better as prose.

Results

Start with a statement of how the data were analysed (e.g. mean, range) and justify this choice of statistics. After that, this section will largely include tables of results/graphs, but it should also include description and a final summary of the main finding in terms of the experimental hypothesis.

Discussion

This section includes two main elements:

- Analysis of your findings (8 marks).
- Evaluation of your methodology (4 marks).

To start with, summarise the main findings, making appropriate points about whether these supported the research hypothesis and why/why not. It is important to make links to theories and previous research here. This is one of the biggest sections in terms of marks and it is important to go into detail.

One good way to approach the analysis is to brainstorm all of the things that occur to you about your results, good or bad. Are they reliable? Do they fit with other studies or theories? Were any results unexpected in some way?

Don't forget to discuss the implications of all of your main statistics, including both the averages and the measures or dispersion. For example, if you found a very high standard deviation, this can suggest that the effect of your IV was not consistent – it had a much bigger effect on some participants than others. Conversely, a low standard deviation suggests that the IV had a similar effect on everybody.

This section should also evaluate your methodology. Ensure that you include at least four to five well-explained points. Ethical flaws must be covered and you could include extraneous variables that should have been controlled, ecological validity, any possible sources of bias, for example, in the sample used, differences from previous studies mentioned in the introduction or any weaknesses of the data collected.

> 🔍 **Top tip**
>
> Ensure that your analysis of results is detailed. Cut words from other sections if you need to, in order to stick to the overall word count.

You should also suggest improvements for future studies. You should then discuss the relevance of the findings, for example, applications and future research. The findings could have some potential benefit to people's wellbeing and this could be explained – studies of memory can help people to study effectively, for example in terms of future research, think about what you would do next if you were a professional researcher (suggestions should be more imaginative than just 'do the same study again'!)

Finally give a brief conclusion – this could come under a separate subheading. Keep the conclusion down to a couple of sentences – don't ramble.

References

Include references to all sources named in your text in a standard format. Make sure they are in alphabetical order by the first author's surname. At this level you should be producing accurate references, so make sure you check them carefully.

Appendices

Many studies will include one or more appendices at the end. These are not awarded marks but must be included for completeness and will contribute to your marks for presentation. Examples include calculations, task sheets, instructions, debrief, consent forms and apparatus.

Higher: example Assignment

The following example shows how an Assignment report can be structured, following the sections and subsections described above. This example is short – at the lower end of the recommended word count – but of reasonable quality. As a Higher Assignment, it deserves a B grade. An A grade write-up would be very similar but more detailed, especially in the discussion section, and the introduction would be more closely linked to the aim rather than talking about the topic in general.

> **Top tip**
>
> Ensure that all sections are completed in your first draft – don't miss chunks out. It is much easier to improve a section than to add it from scratch.

> **Top tip**
>
> In a real Assignment, a contents page would be included as well.

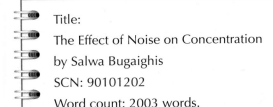

Title:

The Effect of Noise on Concentration

by Salwa Bugaighis

SCN: 90101202

Word count: 2003 words.

INTRODUCTION

Stress can be defined as the body's response when the perceived demands of a situation exceeds a person's perceived ability to cope. Researchers into stress study how things in our environment affect our thoughts, our mood and our health. Things which cause stress are

---

(continued)

called 'stressors'. Stressors can come from our job (occupational), our social life, or from the environment around us. People get stressed from a huge range of situations, such as noisy classrooms, overcrowded trains and arguments with parents.

The study of stress draws heavily on both the biological and cognitive approaches to psychology. Biological psychologists see stress as a bodily response and study the hormones such as adrenaline and cortisol. They view stress as they body's response to things which are detected by the nervous system, and lead to a response by the PNS and endocrine system. Biological psychologists are more interested in how the body reacts to stress than in the cognitive processes – what we think about stress. A lot of research in this area has been conducted on animals, on the basis that they have a similar nervous system and endocrine system to us and therefore the stress response is roughly the same. For example, Selye (1936) studied rats and exposed them to various stressors e.g. spinal shock, surgical injury, and injections of formaldehyde. He found a predictable pattern of biological responses including enlarged adrenal glands, shrunken lymph (white blood cell) system and stomach ulcers (the "physiological triad"). This study and others like it paved the way for an understanding of how stress affects the body. It suggested that all stressors – from background noise to injuries – can have the same effect on the body. However the studies were unethical due to animal cruelty, and Selye was later questioned over research bias when it emerged that he had been funded by tobacco companies, keen to blame health problems on stress rather than on smoking (Bell, 2014).

Noise is an environmental stressor. People might be exposed to noise due to neighbours having a party all night, and this would cause stress. They might be trying to work in the school library when other pupils were annoyingly talking. They might experience stress from the noise of traffic or machinery.

A classic study into the effects of noise on stress was conducted by Glass *et al.* (1969). This study compared reaction to impossible puzzles with unpredictable random background noise. Participants felt frustrated and their ability to solve the puzzles was reduced. This was not found among a control group who heard predictable, regular noises.

The cognitive approach has increased in importance in the study of stress over the past three decades. Cognitive psychologists feel that perceptions and beliefs are of the utmost importance in our behaviour and feelings. This is what the transactional model of Lazarus & Folkman states – people appraise a stressor (primary appraisal) and they also appraise themselves (secondary appraisal), then decide how they will attempt to cope with the stressor. The model can be applied to how we react to noise – the perception of whether or not it is a threat (e.g. panicking that you won't be able to concentrate on homework) affects how stressed a person actually gets.

A more recent study into stress was conducted by Evans and Johnson (2000). They conducted a lab experiment which simulated the effects of a noisy office. The participants they tested showed higher levels of adrenalin after 3 hours, and had poorer posture, and were less likely to attempt difficult puzzles, compared to a control group of participants who had been in quiet conditions. This study has high ecological validity and demonstrates the risks of stress in the real world.

Aim: Due to this previous research it can be seen that noise, especially unpredictable noise, can lead to stress, causing it to be hard to concentrate. The aim of this study is therefore to test the effect of unpredictable noise on concentration, using a recording of unpredictable random bleeps or regular bleeps as people try to solve puzzles, some of which were impossible. This study will find out about the ability of people to concentrate when they are exposed to unpredictable noise, and therefore has relevance to education.

Hypothesis: The experimental hypothesis was that the participants who listened to unpredictable noises would spend less time on the impossible puzzles than those who heard regular noises.

Null hypothesis: The null hypothesis was that participants who heard unpredictable noises would not spend less time on the puzzles. Any differences found would just be due to chance variations.

METHOD

Design:

This was a lab experiment. A classroom was adapted to take the form of a lab. The design of the study was independent groups – participants were either in the unpredictable noise condition or the predictable noise condition. This allowed the same puzzles to be used for both conditions, without practice effects distorting the results. Allocation to conditions was done randomly.

The independent variable of the study was the presence or absence of unpredictable background noise. The dependent variable was the length of time in seconds spent on the puzzles.

Several things needed to be kept constant. Every participant was given the same instructions and the same tasks. The experiment lasted for the same amount of time for every individual participant. In order to control extraneous variables like temperature and distractions, the study was conducted in a small quiet classroom that had been set up as a lab, and each participant was tested separately. Both conditions were conducted at the same time of day (lunchtime).

Participants:

An opportunity sample of 20 participants was used. All of the participants were pupils of a secondary school in Dundee. They were selected by asking people in the cafeteria. Most were known to the researchers, but were not psychology students. The age range was 16–19. The mean age was 18.1 and out of the 20, 12 were male and 8 were female. They were naive to the research, as none had ever studied Psychology.

After they agreed to take part, participants were randomly put into one of the two conditions by tossing a coin, and a time to test them was arranged within the same week.

Materials:

The researchers prepared two short tracks of beeping noises using a computer application. The tracks each lasted for 10 minutes. One had a bleep every 10 seconds, and therefore 60 bleeps overall. The other also had 60 bleeps, but these were spaced at uneven intervals. These were put into an iPod.

A sheet of puzzles was used. It had 8 puzzles on it. Puzzles number 1–6 were straightforward (a pilot study of classmates found that most people could solve each of these within one minute) while puzzles 7 and 8 were impossible to solve. This sheet can be seen at the end of this assignment (see Appendix 2).

(continued)

Procedure:

Participants were tested at school lunchtimes as far as possible, though some were tested during free periods. At prearranged times they were brought to the student laboratory (empty psychology classroom) and seated at a desk, where they were asked to read and sign a short ethical statement and consent form. This informed them of their right to withdraw from the study at any time.

Standardised instructions were then read to each participant. This told them that they would be given puzzles of varying difficulty to do, they had a maximum of 10 minutes to do the puzzles, but they could stop at any time when they were finished or if they decided to give up.

Participants were then handed a sheet of puzzles, face down. They were asked not to turn the paper over until they heard the first 'bleep'. The track was then started, and was played using an iPod with small plug-in speakers. The iPod was around 2 meters away from the participant as they did the puzzles, and the volume was set to a medium level so that it could clearly be heard but was not unpleasantly loud.

A researcher began a timer after the participant had turned over the paper, and stopped the timer when the participant said that they were finished/gave up; if the participant continued to the maximum 10 minutes then they were stopped and '10.00' was recorded as their time.

At the end the participants were debriefed and thanked. The aims of the study were explained to them, and they were reminded of their right to withdraw.

RESULTS:

The results were gathered together and a mean and range were calculated. The mean showed the overall average score, while the range indicated the spread of the scores. This statistic was chosen because it takes all of the raw scores into account. A median was also calculated. This calculation is not distorted by extreme outliers, and can therefore be a more typical midpoint. To measure dispersion in the scores, a simple range was calculated, and again to avoid the problem of outliers and to take every score into account, a standard deviation was calculated too.

These scores can be seen in table 1, below:

	Mean	Median	Range	SD
Predictable noise	473	450	350	95.6
Unpredictable noise	359.5	298	427	159.2

Table 1: Results of study (seconds)

The main findings are shown on the following graph, which provides a useful visual summary. As can be seen, there was a difference between the mean scores for the two conditions of over 110 seconds. Clearly participants persevered longer in the condition where there was predictable background noise during the task. The range and SD were both larger in the unpredictable condition.

The large difference in mean and median scores supports the experimental hypothesis, and the null hypothesis can be rejected.

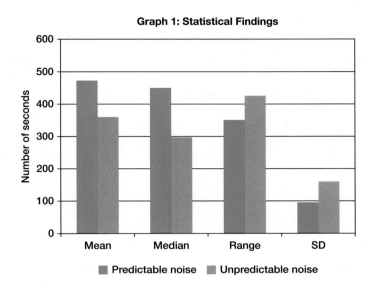

Graph 1: Statistical Findings

Number of seconds

■ Predictable noise ■ Unpredictable noise

DISCUSSION

The results show a clear difference between the two conditions of over 110 seconds (mean). Participants in Condition 2 (unpredictable noise) spent less time on the impossible puzzles than the participants in condition 1. This supports the work of Glass *et al.* (1969). It appears that an inconsistent noise is more stressful than a regular one, resulting in a poorer ability to concentrate on difficult puzzles. The findings support the experimental hypothesis.

The statistics also showed a wider dispersion of results in the noise condition. Both the mean and range were higher. This suggests that there were individual differences in how long people were willing to concentrate despite the background noise.

Together, what these findings suggest is that people will spend less time trying to solve a difficult or impossible puzzle if they can do it in silence. People find noise distracting, and will give up quicker. However, as shown by the range, some people will persevere for longer than others, while some will give up very quickly.

These findings link noise and stress, supporting previous research studies. The stress of background noise apparently reduces people's ability to focus. These findings have practical uses. They may link to the real world because workplaces and classrooms are often very noisy. Factories might have predictable noises due to the regular action of machinery. Classrooms and offices might have unpredictable noises. Noisy neighbours and annoying people on public transport make unpredictable noise that can stress someone out. This study shows that such unpredictable noises are especially likely to harm a person's mental health and concentration.

To evaluate, this study had several weaknesses. The researchers did not check the hearing abilities of participants. If any of them had had poor hearing due to listening to excessively loud music then they would have been less sensitive to noise. There were also some extraneous variables that were not controlled, for example, time of day. People might have been more or less stressed depending on the time of day, and that could have affected their results. Some participants may have had undiagnosed learning disabilities which affected their concentration.

In future studies, participants should all be tested at the same time of day, and a questionnaire should be used to ask about hearing or learning disabilities.

(*continued*)

The predictable noise group spent a mean time of 7.9 minutes working on the tasks, compared to just under 6 minutes by the unpredictable noise group. This suggests that unpredictable background noise makes it more likely that people will get frustrated and give up.

REFERENCES:

Bell, V. (2014). The concept of stress, sponsored by Big Tobacco. Retrieved 01 December 2014 from *http://mindhacks.com/2014/07/14/the-concept-of-stress-sponsored-by-big-tobacco/*

Evans, G. and Johnson, D. (2000). Stress and open-office noise. *Journal of Applied Psychology, 85*(5), 779-783.

Glass, D.C., Singer, J.E. and Friedman, L.N. (1969). Psychic cost of adaptation to an environmental stressor. *Journal of Personality and Social Psychology, 12*(3), 200-210.

Selye, H. (1936). A syndrome produced by diverse nocuous agents. *Nature, 138*, 32.

APPENDICES:

Appendix 1: The following table shows the raw data gathered, alongside statistical calculations:

	Scores	mean	Unpredictable noise x–mean	Squared			Scores	mean	Predictable noise x–mean	Squared	
	190	359.5	−169.5	28730.25			302	473	−171	**29241**	
	186	359.5	−173.5	30102.25			391	473	−82	6724	
	210	359.5	−149.5	22350.25			406	473	−67	4489	
	233	359.5	−126.5	16002.25			421	473	−52	2704	
	270	359.5	−89.5	8010.25			430	473	−43	1849	
	288	359.5	−71.5	5112.25			435	473	−38	1444	
Median:	**298**	359.5	−61.5	3782.25		Median:	**450**	473	−23	529	
	340	359.5	−19.5	380.25			486	473	13	169	
	371	359.5	11.5	132.25			488	473	15	225	
	501	359.5	141.5	20022.25			501	473	28	784	
	559	359.5	199.5	39800.25			578	473	105	11025	
	611	359.5	251.5	63252.25			609	473	136	18496	
	617	359.5	257.5	66306.25			652	473	179	32041	
			SUM:	303983.25					SUM:	109720	
TOTAL:	4674		/n–1	25331.94		**TOTAL:**	6149		/n–1	9143.33	
MEAN:	359.5385		SQ Root:	159.2	SD	**MEAN:**	473		SQ Root:	95.6	SD
Range:	**427**					Range:	**350**				

Appendix 2: Copy of task used:

You have up to 10 minutes to complete these puzzles. You can stop (give up) at any time:

1. Three frogs catch three flies in three minutes. How many frogs are needed to catch 30 flies in 30 minutes?

2. A toad is at the bottom of the well which is 20 meters deep. Every day the toad climbs 5 meters upwards and then fall back by 4 meters. How many days it will take for the toad to reach the top?

3. If x is 3 and y is 4 and $x^2 - 3y + 4 = z$, what is z?

4. Use only the numbers 1, 9, 7 and 5 in that exact order to calculate the numbers 33 and 79. You can use any mathematical symbol (for example, you could make 59 by calculating $1 + 9 \times 7 - 5$).

5. Tom wants to measure out 4 litres of water into a soup pan. He doesn't have a measuring jug, but he does have a 3 litre and a 5 litre bottle. How can he do it?

6. What is the missing number in this sequence: 0, 1, 4, 15, __, 325

7. You have two types of square tile – one type has sides of length 1cm and the other has sides of length 2cm. Find a square with sides of under 10cm which can be covered by an equal number of each type of tile.

8. This diagram shows the walls of five rooms. Cross every line in the diagram once (and only once) using a continuous line. You must cross both internal and external walls:

Finalising the write-up

Final checks

You should allow enough time to check through your Assignment document before you submit it. Remember that it is worth a large percentage of your course marks, so you want it to be excellent.

Backup

This project forms a huge part of your mark for the National 5/Higher course, and it would be disastrous to lose it though a computer problem. Ensure that you keep a backup version (or versions) using a pen drive, cloud storage, emailing drafts to yourself and occasionally printing a hard copy. Save a new version each time you make significant revisions. Don't forget to back it up when it is complete, too, in the unlikely event that it gets lost by your school/college or by the SQA.

> **! Syllabus note**
> This section applies to both National 5 and Higher.

It is a good idea to regularly save your Assignment on a pen drive!

🔑 Key concepts

- Research brief
- Pilot study
- Introduction
- Method
- Results
- Discussion
- Appendices
- Subheadings

🔍 Top tip

Markers can stop marking if you exceed the word limit.

🔍 Top tip

You do not need to include references in your word count.

🔍 Top tip

Note that the 'Discussion' section includes analysis, evaluation and ethics. There are a lot of marks available for this section.

Checklist

This checklist will help you to look out for common problems:

☐ You have a front cover with your name and the title of the study

☐ You have given a definition of the topic of study (e.g. sleep)

☐ You have cited at least two relevant studies in your introduction and included in-line citations

☐ Terminology is used accurately and consistently

☐ You have stated an aim for research on this topic

☐ You have linked the aim to previous research

☐ Check the hypotheses. Are they phrased like the examples on page 232?

☐ Variables are explained in detail (depending on the study, for example, co-variables, or IV and DV plus any variables kept constant)

☐ You have explained why the sampling method is suitable for this study

☐ The method used (e.g. questionnaire/survey/lab experiment) is explained including main strengths and weaknesses of the method

☐ Apparatus/materials required have been explained

☐ Procedure has been explained, with steps to follow

☐ Type of data to be gathered has been explained, as well as how to analyse it.

☐ Potential ethical issues have been identified

☐ Strategies to avoid/minimise ethical issues have been explained

☐ Presentation: a title page and contents are included

☐ References: the studies cited have a reference at the end

☐ Word count: check this using your word processor and state it at the end or on your front cover

Higher only

☐ The discussion includes evaluation of the study

☐ Suggestions for future research studies are included

Appendix: Research materials for Assignment

Example Consent Form

I consent to take part as a participant in this psychology research study. I have received information about the nature of the research and I understand that I have the right to withdraw at any time. I understand that the researcher(s) are working under a code of ethics, which prohibits them from putting me in harmful situations and any data obtained from my participation will be treated confidentially.

Name _____ Date _____

Social behaviour

10 Conformity

The nature of conformity

Conformity usually results from 'peer pressure'

Conformity can be defined as social pressure to change behaviour or beliefs in order to come into line with others in a group. Conformity usually results from 'peer pressure', meaning pressure from your **peers** (people similar to yourself), but we can also feel pressured to go along with groups of strangers, as several studies demonstrate. We are also influenced by **media pressure** – people that we identify with via the media can have a strong influence on behaviour.

Conformity is typically unspoken, that is, we respond to what we observe others doing and change our behaviour to fit in. However others can sometimes ask us to do the same as they are doing, such as, to have another drink or wear different clothes.

Types of conformity

Conformity can be responded to by simply going along with the group situation – or it can affect us more deeply. The term **compliance** refers to the first type – when a person pretends to agree with the group, while maintaining their own beliefs.

If the group has a deeper effect on the person, and they come to agree with the group and adopt the same behaviours even when alone, then the person has shown **identification** with the group, but this may well

> **! Syllabus note**
>
> For National 5, you only need to be able to describe compliance and internalisation.

be temporary – meaning that if the individual leaves the group, the behaviour will stop.

Sometimes a group has such an influence on a person that they permanently adopt the behaviour and carry it out even if they are no longer a group member. This is known as **internalisation** (Kelman, 1958).

Internalisation is when a person permanently adopts a behaviour

Examples

Compliance	Tom notices that everyone else has taken their food off their tray in the cafeteria, so he decides to do the same.
Identification	Dave supports his school hockey team, but then he moves school and starts to support the team of his new school instead.
Internalisation	Ava spends a lot of time with a group of friends who love rock climbing and comes to take up the sport. Long after she no longer sees those friends, she still goes rock climbing.

Motivation to conform

Why do people feel the need or desire to conform? There are times when we feel an urge to do the same as others that is very hard to resist. Where does that motivation come from? According to Deutsch and Gerrard (1955) there are two separate reasons motivating conformity, which might occur separately or both at once:

Informational influence: when uncertainty leads to a person adopting the behaviour of others – they conform because they don't know what to do and they want to be correct.

Normative influence: when a person is not in doubt but is influenced by social norms. The pressure comes from the group, based on a need to be liked and accepted by it.

Classic research into informational influence

Jenness (1932) conducted a study where individuals were shown beans in a bottle and asked to guess their number. There were over 800 beans and it was impossible to count them, so nobody could be entirely sure of their estimate. Participants were then put in groups of three and asked to discuss the number and give a group estimate. When later given the option of changing their first guess, most participants wanted to change to a number closer to the group estimate. They were motivated to be correct because Jenness offered the reward of an A grade for the most accurate guess in their class. It appeared that when unsure of the correct answer, people will tend to be influenced by a peer group – even though there is no reason to believe that the group are any more accurate.

Jenness's study was supported by Sherif (1935), who obtained similar results using an illusion called the auto-kinetic effect where a point of

Top tip

The term 'comply' is also used more generally to mean going along with any kind of social pressure, including obedience. 'Dissent' means refusing to conform or obey.

Discussion point

Distinguish between compliance, identification and internalisation by asking if a person would exhibit a behaviour in private or just in group situations and whether they would continue the behaviour if the social group ceased to exist or they were no longer a member.

Discussion point

What types of groups and situations lead to identification?

Top tip

Normative influence is often called 'normative social influence' or NSI. Informational influence is often called 'information social influence' or ISI.

? Discussion point

Do you consider informational influence to be true conformity? What about internalisation? Or do you think the term 'conformity' should only apply when people are acting against their own wishes and beliefs?

How many beans are in the bottle?

The auto-kinetic effect was first noticed in stars

Top tip

Many sources focus on a later replication of this 'length of lines' study. You can gain credit for these instead of the original study, as long as they are accurately explained. In the replication, Asch (1955) calculated an overall conformity rate of 36.8%, based on 123 participants.

light appears to move in a darkened room. There was no true answer, but when estimates were called out aloud in a group of three, people's estimates conformed to those of group members.

Classic research into normative influence: the Asch experiment

Early studies such as the Jenness (1932) 'bottle of beans' study put people into ambiguous social situations, to see whether people follow the crowd when they don't know what to do or say.

However, a study by Asch (1951) tested whether social pressure would result in people denying something they could see quite clearly with their own eyes. He tested people's judgement of the length of lines. In a simple task, participants were asked to state which one out of three 'comparison' lines was the same as the 'standard' line – 'C' in the example in the Key study below. Asch found that 75% of people conformed on a least one occasion – demonstrating that most people are willing to say something that they know is wrong due to social pressure (see key study).

📖 Key study: Asch's (1951) experiment into length of lines

A photograph of the study

Aim: In contrast to previous studies of conformity, Asch wanted to see whether people would conform to others' incorrect estimates if the task was easy and the correct answer was obvious.

Method: Fifty male American participants were used and they were told that this was an experiment into visual perception. They were placed in a group with seven other individuals. Unknown to the true participant, everyone else in the group was an actor whose responses had been prepared in advance.

The group were shown a series of 18 cards and asked to match the line to a choice of three comparison lines each time. The confederates (actors) had all been briefed to give the same wrong answer on 12 out of the 18 examples – these are described as the 'critical trials'. The true participant was always last or second last to answer. This put them in a position of having to choose between giving the clearly correct answer or conforming to the majority and giving the wrong answer.

Findings: *Two main issues arose. First, the majority group generally had a large influence on the true participant. Over all of the critical trials, 32% were incorrect – despite the fact that participants could see the correct answer very clearly. There was a mean of 3.84 errors out of the 12 trials; in contrast, a control group made a mean of 0.08 errors. Asch believed that the main reason for these findings was that people do not wish to be ridiculed and excluded by a majority. Some participants reported that they started to doubt their own perceptions.*

Second, there were considerable individual differences in how people responded; 25% of participants did not conform at all (by the same token, 75% of participants gave a wrong answer at least once). Asch noted that even when participants gave correct answers, the way they expressed their answers was influenced by the presence of the majority, with participants often appearing withdrawn or embarrassed. The largest number of incorrect responses was 11 out of 12; Asch noted that this participant 'appeared nervous and somewhat confused… The primary factor in his case was a loss of confidence' (p.228).

Evaluation: *The Asch study was a powerful demonstration of how a group can influence our behaviour – even a group of strangers can make people respond very differently to how they would when alone. The study was hugely influential and many other studies have used a similar task. However, it lacked ecological validity, as it was an artificial lab experiment. The task itself lacked mundane realism, as real-life situations where we are pressured to conform tend not to be so clear-cut.*

It may also be the case that the culture of 1950s America encouraged conformity and the findings can't necessarily be generalised to social behaviour in other places and eras. Perrin and Spencer (1981) replicated the Asch study using British engineering students and found a much lower level of conformity than the original study. They suggested that the findings depended on how people interpret the social situation and on their cultural norms.

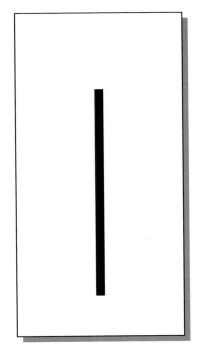

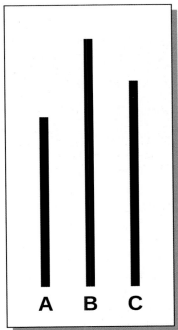

Asch used clear images of lines

Minority influence

Most studies of conformity investigate the effect of a majority on an individual or a small group. But what about the reverse? Moscovici (1981) believed that in the real world, compliance with a majority viewpoint rarely has any long-term impact on a person's behaviour. Instead, it is often minorities that cause a real long-term change by exerting consistent pressure on the majority. Examples could include feminism or the environmental movement.

Minority influence is when an individual or a minority within the group changes the behaviour of the larger group. In a classic study of the phenomenon, Moscovici *et al.* (1969) planted two confederates in a group of six that had the task of naming the colours of a set of slides. The confederates had been told to call certain blue slides 'green'. True participants showed signs of being influenced – 8.42% of their responses followed the minority, considerably more than the control

🔍 **Top tip**

Fake participants in studies such as Asch (1951) are called confederates or 'stooges'.

? Discussion point

Can you think of any examples of minority influence among school or college students?

? Discussion point

Why might pressure from a minority have a greater long-term effect on behaviour and opinions compared to a majority?

group. Interestingly, the effect disappeared if the two confederates were not consistent with each other – influenced responses from the true participants dropped to just over 1%. Therefore, it appears that if a minority is to exert an effect on the majority, it has to present its viewpoint consistently.

The women's suffrage movements is an example of minority influence

Key concepts

- Conformity
- Peer pressure
- Media pressure
- Compliance
- Identification
- Internalisation
- Normative influence
- Informational influence
- Minority influence

✔ Questions

1. Which type of influence means that we conform in order to be liked and accepted – informational or normative?

2. What type of conformity occurs if you feel part of a group but stops if you leave the group?

3. What term means that someone refuses to conform?

4. What type of objects did participants have to estimate in Jenness's study?

5. How many of Asch's participants conformed at least once?

6. If you laugh at a joke that you don't find funny, just because everyone else is laughing, which type of conformity is occurring?

7. If a person becomes a socialist because their school friends are, and then maintains these political beliefs throughout life, which type of conformity is occurring?

8. Which type of influence has a long-term effect on behaviour, according to Moscovici?

9. Was Asch's study a lab or a field experiment?

10. Who were the participants in Perrin and Spencer's replication of the Asch study when no conformity was found?

GO! Activities

1. Over the following week, take notes of situations where you observe informational or normative influence. Do you sometimes see both together? Be prepared to discuss this with fellow students.

2. Find out more about Jenness's study. Could you replicate it with students today? Do you think the results would be the same?

3. How does conformity affect other areas of Psychology? For example, does it affect sleep habits, attitudes to psychopathology, or other areas of social psychology such as prejudice? Write a short summary or blog post on this issue.

Explanations of conformity

What makes some people conform when others don't, or conform on some occasions and not others? In other words, what **factors** affect levels of conformity?

The factors that affect conformity can be divided into two types: **situational factors** and **individual differences**. Situational factors are things that vary from one situation to another, while individual differences refers to the fact that some people are more likely to conform than others due to things such as their personality.

How does group size affect conformity?

Key situational factors

Asch's study helps to illustrate some of the key factors that make conformity levels rise or fall depending on the situation.

Group size

The most obvious situational factor is group size – it might be assumed that a large majority will have a much bigger influence than one or two people. Asch (1951) put this to the test by varying the number of participants in his 'length of lines' experiment. He found that with fewer than three confederates, the level of compliance diminished greatly. However, increasing group size only made a difference up to a certain point:

- With only one confederate, there was almost no conformity.
- With two confederates, the conformity rate was 12.8%.
- With three confederates, the rate rose to 33.3%.
- The addition of further confederates made only a slight difference to results.

In his replication of the study, Asch (1955) varied the number of participants from 1 to 15 and found very similar results (see graph).

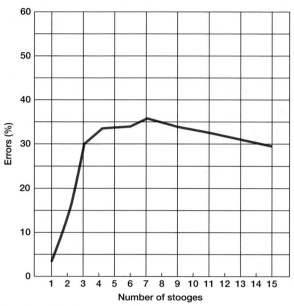

Results of Asch's 1955 study

In summary, the rise in group size from three to four is critical. After that, adding an additional person (e.g. increasing group size from five to six) only made a slight difference. It could be that beyond this point, the others are perceived as 'a group' rather than as a particular number of individuals. It is also possible that true participants may suspect a trick if a large number of the other participants all give the same wrong answer; in the real world, a larger group may have more of an influence (Baron & Byrne, 1997).

Social support

In another variation of Asch's basic procedure, he instructed one confederate to act as an ally to the true participant by disagreeing with the others so that the majority were no longer unanimous. The ally was seated fourth, and therefore answered before the true participant. This produced a sharp decrease in total conformity, which fell to 5.5% (Asch, 1951). Interestingly, the participants reported greater feelings of warmth and liking towards the ally, but did not believe they had been influenced by him (Asch, 1955).

How would conformity affect this driver?

Secrecy of response

Asch's classic study mainly tested public compliance. In another variation of the study, a participant was told that they had arrived late and they had to write their answers down privately, while everyone else spoke theirs aloud. The experiment was otherwise identical to the original study, with confederates giving incorrect answers. The conformity level fell to 5%. This suggests that in real situations where we can hide our response or avoid responding in front of other people, compliance is much less likely to occur.

Conformity tends to fall when participants are able to write their answers down secretly

Similarity of group

Experiments on conformity tend to use strangers, but away from the laboratory, we are most likely to come into contact with, and be influenced by, people that we have something in common with, such as friends and colleagues.

Abrams *et al.* (1990) found that if participants feel that they share characteristics with the majority, they are more subject to normative influence in an Asch-type situation.

Even just being in the same situation as another person – for example, on the same plane or train – means that we have something in common and may assume that they are similar to ourselves.

We may assume that someone on the same bus is similar to ourselves in some way

Individual differences in conformity level

Looking at the classic research on conformity described above, it is hard to escape the idea that some people are more susceptible than others to social pressure; 75% conformed at least once in the Asch study but how were the remaining 25% able to maintain their independence on every trial?

This question links to an important concept in psychology more generally – that people's behaviour is strongly affected by **individual differences**. Some of the main individual differences to consider here (as in other topics) are age, sex, cognition, personality and culture. These are the things that make us fundamentally different from one another and all of these things could potentially cause people to conform.

> ### 🔍 Top tip
>
> Use the 'S' initials of these factors to help remember them – **s**ituational: **s**ize, **s**upport, **s**ecrecy, **s**imilarity. Write these on an index card or a page of your notebook.

Age

Some age differences have been found in conformity. A review of studies reported that conformity levels remain static between the ages of 10 and 14, after which, the ability to dissent rises steadily up to age 18. Thereafter it remains steady through early adulthood (Steinberg & Monahan, 2007).

When considering age, it is important to consider the age of the group. We conform more to people like ourselves in a Jenness-type experiment. For example, would you conform to a group of young children? What about a group of people a year or two older than yourself? In this sense, age is also a *situational* factor in conformity, affecting the context of the situation.

How likely are you to conform to a younger sibling?

Personality

Certain personality characteristics link to conformity levels. Santee and Maslach (1982) found that people who have higher self-esteem were less likely to conform. Burger (1992) showed that people who value control are less likely to conform: participants rated as high in their personal desire for control conformed less in an Asch-type experiment where they had to rate the funniness of cartoons.

However, in the Stanford Prison Experiment (see p.294), Zimbardo *et al.* (1973) did not support the idea that social behaviour comes from personality. They concluded that behaviour is mainly influenced by social context.

Women tend to conform more to promote group harmony

A rally in support of same-sex marriage in Sydney, Australia, May 2015

🔍 Top tip

Ensure that you can explain both situational factors and individual differences. Cultural factors must be included, as this is a mandatory part of the course content.

❓ Discussion point

What subcultures exist where you live? Consider groups related to age, occupation, fashions and hobbies. Are you a member of a subculture? Do people from subcultures appear to conform more or less than the majority? Do some of them display counter-conformity?

Collectivist cultures tend to show higher levels of conformity than individualist cultures

Sex

Some researchers have found sex differences in conformity, with women tending to conform more compared to men (Mori & Arai, 2010; see key study). Eagly (1987) suggested that this happens because women tend to take a communal role and promote harmony in the group, while men are more comfortable maintaining independence. However, the behaviour of males and females varies greatly over time and depends on culture. Some older studies of gender differences in conformity may be culturally biased and outdated, while even more recent ones, such as Mori and Arai (2010), cannot be generalised to all cultures.

Thought processes

There are differences in cognitive processes from one individual to another in a conformity situation – everyone interprets the situation differently. This was noted by Asch (1955) who stated that some participants genuinely doubted their own judgement, while others knew that they were right but followed the crowd in an attempt to avoid disapproval.

Hornsey *et al.* (2003) found that if someone had a strongly held conviction about an issue, they are less likely to conform. They studied 205 Australian university students who had reported being in favour of same-sex marriage and showed them faked graphs supposedly of other students' views that seemed to show that the majority disagreed with them. In terms of how they would act privately, those with weak beliefs conformed, while those with stronger beliefs did not. In terms of public behaviour the difference was even greater – those with strong beliefs in favour of the topic showed **counter-conformity**, meaning they became even more strongly in favour of same-sex marriage than before, in defiance of the supposed majority who were against them.

Culture

One problem with interpreting the classic research by Jenness and Asch is that they studied young Americans in the mid-20th century and findings can't necessarily be generalised beyond that cultural context – a culture that has been described as highly conformist (Perrin & Spencer, 1981). Follow up studies have not always replicated the findings, perhaps because of varying cultural attitudes about the value or necessity of maintaining group harmony.

One consistent cultural difference is that collectivist cultures tend to show higher levels of conformity than individualist cultures. Collectivist cultures – including most Central American and South East Asian countries – value the family and society over the needs of the individual while individualist cultures – including most Western countries – have the opposite emphasis. Smith and Bond (1993) reviewed conformity research from around the world and found Belgians to have the lowest level of conformity and Fijian Indians the highest. Some subcultures are strongly associated with counter-conformity – punks are a good example of this. It may be the case, though, that members of the subculture conform to each other (see chapter 2 for more information about culture).

📖 Key study: Mori and Arai (2010): length of lines study

Aim: This study aimed to replicate Asch's experiment without the need for actors, to ensure that nobody was acting unnaturally. It also included both males and females, thus contributing to our understanding of individual differences in conformity.

Method: The researchers replicated an Asch-type situation with length of lines but with an important twist – there were no actors. Instead, everyone wore a pair of specially designed filter glasses that allowed them to look at the same image but see different things. This meant that everyone was a true participant – but one had been given a different type of filter glasses that meant that they perceived a different correct answer. 104 Japanese student participants were used in groups of four. Participants stated their answers aloud, with the minority participant going third.

Specially designed glasses were used in the experiment

Findings: For female participants, results were similar to those of Asch (1955), with conformity to the majority shown on 4.41 out of 12 critical trials (versus 3.84 in the original). However, it was found that the male participants did not conform to the majority view. Another difference from the Asch findings was that it made very little difference whether the majority were unanimous or not. In other words, having an 'ally' did not make the radical difference shown in Asch (1951) and led to a small reduction in conformity rate.

Evaluation: The researchers explained the gender difference in terms of the different expectations and social roles of males and females. They concluded that the reduced conformity in males compared to the Asch study may reflect generational changes since the 1950s. Culture could also be a factor, as gender roles can be different from one culture to another.

In this study, the participants knew each other (compared to the strangers used in the Asch study), which could have affected results. Mori and Arai believe this was a strength of the study because how we conform to our friends and acquaintances is more relevant to real world problems than conformity to strangers.

Summary and analysis

The Asch experiment has certain limitations mentioned in the previous section and its findings cannot necessarily be generalised to all situations. Nevertheless, the way that the study varied several aspects of the procedure provides useful objective evidence to help you analyse situational factors. For example, it can be used to support a claim that group size affects behaviour or that having social support can make us less likely to conform.

It is useful to consider the categories of individual difference such as age, personality and culture. In real situations, these factors may all play a role and may interact with each other, making it hard to be sure which is the most important.

⚷ Key concepts

- Factors in conformity
- Situational factor (conformity)
- Individual differences
- Counter-conformity

✔ Questions

1. At what point in Asch's study did rising majority group size make the biggest difference to conformity?

2. True or false: writing answers in secret made no difference to conformity level in Asch's study?

3. True or false: having the support of an ally dramatically reduced conformity?

4. Name three types of individual differences that can affect conformity.

5. Which study showed that low self-esteem affected conformity level?

6. What is meant by 'counter-conformity', as shown in the Hornsey *et al.* study?

7. Which group of cultures tend to show higher levels of conformity?

8. How did Mori and Arai (2010) avoid the need for confederates in their study?

9. What two major differences were there in the findings in Mori and Arai compared to the original study by Asch?

10. Who were the participants of Mori and Arai's study?

🔵 Activities

1. Draw up an A3-sized poster on either the Jenness, Asch or Mori and Arai study. Ensure that you include the aim of the study and the background. Choose a suitable image and describe the procedure. This could be used to decorate your study area and will help you to remember the details of the study.

2. Make a mind-map in your notes of the main individual differences that can affect behaviour – personality, age, sex, thinking style, culture. As well as individual differences in conformity, you could link these to other topics such as stress or sleep on your mind map.

Obedience

Obedience is a form of social pressure, but unlike conformity, it normally involves a direct command or instruction. While pressure to conform comes from peers, obedience is the result of an **authority figure** – someone in a position of power – telling you what to do. In addition, the person giving the order is typically not doing the same thing themselves. It is a case of 'follow my instructions' rather than 'follow my example'.

Obedience to rules and to authority figures is a key part of everyday life, and is arguably a useful thing that allows society to function effectively. For example, rules about behaviour in school allow everyone to learn without disruptions, while rules about paying tax allow the government to collect money that can then be spent on socially useful things such as health care. However, if an authority gives a harmful instruction and people obey it, then obedience becomes problematic. One of the biggest questions for social psychologists since the mid-20th century has been why people followed instructions to commit atrocities such as the Nazi Holocaust (i.e. the mass murder of Jews, disabled people, gypsies, communists and homosexuals under Hitler's regime in the Third Reich).

Legitimate authority

Many parts of society, such as schools and workplaces, are structured as **hierarchies**, meaning that people with lower ranks or status are expected to obey those in higher positions. For example, employees usually obey their manager and school pupils usually obey their teachers and headteacher. These figures are considered in society to be **legitimate authority** figures.

Sometimes, however, the legitimacy of an authority figure is not clear – someone may give an order but people are not sure whether to obey or not, asking themselves, 'does this person have the right to tell me what to do?' This problem is familiar to student teachers or babysitters, as children may not recognise them as authority figures, and therefore, behave more disobediently than usual!

Someone who receives an order tends to look for clues in the situation and a major one is the way someone is dressed. Bickman (1974) conducted a study where actors gave orders to passers-by, such as '*pick up that litter*' or '*give that person a dime*'. There were three conditions – actor dressed as security guard, in a milkman's uniform or in casual clothes. The security guard outfit led to the greatest level of obedience. Even though a security guard is not a legitimate authority – they don't have the right to tell members of the public to pick up litter – their uniform conveyed a sense of power and legitimacy.

Obedience is the result of an authority figure telling you what to do

!**Syllabus note**

This part of this topic is only required at Higher, not National 5.

🔍 **Top tip**

Although it forms part of the same topic, obedience is **not** a type of conformity. Both conformity and obedience are types of **social pressure**.

The commandant of the concentration camp in Landsberg Germany stands among dead prisoners

Employees usually obey their manager

Sociologist Max Weber said that legitimate authority and the right to give orders comes from three main sources (cited in Howitt *et al.*, 1989):

- Tradition: in each society, some groups are considered to have the right to give instructions, for example parents.
- Legal: some people have a legal authority, and it is rational for others to obey them because failing to do so would have negative consequences such as punishments.
- Charisma: some people have great personal charm and manage to persuade others that they should be listened to instead of the traditional authorities, sometimes claiming religious inspiration or moral superiority. Political rebels and religious dissidents fall into this group.

However, there are some limitations to this view. It is a descriptive summary, which doesn't really explain *why* people obey instructions from these sources. Also, as is clear from the Milgram study (see below), the power of the authority figure plays less of a role than variations in the social situation and factors such as experience.

Children may not recognise a babysitter as a legitimate authority figure

The Milgram study of obedience

According to social psychologist Stanley Milgram, orders can result in a clash between a person's morals and the social situation. He wanted to know if there was something uniquely obedient about German soldiers and concentration camp guards who had followed immoral orders during the Second World War.

Milgram devised an experiment where people would be asked to deliver increasing levels of electric shocks on the demands of an experimenter – although the shocks would be faked, the participants would think that they were real. He asked his colleagues, researchers and PhD students, whether people would obey and most said that only a tiny minority of people would obey, and those would be psychopaths. Essentially, the experts had predicted that the American participants would not obey immoral instructions and that German people during the war were somehow different. In fact, his volunteers proved highly obedient to authority (see key study).

In Bickman's study the security guard's uniform conveyed a sense of legitimate authority

? Discussion point

Who are the legitimate authority figures in your life?

📖 Key study: Milgram's (1963) study of obedience

Aim: *Milgram wanted to know how obedient ordinary people would be to an authority figure. This would allow him to have a baseline level of obedience in a normal population, for comparison in later studies.*

Method: *Milgram recruited 40 volunteers by advertising for a 'memory and learning experiment'. An experimenter introduced each participant to 'Mr Wallace', who they were told was another participant – but was actually a confederate working for Milgram. The pair was then told that one of them would take the role of a 'teacher' and one would be a 'learner' in the memory experiment. The teacher, they were told, would have to give an electric shock to the learner each time they got an answer wrong. The participant was given a mild 15-volt electric shock as an example. The pair drew lots – but this was fixed; Mr Wallace was always placed in the role of learner and the true participant placed in the role of teacher.*

A photograph from the study

The electric shock apparatus had a series of switches, the first of which was labelled 15V, and participants were asked to increase the shock level with each wrong answer. There were labels below the switches, for example, 375V – 'Danger, severe shock'. The last switch was labelled 450V. The confederate deliberately got many answers wrong and the participants found themselves under pressure to give stronger and stronger shocks.

The confederate participant grunted with pain at first, and as the faked shocks continued, began to shout in protest, including saying that he had a heart condition and refusing to take any further part. After 315V, he was silent. If the true participant hesitated, the experimenter could use a verbal prod such as 'the experiment requires that you continue', or 'you have no choice, teacher – you must go on'.

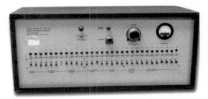

The electric shock apparatus used

Findings: *Twenty-six out of 40 (65%) continued up to the maximum shock level of 450 volts. Many showed signs of becoming highly stressed but nobody stopped before 300V.*

Evaluation: *This was a groundbreaking and highly influential study that was well controlled in a lab. However, it can be criticised on ethical grounds, as participants were both stressed and deceived. In his defence, Milgram stated that in a subsequent survey, 84% of participants said that they were 'glad to have been in the experiment' and that participants showed no signs of long-term harm in psychiatric assessments (Colman, 1987).*

The dose requested by the doctor was twice the maximum shown on the label

The obedience rate was higher in the prestigious setting of Yale University

Was the Milgram study realistic?

Milgram's study was a fascinating demonstration of obedience in a lab but it is not clear if it can be directly compared to everyday life – it lacked ecological validity. Orne (1962) doubted whether Milgram's participants really believed in the electric shocks and suggested that such a high level of obedience in the face of harmful consequences would not be found in the real world.

However, another research study in the 1960s demonstrated a very high level of obedience in the real world. Hofling *et al.* (1966) conducted a field experiment on nurses. A fake drug labelled 'Astroten' was left in the ward and each nurse received a phone call from an unknown doctor, calling himself 'Dr Smith'. The doctor told the nurse to prepare a dose of the drug (which was double the maximum dosage indicated on the label) and give it to a patient, 'Mr Jones'. Despite having the opportunity to refuse, 21 out of 22 nurses prepared the medication and they were going to administer it until stopped by the experimenter.

Why people obey: effects of the situation

We like to feel that we have a choice over our actions and that whether we obey an immoral command or not is due to our own moral values. Some participants in Milgram's study did refuse to obey. One participant, Jan Rensaleer, was an electrical engineer, and refused to continue, stating '*I know what shocks do to you*' (Milgram, 1974, p. 52).

However, the overall findings of his work led Milgram to believe that individual factors have a very limited role in obedience behaviour. People don't obey because of their personality, he thought, but because of the social situation they find themselves in. His results went against the idea that Nazi soldiers were somehow different from other people and suggested that in particular circumstances, nearly everyone will obey authority.

According to Milgram, there were several variables that could have affected the results and in order to test the role of each variable he repeated his experiment 20 times with a slightly different procedure each time. Every time he used a different 40 participants, and obedience level was always based on *the percentage who went up to the maximum shock level*.

Legitimate authority

Milgram (1974) thought that one reason for the high level of obedience in his original study was that its setting was prestigious – Yale University. What would happen if it was conducted in a more everyday setting? He replicated the experiment in an office in the city centre, with the experimenter wearing casual clothes. Obedience rate dropped to 52% – a fairly small difference that suggests that the appearance and social power of the experimenter was not the main cause of obedience.

Proximity

Milgram felt that having a wall between the participant and Mr Wallace acts as a **buffer**, making it easier to deliver the shock, as the suffering is not immediately visible. One variation of the experiment – the 'proximity' variation – involved the teacher sitting in the same room as Mr Wallace, so they could see as well as hear him. However, obedience rate only fell to 40%, and even when the teacher had to hold Mr Wallace's arms down, believing that shocks were delivered through metal plates on the chair arms ('touch proximity'), obedience rate stood at 30% (Milgram, 1974). It appears that the lack of a buffer has an effect but that there is still a lot of obedience.

Children tend to be less obedient if their teacher or parent leaves the room

Presence of authority

In the classic version of the study, the authority figure, that is, the experimenter was in the room (note that the 'experimenter' was an actor as well and not Milgram himself). Life experience suggests that if the authority figure is removed, obedience tends to fall, just as when children stop working if their teacher or parent leaves the room. In the 'remote authority' variation, the experimenter gave initial instructions and then left the room, delivering further instructions by phone. The obedience rate fell to 20.5% (Milgram, 1974).

Peers

Milgram wanted to see how peer pressure would interact with obedience. To do this, he added two confederate teachers who were instructed to dissent at specific points (150V and 210V). The obedience rate fell to 10%. However, in another variation, a confederate teacher pressed the electric shock switches, so that the true participant just had to read the questions, thereby playing along with the suffering of the 'learner' but not directly causing it; 92.5% continued to the maximum level in this variation (Milgram, 1974).

Why people obey: effects of society

Agency theory

According to Milgram, people's decision to obey or dissent from an authority figure can depend on the mental state in which they find themselves. Most of the time, we act based on our own wishes and desires. Milgram called this the **autonomous state**. However, at times of stress and conflict, there is a tendency to look for the person in charge – the authority figure in the situation – and follow their orders. This happens because we are used to hierarchical systems throughout society where there are both leaders and followers. Therefore, when people are under moral strain such as in the Milgram experiment, they relinquish their own moral responsibility and act on the basis of this authority figure's commands. This is known as entering the **agentic state**:

- Autonomous state: seeing yourself as being in power; acting on your own wishes and morals.
- Agentic state: seeing another person as having power; acting on behalf of their principles/commands.

At times of stress and conflict, there is a tendency to look for the person in charge

Parenting style will have an affect on a child's level of obedience

Top tip

Find out more about the Stanford Prison Experiment and its follow-up, the BBC Prison Experiment. As well as being relevant to obedience, they are also useful evidence for the prejudice topic – the two groups quickly became hostile towards each other, rather like in Sherif's 'summer camp' experiment (see p.324).

Socialisation

One of the reasons we enter the agentic state is that society has taught us to respect and obey authority figures. Childhood is the time when we learn society's rules, including learning who is considered to be an authority figure and who is not – parents, teachers and so on. The effect of childhood experiences on making us behave according to social norms is known as **socialisation**. It is the result of collective social pressures from family, teachers, peers and other significant people encountered as a child grows up. As Andersen and Zimbardo (1984, p. 200) state:

'The 'good child' learns his place in all social settings, stays put in her seat, is polite, speaks only when spoken to, is cooperative, does not make trouble, and never makes a scene. As children we are rewarded for going along with the group and for not insisting on getting our way. It is the wiser course of action, we are taught, to go with (or around) power, not to challenge it.'

Parenting

One of the biggest influences on a child's socialisation is its parents. However, not all children are raised in the same way by their parents. Some are encouraged by their parents to think for themselves and make rational choices. This is called **democratic parenting**. In this parenting style, rules are not absolute; instead, children are encouraged to negotiate reasonable boundaries.

Other parents teach their children that obedience to, and respect for, authority figures is the top priority and that rules should be obeyed and not discussed. This is known as **authoritarian parenting**.

However, it is hard to put parents into a particular category. In addition, as we grow older, peers begin to become more influential. Nevertheless, the beliefs about the world that we learn in early childhood tend to stay with us.

Summary and analysis

The variations of Milgram's basic study provide powerful evidence of the role of situational factors in obedience. They are supported by the hospital study of Hoffling *et al.* (1966), which demonstrated that obedience plays a role in real life settings.

Another study that showed the importance of the situation was the Stanford Prison Experiment by ZImbardo and colleagues (Zimbardo *et al.*, 1973). Student volunteers were randomly divided into two groups – prisoners and guards – and put into a mock prison, which was actually set in the basement of Stanford University Psychology Department. The researchers observed the students changing their behaviour to suit their new roles, with prisoners becoming demoralised and depressed while many guards became aggressive and demeaning, and used their power to humiliate the prisoners.

However, despite the importance of the social situation, individual factors can play a role in obedience too. You have already seen the how the personal experience level of some of Milgram's participants made them more likely to dissent. Sex differences have been found too, with Kilham and Mann (1974) reporting significantly lower levels of obedience among women in a Milgram-type experiment.

Kohlberg (1969) described the importance of an individual's level of moral development in whether they obey authority or not (see box below). He stated that only some people reach the highest level of moral development – **post-conventional reasoning** – and that these people are better able to disobey an immoral command.

- Pre-conventional reasoning: the individual's view of right or wrong depends on the standards of adults around them, and on the outcome of their actions. At this stage, typical in children under the age of 9, anything that results in punishment is 'bad', and anything that results in a reward is 'good'.
- Conventional reasoning: the individual's view of right-or wrong has come to be based on the standards of their society as a whole – they see law breaking as always wrong, for example, while obeying the rules is seen as good behaviour.
- Post-conventional reasoning: at this stage, the individual goes beyond the norms of their society and comes to realise that rules/laws themselves are not always morally right. Such individuals may consider it morally correct to break a law if it results in a greater good.

✔ Questions

1. True or false: obedience usually results from unspoken social pressure?

2. Two sources of authority according to Weber are traditional and legal – what is the third?

3. What is the name of a social structure where people with lower ranks or status are expected to obey those in higher positions?

4. How many participants took part in Milgram's original (1963) study?

5. How many of the participants obeyed up to the maximum level?

6. What were the main ethical issues with the Milgram study?

7. In what setting did the Hofling *et al.* (1966) study take place?

8. Which variation of Milgram's basic procedure produced the highest level of obedience?

9. What are the two states that form Milgram's agency theory?

10. True or false: democratic parenting encourages children to blindly obey authority?

🔑 Key concepts

- Obedience
- Authority figure
- Social pressure
- Hierarchy
- Legitimate authority
- Buffer
- Autonomous state
- Agentic state
- Socialisation
- Democratic parenting
- Authoritarian parenting

> **GO!** Activities
>
> 1. Think of three examples of when obedience is a positive/useful thing in society and three examples of when it can be negative/harmful. For example: 'obedience is a bad thing if someone obeys their partner in an abusive relationship.' Compare your answers with a classmate. Do you agree about when obedience is good or bad?
>
> 2. Draw up a table summarising the main variations (including the original) of Milgram's study ('proximity', 'peer gives shock', etc.) and the obedience level that was found with each one.
>
> 3. Give a real example of how the following factors can affect whether people obey or not:
>   - power of the authority figure
>   - presence/absence of the authority figure
>   - proximity to victim
>   - personality/personal experience
>   - peers
>   - parenting style
>
> If possible, draw the examples from your own experience.

! Syllabus note

This part of this topic is only required at Higher, not National 5.

🔍 Top tip

This applied area of the topic relates to both resisting conformity and resisting obedience.

Resisting social pressure

Having seen how powerful an effect conformity and obedience can have on people's behaviour – from making us deny the evidence of our own eyes to risking another person's life – it should be obvious that at times, for example when pressured to take part in bullying, substance abuse or crime, it would be helpful if individuals were able to **resist social pressure** and to stick to their own beliefs and choices.

Social pressure has such power over us that it is, perhaps, no surprise that is used for harmful purposes by some individuals in society. Unscrupulous salespeople, politicians or abusive partners may use social pressure to get what they want. For convenience, these people will be all be referred to as **manipulators**.

The variations of Milgram's classic obedience study showed that the biggest effect came not from changing the authority figure, but from adding peers who complied or dissented. This suggests that combining both obedience and conformity makes for a very powerful mixture. As will be seen in the following section, this combination of social pressure is used by groups such as **cults** to distort people's behaviour.

What is a cult?

The concept of a **cult** is hard to define, as different groups each have their own characteristics. There is a tendency for the term 'cult' to be used as an insult about any group that we don't agree with.

However, researchers have tried to establish an objective definition. Overall, a cult is a group with beliefs and behaviours that are considered abnormal by the majority of society. Although the term originally applied to religious groups, some cults are not religious. A terrorist group could be considered a cult. Hassan (2012) distinguished between two main types:

- Benign cults: these groups are unconventional and may seem 'weird' to the majority but do not harm their members or other people and they may actually be beneficial. The early days of some political movements may fit the definition of a benign cult.
- Destructive cults: as well as being unconventional, these groups engage in one or more harmful actions such as crime, abuse of their members or terrorism. These tend to be the groups that we think of as cults and they are of particular relevance to this topic.

Rather than use the label 'cult', Almendros *et al.* (2007) advise focusing on the behaviour of the group. This can help to focus on the abusive and controlling behaviour of groups that are not usually considered to be cults, such as gangs, people traffickers and certain political extremists.

How to recognise a cult

Hassan's (2012) **BITE model** describes four key characteristics of destructive cults:

B – Behaviour control. This could include trying to regulate the member's movements, where they live, what they eat, who they have sex with, when they sleep and what they do in their free time. Permission may be required before taking any major decisions. Generally, rigid rules are imposed and individualism is discouraged.

I – Information control. This could include deception and lies (including lying about the nature of the cult), minimising access to non-cult sources of information and use of cult-generated propaganda. They may also encourage confessions but withhold forgiveness, and encourage members to spy on other members.

T – Thought control. The main point is that members have to accept the cult's view of reality as the truth. They instil simplistic 'us vs. them' thinking, change the person's name and identity and use techniques to discourage free thinking including denial and rationalisation, plus prayer and meditation. Criticism of the leadership/ideology is forbidden.

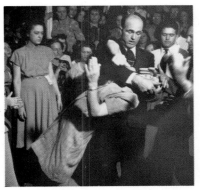

A cult member receiving 'healing' in 1948

? Discussion point

Note that to be considered a cult, a group must have both beliefs and behaviours that are considered abnormal. Should gangs and terrorist groups be classified as cults? Would a broader definition be more useful?

Cult leader Charles Mason under arrest in 1969

The Thugs were a cult in India that existed for over 450 years

? Discussion point

Similar techniques may be used by other groups in society who are not considered cults because their actions and beliefs are not considered abnormal. Is this still a problem? For example, if a charity used the techniques that cults use in order to recruit members and fundraise for good causes, would this be a problem? Should they be considered a cult?

Make the link

…with the topic of psychopathology (chapter 4): cults are groups that deviate from social norms and the problems defining them are similar to the problems defining abnormal behaviour in individuals. Cults and abusers try to distort their victims' view of normality and some individuals involved may fit a psychiatric diagnosis such as antisocial personality disorder.

Over 900 members of the cult died in a mass suicide

E – Emotional control. Members are taught to block out feelings that may lead to homesickness or doubt and they are made to believe that problems are always their own fault, with strong promotion of guilt and fear. In particular, members are taught to fear independent thought and the outside world/non-group members, as well as to fear leaving the group. Leaving is presented as characteristic of the weak, unspiritual or those who are seduced by sin. In some cases, there are real threats of harm to anyone who leaves.

However, Hassan points out that not all of these characteristics need to be present; in some cases, people live apparently normal lives in their own homes but are still mind-controlled cult members, unable to think independently.

Remember how in the 'ally' variation of Asch's study, participants reported greater feelings of warmth and liking towards the ally but they were completely unaware of how much they had been influenced by him? An effective manipulator does not make it obvious that they are manipulating you, but instead portrays themselves as someone who is on your side and who understands your concerns (Andersen & Zimbardo, 1984). **Love bombing** is a term meaning the lavish positivity shown to new cult recruits.

The Peoples Temple cult and 'Jonestown'

Presenting himself as a minister and charity worker, Jim Jones started 'Peoples Temple' branches around the USA, running soup kitchens and food banks. He particularly targeted members from ethnic minorities, recognising that that they were often dissatisfied by mainstream American society. Behind closed doors, Jones was exerting increasing control over members' lives. He insisted on their spending more and more time with Temple members, including at Christmas, and tried to get them to cut contacts with their family. Anyone who was not a Temple member was portrayed as sinful and dangerous.

Claiming that the USA was at risk of a nuclear war, Jones persuaded hundreds of members to move to a commune that he established in Guyana, South America, calling it 'Jonestown'. Members were offered a utopian society, away from the pressures of American life. In practice, when they arrived, things were very different. Members were treated with increasing brutality by Jones' inner circle. Members had to spend long hours working on the fields of the new settlement and many became ill with tropical diseases. Worse was to follow however – Jones had developed a theory that if the cult members died together, they would ascend to paradise. Coming under increasing pressure from the US authorities, the group drank a fruit drink known as 'kool-aid' that had been poisoned using cyanide. Even cult members' children were forced to drink it. Those who did not obey were shot. In total, over 900 people died.

Analysis: how cults and manipulators control us

As you have seen, a number of factors in the social situation make conformity and obedience more likely. Cults use these factors to their advantage and set up situations where most people are likely to comply with their wishes. Singer (1979, p. 73) states that the most widespread, highly structured cults are essentially very similar and that they typically use a set of 'brainwashing' techniques for mind control, noting that *'recruitment and indoctrination procedures seemed to involve highly sophisticated techniques for inducing behavioral change.'*

However, Andersen and Zimbardo (1984) take a different view. They state that control is based on ordinary, everyday processes. Skilled manipulators learn to use the individual weaknesses of their victims. In large groups, it becomes more efficient to let the processes of ordinary social pressure take over, with leaders taking a lower-profile role and relying on the new members conforming to the fanaticism of more established members.

Hassan (2012) notes that cults use a number of techniques, targeting the vulnerable and employing the use of sleep deprivation and separation from loved ones as part of a campaign of distorting members' ability to make clear judgements. He also suggests that lengthy chanting sessions produce a suggestible, hypnotic state.

Boulette and Andersen (1985) draw a comparison between cult membership and people who are in abusive relationships. The victim of an abusive relationship has several features in common with the members of a destructive cult, including:

A member of a 'snake cult'

- Their view of normality is gradually distorted.
- Guilt and self-blame are used to motivate compliance.
- Kindness and cruelty are alternated to throw the victims off balance.
- Victims are isolated from their support network.
- Fear and intimidation are used to encourage obedience.

Resisting pressure

Researchers into cults and other forms of controlling/manipulative behaviour have identified strategies and skills that can be used to resist them.

> **? Discussion point**
>
> How many of the features identified by Boulette and Andersen can be seen in experiments such as Milgram (1963)?

Education

Education can be used to inform people – especially young people – about cults and manipulators. The first and most important is **raising awareness**. Just being aware of what cults and other manipulators do makes people less likely to succumb. This is one reason that cult recruiters tend to lie about their identity at the start, presenting themselves as a charity or a support group, for example. The easiest time to resist a cult is at the beginning – it is better to not get involved in the first place, rather than to try to get out once they have started controlling your behaviour. The same applies to other manipulators in society.

Education can also furnish people with skills and knowledge that makes them less vulnerable to persuasion. Assertiveness training is a form of education that equips people with skills to resist coercion. For example, the 'broken record' technique involves repeating a simple statement such as '*no, I don't want to join*' until the other person gets the message. This gives the manipulator nothing to work with – no opportunity to twist your words (Tucker-Ladd, 2010).

Studies in the previous sections have shown how people with a high level of self-esteem, knowledge and belief in their own values are less likely to succumb to pressure, as are those who are democratically parented. Education can play a role in encouraging confidence and promoting democratic parenting over authoritarian parenting.

Role models and group support

As several studies in the previous sections have shown, having other people around that either comply or resist social pressure can make a massive difference to behaviour. Disobedient peers act as **role models**, making it easier for others to do the same.

It will be helpful if others refuse to obey. For this reason, manipulators try to find people who are isolated. Cults often ask their members to cut contact with their families, at least for a period of time and surround new recruits with the most fanatical believers that all fully support the leader. Salespeople may try to catch people alone and get them to commit to buying things before they have had a chance to discuss it with family and friends.

Having the chance to discuss issues with others can make it much easier to resist. For example, following Hofling *et al.*'s (1966) study of obedience (see p.292), Rank and Jacobson (1977) found that only 11% of nurses obeyed when they were allowed to discuss the instruction with a colleague first. At-risk children could be encouraged to talk with friends, over phone lines or with guidance staff at school when they are being pressured to do something that makes them uncomfortable. Workers should take every opportunity to discuss problematic orders with peers.

Moral reasoning and values

The conformity study by Hornsey *et al.* (2003) is useful evidence here – if people had a strong moral belief, they were less likely to succumb to social pressure to do something that went against their values. One

Children should be encouraged to seek support if they are being pressured into doing something that makes them uncomfortable

? Discussion point

Does/did your school encourage unquestioning obedience, e.g. of uniform rules?

reason that young people are often vulnerable to cults and manipulators is that they are often confused, victims of abuse or may have drifted away from their childhood religion or values (Hassan, 2012).

Kohlberg (1969) notes that people who disobeyed Milgram's experiment had mostly reached a post-conventional level of moral reasoning (see previous section).

As mentioned in the previous section, socialisation can play a large role in obedience. Many young people are brought up to obey social and religious rules unquestioningly, and these habits, however well meaning, puts the individual at risk of cults that also demand unquestioning obedience. Again, education can play a role – rather than promoting a specific set of cultural rules and values that can then be replaced by a more harmful one, families and educators can work to develop post-conventional reasoning in young people by encouraging democratic questioning and debate of values and rules.

Families can help children by encouraging them to question

Questioning motives

Manipulators and cults lie about their true aims and people need to critically question the motives behind their actions. Cults offer something appealing at the start – unconditional friendship and community to the person who feels isolated and a simple answer to life's problems to people who are feeling confused. However, like with 'great deals' offered by advertisers and salespeople, the offers are really too good to be true. Former cult members have reported manipulation by the cult as the main reason they were recruited (Almendros *et al.*, 2007).

Manipulators are good at using compliance to get people to agree. Andersen and Zimbardo (1984) state that it is important people avoid making decisions under stress and avoid making decisions when in the presence of the person who triggers the stress.

A similar situation occurs when people make a commitment to buy something that they don't want or need. Having agreed, they may feel doubts, but want to appear consistent in their behaviour and so avoid saying that they have changed their minds. Both cult leaders and other manipulators are often benefiting financially from the people they control – people should ask from the start, 'who is profiting here?'

Manipulators such as sales people are good at getting people to agree

Responsibility for own actions

Following on from questioning motives comes taking responsibility. Cults generally try to get people to switch off their own sense of values and freedom of thought and action, and let the cult leader tell them what to do. It is apparent from Milgram's study that for many people there is a certain comfort in being told what to do – if they enter the agentic state, they no longer feel responsible for the negative outcomes of their actions (Milgram, 1974).

However, it is important not to blame the victim and suggest that they should simply take more responsibility. Cults target the young and the vulnerable – cult recruits tend to have suffered a traumatic experience in the year prior to being recruited (Singer, 1979).

Key concepts

- Resisting social pressure
- Manipulators
- Cults
- Love bombing
- Education
- Raising awareness
- Role models
- Moral reasoning
- Questioning motives
- Responsibility for own actions

Questions

1. What two things are abnormal in a cult?

2. Give an example of a manipulator.

3. What are the four factors of the BITE model?

4. What was the name of the settlement Jim Jones set up for his cult followers?

5. Name a similarity between cults and abusive relationships.

6. Name three main strategies for reducing social pressure.

7. Why do cults sometimes hide their true identity?

8. What behaviour can education promote?

9. Which study replicated Hofling *et al.* (1966) and showed that being able to discuss actions reduced obedience?

10. Which study showed that people with strong beliefs are less likely to conform?

Activities

1. Research another well-known destructive cult, such as the Manson Family or Heaven's Gate. There are good documentaries available, as well as a great deal of information on the internet. What kind of people joined and why? What characteristics did the cult have, and how did it control its members? Does it fit with Hassan's 'BITE' model? As with any research, be critical about the quality of your sources. If your teacher/lecturer agrees, you could give a short talk about what you find out.

2. Link the information in the following box to these headings. Items may link to more than one heading:
   - education
   - role models/group support
   - moral reasoning/confidence in own beliefs
   - questioning motives of advertisers/politicians/cults
   - responsibility for own actions

a) In a follow up to Asch's study, Perrin and Spencer (1981) found that engineering students were much less likely to conform. This relates to their self-confidence in their own ability to make visual judgments.

b) Hornsey *et al.* (2003) found that students with strong political beliefs were less likely to privately conform to majority political statements and in public showed 'counter-conformity'.

c) Milgram's study used a series of four prompts, such as *'you have no other choice, you must go on.'* If a participant continued to refuse after all four prompts, the experiment was stopped. The broken record technique involves repeating a statement that was ignored/rejected using the exactly the same words (e.g. 'I'm sorry, but I won't do it').

d) In a partial replication of the Hofling *et al.*'s nurses study, Rank and Jacobson (1977) found that only 11% of nurses obeyed when they were allowed to check with a colleague first.

e) In Milgram's study, people moved to an agentic state – acting as an agent of the authority figure. To resist authority, people must maintain an autonomous state – acting based on their own morals.

f) Jan Rensaleer, an engineer who took part in Milgram's experiment, stopped at 225V, stating *'I know what shocks do to you'*.

g) Kohlberg (1969) stated that some people develop a higher level of moral reasoning than others. He called the highest level 'post-conventional moral reasoning'. He interviewed Milgram's participants and found that those who had resisted authority were able to reason at this higher level.

h) Nazi unit 'Reserve Police Battalion 101' were ordered to kill Jewish civilians but given the option of other duties. Despite disobedient models, 80% obeyed.

i) Cult recruits are often encouraged to divide the world into black-and-white distinctions, with cult leaders claiming to lead a moral fight against corrupt authority. Andersen and Zimbardo (1984) found that obedience could be resisted if people reject that view and avoid making decisions when under stress.

j) Elizabeth Olson, who starred in a film based on a cult, says *'people don't get sucked into these groups because they look bad from the outset. There's always something … being offered, like love, community and acceptance. Then the abuse starts. But if there are people telling you the abuse is okay, your view of what is normal and acceptable changes.'* http://bbc.in/xFXyY4.

k) The 'low ball' technique is where salespeople state a low up-front cost to draw people in (e.g. it only costs £50), and reveal add-ons later when the buyer is already committed (e.g. plus VAT, fees and insurance). In some ways, Milgram's study had an element of low-ball, as does cult membership.

3. Make up a mnemonic to help you remember the five strategies discussed in this section. Find another quote or research finding that illustrates each one.

> **GO!** **End of topic project**
>
> In your class or another suitable group, conduct a simple experimental study, as follows:
> * First, identify a suitable stimulus, such as that used in the Jenness or Hornsey *et al.* studies.
> * Now identify a way of applying group pressure – for example, a faked list of prior responses.
> * Using opportunity sampling, find participants to look at, and respond to, the stimulus.
> * Make a distinction between two groups, for example, with versus without social influence (fake guesses or no fake guesses).
> * Analyse results and draw conclusions.
> * Write a summary of the study and your findings. Find at least one relevant background research study that is not from your notes or textbook.

✔ End of topic specimen exam questions

National 5

1. Give one example of a situation where people might conform.   2 marks

2. Explain two types of conformity.   4 marks

3. Analyse one research study into conformity.   5 marks

4. Explain the difference between minority and majority influence.   4 marks

5. At school, some people conform more than others. Explain why this is the case. 6 marks

Higher

1. Some people are more vulnerable to peer pressure than others. Explain two or more factors involved in conformity that could account for this difference.   8 marks

2. Analyse one research study relevant to conformity.   8 marks

3. Explain the concept of obedience, referring to research evidence and factors that affect obedience.   20 marks

4. Explain how knowledge of conformity/obedience has been applied to strategies for resisting social pressure.   10 marks

The total exam mark allocation for the Social Behaviour unit will be 20 marks; however, there is no way of knowing in advance how this will be split between this topic and your chosen optional topic.

11 Prejudice

Prejudice, stereotypes and discrimination

Prejudice is an attitude, usually negative, towards another person based on their perceived membership of a group. Note that in social psychology, the term **in-group** is used to refer to any group that a person is part of, while **out-group** means a group that they are not part of. These terms are widely used in this topic.

In his classic work on prejudice, Allport (1954) notes that an in-group is any group about which we would use the word 'we', but notes also that these are flexible – people will broaden and narrow their definition of their in-group depending on the situation. For example, on a local level, someone in a different part of town is an out-group member, but if you are focusing on your whole town/country versus other towns/countries, the same person is seen as an in-group member.

Generally, prejudice is used to refer to negative judgements. It is linked to two other key concepts – stereotypes and discrimination.

Cognitive, affective and behavioural

Prejudice is an **attitude**, meaning that it is an emotional reaction to a type of person, object or situation, usually based around our likes and dislikes. **Examples of attitudes:**

> **!Syllabus note**
>
> As well as 'Conformity', you need to study one optional topic in Social Behaviour. Prejudice would be a suitable choice. The optional topic should be tackled in a similar way to conformity, that is, you should be aware of key concepts, theories, research studies and (for Higher) a real-world application of the topic.

Prejudice is an attitude, usually negative, towards another person based on their perceived membership of a group

- R does not like parties.
- A thinks that school is a waste of time.
- D thinks that all politicians are corrupt.

Note that some researchers use the term 'prejudice' to refer to both thoughts and feelings, while others refer just to the feelings, and define it as part of the broader concept of **intergroup bias**, that is, any behaviour – thought, feeling or action – that favours one's in-group over out-groups (e.g. Hewstone *et al.*, 2002). According to this point of view, intergroup bias can be divided into three main aspects:

Cognitive. The cognitive aspect of intergroup bias is the thoughts or beliefs a person has about an out-group. An example would be the belief that women are more emotional than men are (or vice versa). As discussed in chapter 2, a schema is a cognitive term meaning a set of ideas, knowledge and beliefs; a schema about a particular out-group is called a **stereotype**.

Affective. The term 'affect' (as a noun) means emotion. This aspect means a person's biased feelings towards the outgroup, such as judging them, fearing them, hating them or viewing them as making a positive or negative contribution to society. As discussed above, this aspect is usually called **prejudice**.

Behavioural. This aspect refers to what people actually do towards an out-group – any actions that involves treating the members of that group differently. The most obvious example is **discrimination**, that is, treating the out-group unfairly or oppressing them. This could happen either directly, or indirectly by showing **favouritism** to the in-group. Another major behavioural aspect of intergroup bias is **aggression**, ranging from physical and verbal assaults to genocide (Hewstone *et al.*, 2002).

It is possible for a person to display differences between these different aspects, with some more positive than others. For example, a person could think that young people are lazy but not dislike them for it (cognitive but not affective) or they could hate communists but never act on their hatred (affective but not behavioural).

The remainder of this section looks at stereotypes, prejudice and discrimination in more detail.

Stereotypes

As mentioned above, a 'stereotype' relates to the cognitive aspect of intergroup bias. A stereotype is an over-simplified, distorted or inaccurate schema of a particular group. Common examples include stereotypes of men or women, stereotypes of age groups (e.g. of teenagers) and stereotypes of nationalities. Groundskeeper Willie from *The Simpsons* is a good example of a Scottish stereotype and it is not unusual for stereotypes to form the basis of humour.

The term is also used to describe specific people/characters in the media and elsewhere – we might say that the characters in a bad novel or TV programme are stereotypes, meaning that they show socially conventional examples of sex roles, social class, nationalities, etc.

Not liking parties is an attitude

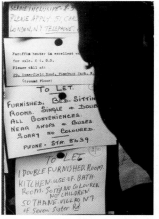

The belief that women are more emotional than men is a stereotype

Advertisements discriminating against people who are not white, London, 1967

The process of stereotyping involves generalising from a stereotype to an individual person. When they are aware of a social stereotype of a group, people may then apply that to members of the group, so that assumed characteristics of the group are applied to members of a group. For example, if somebody believes that men generally like eating meat, they might assume that a specific man will not want to eat a vegetarian meal. Of course, this assumption may be incorrect. This highlights two main problems with stereotyping:

- The stereotype itself may be inaccurate.
- Even if the stereotype is broadly true as a generalisation, it might not apply to a specific member of the group.

Stereotypes can relate to any group within society of which people are aware. There are stereotypes of both high and low status groups. Many jobs and careers have stereotypes associated with them – scientists might be assumed to be 'mad', teachers to be stressed or politicians to be dishonest. There are also stereotypes of styles, clothing, disabilities or hobbies, for example, the stereotype that people who wear glasses are intelligent.

Chartrand and Bargh (1999) describe stereotypes as 'categories gone awry' (p.907), stating that categories are generally useful but a stereotype is a distorted and harmful version of a category.

Effect of stereotypes

Stereotypes can have harmful effects. One issue in education is called **stereotype threat** – this means when awareness of a negative stereotype leads to poorer performance. Ambady *et al.* (2001) found that when girls were reminded of gender differences using a questionnaire, they did more poorly on a maths test compared to a control group (responding to a common gender stereotype that girls are worse at maths). This effect disappeared between the ages of 8 to 10 – when girls tend to have a strong sense of superiority over boys – but reappeared from age 11 onwards. Spencer *et al.* (1999) found a very similar effect with female undergraduates.

Is there anything wrong with **positive stereotypes**? Having a positive stereotype can improve performance (sometimes called 'stereotype lift'). These can cause harm, though, by disadvantaging other groups who do not receive the same benefit – a positive stereotype implicitly judges other groups as negative.

Where do stereotypes come from?

Stereotypes appear to be learned from society as a whole and people are aware of them even if they do not agree with them (Karlins *et al.*, 1969). They are learned early; from the age of 2 or even before, children choose toys that are stereotypically associated with their gender (Caldera *et al.*, 1989). Children's books often portray some stereotypes, and although this situation has improved in recent years, there are still inequalities such as the presentation of females as the main caregivers for children (Anderson & Hamilton, 2005).

Groundskeeper Willie is an example of a stereotype

? Discussion point

Are you aware of the stereotypes of different nationalities? Is it ok to make jokes about these?

A stereotype of a French person

The idea that those who wear glasses are intelligent is a stereotype

Make the link

…with Modern Studies and Politics. You may be able to identify certain stereotypes when politicians talk about national groups, especially in the context of immigration, as well as benefit claimants, teenagers, the elderly, etc.

When girls were reminded of gender differences they did more poorly on a maths test

? Discussion point

Think of some films that you have seen recently. How many male and female characters did they have? Were male characters shown in a more positive way than female characters, for example, more skilled/brave? What other stereotypes did you notice?

Children often choose toys that are stereotypically associated with their gender

? Discussion point

Have you observed friends or other people around you showing confirmation bias? How can it be avoided?

Why do people not just reject inaccurate stereotypes? Under the cognitive approach (see chapter 2), it was explained that some human thought processes show bias and take shortcuts in order to conserve mental resources such as attention. Cognitive researchers believe that stereotypes are a form of shortcut, limiting the need to think about each person individually, and therefore freeing up attention for other tasks (see cognitive miser theory, below). They are then supported by another shortcut – **confirmation bias**. This is where people tend to notice information that fits their stereotypes, while ignoring information that goes against them. In other words, what we notice and remember is biased in a way that reinforces our stereotypes.

📖 Key study: Cohen (1981): confirmation bias

Aim: *Cohen (1981) conducted a study into the memory of stereotyped features of common jobs and how well people remembered conflicting information. The aim of her study was to find out whether stereotypes affect what people remember.*

Method: *Ninety-six student participants were shown a video of a woman who was identified as either a waitress or a librarian. In one condition, the video contained some information that was consistent with the stereotype (e.g. the librarian had spent the day reading/the waitress has no book shelves). In the other condition, the information was reversed and it was inconsistent with the stereotype. Participants were either told the occupation before or after the video.*

Would you guess that this woman was a waitress or a librarian?

Findings: *Recall was as follows:*

	Consistent information	Inconsistent information
Told before	74%	66%
Told after	68%	57%

As can be seen, memory was best for information that fitted the stereotype, especially if they were aware of the stereotype before the video. According to the researcher, this was because confirmation bias was acting on both encoding and retrieval of the information.

(continued)

Evaluation: This was a well-controlled experiment, with participants randomly allocated to conditions and extraneous variables such as video length kept constant. However, a weakness is that as they were undergraduate students, the participants may have had relatively little real-world contact with librarians and waitresses – they may not have known anyone with these jobs on a personal level, making it hard to generalise the results to older adults. There may also have been demand characteristics – participants may have guessed that they were expected to conform to stereotypes.

The findings of Cohen on confirmation bias (1981; see key study) were supported in a meta-analysis of 26 studies by Fyock and Stangor (1994), which showed an overall effect of the stereotype-consistency of information on how well it was remembered.

Therefore, it appears that stereotypes are learned early, they derive from society around us and they are largely inaccurate but can be reinforced by biases in our memory.

Prejudice

Prejudiced attitudes

The word prejudice literally means to 'pre-judge', that is, to judge another person before you have the opportunity to learn the facts. For example, if you decide not to talk to someone, assuming they must be boring because they are older than you are, then you have pre-judged the person and you are showing prejudice. As mentioned above, prejudice is an attitude that can be seen as the affective aspect of intergroup bias but is sometimes used more generally (to include all three aspects).

As with a stereotype, prejudice involves making an **over–generalisation** based on group membership. The prejudiced person has an attitude towards the group and applies that attitude to individual members of the group without finding out their individual characteristics.

Prejudice typically includes feelings of less **warmth** towards the out-group (Fiske *et al.*, 2007). This tends to be associated with an increase in desired **social distance** – the extent to which we wish to separate ourselves from members of the out-group, for example, by not sitting near them, not talking to them or avoiding places where they go. As noted above, however, the prejudice may not always correspond to behavioural aspects of bias.

Prejudice is often targeted at prominent and visible out-groups, such as people of a different nationality, age, sex or race, but it can be based on any perceived group difference. There may be prejudices against very specific groups in your life, for example, people who drink at a pub near where you live, or people who are in the next-door class or a younger year at school/college.

> **? Discussion point**
>
> Confirmation bias can also be a problem in research. Researchers should look impartially at evidence and draw the best conclusions. However there is a risk that a researcher makes up their mind first, then looks for evidence to support their idea (called 'cherry picking' the evidence). Have you ever done this in a study or essay?

> **Make the link**
>
> ...between confirmation bias and the irrational beliefs explained by the cognitive approach (see chapter 2).

> **Make the link**
>
> ...with the topic of memory, especially the study by Brewer and Treyens (1981).

> **Make the link**
>
> ...between research into confirmation bias and National 5/Higher Philosophy.

Assuming an older person is boring is an example of a prejudiced attitude

Supporters of the campaign for equal wages for women outside the Houses of Parliament in 2014

A rally in Baltimore in May 2015 protesting the death of Freddie Gray, a black man who died after being injured in a police van

A protest against homophobia at the Swedish embassy in Berlin, 2014, following the stabbing of members of the 'football fans against homophobia' group in Sweden

The '-isms'

Prejudice can apply to a multitude of groups but tends to be closely associated with four concepts in particular: **sexism**, **racism**, **ageism** and **heterosexism** (or 'homophobia').

Sexism means prejudice against someone of the opposite sex. Typically, it refers to prejudice against women, although in principle the term applies equally to prejudice against men. Some sexist attitudes appear positive (e.g. 'women deserve more protection than men'), but Glick and Fiske (2001) state that such views link to harmful sexism as well; in a cross-cultural study, they found that the countries with the most positive/protective sexist attitudes also showed the highest levels of harmful and violent attitudes towards women.

Racism means prejudice against a target based on their assumed race. In fact, this term is often used loosely, for example, to describe conflict between neighbouring countries that have relatively few if any racial differences (e.g. Scots versus English) when the word **xenophobia** – a fear/dislike of foreigners – might be more appropriate. Sometimes, racism is directed at a specific religious group, for example, Muslims ('Islamophobia') or Jews ('anti-Semitism').

Ageism means prejudice based on age. In workplace and community settings, this often refers to the elderly but there is also considerable ageism against younger people. Ageism is an unusual form of prejudice in that everybody could in the future become a member of the target group as they get older (or has been in the past, in the case of ageism against the young). As with sexism, there is a positive, protective form of ageism towards the elderly that is often seen as patronising.

Heterosexism means discriminating against people based on their sexuality – the heterosexual majority showing prejudice against other sexual orientations. It is sometimes taken to include prejudice against transgender groups. Some people find this a problematic term, as it does not apply in both directions (i.e. homosexual people cannot be 'heterosexist'), and because sexuality itself is complex and people cannot be as easily categorised.

Abrams and Houston (2006) found that British people surveyed were more likely to admit to prejudiced attitudes against some groups than others. In particular, they were happier to admit to prejudiced attitudes against homosexual people, Muslims and women than against disabled people or the elderly. Therefore, it appears that prejudice depends on the social context and social norms and it is not just a characteristic of the individual.

Discrimination

Discrimination is a behavioural aspect of intergroup bias. It means treating other people better or worse because of their membership of a social group, or some personal or physical characteristic such as a disability. Usually, it refers to unfair treatment of minorities or vulnerable people. For example, it would be discriminatory to deny someone a place on a good university course based on a stereotype about their race or social class or to deny a woman a job because she was pregnant if she would otherwise be considered the best candidate.

Discrimination is usually illegal; under UK legislation – the **Equality Act of 2010** – it is against the law to discriminate against people with certain 'protected characteristics'. These include the four 'isms' mentioned earlier in this chapter – sex, age, race and sexual orientation – as well as five others: religion/beliefs, disability, gender reassignment, marital status and pregnancy. It is illegal to deny somebody a service or refuse them equal opportunities based on any of these things. Examples could include:

It would be discrimination not to employ a woman because she was pregnant

- Refusing to serve someone in a shop because of their race.
- Denying an employee a promotion because he/she is an atheist.
- Paying a women less than a man for the same work.
- Not allowing someone to book a hotel room because of their sexuality.

There are certain exceptions – it is legal to specify the race and sex of an actor for a role, for example. More controversially, some religions are allowed to discriminate when choosing religious leaders or teachers for faith schools.

Most of the examples so far refer to **direct discrimination**. Examples of **indirect discrimination** include having policies in an organisation such as a university or workplace, that are unfair to certain groups – for example, refusing to let people wear a headscarf to class or not building suitable access for wheelchair users.

It would be indirect discrimination to have a policy against headscarves in class

Inconsistent views

As mentioned earlier, the cognitive, affective and behavioural aspects of prejudice are separate. Someone could have a prejudiced attitude and yet not discriminate against an individual because it would be illegal to do so. Likewise, someone might discriminate even though they do not hold a prejudiced attitude themselves – perhaps because they work in an organisation that has discriminatory policies.

Mann (1959) states that while the cognitive and affective aspects tend to be closely linked in most people, there are often differences between these two aspects and people's behaviour. One example of this comes from a study by LaPiere (1934) who studied attitudes in the USA in the 1930s at a time when prejudice towards Chinese-Americans was commonplace. In order to test for discrimination, he toured a large number of hotels, cafes and restaurants together with a student and his wife who were both of Chinese descent, and found that they were refused service only once out of 251 establishments. However, when he later surveyed the restaurant owners to ask if they would serve Chinese guests at their establishments, over 90% said that they would not. This provided strong evidence that there can be a mismatch between attitudes and behaviour.

In 2010 civil partners Martyn Hall and Steven Preddy sued the owners of a B&B in Cornwall who would not allow them to stay in a double room together

It is widely assumed by researchers in the cognitive approach that cognitions precede emotions – that people first think about an issue

> **? Discussion point**
>
> Is it discriminatory to give mothers a longer period of time off for maternity leave than fathers get for paternity leave?

In LaPiere's study 90% of hotel, cafe and restuarant owners asked said that they would not serve people of Chinese descent

🔑 Key concepts

- Prejudice
- In-group
- Out-group
- Attitude
- Intergroup bias
- Cognitive
- Affective
- Behavioural
- Stereotype
- Discrimination
- Favouritism
- Aggression
- Stereotype threat
- Positive stereotype
- Confirmation bias
- Positive stereotype
- Overgeneralisation
- Warmth
- Social distance
- Sexism
- Racism
- Ageism
- Heterosexism
- Xenophobia
- Equality Act of 2010
- Direct discrimination
- Indirect discrimination
- Amygdala

and this causes a feeling (e.g. Beck, 1976). However, Zajonc (1980) argues that it is the other way around – we form our feelings and opinions first. This might seem strange at first but it fits with evidence that some feelings can be fast and largely automatic (Bargh & Chartrand, 1999). Zajonc suggests that emotions and cognitions are under control of different systems, which can affect each other in various ways. This idea is supported by some neurological evidence – cognitions are linked to the neocortex, while emotions such as fear, anxiety and anger are linked to the 'limbic system', in particular, the **amygdala**.

✔ Questions

1. What terms are used to refer to the group that we are/are not part of?

2. Define an 'attitude'.

3. What is the cognitive aspect of intergroup bias?

4. Where do we get stereotypes from?

5. Why do people fail to change their inaccurate stereotypes?

6. Who were the participants in the Cohen (1981) study?

7. What does 'prejudice' literally mean?

8. Give two examples of the common prejudice '-isms'.

9. What law makes it illegal to discriminate against people based on their race, age and other 'protected characteristics'?

10. What is indirect discrimination?

GO! Activities

1. Think about which aspects of intergroup bias link to the example situations in the table. Fill in any that apply:

Example	Cognitive	Affective	Behavioural
R decides not to invite someone in her class to a party because they are 'too old'.			
D decides to give his niece a pink doll for her birthday.			
X invites his male friends to play football but does not consider inviting his female friends.			
A children's film has 4 lead characters – a heroic young white male, a pretty white female who needs to be rescued a lot, a wise old man and a funny male from an ethnic minority.			
A toy manufacturer decides that a popular play set is not appealing enough to girls so they bring out a new version featuring toy horses and shopping.			

2. Think of examples of rules/restrictions in the workplace that could lead to indirect discrimination. If you are stuck, try searching for news stories about discrimination online.
   Share your examples with your classmates.

Theories of stereotypes and prejudice

Cognitive miser theory

The **cognitive miser** theory is a theory of why people hold stereotypes. It states that a stereotype is a mental shortcut, made because people cannot or do not wish to make the mental effort to process each person's traits individually.

'Like it or not, we all make assumptions about other people, ourselves, and the situations we encounter … much of the time our expectations are functional, and indeed, we would be unable to operate without them.'

Source: Fiske and Taylor (1991, p.97)

The quote above implies that stereotypes exist to simplify the world. From this point of view, attention is limited and treating everything we encounter as unique and separate would take too much processing power; therefore, stereotypes are useful because they save the mind unnecessary work. This view implies that stereotyping is largely automatic.

! Syllabus note

In this topic, theories are only mandatory for Higher but National 5 students will also find it useful to study at least one theory.

The development of this theory reflects changes in the cognitive approach over the years (see chapter 2). In the 1950s, humans were seen as largely rational, who thought in a scientific way about the world (Heider, 1958). However, we are now aware of a number of ways in which people are biased and unsystematic in their thinking (Tversky & Kahneman, 1974).

Research evidence and evaluation

Bargh and Chartrand (1999) reviewed the evidence and concluded that much of our decision making happens automatically, that is, without intention or conscious awareness.

Aboud (2003) found that in-group favouritism is strongly apparent from the age of 5, supporting cognitive miser theory. This follows Allport (1954, p.29) who stated that strong in-group prejudice is apparent from age 5, and although the child does not fully understand the group differences until age 10, it *'doesn't wait for this understanding before [developing] fierce in-group loyalties'*.

However, not everyone agrees that stereotypes are based on unconscious biases or that they are simply shortcuts, making incoming information easier to process. Rutland (1999) states that stereotypes are a meaningful attempt to make sense of the world around us and that we choose to use them. He considers group categories useful and largely accurate.

Authoritarian personality theory

Why is one person prejudiced while another is not? The **authoritarian personality theory** states that prejudice results from the disturbed mental processes of certain individuals who desire order and are aggressive to minorities (Adorno *et al.*, 1950).

This theory follows the approaches to psychology that emphasise the effect of childhood on behaviour – in particular, the psychoanalytic approach (see chapter 2), which states that childhood and unconscious motivations play a huge role in a person's adult personality. The authoritarian personality theory sees authoritarianism as a syndrome that develops in childhood, resulting in certain key characteristics that make a person more prone to **fascist** tendencies.

The authoritarian personality theory was developed around the time of the Second World War. The researchers wanted to explain the appeal of the Nazis and other fascist parties. Hitler himself can be seen as an example of an authoritarian personality, but more importantly, it applies to people who *follow* harsh, controlling ideologies like that of the Third Reich.

The researchers said that authoritarian individuals had repressed anger and a weaker than usual superego due to strict parenting – they were thought to have over-dominant fathers and strict mothers (van Ijzendoorn, 1989). Because of their fear of authority, they show an exaggerated respect for conventional values and their unconscious anger would be displaced onto weaker targets – usually minorities. The personality type was characterised by nine key traits, as follows:

- **Conventionalism**: traditional middle-class values.
- **Authoritarian submission**: submissive attitude to power and authority.

- **Authoritarian aggression**: hatred and rejection of minorities.
- **Anti-intraception**: dislike of reflective thinking or new/imaginative ideas.
- **Superstition and stereotypy**: belief in fate; tendency to think in rigid categories.
- **Power and 'toughness'**: obsessed with the idea of strong versus weak people.
- **Destructiveness**: general hostility/anger.
- **Projectivity**: belief that wild and dangerous things go on in the world.
- **Sex**: obsession with sexual 'goings-on'.

The overall picture is of people who are angry and hostile, paranoid about anything new and different, and very willing to take orders from traditional sources of power. Such people made perfect followers for fascist politicians.

Research evidence

A key tool used by Adorno *et al.* (1950) was a questionnaire called the **F-scale**. 'F' stood for 'fascism', and the scale aimed to measure fascist sympathies, including aggressive racism and intolerance. Items on the scale consisted of a series of statements, which participants were asked to agree or disagree with. Each statement had been uttered by the researchers' previous research participants, for example, *'people can be divided into two distinct classes: the weak and the strong'* and *'what the youth needs most is strict discipline, rugged determination, and the will to work and fight for family and country.'*

Participants had to respond on a scale from one to six, from 'disagree strongly' to 'agree strongly'.

> **? Discussion point**
>
> Do you agree that people's behaviour is often biased and irrational? How does the idea that humans are irrational affect theories in other subjects such as Politics and Economics?

Aboud found that in-group favouritism is strongly apparent from the age of 5

Oswald Mosley, leader of the British Union of Fascists, with supporters in 1936

What is fascism?

The *F-scale* is based on the idea of **fascism** – the ideology of several political parties beginning in the 1920s and 30s, most notably in Italy, Mussolini's *National Fascist Party* and in Germany, Adolf Hitler's *National Socialist Party* ('Nazi Party'). Both of these leaders and their parties are considered to have extremely right-wing politics with an emphasis on state control and an intolerant, rather than supportive, attitude towards minorities, as well

Hitler and Mussolini

(Continued)

as towards anyone who could not contribute to the industrial economies of the time, such as disabled individuals.

In general, fascist politicians support strict limitations to personal freedom, regulated morality and behaviour and strong state control. Unlike the totalitarian communist states of North Korea or the former USSR, fascist states tended to support capitalism/business interests and favour traditional/religious morals.

Fascism is often contrasted with **democratic** views, held by people who, on the whole, favour personal freedom, diversity and people-power rather than strict control by the state (Meloen, 1993).

One example of this in practice is human rights policies, such as the right to freedom of speech, or to freely join any groups you like. Fascist groups/governments and their supporters are highly likely to ban groups that disagree with them and to oppose free speech.

Make the link

...between fascism/the F-scale and your knowledge of History or Modern Studies

Evaluation

A weakness of the F-scale is that all of the 'agree' options led to a higher F-score, making it hard to distinguish between people who agree with all the statements and people who would agree to anything (see section on response acquiescence bias, p.223). Bass (1955) concluded that this had a large effect on Adorno *et al.*'s findings.

Some findings have been consistent – authoritarians are found to believe very strongly in the rights of the established authorities and they are much more likely to consider illegal government actions as acceptable (Altemeyer, 2006).

This theory is now marginal, with little research support for the view that a strict upbringing leads to prejudice. Altemeyer (1981) has found that of the nine authoritarian traits, only the first three (conventionalism, authoritarian submission and authoritarian aggression) correlate together reliably. He suggests that the term be replaced by 'RWA' – **right-wing authoritarianism**, which should be seen as an attitude rather than a personality type.

By viewing prejudice as an individual trait, the theory doesn't take account of cultural values and the influence of political events. It struggles to explain why the same individual can be prejudiced against some groups but not others. It neglects the importance of social and cognitive processes.

Social identity theory

Social identity theory states that people's behaviour is driven by group membership. People make automatic decisions about which groups they are or are not part of, then show prejudice against other groups to try and put their own group on top, therefore, boosting their own self-esteem.

Origins of the theory

Henri Tajfel was the son of a Polish-Jewish family and most of his relatives died in the Holocaust. He himself survived as a prisoner of war by hiding his own Jewish identity. This traumatic background may have stimulated his interest in prejudice, as he developed a theory of how personal identity links to our membership of social groups.

In experiments on schoolchildren, Tajfel (1970) tried to find the minimum requirements for discrimination to emerge (see key study). The main finding from this research was that people could be prompted to discriminate very easily and for trivial reasons. People seem to be highly motivated to boost their self-esteem by giving their group an advantage over other groups.

📖 Key study: Tajfel's (1970) minimal groups experiment

Aim: *The study aimed to find out what the minimum conditions are for discrimination to emerge. Will people discriminate if they have no good reason to do so, if the task is trivial and both groups are very similar?*

Method: *Tajfel studied schoolboys aged 14 to 15 in Bristol. They were shown 12 images of paintings by the modern artists Paul Klee and Wassily Kandinsky. The boys were then randomly grouped but were told that their choice of artwork was the reason for the grouping.*

Tajfel then put the participants into groups of 16 and gave them a task of allocating small cash rewards to the other boys in the group. Each had to fill out a booklet that allowed them to give small monetary rewards. Choices were designed so that they could pick from these three options:

Henri Tajfel

- *Maximum joint profit: the biggest overall amount of money*
- *Maximum in-group profit: the best reward for the in-group member*
- *Maximum difference: the amounts that caused the in-group to be as far ahead of the out-group as possible*

For example:

Choice	(a)	(b)	(c)
Boy-IN	12	16	14
Boy-OUT	19	13	6

Choice (a) would give the biggest overall reward (31) if the group was not considered. If the aim was to do as well as possible for the in-group, choice (b) would be favoured, while choice (c) would suggest that participants wanted to emphasise group differences.

Findings: *Despite the trivial nature of the groupings, the boys' responses clearly favoured in-group members, giving them higher rewards. Crucially though, the biggest factor was putting their own group ahead, even if it meant getting a lower reward overall. Choices like (c) were picked most – the boys seemed to want to create the biggest advantage of in-group over the out-group,*

Green church and steeple by *Paul Klee*

Composition VI *by Wassily Kandinsky*

regardless of the fact that this sometimes led to a lower reward for the in-group and a lower total reward.

Evaluation: One problem with this study was that the task was highly artificial and short-term, therefore making it hard to generalise to real cases of prejudice. In addition the participants were all teenaged boys and therefore not representative of the population as a whole. However, Tajfel's experiment was helpful in suggesting that prejudice can't be explained in terms of conflict over limited resources – being the top group was found to be more important than getting more money. It demonstrated that we discriminate very easily and for trivial reasons. This finding played a key role in developing social identity theory.

Our political views are part of our social identity

In a crowd of sports fans we may follow the norms of the group

? Discussion point

Which of these two components of identity – individual or social – makes more of a difference in your everyday life? Brown and Turner (1981) note that it can depend on the situation we find ourselves in – for example, when chatting to a close friend we may behave according to our individual identity, while in a crowd of sports fans, we may follow the norms of the group.

The theory

Tajfel teamed up with a group of British psychologists, including John Turner, to develop these findings into a theory. The basic premise of SIT is that we are strongly motivated by our social identity and this can result in us trying to make our groups do better than others. It begins with an automatic process of dividing the world up into 'them and us' groups that Tajfel and Turner (1979) called **social categorisation**. Tajfel (1982) states that social categorisation is necessary and sufficient for discrimination and prejudice to occur and although it can sometimes be harmful, it is essentially a normal thing to do.

The next process is identifying the groups we belong to. Our social identity is one of two components to our self-image:

- Personal identity: a sense of who we are in terms of unique personal characteristics, e.g. appearance, personality, likes and dislikes.
- Social identity: a sense of who we are in terms of groups we belong to e.g. male/female, nationality, political view.

In other words, people's sense of what groups they belong to is a fundamental part of who they are. The process of identifying with certain groups and building up our social identity is called **social identification.** This can have a large effect on behaviour – when people start to identify with a new group, they relate the characteristics of that group to themselves and change their behaviour accordingly (Reynolds *et al.*, 2015). For example, if a teenager moves school and makes a new set of friends, they may change their likes and dislikes to fit in.

According to the theory, social identification is followed by a third stage – people making a **social comparison** between groups they are members of and other groups. This third process plays a key role in prejudice, as it boosts self-esteem if our own groups appear to be superior (Hogg & Abrams, 1988). When people see their groups doing worse, they will attempt to boost their own group, perhaps by harming the other group. They also want to appear clearly different from members of other groups. The drive to maintain a positive social identity – **positive distinctiveness** – leads to intergroup bias.

Evidence

As shown by the Tajfel's (1970) participants, people will begin to treat other people differently if they start to perceive them as out-group members. If they perceive that the in-group is not sufficiently distinct or not superior then they will try to change that via discriminatory behaviour.

Judd and Park (1988) found evidence that people think differently about out-group members. Their study showed that people we categorise as being different from ourselves are evaluated less favourably and are seen as more alike in behaviour and appearance than the in-group.

Evaluation

Although it has its origins in the early 1970s, social identity is very much a mainstream theory today, with the general principles largely unchanged. It has been successfully applied in a large number of areas such as education (e.g. Reynolds *et al.*, 2015). It has successfully argued that our group identity is a vital part of who we are.

However, SIT's view of prejudice as based on a drive to boost self-esteem by promoting the in-group may be over-simplistic. There are numerous other influences on self-esteem, not least a person's position within the group, as well as their individual achievements and image. Rubin and Hewstone (1998) dismissed the idea that intergroup discrimination boosts self-esteem or that low self-esteem motivates discrimination.

In addition, the concept of SIT doesn't entirely explain why interrelations between groups change over time. For example, boys and girls aged 8 show considerable prejudice towards the opposite sex but this reduces by the mid-teens (Ambady *et al.*, 2001). This change is more easily explained in terms of sex hormones and an evolved drive to seek out potential sexual partners than in terms of SIT theory.

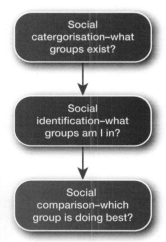

Make the link

…between social identification and the topic of conformity and also with the issue of social norms in psychopathology.

Social catergorisation–what groups exist?

↓

Social identification–what groups am I in?

↓

Social comparison–which group is doing best?

Boys and girls aged 8 show considerable prejudice towards the opposite sex

⚷ Key concepts

- Cognitive miser
- Authoritarian personality theory
- F-scale
- Fascism
- Right-wing authoritarianism
- Social identity theory
- Personal identity
- Social identity
- Social categorisation
- Social identification
- Social comparison
- Positive distinctiveness

✔ Questions

1. Why do researchers such as Fiske and Taylor think we are 'cognitive misers'?

2. Why did Rutland not agree with the idea that a stereotype is a cognitive shortcut?

3. Which approach to psychology is the authoritarian personality theory linked to?

4. According to Adorno *et al.* (1950), what is more important in whether you become a fascist – your upbringing or your social group?

5. Where were the statements on the F-scale taken from?

6. Out of the nine traits of the authoritarian personality, which three reliably correlate together?

7. Name the main processes of SIT theory.

8. Who were the participants in Tajfel's (1970) experiment?

9. Give a criticism of the experiment.

10. Why did Rubin and Hewstone (1998) criticise SIT?

🔵 Activities

1. How prevalent are fascist-type views among your group of students? Try out the F-scale online or make up your own survey. Can you see any link to upbringing?

2. Find out more about the cognitive miser theory – find at least one recent research study or science news article that talks about stereotypes either being useful/meaningful or being a shortcut/distortion. Which view do you agree with? Report your findings and your thoughts on it back to the class.

Reducing prejudice

Psychologists want to help to reduce and, if possible, eliminate prejudice. There are many programmes and interventions that have been used to reduce prejudice and these fall into three main categories:

- **Education**: raising awareness of prejudice, its effects and why it is irrational and harmful.
- **Contact hypothesis**: the idea that prejudice will reduce when conflicting groups increase their level of contact and communication.
- **Superordinate goals**: creating situations where members of different groups have to work together to achieve a shared goal.

Education

Education involves tackling the cognitive aspect of prejudice, and generally occurs in schools, though it could involve any educational setting or context, including books and leaflets. The main aims of education to reduce prejudice are:

- Raising awareness about stereotypes.
- Teaching strategies to reduce prejudiced thought processes.

Research and evaluation

Perhaps the best known example of an educational intervention to reduce prejudice was conducted by a schoolteacher, not a psychologist. Jane Elliott was working in a small town in Iowa, USA, at the time when civil rights activist Martin Luther King was assassinated. Shocked by the event and by the reaction to it – expressions of prejudice against black Americans in the white-dominated media – Elliott decided to tackle prejudice directly among the third grade (age 8 to 9) children she taught. She set up a scenario where children's eye colour would determine how they were treated, allowing everyone to understand what it felt like to be the victim of discrimination (Elliott, 1977). It became known as the **blue eyes/brown eyes exercise**.

On day one, blue-eyed children in Elliott's class were told that they were the social superiors, and received privileges such as extra playtime. Prejudice spontaneously emerged, with name-calling against the out-group. Those labelled inferior did worse at a card-sorting task, suggesting that stereotype threat could have an immediate impact on school performance. On the second day, the roles were reversed, with brown-eyed children being put into the superior role. The effects were repeated, with the blue-eyed children now doing more poorly on the card task.

Elliott's technique worked well with her all-white schoolchildren but it has not always been successful with more diverse groups (Anthony, 2009). It is confrontational and caused some distress in the children—although on the positive side, the original group of children later said that they had found the process educational and it had raised their awareness of prejudice.

> **! Syllabus note**
>
> This part of this topic is only required at Higher, not National 5.

> **! Syllabus note**
>
> This section includes information on practical ways of tackling prejudice. It also provides several good examples of research evidence that could be used in an answer to an exam question.

Martin Luther King addressing the crowd at the Lincoln Memorial in Washington D.C. in 1957

A photograph from the study

Diversity training can be effective in combatting prejudice

Overall, education is the most common intervention against prejudice – most school systems teach children about the issue. It is relatively cheap to do, as it can be conducted as part of the general social education curriculum. However, despite its prevalence in education, prejudiced attitudes are still widespread.

In adults, **diversity training** is a form of education aimed at reducing stereotypes, prejudice and discrimination. Some workers are offered it as part of their job (e.g. certain police forces). People are sometimes ordered to attend such courses after discriminatory or abusive behaviour, such as when Football Association referees' chairman David Elleray was sent on such a course for allegedly making racist comments to a colleague (Percy, 2014). Bezrukova *et al.* (2012) reported that such courses are more effective when integrated with other workplace activities (rather than a one-off, 'stand-alone' format).

The contact hypothesis

According to Allport (1954), we are more likely to form stereotypes if we are ignorant of out-groups, while if we get to know them as individuals, we will become less prejudiced. This idea is known as the **contact hypothesis**.

Clearly, there are times when increased contact can actually lead to conflict, for example, when new groups immigrate into a country or two organisations merge. Allport explained this issue by stating that there are several conditions for successful contact, and without these, contact will not work as a strategy to reduce prejudice. These include working to achieve common goals and having support from authorities/ society. Most importantly, Allport thought that contact must be **equal status contact**, that is, individuals must cooperate on an equal basis, without either group being superior or inferior.

Cook (1978) agreed with these factors, but also emphasised the importance of getting to know individuals in the out-group, particularly ones who do not fit the stereotype held about the out-group. In combination with Allport's ideas, Cook summarised five factors for contact to be effective:

- support from authorities
- personal acquaintance
- introduction to non-stereotypical individuals
- cooperation between groups
- equal status

> **? Discussion point**
>
> Do you have any experience of getting to know people from a group that you previously had no contact with? Did it change your attitude towards that group?

Research and evaluation

Binder *et al.* (2009) conducted a longitudinal study in the UK that showed that contact reduced prejudice in majorities but did not appear to work for minorities. This could be because ethnic minorities in the UK already have lots of contact with the majority white population.

When contact is shown to correlate to lower prejudice, the direction of this relationship is not always clear (Binder *et al.*, 2009) – does contact reduce prejudice or does prejudice reduce contact? Additionally, research can suffer from sampling bias, as highly prejudiced people typically do not want to take part in programmes that promote contact with out-groups (Pettigrew, 1998).

Laar *et al.* (2005) studied Dutch students who had been randomly allocated a university roommate of a different race. After sharing a room for several months, participants became less prejudiced, according to questionnaire data. Although it was a natural experiment, this appeared to demonstrate cause-and-effect. However, it may not be possible to generalise from young students in an individual setting to other social groups. In addition, the level of contact involved in sharing a room is much greater than is possible in most other settings.

In Laar's study students who lived with someone of another race became less prejudiced

Superordinate goals

A **superordinate goal** is where two or more people must work together to achieve a shared goal that cannot be achieved without their cooperation. Muzafer Sherif's 'Robbers Cave' study (Sherif *et al.*, 1954; see key study) is a classic example of this technique in action. The study manipulated boys into a situation of conflict, and then presented situations where they had to work together to complete tasks. Prejudice reduced as a result.

The **jigsaw technique** was developed to reduce prejudice using superordinate goals in the school classroom. The key idea is that every member of a group must have an essential piece of information. Therefore, when a group works on a task (e.g. project work), each member has to contribute and the whole group must work together in order to complete the task. This promotes listening and a respectful exchange of information. Here, the superordinate goal is the completion of the project.

In the USA after desegregation of schools, it was hoped that prejudice levels would reduce due to contact, but they remained high. Aronson and Bridgeman (1979) used the jigsaw technique with 10 classes of elementary (primary) school pupils over seven schools in Texas. Another three classes were used as a control group. Tasks involved working in jigsaw groups, which took 45 minutes as part of their school day. After three weeks of this intervention, the researchers found increases in three key areas:

- self-esteem increased
- students reported higher levels of liking for both in-group and out-group members
- academic performance increased

Meanwhile, there was less evidence of negative stereotypes of other ethnic groups.

> **?** **Discussion point**
>
> Is this different from a shared goal? (See p.409 for feedback.)

The jigsaw technique was developed to reduce prejudice

📖 Key study: Sherif *et al.* (1954): the Robber's Cave study

Aim: *Sherif believed that conflict arises due to groups having incompatible goals, such as countries disputing the same area of land. He had conducted two previous summer camp studies, during which he refined a set of techniques to cause conflict between groups. This summary is based on the third published study, which had the key difference from the earlier studies that the conflicts were resolved.*

Method & Findings: *The participants were 22 middle-class Protestant boys from Oklahoma City. They were carefully selected to be similar to each other in background and schooling. It was also carefully established that none of them previously knew each other. The participants were divided into two groups of 11, again keeping them as closely matched as possible, and taken to the Robber's Cave National Park for their camp – a large isolated hilly area with plenty of space for outings, swimming and boating, which took its name from its past as a hideout for the outlaw Jesse James.*

In week one of the study, the boys were kept separate, for example by staggering meal times. The aim of this stage was to allow a strong in-group identity to form; the groups nicknamed themselves 'Eagles' and 'Rattlers' (i.e. rattlesnakes) and developed group norms including status, nicknames and favourite songs. A recognised 'leader' emerged amongst both groups of boys. Gradually, each group was allowed to 'discover' that there was another group in the area and the idea of competing against them at baseball was raised.

The two groups competed in tug-of-war contests and at other games

In week two, the aim was to cause the groups to come into conflict due to incompatible goals, in particular a tournament that only one side could win. The tournament included baseball, tug-of-war and other contents. Sherif and colleagues announced the tournament gradually, wanting it to appear to be the boys' own idea. The prizes – a trophy, medals and a penknife each – were displayed prominently. The researchers hypothesised that this would lead to negative attitudes and stereotyped views of the out-group. Early in this stage, the boys met the other group for the first time and name-calling began immediately. Some tournament events were judged by the researchers, allowing them to manipulate the scores and keep the contest even. The researchers also noticed that a sense of 'good sportsmanship' was prominent at the start but gave way quickly to name-calling and resentment. The Eagles lost the first two events and proceeded to burn the Rattlers' flag. By the end of the tournament, won by the Eagles, there was such bad feeling that fights broke out and had to be stopped to prevent injury. The Rattlers raided the Eagles hut and stole their medals and knives, though these were later returned to them by Sherif. Both groups were asked to identify friends 'from the entire camp' and in each camp, over 92% of choices were boys from the in-group.

A test of judgement was also used to follow up on stage 2, where each boy had to put beans into a bottle within a time limit and then everyone estimated how many they had managed to put in. Rattlers' in-group estimates were 3.7 higher and the Eagles estimated their own group 7.2 higher on average compared to the out-group, even though the stimuli were faked, and everyone was shown the same number of beans (35).

In week three, Sherif and colleagues set out to replace the conflict with cooperation. To start with, seven unstructured 'contact' situations were arranged, but groups continued to jeer at each other, sit only with in-group members and some meetings resulted in food fights. Then the researchers introduced superordinate goals, most notably a vandalised water supply and a truck that had broken down on a camping excursion. These events were set up but required all of the boys to work together to solve them (for example, the whole group pulling the truck with their 'tug-of-war' rope until it started). The key finding was that after working together with superordinate goals, group hostility dropped away. The boys willingly travelled together in a single truck and laughed about the raids that has caused so much hostility the previous week. They alternated singing the songs that each group had previously adopted. At the end of the last week, they arranged and organised a group campfire, and agreed to travel back to Oklahoma City together on the same bus. In-group identities still existed, but the groups mingled readily, and name-calling had more or less disappeared.

Evaluation: The study had high ecological validity – later, Sherif (1977) commented that a lack of a control in research is less of a risk than a lack of real life relevance! It made a huge impact in social psychology, and the study of prejudice in particular; there have been few, if any, other field studies with such elaborate procedures. It has great real-world relevance as a model for how to reduce prejudice.

A limitation in terms of external validity was that the sample were all boys. However, Sherif cited Avigdor (1951), who similarly found among a group of 10-year-old girls that cooperation led to positive stereotypes and conflict led to negative stereotypes. Also, the sample were children and all of the same nationality, race and religion as each other. This makes it harder to relate to real-life conflicts.

There were considerable ethical issues. Child participants were deceived and put into situations where physical fights broke out. They were also provided with knives as prizes. One task involved depriving them of drinking water. The area contained significant natural risks as well, including poisonous snakes. The conflict was highly stressful; observers noted signs of bedwetting, homesickness and attempts to run away among some participants (Perry, 2014).

Both the jigsaw technique and the Sherif et al. (1954) study seem to suggest that contact alone is not enough. The Robber's Cave study involved a lot of contact, as does an everyday classroom situation in a school, but prejudice and stereotypes can remain strong. These research studies suggest that while contact is necessary, it is not sufficient to reduce prejudice. In the Sherif study in particular, there was no particular difference in status between the two groups of boys, who were chosen to be as similar as possible to each other. This provides strong support of the importance of intergroup superordinate goals.

Sherif's studies linked to his belief that intergroup conflict arises from competing over limited resources (e.g. territory and the tournament prizes in the Robber's Cave study). However, this is generally seen as too narrow, as not all conflicts involve limited resources, and as a theory, it has largely been superseded by social identity theory.

Key concepts

- Education
- Contact hypothesis
- Superordinate goals
- Blue eyes/brown eyes exercise
- Diversity training
- Equal status contact
- Jigsaw technique

✓ Questions

1. What is meant by 'raising awareness'?

2. What physical feature did Elliott use to stimulate prejudice?

3. According to Aronson and Bridgeman, what three things increased when the jigsaw technique was used?

4. Name the factors that make contact successful according to Cook (1978).

5. Does contact work better for minorities or majorities?

6. What happened during the first week of the Sherif *et al.* (1954) study?

7. Name two tasks that were used to reduce prejudice in Sherif's study.

8. Why do you think Sherif chose participants who were all very similar to each other?

9. Name an ethical issue with the Sherif study.

10. What did Sherif think that prejudice was based on?

GO! Activities

1. Sherif's tasks and the jigsaw technique both used superordinate goals. Think of other tasks, perhaps from your own life, which involve superordinate goals. Make a list.

2. Find out about a current issue relating to prejudice. It could be one that affects you directly or from the news/your own reading. Which of the techniques described could realistically be used to reduce prejudice and promote positive interactions? Make a list of practical suggestions. If you have time, you could develop this into a presentation and/or record it as a YouTube video.

End of topic project

Conduct an observational study of prejudice. This can be done using seating distance, as follows:

- Obtain volunteers to take part in a study on health treatments, using adverts or similar.
- Obtain consent from the participants.
- Half of the participants will be briefed about the importance of treating minorities equally and fairly, while the other half will not (randomly decide which condition participants will be in).
- All participants are told that they are first to arrive for a group discussion on health treatments that will be observed. They will be told that the school/college has a visiting speaker who is a health campaigner and used to suffer from schizophrenia.
- Arrange nine seats in a circle. Put a sign on one seat marked 'visiting speaker'.
- Observer how close the participants sit to the visiting speaker's place, that is, how many chairs away from one to four in either direction. In reality, there is no speaker, and once the participant has been sat down and their seat has been noted, they can be debriefed.
- Prepare and deliver a short talk to your class on what you found and concluded from this observation. Refer to at least one relevant background research study that is not from your notes or textbook.

This study is based on Norman *et al*. (2010).

End of topic specimen exam questions

As this is an optional topic, exam questions will be quite general and will not name the topic or its specific theories/research studies, for example:

National 5

1. For your optional Social Behaviour topic:

   a. Briefly explain the topic. 4 marks

   b. Name and describe one research study that has been carried out in your chosen topic. Include the aim, method/procedure and results of the study. 6 marks

2. Choose a topic in Social Behaviour other than conformity. Explain this topic using two or more concepts/theories and the findings of at least one research study. 10 marks

Higher

1. Describe and evaluate one or more research studies from your optional Social Behaviour topic. 12 marks

2. Choose a topic in Social Behaviour other than conformity and obedience. Explain this topic using two or more concepts/theories and the findings of at least one research study. 10 marks

3. Explain how a Social Psychology topic other than conformity and obedience has been applied in the real world. 10 marks

The total exam mark allocation for the Social Behaviour unit will be 20 marks; however, there is no way of knowing in advance how this will be split between this topic and conformity.

12 Non-verbal communication

Within the context of non-verbal communication (NVC), you should know and understand:

- Different aspects of body language.
- Facial expressions and paralanguage.
- Nature and nurture theories of NVC.
- Research evidence including Ekman and Friesen (1971), Meltzoff and Moore (1977), Chartrand and Bargh (1999).
- An application of the concept to technology or society.

You need to develop the following skills:

- Distinguishing between types of NVC.
- Using research evidence to support statements about the topic.
- Identifying how NVC plays a role in real-world contexts.
- Explaining the links between concepts/theories and a real-world application.
- Analysing research relevant to the topic.

! Syllabus note

As well as 'Conformity', you need to study one optional topic in Social Behaviour. NVC would be a suitable choice. The optional topic should be tackled in a similar way to conformity – that is, you should be aware of key concepts, theories, research studies and (for Higher) a real-world application of the topic.

Non-verbal comunication includes facial expressions and body langauge

Aspects of NVC

Non-verbal communication (NVC) means communicating without words. There are several aspects to NVC, such as facial expression, paralanguage and various types of body language.

Body language

One of the most obvious and important aspects of NVC is a person's **body language** – the way they communicate using their bodies rather than (or as well as) words. A person's posture and facial expression, as well as how close they stand to another person, these are all examples of body language. The following section explains four major types of body language that are apparent in everybody when communicating are outlined below.

Proximity. This is how close we are to another person. Generally, people stand closer to those that they like better – and proximity can therefore communicate liking – or dislike – to the other person. On the other hand, standing too close is rated unfavourably – there are social norms regarding how close people can stand without making the other person feel stressed, unless the person is already a close friend (Freedman, 1975). If **personal space** is invaded, people tend to back away (Felipe & Sommer, 1966) and/or show signs of anxiety. People also keep a greater 'social distance' from members of groups that they have prejudiced feelings against (Norman *et al.*, 2010). Proximity seems to be linked to the hormone oxytocin, which appears to cause people who are already in a romantic relationship to keep a greater distance from other members of the opposite sex (Scheele *et al.*, 2012).

Proximity can communicate whether or not you like someone

'Thumbs up' is a gesture

Posture is another aspect of body language. Broadly, this can include things such as sitting, standing or lying down, but on a more precise level, things such as the angle of a person's shoulders, neck and back can signal their mood – a straight back and relaxed shoulders indicating confidence, for example, while slouching does not (Krauss Whitbourne, 2012). Furley and Schweizer (2014) showed participants images of athletes, without giving away the score or showing any clear examples of celebration or disappointment. They found that child participants could guess the score from the body language of the athlete – in other words, they could reliably tell who was winning or losing just by looking at them.

Gesture means the things that we do, primarily with our hands and arms, to communicate non-verbally or in addition to words. Examples include pointing, clapping, 'thumbs up', waving arms around, and, of course, sticking fingers up! A gesture may support the content of speech, such as a rising hand motion when talking about climbing (McNeill, 1992). There are certain ritual hand gestures in religion, politics or the military (e.g. saluting) and they can form part of games (e.g. 'rock, scissors, paper'). Gestures are typically done using the hands, but shrugging shoulders, nodding, shaking the head, etc. are also usually considered to be examples of gestures.

Do you think Andy Murray is winning?

Making eye contact signals that you wish to communicate

Gaze essentially means the direction in which we orient our eyes, but people usually also move their head and their whole body. Looking towards the same object as another person indicates engagement in what they are doing (Rich *et al.*, 2010), while failure to pay attention to someone's gaze is usually interpreted as a sign of not being interested or not listening to what they are saying (Argyle & Cook, 1976). In particular, gazing at another person's face and making **eye contact** signals that you wish to communicate (DeSteno *et al.*, 2012). Kendon and Cook (1969) found that there are individual differences in length of gaze, with some people tending to look at faces for longer than others regardless of who they are speaking to.

Ambady and Rosenthal (1992) believe that these cues lead people to make unconscious but yet very accurate judgements of others. In their research, they discovered a reliable correlation between people's own reports of their personality and short clips of their body language observed by others. They used the term **thin slicing** to mean immediate judgements that are made about a person or situation and observed that taking more time or paying more deliberate attention to an observation did not make people's judgements more accurate – a 30-second observation was just as effective as five minutes.

Therefore, it appears that these aspects of NVC affect us on a very basic psychological level – we make fast, accurate judgements of others based on their body language and we are generally unaware of doing it. And of course, other people are doing the same to us all of the time.

Facial expressions

Facial expressions play a huge role in understanding what another person is feeling. The most obvious one is the smile. It was recognised in the 19th century that there are two key types of smiles – one that involves the mouth muscles and the muscles around the eyes – a so-called **Duchenne smile** – and one that just involves the mouth. Subsequent research shows that a smile involving only the mouth is more likely to be false, while a smile involving both the mouth and the eyes is universally associated with positive emotions (Messinger *et al.*, 2001).

Researcher Paul Ekman has done extensive work on facial expression, stating in the 1960s that there are certain basic facial expressions that are the same for everyone – which are **culturally universal**. Ekman (1999) believes that these indicate universal basic emotions.

Ekman (2009a) also noted that faces display brief **microexpressions** – momentary appearances of emotion on the face, sometimes too fast to see without a slow motion video, which the person then deliberately hides. For example, if someone's boss gives them extra work to do, there may be a momentary sign of anger on their face, which they then hide by deliberately looking happy. Their initial brief micro-expression may be a truer indication of what they are feeling.

Ekman states that there are seven emotions that have universal signals in people's facial expressions, often revealed in their microexpressions:

- anger
- fear
- sadness
- disgust
- contempt
- surprise
- happiness

A smile involving both the mouth and the eyes is universally associated with positive emotions

Polikovsky *et al.* (2009) supported the idea of microexpressions and suggested that they can be a clue to violent and criminal intentions. However, Ekman (2009a) noted that microexpressions are hard to spot and that NVC in general is easy to misinterpret.

The idea of microexpressions suggests that our facial reactions are, to some extent, controlled by automatic emotional responses and that these are quickly suppressed as our awareness of the social situation takes control. Therefore, there are at least two processes controlling facial expressions: one more immediate that leads to automatic reactions, and a slower, more deliberate, cognitive reaction that allows us to think strategically and to modify our own expressions.

Can you tell how this girl is feeling from her expression?

📖 Key study: Ekman and Friesen (1971): the universal nature of facial expressions

Aim: Ekman and Friesen aimed to find out whether facial expressions are universal to all humans.

Method: The researchers studied the **Fore people** in Papua New Guinea, a group that had been isolated for thousands of years, living in a Stone Age culture. The tribe had very little contact with outsiders before the 1950s, and although some had since met and interacted with many outsiders, the researchers picked participants who had experienced very little of such contact. They had never learned a Western language, seen a movie or worked for an outsider. The sample included 189 adults and 130 children – around 3% of the total Fore population. For comparison, researchers also studied 23 adults who had extensive contact with Westerners. A difficulty was that none of the participants could read. Therefore, a task was chosen that involved looking at two to three pictures of facial expressions while the researcher read out a short scenario that indicated an emotion, for example, 'her mother has died and she feels very sad' (p.126). The participant then had to point to the face picture that indicated the emotion. The scenarios were read by Fore translators who were instructed not to prompt.

People may try to hide their feelings by changing their facial expression

Photographs of one of the Fore men studied – can you match the expressions to the following emotions: happy, sad, disgusted and angry?

Findings: *Responses were very similar to those previously found by Western subjects. Importantly, there were no significant differences between the Westernised and isolated groups, suggesting that exposure to Western colonists had not affected Fore perceptions of facial expressions. The one error that was commonly found was in distinguishing fear from surprise. No sex differences were found, except that Fore women were less enthusiastic about taking part in the study. There were also no age differences found, with six to seven-year-old children responding the same as older Fore individuals and with as much accuracy. The researchers concluded that certain facial expressions are universally associated with particular emotions in all human cultures. They accepted that fear had not been well distinguished from surprise and noted that it was unclear whether this is because culture does play some role in modifying innate facial expressions, or because among the Fore people, fearful events (such as an attack by another tribe) are generally also surprising.*

Evaluation: *A strength of the study was the relatively large sample who had very little contact with the outside world. It was also supported by a number of other findings; for example, work with blind children who show the same facial expressions as sighted children. The research supports the views of researchers such as Darwin, Wundt and Asch that facial expressions are universal. However, Smith and Bond (1993) argued that relatively few emotions are truly universal, while Matsumoto (1989) found that Japanese people were poorer at identifying images of negative emotions – perhaps because it is less culturally acceptable to express these emotions in Japan than elsewhere.*

Paralanguage

Paralanguage means things that we do to communicate through speech but not including the words themselves. This includes the volume that we speak at, speed of speech (which can communicate urgency, excitement or interest) and the tone or pitch we are using (a flat tone can make us sound bored).

Laughing expresses a powerful message

As well as the sound of the words we are using, several sounds/expressions we make during communication can express a very powerful message, for example:

- gasps
- sighs
- laughs

Paralanguage is used during a conversation

One type of paralanguage is only used by the listener – the **backchannel** means the sounds or words made by a listener while another person is speaking. Common examples of a backchannel include '*mmm…*' or '*uh-huh*'. These are primarily used to indicate interest, though they also play a role in **turn-taking** – indicating that the listener wants the speaker to stop so that she/he can respond (Crystal, 1997). Turn-taking is a two-way process, however, as speakers may indicate that they are ready for a response from their listener through paralanguage, such as by lowering the pitch of their voice (Ward, 1996).

Although the term backchannel is widely used, Fujimoto (2007) states that it not specific enough to be useful because it contains some contradictions in terms of the type of communication to which it refers:

- Some are sounds ('uh-huh') while others are words ('yeah').
- Some indicate agreement and others disagreement.
- Some signal the speaker to continue and others signal that the listener would like a turn.

✔Questions

1. Four major types of body language were described at the start of this chapter. Two are proximity and gaze, what are the other two?

2. Which of the four types is this an example of: pointing?

3. Which of the four types is this an example of: slouching?

4. How do people usually interpret mutual gaze?

5. Who were the Fore people and what made them unique?

6. How many participants were there in Ekman and Friesen's study?

7. Give one example of why Fujimoto (2007) said that 'backchannel' is too broad a term.

8. Give two examples of 'backchannel' paralanguage.

9. Give three examples of what Ekman considers basic facial expressions.

10. What type of NVC is being used when someone shouts?

🔑 Key concepts

- Non-verbal communication (NVC)
- Body language
- Proximity
- Personal space
- Gesture
- Posture
- Gaze
- Eye contact
- Thin slicing
- Duchenne smile
- Cultural universals
- Microexpression
- Paralanguage
- Backchannel
- Turn-taking

Activities

GO!

1. Use your phone or webcam to make the seven basic facial expressions described by Ekman – take pictures and add them to your study notes. Can you think of a situation when you would make each of those faces? Note those down as well.

2. What do the following gestures mean to you?

3. If someone you knew was going for a job interview, what would you tell them about the following?

- posture
- paralanguage
- backchannel paralanguage
- gaze

Most babies start to smile at around six to eight weeks old

Theories and debates in NVC: nature and nurture

As is apparent from other topics in psychology, there is an ongoing debate between approaches and theories that emphasise the role of nature – our biology and genetics – in behaviour, and explanations that say that culture and/or experience have greater roles. This is known as the nature-nurture debate (see chapter 2).

In terms of theories of NVC, the biological and evolutionary theories place a strong emphasis on NVC being innate and due to 'nature', while cultural explanations suggest that the major part of NVC is learned from society around us, that is, 'nurture'.

The biology of NVC

A major issue in the nature/nurture debate in NVC is the extent to which body language and other NVC functions are controlled by universal biological systems. Evidence here that mainly supports the 'nature' side of the debate is the study of the biology of NVC, closely linked to the biological approach to psychology.

A brain area called the **amygdala** appears to play a central role in regulating our response to other people's NVC. The amygdala is part of the **limbic system**, a brain area near the hypothalamus that is connected to many other areas of the brain. It plays an important role in regulating emotions, especially fear and aggression, in all animals, and in humans it seems to be very important in responding to faces – people who have had their amygdala damaged tend to trust unappealing, unfamiliar faces that other people react negatively to (Adolphs *et al.*, 1998).

The amygdala is important in responding to faces

When viewing faces, the amygdala is probably involved in the rapid 'thin slicing' reactions described in the previous sections. In other words, this part of the brain produces our 'gut feelings' about a person or situation. The amygdala is also involved in recognising body language, as are several other brain areas; **motor cortex** – the area of neocortex that controls movement – is vital for mentally representing the actions that we see (De Gelder, 2006).

Researchers have discovered that our reaction to NVC and the appearance of others appears early. Most babies start to smile at around six to eight weeks old, suggesting that this is biologically programmed in humans. Babies appear to recognise faces and prefer them to non-faces – in experiments, they respond more to face-like pictures than pictures with the same features jumbled up (Fagan, 1976). They also **imitate** the facial expression of adults long before they learn to imitate more generally (Meltzoff & Moore, 1977, see key study). Together, these findings suggests that the way we respond to people's faces and body language occurs at a very basic (unconscious) level, which is under biological control and largely innate.

Evaluation

This theory is supported by evidence that our proximity to others can have a biological effect, as can physical touch. Middlemist *et al.* (1976) demonstrated that people find it hard to go to the toilet if others are too close, while Cohen *et al.* (2015) found that hugging could help protect against illness.

However, the idea that our reactions to NVC are linked to basic biological systems does not rule out the possibility that these functions come under conscious control as we get older, and therefore become influenced by culture.

Cohen found that hugging could help protect against illness

Holland *et al.* (2004) found that activating individual or social schemas led to variations in how much proximity people chose relative to strangers. NVC also varies greatly with culture as described below; suggesting that innate NVC functions can be modified. Biological psychologists, however, would argue that such modifications are minor and do not change the basic nature of NVC functions.

> ### 🌐 Make the link
>
> …between the Cohen *et al.* (2015) study of hugging and the topic of stress.

📖 Key study: Meltzoff and Moore (1977): babies imitate facial expressions and gestures

Aim: The researchers noted that earlier experts on infant development such as Jean Piaget had assumed that imitation does not develop until eight months of age or older. Their aim was to show that it could occur in babies who are only three weeks or less.

Method: The researchers studied six babies aged 12 to 19 days. In a laboratory experiment, the researchers initially displayed a neutral face. They then showed one of four stimulus faces/gestures in a random order:

- *tongue out*
- *pouting face*
- *wiggling fingers*
- *wide open mouth*

Each stimulus was displayed four times over 15 seconds, and for the following 20 seconds, the experimenter made a neutral face again and the baby's reaction was recorded. In order to allow for the possibility that the baby might not be paying attention, this process was repeated up to three times in total if required.

Findings: Undergraduate observers were then shown the video recordings in a random order and they were asked to estimate which of the four gestures they thought the baby was copying. They were significantly more likely to guess the correct gesture than the other options. The researchers concluded that babies could imitate at a very early age – much earlier than previously thought.

A photograph from the study

Evaluation: A strength of the study was its careful control of possible confounding variables that had to be avoided, for example:

- *The effects of two similar facial expressions were compared, for example, tongue sticking out versus wide mouth.*
- *Distance between the baby and the adult was kept constant.*
- *Observers were shown the baby's face only on a video recording and they were not told what gesture the infant had been shown.*

The study was highly influential in showing that some NVC occurs very early and it is apparently linked to others' NVC at a very young age. It led to the development of a model of infant imitation that has been used by researchers Breazeal and Scassellati (2002) in teaching robots to imitate (see next section). However, Jones (2009) disputes the findings. She points out that imitation of finger wiggling and the pouting face have not been reliably replicated, while sticking the tongue out is a very typical response in babies to anything that interests them – it does not necessarily mean that they were imitating.

Evolutionary theory

The evolutionary theory of NVC tries to explain why we use NVC the way we do. Drawing on Darwin's theory of natural selection, it suggests that functions such as facial expressions and body language have evolved because they gave our ancestors a survival advantage.

Darwin considered human behaviour to consist of evolved traits that, as in animals, have given an advantage to our ancestors. In terms of NVC, Darwin made four key claims that have been supported by subsequent research (Ekman, 2009b):

- There are several basic emotions that are fundamentally separate from each other.
- Facial expressions are the main way of conveying these emotions through NVC.
- Facial expressions are culturally universal.
- Gestures are cultural conventions, learned within a social group.

Darwin believed that all human emotions were linked to our origins as apes and he saw parallels with expressions of emotion that he observed in other primates. It is difficult to study emotion in primates as it can only be done through observation, however Ekman (1999, p.54) states there is *'no convincing evidence'* that humans have any emotions that are not also present in our near relatives such as chimpanzees.

As well as facial expressions, body language in grief among other apes is strikingly similar to that in humans. Chimpanzees have been observed stroking the hands of ill relatives, hugging bereaved individuals and sitting in a nightly 'vigil' after a death (Anderson *et al.*, 2010). Their posture and proximity to the dying and deceased also changes, with a tendency to avoid places associated with death. Chimps also make a 'begging posture' with outstretched hands (Premack & Premack, 1983). As chimps share many of the same genes as humans but do not experience human culture, these similarities suggest that at least some aspects of NVC may be under genetic control. Human language may even have evolved as a quicker and more efficient alternative to communication via physical touch and gesture as our social groups became larger (Dunbar, 1996).

Evaluation

Although the principle of natural selection is generally accepted, researchers do not always agree on why NVC functions evolved – what use these behaviours had for human ancestors. Ekman (2009b) states that emotional facial expressions are largely universal because it was essential during human evolution that individuals have clear signals to the social group of what they were feeling and what they might be just about to do. Zajonc (1985) disputes this view, arguing that humans, having evolved sophisticated verbal communication, would not have needed a great range of facial communication, and in addition, it would not have been an evolutionary advantage to let enemies know one's intentions.

Zajonc suggests instead that movements of facial muscles evolved to help regulate blood flow to the brain, rather than to tell other people what we are feeling. This is supported by the work of Byrne and Corp

Emotion in primates can only be studied through observation

Chimps make a 'begging posture' with outstretched hands

(2004), who think that the evolution of human intelligence was driven by the need to deceive rather than to inform others.

However, Ekman (2009b) argues that hunter-gatherer cultures in our evolutionary past did not have much reason or opportunity to lie, as lies would be easily found out and the costs of being rejected by the social group would be huge. These issues affect some of the applications discussed in the next section.

Cultural explanations

As noted in the previous section, some facial expressions are thought to be culturally universal, that is, the same in everyone regardless of their upbringing and culture. However, it is clear that culture can make a huge difference to many aspects of NVC. **Culturally influenced NVC** cues include, most obviously, gesture – gestures can have very different meanings in different cultures and even things that seem fairly simple, such as sticking your tongue out, can range widely in how they are interpreted.

Meanings of sticking tongue out:

* Western cultures: seen as cheeky and provocative.
* Tibet: seen as friendly.
* Māori: seen as angry/defiant and used as part of the 'haka' war dance.

How would you interpret this gesture?

This can of course cause problems to a traveller – as you may know if you have been abroad, attitudes to things such as public hugging, kissing and holding hands can vary between cultures, for example the norm of kissing-to-greet in some Mediterranean countries. These behaviours can also vary within cultures; in some situations within your own culture it may be more socially acceptable than others to hold hands or make rude gestures – among a group of teenage friends rather than a work meeting, for example.

There is also considerable variability in other NVC functions. Ward (1996) notes that backchanneling is twice as common in Japanese language conversations as it is in English. Jourard (1966) found that attitudes to being touched and to touching others differed depending on a person's sex and religious background. Such cultural preferences may also change over time, like other types of social norms.

Kissing-to-greet is very common in some Mediterranean countries

How exactly do people learn gestures and other culturally influenced NVC? Alfred Bandura developed the work of the behaviourist approach (see chapter 2) to explain how people learn from those around them, not just from stimuli in the environment. One key concept from this research is known as **social learning**. This means that just as an action can be rewarded directly, we can observe others doing an action and being rewarded and we are more likely to do it ourselves.

Evaluation

It may seem surprising nowadays, but some historical writers considered cultural differences in NVC to be based on racial groups – an idea that was also popular in Nazi Germany. Writing at a time when the Nazis were in power, Efron (1941) dismissed this idea, noting that cultural differences in NVC among Jewish and Italian communities in New York largely disappeared as they assimilated into the broader American community. The fact that people can change and adapt and that cultures change their NVC over time supports the idea that these are learned from society, and not innate.

A problem with cultural explanations is the existence of universal aspects of NVC. However, even though these are to some extent biologically programmed, it doesn't mean that everybody interprets the meaning of those expressions in the same way. In a quasi-experiment, Matsumoto and Kudoh (1993) showed US and Japanese students the same photos of faces. There were differences between the two groups of students in how they attributed feelings and personality traits to the faces. For example, the Americans were more likely to say that a person with a Duchenne smile was very sociable.

Therefore, these researchers think that although NVC may have a biological basis, a major part of it is learned through experience and our culture ultimately plays a bigger role than innate behaviours.

Italian immigrants arriving in America

✔ Questions

1. What is the name of the debate about how much of our behaviour is innate and how much is learned?

2. What part of the limbic system plays a key role in the biology of emotions and NVC?

3. Given an example of NVC that develops early in nearly all babies.

4. What did Holland (2004) find out about proximity?

5. True or false: Ekman believes that human emotions are different from emotions in chimps.

6. Give one example of NVC that is similar in both chimps and humans.

7. Zajonc disagreed that facial expressions evolved to communicate emotion. What two reasons did he give for this view?

8. What did the Nazis believe about cultural differences in NVC?

9. Give an example of what sticking out one's tongue means in other cultures.

10. Which researchers found a difference in how American and Japanese students interpreted a Duchenne smile?

🔑 Key concepts

- Limbic system
- Amygdala
- Motor cortex
- Imitation
- Culturally influenced NVC
- Social learning

Uses of NVC research

Research into NVC is of general interest, as it has the potential to help people to understand their own communication better and to communicate more successfully. People generally want to use their own NVC to their best advantage and to help them understand others. Three areas in particular have attracted considerable attention: social interaction, policing and technology.

Work and social applications

It appears to be important to look regularly and steadily at the interviewer in a job interview

Kendon and Cook (1969) found that gaze and eye contact affects how people are evaluated. People who spent more time looking at a conversation partner were judged more positively in their study, but only if they used long, steady gazes – people who looked at the partner a lot but did so in many short glances were less well liked. Therefore, it would appear to be important in meetings and job interviews to look regularly and steadily at the other person (this does not necessarily mean eye contact where both people simultaneously gaze at each other, which happens quite infrequently in any encounter).

People who mimic the body language and speech of others tend to be judged more favourably (Chartrand & Bargh, 1999; see key study). Fortunately, we largely do this unconsciously and automatically – a process that Chartrand and Bargh called the **chameleon effect**. In particular, we imitate the posture, facial expression and mannerisms of other people – and this happens especially when people are high in empathy (i.e. they are sensitive to the emotions of others).

We find people who mimic our body language more attractive

Some researchers have studied the chameleon effect as a strategy to help when dating. Gueguen (2009) recruited three female confederates to copy men's NVC during a speed-dating event. They were instructed to mimic both body language and speech. The findings of the study were that the women were rated as more sexually attractive by the males who had been mimicked than those that had not and they were more likely to be given contact details. Similarly, Bertamini *et al.* (2013) showed computer-generated images of people either sitting or standing and they found that they were more likely to be rated as attractive if the viewer was in the same posture as the person in the picture.

The same principle can be applied much more widely, including in work situations and interviews. However, there are drawbacks to deliberate imitation of NVC – if the person realises that they are being mimicked, they will actually like the mimicker less (Barco, 1999). One way to gain the benefit more subtly would be to move the same body part but not copy the actual gesture or position; Sparenberg *et al.* (2012) found that just moving the same limb is enough to trigger the same benefits, regardless of the precise movement.

Key study: Chartrand and Bargh (1999): the 'chameleon effect'

Aim: The researchers believed that there was a direct link between perception and behaviour, so that we can copy our surroundings (other people) without any conscious awareness of doing it, like a chameleon changing colour. This, they believed, happens in order to promote social bonding. The aim of their study was to test this hypothesis. They referred to research that showed that married couples become gradually more alike in appearance and suggested it could be due to similar facial lines appearing after years of unconsciously mimicking each other's facial expressions.

Methodology: In a lab experiment, 35 participants were told to free associate about a set of photographs together with a partner. Unknown to them, the photo task was just a distractor, and their partner was actually a confederate of the researchers who had been told to display certain NVC behaviours – smiling, rubbing their face or shaking their foot – during the task.

Findings: Observations showed that participants were much more likely to rub their face than shake their foot if the confederate was rubbing their face and vice versa (see graph). Participants also showed a strong tendency to mimic smiling but interestingly, smiles did not appear to affect imitation of the other actions – participants were just as likely to copy a non-smiling confederate as a smiling one. When interviewed afterwards, none of the participants had noticed the behaviours that they had copied, supporting Chartrand and Bargh's view that we can mimic NVC unconsciously.

The researchers also believed that the chameleon effect has a useful function – boosting how likeable we are to others. In order to test this, they conducted a follow-up study where a confederate either deliberately mimicked the true participant or displayed neutral NVC. Participants were then asked to rate how much they liked the confederate on a scale of 1 to 9. Liking scores were significantly higher for the confederate who mimicked than for the one who did not (a mean of 6.62 versus 5.91).

Participants were much more likely to rub their face if the confederate was doing so

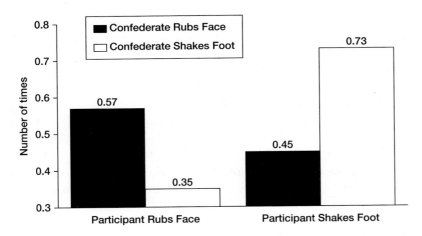

Results of the study

Evaluation: As a lab experiment, this was well controlled – unlike naturalistic observations of imitation, it was possible to determine cause-and-effect. It demonstrated that imitation could occur without any intention to do it and without knowing the other person. Results in the first experiment were highly statistically significant (i.e. very unlikely to have occurred by chance). The difference in the second experiment was smaller, though still significant. A potential difficulty comes in generalising to the real world, as this study used an artificial situation and a confederate who was unknown to the participant. The ethics (deception) could also be criticised.

Policing

From a legal or police perspective, it would be extremely useful for crime prevention or interviewing witnesses if it was possible to 'read' body language. TV shows such as *Lie to Me* suggest that people can be trained or have natural skills in interpreting people's microexpressions and figuring out what they are thinking. While microexpressions are real and these ideas make for good entertainment, the idea that our body language can be so simplistically interpreted is a myth. For example, the body language that indicates lying could also indicate that someone is simply feeling very stressed by an interrogation (Navarro, 2014).

The study found that CCTV operators trained in NVC were much better at predicting when a crime was about to take place

Grant and Williams (2011) studied CCTV operators' ability to predict when a crime was about to take place and they found it to be little better than a 50:50 chance, and not significantly better than members of the public. However, it improved when they were trained to focus on certain aspects of NVC, in particular the body language of people involved in a conversation/interaction, and the faces of those standing nearby. Such improvements have potential to aid crime prevention and faster police responses to crimes. The groups used in the study were small, however (12 participants in each).

Most people are very poor at juding whether someone is lying or not

Ekman (2009a) has studied why people are so poor at judging whether someone is lying or not. Similarly to Grant and Williams, some professionals – including FBI agents and judges – were found to have only a little over a 50% chance of correctly judging whether a suspect was lying or not in a lab experiment. Interestingly though, there were some groups studied – including trained interrogators and forensic psychologists – that had a much greater success rate, at 80% or above (Ekman, 2009a, p.123). This finding suggests that NVC cues to lie detection such as microexpressions are visible to everyone, but that most people tend to miss them.

Overall, it appears that despite the potential benefits for crime prevention and detection, NVC cues are not always noticed or understood by legal and crime professionals but training has the potential to improve that situation.

Technology

The chameleon effect even appears to apply to computer-generated people

Communication technologies, once limited to text, are increasingly making use of NVC functions. Traditional emails and texts are notorious for being misread in terms of mood and humour, but it has become common, at least in personal messages, chat and social networking, to use **emoticons** – small icons of facial expressions that represent moods.

A development in this area is to add a realistic face with NVC cues to voice recognition/speech apps that are now widely available for smartphones. This combination provides a challenging extension of the **Turing test** (Bailly *et al.*, 2010) – a classic research problem in artificial intelligence in which developers try to 'fool' people into thinking that they are communicating with a person, when it is actually a computer (see chapter 7).

Curiously, the chameleon effect (see previous section) appears to generalise to computer-generated faces. Bailenson and Yee (2005) equipped 69 student participants with a virtual reality helmet that showed a 3D human-like head and shoulders that spoke about a planned university campus. In one condition, it mimicked their head movements and these participants rated it as more likeable and persuasive than a control condition.

Emoticons are commonly used to convey mood

The term **robot** tends to evoke an image of a blank, metal, expressionless face. However, researchers have investigated ways of controlling the expressions of robots and they are using an understanding of NVC to do so. One of the first such robots was 'Kismet', designed by Cynthia Breazeal and her colleagues at MIT in the 1990s. Kismet was the first truly **social robot** – although it didn't speak, it possessed a moveable head, mouth, eyes and ears, allowing it to make the basic facial expressions described earlier in this chapter. It could respond to speech through body language signals such as gaze and nodding. Its abilities were fairly basic, but it paved the way for more sophisticated robots that have been developed since. Breazeal and Scassellati (2002) noted that their robots had to imitate as a human baby does, which meant programming the robot with certain key abilities:

Kismet, now in the MIT museum in Cambridge, Massachusetts, USA

- Recognising which features/gestures in a situation are relevant.
- Perceiving the movements of a human in an interaction.
- Relating these movements to its own limbs/face.
- An ability to refine a movement/skill that has been learned.

As robots have developed, researchers have realised the importance of NVC in gaining a sense of **engagement** during an interaction, that is, feeling that the robot is paying attention and ready to communicate. Rich *et al.* (2010) conducted a video study of human conversation to get a sense of how two people engage each other's attention – for example, both looking at the same object. They then applied the findings to a robot-human interaction. By recognising human responses, robots were able to use engagement strategies such as mutual gaze and pointing.

Gordon and Breazeal (2014) found that in a real world environment, a robot programmed to respond to feedback was able to learn which behaviours led to the longest interactions with passers-by (the answer – a sad face!) DeSteno *et al.* (2012) found that use of NVC cues can

Another robot, Asimo, can respond to human gestures, such as a handshake

? Discussion point

Bill Gates has suggested that artificial intelligence could become a threat to humans in the future (Griffin, 2015). Do you think there is a risk involved in programming robots to communicate?

directly affect the sense of trustworthiness of the robot – and that the same effects generalise to human-human interactions. So curiously, as well as using NVC knowledge to design robots, the robots could also become a powerful tool for new research into NVC in the future.

Designing robots to communicate using NVC as well as language has many potential practical benefits in terms of engaging users and getting information across in a way that does not require any training to interpret (Brooks & Arkin, 2007). However, as well as technical/mechanical challenges, a potential problem is that different cultures and subcultures assign different meanings to such things as gesture and paralanguage, as described in the first section. Therefore, any robot programmed to use these NVC functions may be culture-specific.

⊶ Key concepts

- Emoticon
- Turing test
- Robot
- Social robot
- Engagement

✓ Questions

1. Do people respond better to being looked at in short, frequent glances or a smaller number of longer gazes?

2. What task did Chartrand and Bargh's (1999) participants do during their 'chameleon effect' experiment?

3. How aware were Chartrand and Bargh's participants of having mimicked their partner's movements?

4. How good were CCTV operators at spotting signs of crimes using NVC?

5. True or false: Ekman said that it is impossible to detect lies using NVC.

6. Does the chameleon effect work with computer-generated faces/bodies?

7. What was Breazeal's early 'social' robot called?

8. What facial expression led to the longest engagement with Gordon and Breazeal's (2014) robot?

9. Give one evaluation point relating to the use of NVC cues in robots or other technologies.

10. Is it a good idea to copy another person's movements precisely in order to make them like you more?

GO! Activities

1. Find out more about the use of NVC in robots. If you can, watch clips of the robots Kismet, Leonardo and Jibo, designed by MIT researchers. What NVC do these robots use? How do you expect robots to develop in the future? Prepare an essay, poster or blog post on this issue.

2. How do you think research into the chameleon effect links to the three theories described in the previous section? Does it support nature or nurture? From an evolutionary point of view, why would it have been an advantage to our ancestors? Write your thoughts on this in your notes.

3. Experiment with the chameleon effect: next time you are sitting opposite a stranger in a waiting room or on a train, try varying your body language, for example, by folding your arms or by crossing your legs at the ankles. Do they copy you?

GO! End of topic project

In your class or another suitable group, conduct a simple observation study into NVC, as follows:

- First, identify a suitable piece of video footage. For ethical reasons, do not use footage of anyone you know. It is best to avoid any acted/scripted behaviour such as dramas/soap operas/music videos. Some better options include:
  - an interview, for example of a politician
  - a piece of sports footage
  - a conversation during a reality TV show
- Now prepare an observation schedule (see chapter 8). Brainstorm likely NVC cues that you may see – posture, gaze and so on. For this type of observation, a good choice would be to make a tally mark each time a behaviour occurs. Alternatively, you could write verbal descriptions at 30-second intervals.
- Compare your results between the two observers, checking for inter-observer reliability. If necessary, watch the clip again.
- If you can, play the video in slow motion and watch for microexpressions!
- Draw conclusions.
- Prepare and deliver a short talk to your class on what you found and concluded from this observation. Refer to at least two relevant background research studies – ideally including one that you have found out about yourself outside of class!

✔ End of topic specimen exam questions

As this is an optional topic, exam questions will be quite general and will not name the topic or its specific theories/research studies, for example:

National 5

1. For your optional Social Behaviour topic:

   a. Briefly explain the topic.   4 marks

   b. Name and describe one research study that has been carried out in your chosen topic. Include the aim, method/procedure and results of the study.   6 marks

2. Choose a topic in Social Behaviour other than conformity. Explain this topic using two or more concepts/theories and the findings of at least one research study.   10 marks

Higher

1. Describe and evaluate one or more research studies from your optional Social Behaviour topic.   12 marks

2. Choose a topic in Social Behaviour other than conformity and obedience. Explain this topic using two or more concepts/theories and the findings of at least one research study. 10 marks

3. Explain how a Social Psychology topic other than conformity and obedience has been applied in the real world.   10 marks

The total exam mark allocation for the Social Behaviour unit will be 20 marks; however, there is no way of knowing in advance how this will be split between this topic and conformity.

13 Relationships

The nature of relationships

A **relationship** can mean any social connection that we have with another person. Of course, it includes **romantic relationships**, but also the relationships that we have with friends, colleagues and even enemies.

Social relationships can be very beneficial. They provide **social support** that helps to reduce stress. Cutrona (1996) found that stress levels were lower among people who experienced a lot of social interaction. Loneliness tends to lead to feelings such as helplessness, boredom, insecurity or depression (Rubenstein *et al.*, 1979) and overall, it is a factor in ill health comparable with smoking or alcohol consumption (Holt-Lunstad *et al.*, 2010).

Relationships can also be a cause of stress and conflict. This chapter will consider relationship problems and the ways in which psychologists can try to help people improve their relationships.

Remember that the term 'relationship' has a broad definition in psychology. This section begins with the broadest sense of the word and then considers closer interpersonal relationships and finally romantic relationships.

Affiliation

Affiliation is a very broad term meaning the desire to form connections with other people to avoid social isolation or for strategic reasons.

> **! Syllabus note**
>
> As well as 'Conformity', you need to study one optional topic in Social Behaviour. Relationships would be a suitable choice. The optional topic should be tackled in a similar way to conformity – that is, you should be aware of key concepts, theories, research studies and (for Higher) a real-world application of the topic.

Social support helps reduce stress

Shy people may be defending themselves against the unpleasantness of social rejection

Strategic affiliation may be highly significant in the workplace

Affiliation as a need

Some researchers, for example, Maslow (1943), believe that affiliating with others is a very fundamental human need. Maslow states that after a human's most basic needs such as food and shelter have been met, then people are motivated to seek love and belongingness (see chapter 2: humanist approach). Baumeister and Leary (1995) agree that

Relationships can be a cause of stress and conflict

humans have a need for **belongingness**, which, they say, is biologically prepared, and can be compared to the social behaviour of other animals. They point out that although shyness seems to go against the idea of a need for affiliation, shy people are actually very socially-oriented, and may be defending themselves against the unpleasantness of social rejection.

Social identity

Tajfel and Turner (1979) believed that a person's concept of who they are depends fundamentally on their membership of groups. They call this a person's **social identity**. If someone else is seen as a member of the same group, this makes us more likely to affiliate with them and more likely that we will have an influence on their behaviour (Haslam *et al.*, 2009). We are also more likely to gain social support from people who see us as members of the same group.

Strategic affiliation

Sometimes we form social relationships out of necessity. DeScioli and Kurzban (2009) state that friendships can be seen strategically, as **alliances** that can be of benefit in potential conflict. Supporting this hypothesis, they found evidence that people have a ranking of their friends' importance, which they conceal from these friends. People ranked their friends based on their perceived social ranking in the whole group, as well as perceived similarity to themselves. Similarly, Taylor *et al.* (2000) believed that the drive to affiliate with others is prompted by survival needs. They suggest that this was particularly relevant to women, while a 'fight-or-flight' response was more advantageous to males during evolution (see chapter 6). As well as among friendship groups, strategic affiliation may be highly significant in the workplace.

Attachments

We affiliate with a broad range of people – some of whom we do not actually like. However, what about our deeper, more personal social relationships? These more significant relationships feature an **attachment** or 'attachment bond'. An attachment is an emotional connection that we have with another person – typically family members, partners and close friends. The term is often used when in ordinary speech, we would say 'love', but it is preferred by researchers as a less subjective term. A person's earliest attachments are formed to the **caregiver**(s) that look them as small children, from whom separation causes distress and sadness (Ainsworth & Bell, 1970). One feature of getting older is that we are able to tolerate separations from loved ones. However, the loss of an attachment bond through a social break-up or death can result in grief at any age.

Parental attachments

The British psychologist John Bowlby developed a comprehensive theory of attachment in childhood. He said that attachment bonds must develop before the age of 2 (the 'critical period' for attachment) to avoid permanent psychological damage. He also said that an infant's first attachment shows three key features (Bowlby, 1958):

An attachment is an emotional connection that we have with other people, such as family members

- The parent acts as a secure base from which the infant can explore the environment. Infants cling to adults who can protect them against danger.

- The infants show social releasers, such as smiling and crying, to get parental attention.

- The attachment helps the child develop a schema for how relationships work.

Bowlby felt that infants initially form a single attachment with their mother (although he recognised that for babies with no mother, another carer could form a substitute). He stated that 'mother love' is essential for mental health (Bowlby, 1953). This idea, known as **monotropy**, has been criticised as placing the blame on mothers for any problems a child has with attachment or for their later psychological problems. A study by Schaffer and Emerson (1964) cast doubt on the theory; they observed 60 infants in their homes in Glasgow once per four weeks for a year, and then again at age 18 months. They found that 35% of infants did not show a single main first attachment to the mother. Lamb (1981) states that an infant's attachments to its father is different to, but not necessarily weaker than, its attachment to its mother.

Lamb found that an infant's attachments to its father is different, to its attachment to its mother

Mary Ainsworth developed Bowlby's theory by providing a theory of why some infants develop a **secure** attachment and others are **insecure** – she believed that this is due to how responsive mothers are to their infants' needs, in terms of noticing them, responding to them quickly and accurately interpreting these needs (Ainsworth *et al.*, 1971). She argued that insecure children fall into two categories – an **avoidant** type, who avoided contact and comforting, and an **insecure-resistant** type, who could not stand separation and were overly clingy.

Ainsworth and Bell (1970) investigated this theory using an observational study of how babies reacted to strangers that become known as the **strange situation** test (see key study).

❓ Discussion point

How do people react to fathers as caregivers for babies and how do these reactions differ from how mothers are treated?

🔬 Make the link

…with the approaches to psychology. Bowlby's was influenced by both the psychoanalytic and the evolutionary approaches.

📖 Key study: Ainsworth and Bell (1970): the strange situation

Aim: *Ainsworth and colleagues had conducted observations of family homes and concluded that there were three types of attachment. They wanted to test this in a controlled environment, using a test that contrasted a baby's need for attachment with his/her desire to explore the environment.*

Method: *This was a laboratory-based structured observation of a baby with its mother and a stranger. There were several phases, most of which lasted for three minutes:*

- *The mother and baby are introduced to a room with a large square of clear floor space with toys. The baby is put down on the floor and is free to explore.*

- *A stranger enters and speaks to the mother, then approaches the infant with a toy.*

- *The mother leaves the child alone with the stranger and the stranger tries to interact with the child, and then the mother returns. This happens twice and in between there is a phase when the baby is left alone.*

Some of the babies in the study were very distressed when their mother left

Findings: *The findings of the study confirmed the idea that there are three main attachment types. Securely attached infants explored happily when their mother was present, were distressed when to be left with the stranger and enthusiastic on the mother's return. Avoidant infants explored happily when their mother was present, were not fearful of strangers and avoided contact on the mother's return. Insecure-resistant infants were unwilling to explore. They were highly anxious of strangers and showed anger at the mother's return. Ainsworth and Bell concluded that there are a range of attachment types and some aspects of attachment behaviour are only apparent when an infant is under threat or stress.*

Evaluation: *This was a systematic and large-scale study that provided strong objective evidence of different attachment types. Another strength is that some of the babies had also been participants in a longitudinal naturalistic observation in their homes, allowing the researchers to link the three types to maternal sensitivity in everyday life. The lab-based nature of the study might have caused some infants to behave unnaturally, however. In addition, there is an element of cultural bias, because participants were American and all were white and middle-class. The study focused exclusively on the mother rather than other carers and assumed that her behaviour can shape the child's behaviour, rather than innate personality factors. From an ethical point of view, the study caused stress to the infants and they were too young to be able to refuse to take part.*

Attachments through childhood

Attachment behaviour changes quickly during infancy – a single bond with a main caregiver forms in the second six months of life, but other attachments form soon after (Schaffer, 1996):

Name of stage	Age	Key features
Pre-attachment	0–2 months	The baby is content as long as it is well looked after.
Attachment-in-the-making	2–7 months	The infant recognises familiar people but it is still content with strangers.
Specific attachment	7 months +	The infant wants their primary caregiver and shows stranger anxiety.
Multiple attachments	9 months +	Attachments to other familiar people develop but the primary caregiver is still preferred.

In early childhood, attachments outside the family – for example, friendships – start to develop, but these change in character throughout childhood (Berndt, 1982). For example, early childhood friendships are more competitive with individuals aiming to get more for themselves and to win games, while by adolescence, cooperative/fair solutions are preferred.

Friendship bonds are at their strongest during early adolescence (prior to age 16) and they have a major impact on the developing personality of the individual (Berndt, 1982). Parental bonds weaken and romantic attachments begin to emerge.

However, Rubenstein *et al.* (1979) found that adolescence was also the time when loneliness levels were highest – more so than among the elderly, contrary to the stereotype of elderly people being lonely.

Early childhood friendships tend to be competitive

Adult attachments

As adults, relationships change considerably, as people form very strong bonds, sometimes life-long, with others outside their immediate family. For many people, the most significant relationship at this stage is a pair bond with another, that is, a romantic relationship.

Romantic love typically processes through stages, with a predictable series of changes in the brain (not the heart!):

Attraction. When someone feels sexual attraction (or 'lust'), their brain becomes aroused in a similar way to a person who wins at gambling or takes drugs. This **attraction** stimulates the brain's pleasure centre, the **nucleus accumbens** and their sensitivity to

The most significant relationship for most adults is a romantic relationship with another person

Studies have found that in dangerous situations we are more likely to find anyone we meet attractive

Marriage is a long-term attachment

? Discussion point

Do you believe that people's behaviour in romantic relationships can be described in terms of Ainsworth's classification of three types – secure, avoidant and insecure-resistant?

You can study attraction bevaviourally by looking at physical closeness

pain reduces (just viewing an attractive face can have a similar effect on this system to taking a painkiller!). Noradrenaline is released and the body is generally in a more exited/aroused state. Interestingly, being in a situation that causes the body to be aroused or even scared, for example, walking across a high bridge, increases the chance that we will find someone that we meet attractive – possibly because the same brain systems are already active (Dutton & Aron, 1974).

Love. Once we have fixed on a particular partner, there are certain processes that change in the brain as the relationship is either established or not. Chemically and behaviourally, the individual exhibits similar features to someone with obsessive-compulsive disorder, including obsessive thoughts and repetitive behaviours; in other circumstances, the lovers might be assumed to have OCD (Marazziti & Canale, 2004). This process may be useful in establishing a successful long-term bond.

Long-term attachment. While other hormones return to normal levels, the hormone oxytocin is elevated – just as it is when parents are bonding with a new baby. This hormone is further boosted by physical closeness including kissing. Adults who have multiple sexual partners may try to avoid a bond being formed by minimising frequency of contact and avoiding certain types of physical contact, for example, kissing (Hazan & Zeifman, 1999).

As discussed in chapter 2, Sigmund Freud thought that our early childhood could affect later behaviour. Hazan and Shaver (1987) also believed that childhood social experience can affect our relationships later and claimed that the same attachment types discovered by Ainsworth can apply to adult romantic relationships. In a questionnaire study, they found that romantic relationship behaviour has a key similarity to the attachment types in babies:

- Some individuals form a secure bond.
- Some are 'clingy', that is, insecure-resistant.
- Some are avoidant – tending to keep others at a distance and avoid closeness.

Factors that affect attractiveness

As mentioned above, finding another person attractive is the beginning of a process that can lead to a romantic relationship being formed. However, what causes us to find some people more attractive than others?

Psychologists have considered several factors that could affect attraction, ranging from physical appearance to behaviour and status. Attraction can be studied either subjectively, for example, by asking people who they find attractive – or behaviourally, such as looking at people's physical closeness to another person.

Facial symmetry	Rather than being unusual, people who are viewed by others as physically attractive actually have very typical, average features, and the two sides of their faces tend to be highly symmetrical (Langlois and Roggman, 1990).
Responsiveness	We are more likely to want to form a relationship with people who are especially responsive to our needs.
Similarity	How alike people are. Contrary to the popular notion that 'opposites attract', similarity has a positive effect on social relationships and we tend to be attracted to people who are like ourselves – in personality, ethnicity, interests, etc. This can include appearance (see 'Matching hypothesis' below).
Familiarity	In terms of emotions, we tend to react more positively to familiar stimuli (Zajonc, 1968), so if a person's face is familiar, they will be more appealing to us.

Although this issue has mainly been researched in terms of romantic relationships, attraction is also a factor in friendships and other connections. In particular, more attractive males tend to have more friends of both sexes (Berscheid et al., 1971; see below). If there is a work colleague that you choose to spend time with, it may be because you find them attractive on some level or that you are just affiliating with them to help advance your career.

We tend to be attracted to people who are like ourselves

Matching hypothesis

Closely linked to the concept of similarity, the **matching hypothesis** states that people will tend to select romantic partners of the same level of physical attractiveness as themselves. This is because the choice of a potential partner may be affected not just by that person's desirability but also by the likelihood of success in attempting to form a relationship with them (Walster et al., 1966). In other words, the matching hypothesis says that people tend to make realistic choices, rather than aiming for people who are out of their league!

In one study, photographs of real-life engaged couples were judged based on similarity to one another in attractiveness. Judges consistently rated them as more alike than randomly paired photographs (Murstein, 1972). However, with couples that already exist, it is difficult to know what other factors may have played a role (e.g. personality, familiarity, etc.).

More attractive males tend to have more friends of both sexes

Walster et al. (1966) failed to find support for their hypothesis using an artificially set up student dance – they found that students tended to want the most attractive partner possible. However, a study by Berscheid et al. (1971) tried to remedy problems in the Walster study and did find support for the matching hypothesis (see key study).

The study was based around choosing dates to a dance

📖 Key study: Berscheid *et al*. (1971): the matching hypothesis

Aim: The researchers wanted to test the matching hypothesis. They believed that Walster et al. *(1966)* failed to support the hypothesis because their experimental set up had not been realistic.

Method: In the first study, adverts were circulated for a 'computer matching dance', and from the applicants, 170 female and 177 male participants were selected, all first year university students. Some were given an element of realistic risk by telling them that the partner may not agree to go with them. In a second study, 113 mixed male and female participants were each shown six opposite sex photos and asked to choose a date. In one condition, they were told that they would automatically get their choice, and in another condition, that the date would happen only if the partner agreed. All participants were rated on a nine-point scale for physical attractiveness by four student accomplices.

Findings: Overall, the researchers found evidence supporting the matching hypothesis – participants who had been rated as more physically attractive tended to choose more attractive dates. Surprisingly, the elements of risk/realism made no difference to the outcome – participants did not choose less attractive dates, even if warned that they could be rejected. The researchers concluded that previous studies didn't find support for the matching hypothesis because they had not focused enough on a partner's initial choice. The researchers also surveyed their participants and found that attractive males had more friends, while attractive females had been on more dates.

Evaluation: The two studies provided useful experimental support of the matching hypothesis. The first study used a large sample size and both were well controlled. However, a limitation is that they used photographs to judge attractiveness – in real life, students would tend to meet potential dates face-to-face. There are cultural differences in what people find attractive, making it hard to generalise from American students in the 1970s. The students were young and knew this was an artificial one-off date for an experiment, again making findings hard to generalise.

Relationship universals and variations

So far, it has been assumed that the same processes in attachment and attraction affect everybody, but there are many **cultural variations** about how relationships are conducted in different parts of the world. This section will look at what is **universal** – what occurs in every human society – and what varies by culture.

Relationship universals

The following are some of the aspects of relationships that can be considered the norm in every human society, and are therefore, **culturally universal**:

- Age differences in romantic relationships: males prefer younger females and women prefer older males (Buss, 1989).
- Facial appearance: symmetrical faces with features signalling health are found to be attractive (Perrett *et al.*, 1994).
- Most people form long-term pair bonds (Walker *et al.*, 2011).

When traits are culturally universal (or near universal), it is often assumed that these traits may have an evolutionary basis. Supporting research studies tend to treat heterosexual relationships as the norm, possibly causing bias in the selection of participants.

Cultural variations in relationships

The following are some of the aspects of relationships that vary widely between societies:

- Whether love is seen as a romance or companionship (Goodwin, 1999).
- The way that couples/marriages form, independently or via family arrangement (Walker *et al.*, 2011).
- Attitudes towards prior relationships (Buss, 1989).

Parenting also varies with culture, and attachment types in children vary in prevalence. In a review of studies, Van Ijzendoorn and Kroonenberg (1988) found the highest proportions of securely attached children in Britain and Sweden. European countries tended to have higher levels (20% plus) of avoidant children than insecure-resistant, while in Israel and Japan, the opposite pattern was found.

According to Ainsworth's theory, this could relate to cultural differences in parenting style and responsiveness in different countries. In some countries only one or two studies have been done, making it hard to draw firm conclusions.

The role of the internet

The internet is an aspect of modern day culture that has had a major impact on relationships. **Internet dating** – meeting potential partners through websites – is now a highly prevalent way of forming romantic relationships, with over five million people in the UK signed up to internet dating sites. Typically, such sites allow people to browse profiles that include a photo and short description.

The internet is also increasingly a medium for all types of relationships to be maintained and developed, through social networking sites such as Facebook and Twitter, and discussion forums. However there are pitfalls as well – Clayton (2014) found that high levels of Twitter activity was correlated to couples breaking up and suggested that disagreements over Twitter activities played a role in such conflicts.

Most people find symmetrical faces attractive

Japan has a higher level of insecure-resistant children than European countries

🔍 Top tip

In the Higher and National 5 exams, any relevant research studies will be credited – they don't need to be the ones you have studied in class.

Over five million people in the UK are signed up to internet dating sites

Social media use can cause conflict in relationships

Key concepts

- Relationships
- Affiliation
- Attachment
- Caregiver
- Grief
- Monotropy
- Social releasers
- Stages of attachment
- Secure attachment
- Avoidant
- Insecure-resistant
- Nucleus accumbens
- Attraction
- Familiarity
- Similarity
- Matching hypothesis
- Cross-cultural Cultural variations
- Cultural universals
- Internet dating

Questions

1. Does having an affiliation with someone mean that you like them?

2. Which is the broader term – attraction or affiliation?

3. Name a researcher who thought that affiliation is a basic human need.

4. What are the key features of infant-parent attachments, according to Bowlby?

5. Give one feature of attachment behaviour in later childhood.

6. What brain area is particularly active in the early stages of love/romantic attachment?

7. Which of Ainsworth's types of attachment can be linked to adults in romantic relationships being 'clingy'?

8. Do opposites attract?

9. Give two examples of types of websites that can play a role in relationships.

10. Which was the most common of Ainsworth's three attachment types?

Activities

1. Matching hypothesis – find out three to four examples of famous couples or couples from dramas/sitcoms. Do they match in terms of physical attractiveness? If not, what other factors may have affected these relationships?

2. What effect does it have if children fail to form an attachment bond in infancy? Find out about evidence regarding children brought up in orphanages or being very severely socially deprived.

3. Find out about how minority relationship types can lead to prejudice. For example, what kind of attitudes do people have towards those who are gay, single or in 'open relationships'? You could conduct a short survey into one such aspect and report back to your classmates.

Theories of relationships

Social exchange theory

Social exchange theory, proposed by Thibaut and Kelley (1959), suggests that human relationships can be looked at as a series of exchanges, in which each partner tries to get a good deal. It helps to explain why relationships change over time, as the relative costs and benefits to each partner change.

Social exchange theory is an example of what are generally called 'economic theories' of human behaviour. These theories see relationships and other human behaviour as a series of rational choices based on conscious thought processes. They are influenced by the cognitive approach to psychology and view humans as essentially rational. The study of Economics looks at decision making in areas such as personal finance on the assumption that people want to maximise profit and minimise losses. Similarly, economic theories state that when people form and maintain relationships, they fundamentally want the best deal for themselves.

Costs and benefits

According to Thibaut and Kelley, a relationship involves a series of social exchanges between partners. What this means is that when we ask someone on a date, form a relationship or move in together, we are essentially weighing up what we will gain and what we will lose. In these transactions, each partner can get either a good or a bad deal; every individual will try to minimise their **costs** and get as much **benefit** as possible out of the relationship. This might change as a relationship progresses – greater familiarity could cause some costs to reduce (e.g. less risk) but also some benefits to reduce (e.g. not new, so less exciting).

The table below gives some examples of typical costs and benefits, but these depend entirely on the situation. For example, in some cases, money may be a cost (having to subsidise a partner) but in other cases, it will be a benefit (being funded by a generous partner).

Rewards	Social support, childcare, companionship, fun, sex, improved reputation, money
Costs	Effort, time, money, missed opportunities with other potential partners

When we ask someone on a date we might weigh up what we will gain and what we will lose

Someone who has had a series of lazy boyfriends/girlfriends develops a lower comparison level to judge new ones by

At first, this theory does not explain why some people have much more successful relationships than others do and why people stay in bad relationships. Thibaut and Kelley explained that a person judges the relationship they are in against a **comparison level** (**CL**), a schema for relationships that is unique to the individual. As the CL prompts people to decide whether relationships are acceptable based on their past experiences, everyone's judgement will be slightly different. For example, if their parents' relationship featured a high level of conflict and violence, then they may view a medium level of conflict and violence as being acceptable. Someone who has had a series of lazy boyfriends/girlfriends develops a lower comparison level to judge new ones by.

Explanation of attraction

Economic theories try to explain the factors that affect attraction in terms of costs and benefits. For example, similarity may have a function such as facilitating communication and making it easier to find shared activities (Rubin, 1973). The matching hypothesis is explained as follows: people want the best deal they can get but avoid costs, such as time wasting and disappointment, by aiming only as high as they can achieve.

Relationship stages

According to Thibaut and Kelley, the costs and benefits of relationships change over time. For example, the early **stages of a relationship** have high costs and a high risk of rejection, while in a longer-lasting relationship, demands are lower and costs are more predictable. This leads to a series of four stages that a relationship will progress through: sampling, bargaining, commitment and institutionalisation (see sidebar).

Evaluation

Social exchange theory helps psychologists explain why so many people stay in bad or abusive relationships (investment is high and alternatives are unattractive). However, people do not seem to accurately retain a record of what they are 'owed' in relationships (DeScioli & Kurzban, 2009).

The theory can explain the matching hypothesis in principle but struggles to explain the findings of Berscheid *et al.* (1971), which showed that the risk of rejection made no difference to people's choices.

The theory suggests that there tends to be more romantic gestures (e.g. gift giving) at the start of a relationship because potential rewards are higher. This contrasts with the biological evidence discussed in the previous section, which suggests that brain chemistry involved in falling in love leads to obsessional thoughts about the partner.

There is mounting evidence that humans don't actually behave as rationally as the theory suggests. Miller (2005) states that it is unrealistic to reduce human relationships to a series of rational choices, while many aspects of attraction seem to be culturally universal and not due to conscious choice (Perrett *et al.*, 1994).

Sampling: considering costs and rewards and comparing other potential relationships.

Bargaining: giving and receiving rewards, and considering whether deeper commitment is worthwhile.

Commitment: as intimacy increases, the relationship becomes more predictable and costs are lowered.

Institutionalisation: norms are established as the pattern of exchange within the relationship.

Evolutionary theories

According to the evolutionary approach, humans have a basic need to form social relationships of various kinds. To put it simply, we are social animals like other primates, and we have evolved a basic motivation to interact with others. Research into relationship universals supports this view.

The **evolutionary theory of relationships** states that human relationship behaviour has been shaped by Darwinian natural selection. A major aspect of this is that people will engage in behaviour to maximise their **reproductive success**. However, this can be a balance between producing a lot of offspring, or fewer offspring and caring for them well. Bowlby's theory of attachment is also influenced by evolutionary theory – it suggests that bonding with children is an innate strategy to boost the infant's chances of survival, just as baby birds open their beaks wide to be fed.

We tend to give more gifts at the start of a relationship

Bowlby's theory of attachment is influenced by evolutionary theory

Parental investment

One aspect of the theory is that for biological reasons, males and females invest different amounts of resources in having and raising children and that these differences have led the two sexes to evolve different behavioural strategies (Trivers, 1972). **Parental investment** means investing resources in raising offspring at a cost to the parent. Once a baby is born, both parents have a genetic stake in the child's survival, as every child gets exactly 50% of its genes from each parent. Indeed, parenthood in the whole animal kingdom can be seen as an evolved strategy to improve the survival chances of offspring! However, in the vast majority of species, fathers do no childrearing whatsoever. In contrast, Quinlan (2008) notes that in humans cross-culturally, the societies with the highest degree of relationship stability are the ones where males contribute approximately 50% of the resources needed to look after their children.

Even in societies that have relatively equal roles for males and females, females biologically put in more parental investment, as nine months of pregnancy is typically followed by a period of breastfeeding. This **differential investment** is increased if the mother is also the primary carer for her offspring. Another sex difference is that women can have fewer offspring over the lifespan than a man can, meaning that, theoretically, the best evolutionary strategy in terms of survival of her genes would be to look after the children well and seek a partner who is willing to provide support. Male reproduction is less constrained biologically and males could potentially have a large number of offspring with many women – but doing so might come at a cost in terms of a reduced ability to care for the children, thus not ensuring their survival.

The cost of parental investment also implies that in a long-term relationship, there will be an advantage to both partners to ensure that the other stays faithful. For a male, this is to ensure that any children have his genes, so he is not providing care for someone else's offspring. For a woman, this is because she would have to invest more in her children's care if their father didn't stay.

> ### 🔍 Top tip
>
> This topic features two theories that contrast very clearly with each other. Try to think of examples of relationship behaviour and consider how these could be explained in terms of social exchange or in terms of evolution.

Both parents have a genetic stake in a child's survival

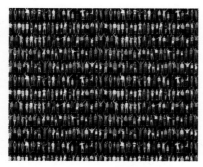

Dunbar's number is the idea that a human's friendship group is limited to around 150 individuals

Primates with larger social groups need larger brains in order to keep track of relationships

A study found that people send Christmas cards to 153.5 people on average

Dunbar's number

Dunbar's number – based on the work of researcher Robin Dunbar – is the idea that a human's friendship group is limited to around 150 individuals. People can have more contacts than that, but it is the upper limit for how many people we can maintain close contact with, including family members and close contacts (see the evolutionary approach, chapter 2).

Such a limit is thought to be based on the size of our brains. The **social brain hypothesis** states that the human brain evolved to be larger because people gained a survival advantage from keeping track of social relationships. This contrasts with previous researchers such as Morris (1967), who suggested that humans evolved large brains because of the challenges of surviving and hunting. Dunbar (1998) stated that the number is a trade-off between the benefits of a bigger group and the costs of a larger brain. Having a large brain is costly in energy but having a large group is beneficial for lots of reasons, including protection. At some point over the past 100,000 years, humans have evolved this biological upper limit. Beyond around 150, it is simply not possible for our brains to keep track of the relationships with others – and crucially, keep track of the relationships they have with each other.

So is there any evidence that brain size links to group size? Dunbar (1992) studied the group size of a range of primates and found that the size of the neocortex in each species was correlated – the bigger the social group, the bigger the neocortex of the brain. As a comparison, chimpanzees have a maximum group size of 50, and around one-third of the neocortex size that humans do (Dunbar, 1992). In contrast, there was no clear relationship between brain size and the complexity of the environment where they obtained their food. This is strong evidence that primates with larger social groups need larger brains in order to keep track of relationships.

Dunbar's number has been supported by the finding that a group size of around 150 seems to be fairly typical in humans through history – from the settlements recorded in the Domesday Book, to the tribal groups in hunter-gatherer societies (Dunbar, 1993). In a neat application to the modern world, Hill and Dunbar (2003) looked at the size of networks to which people send Christmas cards. It fitted the theory – 153.5 was the mean total population of all households receiving cards from each individual. Although people often have a much larger group of contacts on social media, Gonçalves et al. (2011) found that the number of people we regularly contact through sites such as Twitter remains under 200.

Innate nature of attachments

Evolutionary approaches also imply that many aspects of human relationships are innate – designed by evolution to maximise the chances of surviving, reproducing and raising healthy offspring. According to this view, beauty is seen as pre-programmed preference for features that indicate health and fertility (Perrett *et al.*, 1998). This can include facial symmetry, which is thought to indicate health.

We may also be influenced by factors that we are unaware of, such as the **pheromones** – air-bound hormones the body can release – in another person's smell! Wedekind *et al.* (1995) conducted a study of the effects of pheromones on partner preference; 49 women were asked to rate the attractiveness of the odours of t-shirts that had been worn by men who either had a similar or dissimilar human leukocyte antigen (HLA) type. (From the point of view of the immune system of potential offspring, it is better if partners have a different HLA type.) Women rated the odour of the HLA-dissimilar men as more pleasant. This suggests that pheromones have an unconscious effect on attraction, prompting us to select partners who will improve the survival chances of potential offspring.

If relationship behaviour is innate, this helps to explain why certain aspects of maternal behaviour are universal. As Bowlby argued, social releasers improve a child's survival advantage. This contrasts with an older, behaviourist view that babies form an attachment based on the reward from being fed. Harlow (1959) tried to distinguish between these two ideas with an experiment on monkeys and found strong evidence that infants need physical contact with a parent, rather than simply desiring to be fed (see key study).

? Discussion point

Do you have a social group of around 150?

Pheromones have an unconscious effect on attraction

A photograph from the study

📖 Key study: Love in infant monkeys: Harlow's (1959) experiments into attachment

Aim: *The dominant view at the time, from the behaviourist approach, was that infants form social bonds with their carers due to classical and operant conditioning. For example, Dollard and Miller (1950) believed that food is a primary reinforcer, something that is directly rewarding because of its importance to a species' survival. A carer who provides the food is a secondary reinforcer who becomes associated with a primary reinforcer, until their presence becomes rewarding. Harlow disagreed – he said that a baby has an innate need to bond with a parent and gets pleasure from contact/cuddling.*

Method: *Harlow conducted a study in which infant monkeys were taken away from their mother and placed in a cage containing a cold, wire mother-like figure with a feeding bottle, and a soft cloth mother figure that did not. If attachments are formed through association with feeding, then the infant monkeys should become attached to the wire 'mother'.*

Findings: *It was found that the infant only used the wire mother to feed. Rather than forming an attachment to the wire mother, the infant spent most of its time – around 23 hours per day – clinging to the cloth figure, even though it provided no food. It also ran to the cloth mother when frightened. This outcome suggests that rather than learning attachment through conditioning, monkeys, and perhaps humans as well, have an innate drive for 'contact comfort'.*

Evaluation: *Harlow's theory has had a huge influence and it has become widely accepted that some aspects of attachment bonding are innate, at least in infants. However, it has been criticised for being very cruel to the monkeys. There are also issues with external validity of his studies, that is, the findings from monkeys cannot be generalised to humans with any certainty.*

This theory of social relationships cannot easily explain same-sex relationships

Evaluation

This theory of social relationships is based on the well-established theory of evolution by natural selection. Many people will not feel comfortable with the idea that their relationship behaviour is outside of their conscious control. However, it does help to explain relationships that do not seem to be based on rational choices, such as abuse victims and people who suffer from 'Stockholm syndrome' – the condition where hostages develop an attraction to their captors.

Nevertheless, the theory cannot easily explain **same-sex relationships**, because it states that relationships essentially exist to have children and pass on one's genes. It is therefore limited in how well it can explain all relationships. The concept of differential investment tends to ignore the broader social context (e.g. the role played by friends/family in a person's choice of partner).

Another limitation of the evolutionary theory is that there are considerable cultural differences in what is considered attractive. If our relationship behaviour is innate and due to the evolutionary drive to pass on genes, it is hard to understand why it should be so easily influenced by culture, such as the current trend for extreme thinness in women (which is not beneficial for childbearing).

Dunbar's number does seem to be applicable to a large number of situations, from hunter-gatherer tribes to Twitter engagement. However, it is based on correlational studies of brain size that do not prove cause-and-effect, while de Ruiter *et al.* (2011) have argued that although the neocortex plays an important role in social functioning, its size does not directly determine social skills.

✔ Questions

1. Give two examples of potential costs of a relationship.

2. Give two examples of potential benefits of a relationship.

3. What are the four stages in social exchange theory?

4. Does the matching hypothesis support social exchange theory?

5. What is a comparison level?

6. Give one example of how males and females may have different evolutionary strategies.

7. What is the maximum number of close relationships we can have, according to Dunbar?

8. What is the evolutionary explanation for physical attractiveness?

9. What is meant by differential investment?

10. Did Harlow's monkeys form an association through conditioning or due to an innate need for comfort?

⚲ Key concepts

- Social exchange theory
- Costs and benefits
- Comparison level
- Stages of a relationship
- Evolutionary theory of relationships
- Reproductive success
- Parental investment
- Differential investment
- Dunbar's number
- Social brain hypothesis
- Pheromones
- Same-sex relationships

Relationship conflict

As a long-term bond, most relationships experience conflict at some point and some people have considerable problems in maintaining harmonious personal relationships. Psychologists have tried to identify why conflicts occur, and they can either help people directly through counselling or indirectly through self-help.

Relationship problems

Family or romantic relationships can be damaged by the harmful or destructive behaviour of one or both partners, for example, infidelity, manipulative behaviour or violence.

Infidelity and jealousy

In romantic relationships, **infidelity** (i.e. cheating on their partner) is a major cause of harm to a relationship. Kim (2015) notes that cheating is statistically more likely among those who have cheated before, and among people with a '9' at the end of their age (e.g. 49)! It is also more common among wealthier males and poorer females. Of course, these are just statistics – it does not necessarily mean that you will cheat if you fall into these categories.

Jealousy is a set of feelings, especially anger, associated with anxiety over infidelity. As mentioned in the previous section, this fits well with the evolutionary theories that state that partners want to minimise their reproductive investment. Buss (2000) describes jealousy as universal and necessary. People can also feel jealousy over friendships.

Jealousy is associated with anxiety over infidelity

Passive-aggressive behaviour

Passive-aggressive behaviour can be defined as being deliberately uncooperative, while not doing anything overtly aggressive or breaking any rules. Examples include not talking to people, not replying to messages or slamming doors. The passive aggressive person tends not to be upfront about the negative emotions they are feeling, saying '*I'm not upset/angry*' or '*that's fine/whatever*' when their behaviour, tone or body language indicate otherwise (Whitson, 2010). They may also procrastinate or deliberately do tasks badly, either at home or in the workplace.

Emotional blackmail is a particular form of passive-aggressive behaviour where people try to maintain control over partners and friends using a combination of three emotional 'tools' – fear, obligation and guilt (Forward, 1997), which can be shortened to the acronym 'F.O.G.'

Once described as a personality disorder, passive-aggression is now recognised as a type of behaviour that occurs commonly in a great many 'normal' people – a good example of how society's definitions of what is abnormal have changed over time (see chapter 4).

Abusive behaviour

Intimate relationships may feature abusive behaviour – verbal, physical or sexual. These acts tend to be used as strategies in conflict; therefore, they are more likely in relationships that feature a lot of conflict. There is also a link with poverty (Jewkes, 2002). Glick and Fiske (2001) link hostile sexist attitudes to aggression and they argue that hostile sexism tends to be directed at groups of women who are seen to be a threat to men's powerful position (e.g. career women).

As many as 40% of teenagers have experienced some form of relationship-based violence or abuse and it tends to occur when young people are tolerant of this behaviour or consider it ok in certain circumstances (O'Keefe, 1997). Programmes such as 'Expect Respect' try to reduce this by supporting at-risk teenagers, while working with schools and communities to tackle cultural acceptance of abusive behaviour.

Games versus intimacy

Berne (1968) describes many human interactions as **games** where there is some trick or deception involved. Berne (1968) states that there are three main **ego states** that a person can adopt:

- parent
- adult
- child

Communication can't continue freely if two people's ego states are not compatible. For example, if you try to speak to someone adult-to-adult and they respond like a parent speaking to a child, there is a communication breakdown. Berne describes this mismatch of ego states as '*the type of transaction which causes most of the troubles in the world*' (1975, pp.35–6).

? Discussion point

Is infidelity best explained by social exchange theory or by evolutionary theories?

Passive-aggressive bahaviour includes not talking to someone

expect respect
education toolkit

recommended for teachers of PSHE and healthy relationships education

THE HIDEOUT · women's aid *until women & children are safe*

The Expect Respect toolkit

? Discussion point

What ego states do you recognise in your own communication, for example, with friends, parents or teachers?

Some people willingly associate with harmful people because they enjoy complaining

Separation has many effects, including anxiety

Separating children from family members can lead to behavioural disruption as well as psychological effects

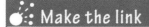

Make the link

...between the Diamond *et al.* (2008) study and the topic of sleep.

The games reflect social situations that on the surface are normal and acceptable communication but are actually insincere 'tricks' where people want a social reward/payoff. Example games that Berne describes include:

'If it weren't for you' – here an individual blames another, usually a partner or parent, for their problems. They say that if it was not for the other person, they would be more successful. They 'win' by avoiding blame for their own failings and presenting the idea that it would be pointless for them to expend more effort.

'Ain't it awful' – here the person willingly associates with harmful people such as bad friends or employers because they enjoy complaining. The payoff is the enjoyment of complaining, as well as not taking responsibility for their own problems.

Berne states that situations such as alcoholism, being caught for petty crimes, religious activity, charity and sexual behaviour can all involve an element of game playing. In contrast, true intimacy is only possible when there is an honest give-and-take in communication, without an ulterior motive or an attempt to exploit the other person (Berne, 1975).

Separation

Separation means a temporary breaking apart of two people who have an attachment bond. In adults, separation has an effect particularly on those who fit the insecure-resistant type, according to Hazan and Shaver's research. Diamond *et al.* (2008) studied 42 couples experiencing ordinary, travel-related separations. Both partners' sleep patterns were affected, reducing in quality during the separation compared to before and after. Mood was affected and individuals with high separation anxiety showed increases in levels of the stress hormone cortisol.

Children also experience separations from friends and family members. The younger children are, the more distressed they tend to be by separations from their loved ones, especially the primary caregiver. Historically, especially from the 1830s to the 1930s, families who entered workhouses would be separated from their parents and sometimes from siblings, and only allowed brief visits (Hodgman, 2010). Even nowadays, children who are placed into care are sometimes separated from their siblings, leading to behavioural disruption as well as psychological effects (Leathers, 2005).

Some of the best-known research into separation has focused on the effects of very young children being separated from their main caregiver (e.g. Robertson & Robertson, 1971; see key study). This has tended to show that separations are very upsetting, but a short separation causes no long-term harm, and the distress can be reduced by providing a substitute attachment figure.

📖 Key study: Robertson and Robertson (1971): the study of John

Aim: Robertson and Robertson aimed to find out the effects of a short separation on infant-parent attachment bonds. Following Bowlby's theory, they believed that separations would be harmful for a child's attachment with its mother.

Method: They observed a 17-month-old boy named John, whose parents had chosen to put him into residential care for nine days while his mother was in hospital for maternity – something which was common at the time (as was a long hospital stay for childbirth).

Findings: John tried unsuccessfully to get a nurse to 'mother' him, and protested aggressively when his father left after short visits. From the third day, John became very distressed and cried sadly for long periods. By the seventh day he was in despair, he would not eat and didn't even play. He did not respond to attempts to cheer him up and he lay silently on the floor. When he was reunited with his mother, he was angry and did not want to sit with her. According to the researchers, John's behaviour showed three stages of childhood separations:

- *Protest – angry outbursts, clinging to the parent when they leave.*
- *Despair – calmer behaviour but inwardly upset; responds less to others.*
- *Detachment – begins to respond to others again but in a superficial way; initial attachment starts to be harmed.*

Evaluation: This study was highly influential, encouraging hospitals to relax their strict visiting hours. It supported Bowlby's idea of the importance of an infant's main attachment for mental health. It may seem unethical, but it should be pointed out that the researchers only observed John and they did not force his parents to leave him in an institution – it was common practice at the time. The researchers believed that John's problems were due to bond disruption and could have been reduced by providing a substitute carer while his mother was away. In a follow-up study, a girl was provided substitute emotional care and she became considerably less distressed, supporting the researchers' conclusions.

A photograph of John from the study

During 'grave-dressing' it might be necessary to divide the things the couple share

Counselling can help with relationship problems

Break-ups

When relationships break up there is a process with a beginning and end, and several **stages of a break-up** can be recognised. Duck (1998) states that break-ups involve the following four main stages:

- Intrapsychic: one or both partners feel dissatisfied with the relationship but keep their thoughts largely to themselves.
- Dyadic: the partners confront each other about the problems, typically leading to arguments.
- Going public: the couple make it official by telling others that the relationship is breaking up. This can take its toll on others, especially children, but also announces each partner as potentially available for new relationships.
- Grave dressing: the couple take steps to tidy up the aftermath. This can include 'saving face' – each partner presenting an account of the break-up to others that shows them in a good light. It may also be necessary to separate aspects of the relationship that are interdependent, for example, home/childcare.

This is important for relationship counselling, as being able to recognise a couple's current stage will have an effect on what advice or action will be most useful (see next subsection). Duck's stages usefully focus on the effect of a break-up on a person's sense of social wellbeing and how they try to manage their image. However, every relationship is unique and many will not follow this general pattern neatly, making the issue more complicated.

Counselling

Counselling is a service offered to people who need help with their relationships and other life problems. Counselling is not necessarily aimed at resolving medically recognised mental health problems, but problems with interpersonal relationships including family conflict or bullying, or other problems such as addiction. However, there are huge overlaps with psychological therapies in terms of the processes involved and the background of practitioners, and the terms are often used interchangeably.

Some trained counsellors specialise in **relationship counselling**. This form of counselling tends to be associated with romantic relationships, at least within our culture, but similar principles could apply to friendships, family relationships or issues with colleagues. Relationship counsellors will try to help people to develop stronger, more harmonious relationships and to make positive decisions regarding friendships and break-ups.

Approaches to counselling

Many counsellors use a combination of different approaches and strategies in their work and there are three main approaches to counselling/therapy that are widely used. They are based on major psychological approaches (see chapter 2):

- Psychoanalysis: based on the idea that many of our problems have their roots in childhood and unconscious conflicts, psychoanalytic therapy/counselling attempts to uncover and resolve these problems.

- Cognitive-behavioural therapy (CBT): a short, problem-based intervention that tries to help people develop more positive thinking styles and cope with specific symptoms such as anxiety.

- Person-centred counselling: based on the humanist approach to psychology, the key idea taken by these practitioners is that each individual has to make their own choices and the role of the counsellor is to provide a supportive and honest context.

There are several different types of relationship counselling

Each type of counselling makes different assumptions about the causes of problems and how to solve them. Person-centred approaches in particular are 'non-directive', meaning that the counsellor/therapist will avoid giving advice to their client, for example, about whether they should cut contact with an abusive friend. The assumption is made that the individual needs to take responsibility for such decisions. CBT is focused on developing more effective behaviours and reducing symptoms such as anxiety. CBT therapists may ask their clients to try **behavioural experiments** – to test out the effects of changing their own behaviour. Psychoanalysis focuses on exploring anxiety that links to childhood experiences.

Becoming a **counselling psychologist** involves doing a university degree in psychology followed by further specialist training such as a postgraduate diploma. It is also possible to train in counselling without a degree, for example as a volunteer with a charity, but the level of pay will be lower (if any) and the range of jobs available will be reduced.

Evaluation

For couples, agreeing to counselling can have an additional benefit that it indicates a commitment to improve the relationship. A limitation with counselling, though, is that it is costly and requires a time commitment from people who may already be busy and stressed. It is also somewhat public, which people may find embarrassing. An alternative is **self-help** – the use of resources such as books and websites to help oneself through relationship problems. In reality, the person is not really helping themselves but getting help from the expert who created the resource. Resources vary in quality but this is a cheaper and more flexible option for some people.

⚷ Key concepts

- Infidelity
- Jealousy
- Passive-aggressive behaviour
- Emotional blackmail
- Games
- Ego states
- Separation
- Stages of a break-up
- Counselling
- Relationship counselling
- Behavioural experiments
- Counselling psychologist
- Self-help

✔ Questions

1. Give one example of a passive-aggressive behaviour, and one example of a passive-aggressive thing that someone might say.

2. Give an example of a group who are more likely to be unfaithful in a romantic relationship.

3. Name one of Berne's social 'games'.

4. What are the three 'ego states' that Berne described?

5. What three emotional tools do people use when trying to control others through emotional blackmail, according to Forward (1997)?

6. Define separation.

7. What are the first two stages of Duck's model of break-ups?

8. What factors can affect the impact of separation on people who have an attachment?

9. How long did John stay in residential care for?

10. Name one of the three main types of counselling.

GO! Activities

1. Can you see any connection between concepts such as emotional blackmail and the use of coercion described in the conformity topic (chapter 10)? If so, would similar strategies be useful for resisting these? Write your response in note form.

2. Why do you think certain groups are more likely to cheat or to commit relationship violence? And what explanations, evolutionary or otherwise, could there be for the types of people who are more likely to do these things? Focus on one example, find out more using the internet and give a short presentation to your class.

GO! End of topic project

In your class or another suitable group, conduct a simple observation study into relationships, as follows:

- First, identify a suitable piece of video footage. For ethical reasons, do not use footage of anyone you know. It is best to avoid any acted/scripted behaviour such as dramas/soap operas/music videos. Some better suggestions include:
  - an interview e.g. of a famous couple
  - a piece of sports footage
  - a conversation during a reality TV show
- Now prepare an observation schedule (see chapter 8). Brainstorm likely relationship behaviours. For this type of observation, a good choice would be to make a tally mark each time a behaviour occurs. Alternatively, you could write verbal descriptions at 30-second intervals.
- Draw conclusions
- Prepare and deliver a short talk to your class on what you found and concluded from this observation. Refer to at least one relevant background research study – ideally including one that you have found out about yourself outside of class!

✔ End of topic specimen exam questions

As this is an optional topic, exam questions will be quite general and will not name the topic or its specific theories/research studies, for example:

National 5

1. For your optional Social Behaviour topic:

   a. Briefly explain the topic.   4 marks

   b. Name and describe one research study that has been carried out in your chosen topic. Include the aim, method/procedure and results of the study.   6 marks

2. Choose a topic in Social Behaviour other than conformity. Explain this topic using two or more concepts/theories and the findings of at least one research study.   10 marks

Higher

1. Describe and evaluate one or more research studies from your optional Social Behaviour topic.   12 marks

2. Choose a topic in Social Behaviour other than conformity and obedience. Explain this topic using two or more concepts/theories and the findings of at least one research study.   10 marks

3. Explain how a Social Psychology topic other than conformity and obedience has been applied in the real world.   10 marks

The total exam mark allocation for the Social Behaviour unit will be 20 marks; however, there is no way of knowing in advance how this will be split between this topic and conformity.

Key skills

14 Key skills

Skills such as literacy, analysis, evaluation and applying knowledge are particularly essential for the exam

There are several skills that are developed during this course including literacy, writing, numeracy, information handling and personal learning. These will be developed throughout the year including on the Assignment project.

Skills such as literacy, analysis, evaluation and applying knowledge are particularly essential for the exam.

Main skills developed in the course: overview	
Numeracy	Numeracy skills are important in handling the data for your Assignment. You will learn how to calculate statistical concepts discussed in chapter 8, such as the mean, and be able to explain and evaluate these statistics. You may need to comment on data in a table or chart in the exam. Ensure that you practice if you are not confident with number work.
Literacy	The literacy skills developed throughout this course and in your other subjects will be important in writing a successful Assignment and in tackling extended answers in the exam. Many students with good knowledge are let down by their literacy skills. You can develop your literacy by reading more, by writing essays and getting feedback. In the exam, you will not be penalised for spelling and grammar, but it is important to be able to write extended/essay answers, especially at Higher. A common problem is writing answers that are too short. The next section will explain how to structure and plan longer exam answers.
Understanding	Understanding and taking in information is considered a thinking skill. It can be challenging, especially if you are new to this subject, to take in and remember the detail of theories and the names and publication years of many research studies, as well as understanding how they relate to each other. As with any skill, this improves with practice. There is a section in this chapter on memory and mnemonics, which will help you to improve the way you use your memory and make your revision more effective.

Analysing and evaluating	Analysing concepts and theories involves identifying and commenting on features of theories and research or on the way these features relate to each other. Evaluating involves identifying what is good or bad about theories, research, etc. Both are important skills in psychology and gain a lot of credit in exam answers. Do not make the mistake of thinking that the psychology exam is just about writing down as many facts as possible! Analysis and evaluation are considered higher-level skills, that is, they are more difficult and important than memorising facts. Evaluation of research studies is especially important in this course and a later section in this chapter discusses this in detail.
Applying	Another key skill is being able to apply knowledge to a situation. In other words, it means identifying links between theories and real life. Psychology research tends to have some practical use, such as the application of memory to legal situations or of psychopathology to therapy. This skill is discussed in more detail under 'Added value', later in this chapter.

Applying knowledge is a key skill

Tackling exam questions in psychology

You want to gain a good pass in the exam and have the best chance of an A grade overall in your course, but developing your knowledge of the topics is only part of the process – you also need good exam technique. This section looks at how to tackle common questions, what skills are required and how to summarise, analyse and evaluate research studies.

You will need good exam technique to get your A!

Short answer questions

Short answer questions are generally very specific about what is required and it is usually clear what the available marks are for. For example:

Describe one strength and one weakness of the psychoanalytic approach to studying dreams and dreaming.

2 marks

Explain two calculations that the researcher has carried out to summarise the raw data.

4 marks

In the first question above, it is apparent that there is one mark for each evaluation point. The points you make do not need to have an extended explanation, but you should try to answer them fully, in a sentence or two, rather than giving one word answers. Compare these two possible points that could be used as a weakness in the above question:

> Better: *Freud's idea of wish fulfilment does not really explain nightmares, because if dreams are about what we wish for, then why would we dream about something bad?*

> Weaker: *It can't explain nightmares.*

Therefore, it is fine to keep these answers short but make sure that they are fully explained.

The second answer also asks for two points to be made but this time they are worth two marks each. A similar approach is required but slightly more information should be given. If there are two marks available for such questions, try to make two separate points, as in the following example:

> *The mean was used – this is calculated by adding up the total of the scores and dividing the total by the number of scores. The mean allows a researcher to get an idea of a typical mid-point of the data that takes every score into account.*

> *The range was also used – this is calculated by subtracting the lowest score from the highest score. The result gives an overall idea of how spread out the data are.*

Both of the above answers do two things – state how the statistic is calculated and state why it is used – and these responses are therefore worth two marks each.

Extended answers

It can be harder to tackle questions that require extended answers and it starts to become very important to structure your answer. For most concepts in psychology, an answer can be structured as follows:

- Identify the concept.
- Explain the concept (two to three sentences).
- Give a real-life example.
- Back up with research evidence.
- Evaluate the evidence.

This will work well for fairly simple concepts or as part of a longer answer. For example, a description of a factor that affects conformity:

> **Explain one factor in conformity.**
>
> **6 marks**

> *Identify the concept: One factor in conformity is the size of the majority group.*

> *Explain the concept: People feel more pressure to change what they do when faced with a large majority group with different views or actions. They are much more likely to conform to the majority when they are in a large group of peers – three or more – than when they are with just one or two other people. Asch called this 'the magic number 3'.*

Top tip

It is very easy for a marker to give just one mark out of two if an explanation is incomplete, so it's better to say too much than too little.

It is very important to structure your answer

Give a real-life example: An example of this is when you are with friends and everyone wants to do something but you do not, such as watch a TV show that you do not enjoy. With one or two other people, you might argue but if with three or more you would just go along with it.

Back up with research evidence: Asch (1951) demonstrated this in his 'length of lines' experiment, where people had to judge which of three lines was the same length as another line. In one version of his study, participants were put in groups of six, where the other five participants were confederates who had been told to give the wrong answer several times. There was a 32% conformity rate. However, when Asch repeated this with only two confederates, the conformity rate dropped to 13%.

Evaluate the evidence: Asch's study clearly shows that a smaller group exerts less social pressure on our behaviour. It was a lab experiment so all other variables were kept constant, allowing a clear conclusion. However, it was an artificial situation and it is hard to say how well the conclusions can be applied to real life settings such as the workplace.

If the question is just on a theory, then the same structure can be used, but it will be necessary to spend more than two to three sentences explaining. Most theories include several components and it will be necessary to go through each component in turn, explaining what it does, as well as making relevant points about the theory as a whole:

- Explain key points about the theory as a whole.
- Name and explain each component of the theory.

The rest of the answer can use the same structure as above – give examples, support with research evidence and evaluate.

Another important variation comes when explaining a key **research study**. These are covered in the next section of this chapter.

Essay answers

It is vitally important to be able to answer an exam essay well, as they are worth such a large number of marks. Three things in particular often let people down:

- lack of detailed knowledge
- essay is too short
- not enough evaluation

This is especially true in the option topics, which tend to feature long, fairly broad questions. You need to think in advance how you will use your knowledge to answer certain common essay questions.

If the essay involves explaining several components – for example, factors that affect sleep – you can use the same structure as described above and simply repeat it for each paragraph.

However, many essay questions in this subject have a more complicated structure, requiring you to integrate approaches, theories and evidence, such as this example:

> **Top tip**
>
> Write this structure onto an index card.

> **Top tip**
>
> This answer does not give very much detail on Asch's study and it is not perfectly accurate, but it is sufficient for the question.

Exam essays are worth a large number of marks, so it's important to know how to answer an essay question well

> **Choose an individual topic other than sleep, dreams and disorders. Explain this topic using two psychological approaches and/or theories.**
>
> **14 marks**

To tackle this question, you will need to choose:

- what topic to explain
- which approaches or theories to use
- at least one piece of suitable research evidence

If you have prepared well, some of these choices should be almost automatic. You will have revised one optional topic besides sleep and dreams (see option topics in chapters 4 to 7). You will also have studied three approaches and two theories/models, as well as research evidence including several 'key studies'.

In terms of which theories and approaches to include, the question allows for various options:

- one of each
- one approach and two theories
- two approaches and one theory
- two of each

You need to think in advance how you will use your knowledge to answer certain common essay questions

If a smaller number of theories/approaches are included in total, then more depth and detail should be included.

There are 14 marks available in the example essay question. The following essay plan allows for two marks for an introduction paragraph and three marks each for another four short paragraphs plus a conclusion.

Paragraph 1

Here you state what topic you will explain in the essay. Give a detailed definition of the topic, or a brief summary of one or more main concepts.

Paragraph 2

Go into more detail about two key concepts in the topic. For example, LTM versus STM in memory, fight-or-flight and stress management in stress. Give details and terminology and briefly mention one piece of supporting research.

Paragraph 3

Explain the first approach. This might follow on naturally from the info in paragraph two – for example, in stress, fight-or-flight links to the biological approach to psychology. First, aim to mention three key facts/ideas about the approach. For example, you could state (1) how the biological approach explains behaviour in terms of genetics, (2) the interaction of neurons and structures in the brain and (3) the effects of hormones on behaviour. Next, link the approach clearly to the topic. For stress, the role of hormones adrenalin and cortisol could be described.

Paragraph 4

Similar to paragraph three, but using a different approach, such as the cognitive approach. Again, mention three key facts/concepts then link the concepts to the specific topic.

Paragraph 5

Here you give a brief overview of one of the theories in this topic, choosing whichever one seems most relevant to the concepts mentioned so far. Again, try to mention three key aspects of the theory. You could mention if the theory links to one of the approaches you have previously described and why – for example, the transactional model of stress is a cognitive theory because it focuses on how thought processes affect stress levels.

Paragraph 6

A conclusion – this is considered good style but keep it short. You have already made your points and hopefully picked up all the available marks, so don't waste time repeating yourself.

One further issue that may arise is that questions, especially extended or essay questions, may ask you to use your knowledge to explain a scenario. For example:

- Use your knowledge of factors in conformity to explain how peer pressure can be more of a problem for some teenagers than for others.
- Use your knowledge of sleep to explain why people who travel internationally and drink a lot of caffeine may have sleep problems.

Below is an example essay for a question that provides this kind of scenario.

Example essay

> **David is a medical student who is finding it hard to get to sleep. Explain some possible reasons for this problem and some of the ways that psychologists might attempt to treat this problem.**
>
> **14 marks**

David appears to have insomnia, a problem with sleep that can have several possible causes. Sleep is a state of reduced awareness, when the body is less active and less responsive to the outside world. We spend a quarter or more of our lives asleep, but some people like David have problems with sleep, known as sleep disorders.

Sleep can be affected by environmental factors such as drugs, zeitgebers or shift work. Zeitgebers are the things that prompt the brain to know whether it is night or day, such as light. As a medical student, David may have to work at night a lot. Then when he tries to sleep during the day, it is light outside and his body is not producing the sleep hormone melatonin so he won't feel drowsy. Another factor is drugs such as caffeine. Night shift workers may take stimulants to

? Discussion point

Can you think of other essay questions that this plan could be used for?

🔍 **Top tip**

Try this plan out and compare your responses with classmates.

A question may ask you to use your knowledge to explain a scenario

Top tip

Note how paragraph three moves from general to specific information. There are general points about the approach, followed by specific links to the topic. This is a key skill and it will require practice and feedback from your teacher.

Top tip

Everything is clearly linked to the scenario. Scenarios like this will be chosen to be easily recognisable – you are not being tested on your knowledge of what being a medical student is like, but you should try to use the example to bring in knowledge from the course.

? Discussion point

In a group or with your teacher/lecturer, try to think of other scenario-type questions.

Top tip

Note how the overall structure is the same as the one presented earlier, with a short introduction and four further main paragraphs, each making around three key points, followed by a brief conclusion.

keep them awake. Then they will find it hard to sleep – caffeine can stay in the bloodstream for many hours after drinking a strong coffee! So after a long shift he may find it hard to drop off.

There are different approaches to understanding sleep and sleep disorders, and one of the most important explanations is the biological approach. This explains that sleep is controlled by certain parts of the brain and body. An area of the brain called the suprachiasmatic nucleus controls the sleep-wake cycle. It gets information from the eyes about when it's dark, and triggers the body to release the sleep hormone melatonin. We therefore find it harder to fall asleep if it's light outside or the lights are on. The approach also explains that stimulants such as caffeine block adenosine receptors in the brain, stopping our body from realising that it needs sleep.

Sleeplessness can affect our mood and make it unsafe to drive, so it could be risky for David to drive home after work. Many accidents are caused that way. Sleep can also lead to health problems (Czeisler et al., 1990). In extreme cases like 'wakeathon' participant Peter Tripp or people who are tortured with sleep deprivation, a lack of sleep can lead to hallucinations and affect a person's mental health. It is important that David addresses his insomnia, though fortunately as a student doctor he will probably recognise the symptoms – generally, insomnia means an inability to get to sleep or that the person cannot stay asleep.

Sometimes sleep problems are not due to zeitgebers or lifestyle, but there is a deeper problem. It could be that there is a medical problem with circadian rhythms – David could have what is known as a circadian rhythm disorder. This is when people do not have a 24-hour cycle from their body clock, but something else like a 25-hour cycle. This could lead to them going to bed later and later every day. This can cause major difficulties with work, so even if he has a regular 9 to 5 job, David would have problems as sometimes his body would want to be asleep during the day.

There are various ways to treat sleep disorders. One way involves light therapy. This is where strong light is used to trick the brain into thinking it is daytime during a night shift. Czeisler et al. (1990) did a study of shift workers, and found that being exposed to really bright light during their shift helped to change the body clock so that they were sleepy during the day and awake at night. This would be helpful for doctors such as David. Another possibility is CBT. It is possible that David's insomnia is caused by worries and anxiety. For example, he could be disturbed by some of the medical cases he has to treat in his job, or simply worrying about the future. If so, a few sessions with a CBT therapist would be helpful. CBT is a short intervention, so six to 10 sessions may be enough. As he is a student doctor, he might be able to arrange it through work, as CBT is available on the NHS.

Hopefully, with the correct treatment David will get over his sleep disorder. It may be that he will need to find a more regular job though, that does not mess with his circadian rhythms by having him stay up all night on shifts.

Understanding research

Understanding research is essential in the study of psychology. Without evidence, we cannot say very much at all about human behaviour. Therefore, you should work on developing detailed knowledge of the research. As well as having knowledge about the evidence, though, you also need to be aware of its strengths and weaknesses. This section will discuss the skills of analysing and evaluating evidence.

Understanding research is essential in the study of psychology

Creating a research file

The topics in this textbook each contain three to four summaries of key research studies. Some are mandatory (e.g. Dement and Kleitman, 1957), while others have been selected because they are theoretically important, well known to teachers and examiners and easy to understand. However, if you come across other interesting studies, feel free to add those to your notes. It can be interesting to use some very up-to-date studies, for example.

It is strongly suggested that you make your own notes on studies. Reading or highlighting the examples in this book is not a good way to encode the information to your memory or to develop evaluative skills. Instead, follow this process:

- Read about the study.
- Close the book and write a draft summary including an evaluation in your own words.
- Refer back to the book to check any details that you couldn't remember (e.g. number of participants) and add these to your summary.
- Write a shorter summary into a separate notebook/index cards.

Index cards are an excellent way to revise studies, as they make it easy to change the order of the studies, and therefore test yourself without it becoming repetitive. A jotter (perhaps the back pages of your main jotter), a ring binder with loose leaf A4 paper or even notes on your phone could also work well.

> ### 🔍 Top tip
>
> For each new study you read about, try to think of another strength or weakness besides those mentioned in the textbook. You can check these with your teacher/lecturer.

You can make revision notes in different ways

🔍 Top tip

See the end of this section for an example of a study on conformity described and evaluated as a main answer.

When considering how to summarise research, remember the two main ways you might use a research study in an exam answer:

1. As evidence to back up a point that you make. Here, a short one to two sentence summary of the research alongside a brief strength/weakness of the study will usually be enough (as in the example essays earlier). Any more, and you may be taking up too much time on the study, and not actually answering the question!

> **Example of using a research study to back up a point:**
>
> *The behaviourist approach explains a lot of our behaviour in terms of simple associations formed between two stimuli. This is known as classical conditioning. An example is when Watson and Rayner (1920) taught little Albert to associate fear and a small animal. Albert learned to fear something that he had previously liked, due to learning an association.*

2. As a main answer. Sometimes you will be asked a question such as *'Describe and evaluate a research study into sleep'*. You will need to know the key research in enough detail to tackle this sort of question. Key information should always include:

   - aim
   - methodology, including participants
   - findings/conclusions
   - evaluation

To help you, these points are highlighted in all of the key studies in this book. You could also get credit for identifying relevant background theories and research.

Analysis of research

Factual knowledge of studies is not enough – you need to be able to think about the research more deeply, understanding why it was carried out and what it showed. In general terms, **analysis** means identifying component parts and explaining how they work together. When discussing a research study, analysis could include:

- Identifying the theory that the research was based on and explaining why it supports this theory.
- Identifying aspects of method/procedure used and explaining why they were used.
- Comparing aspects of the study to other studies.
- Identifying details of the results and explaining what these mean.

Often an analytical point will start by stating a fact, but the key thing is to say something interesting about that fact. For example:

- Asch's study was different from previous research studies into conformity, as it used a task where the answer was clear and unambiguous. This allowed Asch to know whether people would be influenced even if they knew the correct answer, and therefore demonstrated normative social influence.

- Dement and Kleitman's study used only nine participants. This is fairly typical for sleep studies, as they are very time-consuming and require complex apparatus.

- Mori and Arai (2010) used two different types of glasses that caused participants to see the same lines as if they were of different lengths. This contrasts with earlier studies that relied on actors, and meant that nobody was lying or acting unnaturally.

- Czeisler *et al.* (1990) found that people's body clock, on average, had shifted forwards by around nine hours. What this means is that the light therapy had successfully shifted each participant's circadian rhythm, so that rather than just staying awake all night, their body responded as if it was actually daytime.

Analysis means identifying component parts and explaining how they work together

This skill differs slightly from evaluation, which is more about saying whether the research is good or bad for various reasons. As an analogy, if you were taking apart an appliance such as a computer, you might *analyse* what the different parts do and why they were designed that way. *Evaluation* would involve saying how well the computer works – is it fast, does it break down easily, was it cheap to buy, etc.

> ## 🔍 Top tip
>
> Don't worry too much about the difference between analysis and evaluation, as there is often some overlap between the two.

Evaluating research

It is best to develop evaluation **as a skill**. It is much more efficient in the long run to learn *how to evaluate* than simply to memorise strengths/weaknesses for each study. For one thing, this skill will help you to evaluate other studies that you come across in the future, including newly published ones. It will also help you to evaluate your own research for the Assignment.

There are four aspects of any study that you can tackle in your evaluation:

Criticise the ethics of the study

Consider any ethical problems such as deception and stress. It is less common to *praise* the ethics of the study ('it wasn't cruel or deceptive') but it could be a valid point if this is unusual in the research area. For example, as many studies of conformity involve deception, a study that avoids using deception could be praised for good ethical practice.

Example: *Selye's research on rats caused rats to be in extreme pain and some of them died. This is unethical, as there was considerable harm to the participants.*

Praise or criticise the methodology

Consider the internal validity of the study – did it demonstrate cause and effect? Were there extraneous/confounding variables? Identifying

There are four aspects of any study you can tackle in your evaluation

the method used will be useful here. Laboratory experiments are controlled and they demonstrate clear cause and effect, while other studies, such as natural experiments and correlation studies, generally do not. You could also comment on a task for being quick and efficient or for being slow or hard to replicate.

Example: *As a natural experiment, Raine et al.'s (1997) study of brain abnormalities in murderers cannot demonstrate cause and effect. It is not possible to know that these people committed murders because of the differences shown in the scans – there could be some other variable affecting their behaviour.*

Discuss whether findings can be generalised from the sample to the population (external validity)

Consider the sample used – large or small, human or non-human. What age were they, what culture did they come from and was the study conducted a long time ago? All of these issues affect whether findings can be generalised to the broader population in today's society. In addition, the setting of the study, for example, a lab, can make it hard to generalise to real life (i.e. low ecological validity), as can the use of artificial tasks (i.e. a lack of mundane realism).

Example: *A strength of Friedman and Rosenman's (1974) study was that it used a huge sample of more than 3,000 participants, leading to reliable results. However, the sample were all middle-aged men and it is difficult to be sure whether the findings apply to other groups such as young women.*

Compare results to other studies/theories

Many studies are done in order to support a theory. Did the study, for example, usefully distinguish between two theories, showing that one theory was better than the other was? If so, the study helped to make progress in its field and this is a strength. In contrast, perhaps a weakness is that the study is outdated and its findings have since been disputed.

Example: *The word length effect study by Baddeley et al. (1975) was one of the first to show that the idea of short-term memory holding seven items was over-simplistic. The study showed that it depends on the length of the item, so previous theories of memory were flawed.*

These four points should provide a powerful guide that will help you to evaluate any research study in psychology. Write them on your jotter or notebook, perhaps inside the front cover and practice applying them to new studies that you read about in the news or online.

Sample answer

> **Analyse a research study in conformity.**
>
> **10 marks**

For this question, Mori and Arai (2010) might be the obvious choices as the mandatory study for both Higher and N5 but any can be used. The following example uses the Asch (1951) study for the main answer, while the Mori and Arai study is brought in as a comparison:

It is important to develop the skill of evaluation

Top tip

Check back to chapter 8 for an explanation of internal and external validity.

Top tip

It is always good to state the aim.

One study into conformity was conducted by Asch (1951). The aim of the study was to determine conformity levels when the correct response was unambiguous. Unlike Jenness (1932), who gave participants an impossible task, Solomon Asch asked people to compare simple lengths of lines. When alone, there was around 99% accuracy, but when in a group of seven 'confederates' of the researcher who all answered wrongly on 12/18 occasions, 32% of answers conformed (i.e. were incorrect) and 75% of the sample conformed at least once.

Asch's study was a useful demonstration of normative influence. It shows that even in situations where we are not unsure of the right answer, the group has considerable power to change our behaviour. This is because people have a desire to fit in and be liked by the group, and wish to avoid the ridicule of being different. Real-life examples could include joining in with bullying, pretending to like things that you don't, or smoking because all of your friends are doing it.

However, as Asch's study was artificial, it cannot fully be compared to these real life situations. The task itself lacked mundane realism – comparing lines is not the same as bullying someone, because there are no real-world negative consequences of the action. The experimental situation lacked ecological validity, as it is very unusual to be placed in a group of strangers before making a decision. In everyday conformity, we tend to be pressured by friends or colleagues.

A follow-up variation of the study gave the true participant an 'ally' who was instructed not to agree with the majority. In this condition, conformity dropped to 5.5%. This is more realistic, because in real life, there is often a mixture of responses to a situation, and unanimity is rare.

Perrin and Spencer (1981) replicated the study with science and engineering students, and found almost no conformity. This suggests that people who are confident in their knowledge and skills will not conform on judgements of facts. Perrin and Spencer felt that Asch's findings linked to the conformist culture of 1950s America. It is therefore hard to generalise from his sample to modern-day conformity.

In terms of methodology, Asch's study was inefficient due to the need for several actors every time a real participant was tested. Mori and Arai (2010) used a more efficient procedure where all participants were real, and differences among what they considered to be the correct answer were achieved using distorting glasses. The findings of this replication gave further support to the importance of culture in conformity, as among their Japanese participants, the females conformed to the same level as Asch's male participants but the males did not conform at all. It appears that gender roles and cultural attitudes can change over time, and that these things can have a major impact on conformity, again limiting the extent to which Asch's classic findings can be generalised to modern society.

Finally, there were ethical issues with Asch's study. He used deception, telling participants that they were being tested in their perceptual skills. This was necessary in order to test conformity however, and

Top tip

A two-sentence summary of the method and findings is given in this sample answer. This is not analysis, but sets out the context, and should not take much time. Practice giving a two to three sentence summary of method and findings of major studies in each topic.

Top tip

Note how the sample answer analyses the study in terms of a key concept, normative influence, and gives examples.

Top tip

Note that although the question asked for analysis, evaluation can also get credit, as it is a related skill to analysis. See pp. 376–7 for an explanation of these skills.

Top tip

This answer also evaluates a variation of the same study – a similar thing could be done with a variation of the Milgram research.

Top tip

Note how the Asch research is compared with later studies, illustrating the value of knowing a broad range of research on the topic, not just the mandatory studies. If you were analysing Mori and Arai (2010), a similar point could be made, that is, discussing how its results differed from those of Asch.

Top tip

An evaluation is not complete without some mention of ethics.

Top tip

Don't forget to mention some strengths of the study.

participants were not greatly stressed by the procedure. Even today, ethical guidelines such as those from BPS recognise that in certain areas of psychology such as conformity it may be necessary to withhold some information about the aims of the study from participants in order to avoid biasing the results.

Despite these problems, Asch's study was theoretically important, and set up a standard method that has influenced later studies such as Mori and Arai. He was the first to demonstrate experimentally that normal people will deny the evidence of their own eyes in order to be accepted, and for that reason, the study is a classic.

Mnemonics

This section looks at why we forget things and how to use your memory effectively. It should be of use in helping you to learn material effectively from both this and other courses. If you are studying the memory topic, you could also use it as an example of how understanding of memory has been applied in the real world.

As you may have learned, information that we learn is encoded into a memory trace, stored, and then retrieved when needed. **Forgetting** is the flip side of memory – it is what happens when things cannot be retrieved from memory or when memory is inaccurate. **Short-term memory** (STM) is the immediate memory for a few items, such as when you are taking down notes in class. **Long-term memory** (LTM) means permanent storage. What this means is:

- STM is important for taking in and processing new information but it is not used for recall after more than a few minutes.
- LTM involves permanent storage and it is required for all of the information and skills you need for the exam.

Memory Failures

Think of a time when you went to another room and then thought *'what did I come here for…?'* It appears that things can disappear from STM really quickly. STM also has a limited capacity (Miller, 1956), new information will take up all of the space and old information will be pushed out. An analogy is trying to squeeze items into a full suitcase – and other things popping out!

Long-term memory can last for decades, but things can be forgotten if they were not learned effectively. Similar items might be confused ('interference') or may have been forgotten due to insufficient or ineffective revision. LTM can also fail in times of stress.

Your mind going black could be a sign of stress – you could learn some relaxation techniques to help with this

The following table summarises some of these issues:

Problem	Explanation/solution
I revised for two hours but I was really tired and I couldn't focus.	Attention is essential for encoding new information to memory. If your attention level drops – or if you are distracted by other things - you will not take anything in, so it will be a waste of time. Dividing your time into several short revision sessions can make it easier to focus and make links with other knowledge rather than just going over things repeatedly (see 'Elaboration' in the next section).
I took notes in class but I didn't really understand.	LTM is based on meaning. Anything that is meaningless or poorly understood can be held in STM but will not be encoded to LTM. Therefore, it is vital to ask questions and get a good grasp of new topics.
There was so much information; I didn't know where to start.	If you try to tackle an entire topic in one day, you are trying to take in too much information at once. STM capacity is limited, and it is better to break things down into smaller chunks. In addition, learning relies on sleep in order to consolidate changes in the brain – so you cannot remember everything in one day!
I got things mixed up in my test.	LTM is susceptible to interference between very similar items. Unlike a computer, the human mind struggles to store similar sets of information without getting them confused. The more similar things are, the harder it is to distinguish them in our memories. You can make information more distinct by setting it out in different ways on the pages of your notes. Page after page of highlighted writing is easily mixed up. Make sure to emphasise the differences between concepts and check with your teacher/lecturer if unsure.
I thought I knew it but it turned out I was wrong.	Bartlett (1932) found that anything unfamiliar tended to be simplified, omitted or made more familiar. People's minds distort information based on schemas. This may happen in Psychology – perhaps you will stick with your assumptions (such as the incorrect assumption that STM is used for exam recall) and ignore the factual information from your teacher/lecturer!
I thought I knew it but I couldn't remember it later.	Problems with retrieval: it may happen that long-term memories have been stored accurately but cannot be retrieved when needed. Retrieval is more likely to fail when there is a lack of a **cue**, that is, a reminder of something that triggers off retrieval. It could be the first letter of an answer, for example. If you were struggling to remember the lyrics to a song, hearing the first line would be a cue that would make it easier to remember the rest. The use of **mnemonics**, where you create a phrase that helps you to remember the first letters, for example of parts of a theory, can help to provide cues in an exam situation.
My mind just went blank!	Stress. Have you ever been flustered and unable to remember someone's name that you are sure you should know? This shows that stress can interfere with retrieval of factual information. From a biological perspective, the release of cortisol during the stress response negatively affects the hippocampus, a structure that plays a key role in LTM. Some relaxation techniques – such as deep breathing and meditation – can be used during an exam, while others (e.g. exercise) are ideal to break up your revision time (see chapter 6 for more on stress management).

Pinning notes on your wall can really help with revision

Using visual notes can help you to remember information

Types of mnemonic

A mnemonic just means a memory strategy. There are several different types; two of the most useful ones for your studies are as follows:

Acrostics

Some terminology in this course will be hard to remember, such as the names of the stages of a theory, researchers of the key studies in one topic or features of a research method.

Using acrostics means making phrases with the first letter or letters of the items you are trying to remember. For example, the features of the case study method could be remembered as:

Q-U-I-L-T

Qualitative – **U**nusual/unique cases – **I**nterviews/in-depth – **L**ongitudinal – **T**ests

Several key ethical considerations could be remembered as:

B-I-T-C-H

Briefing – **I**nformed consent – **T**reatment of children – **C**onfidentiality – **H**arm

Visualisation

Visual memory is very powerful, but unfortunately, much of what we have to learn in school and college involves verbal information. You can improve recall by combining visual and verbal encoding (Paivio, 1969). Therefore, it is a good idea to try to make visual images for the material in the course. You could make visual notes. If you make your notes very visually distinctive, you may find it easier to remember items in your mind's eye when you are sitting in an exam hall! Use cartoons, different styles and layouts, different types of paper, etc. Try associating key concepts with the images in this book or in your handouts. Mind maps and spidergrams are useful ways of making your notes visual and distinctive.

Other memory tips

What else can you do to improve your memory for information ahead of the exam? Psychology research has suggested three things that are particularly important. Again, these can apply to all of your school/college courses:

Elaboration

As mentioned above, LTM is based on meaning, and information is linked together into meaningful schemas. The result of this is that simply reading over things is an ineffective study strategy – even though you understand them at the time, you have not linked the information to anything that you already know.

Elaboration involves making meaningful connections between new information and things you already know. Craik and Watkins (1973) found that this made a much bigger difference to LTM compared to just spending more time trying to remember the item.

Elaborative links could include real life examples of psychological concepts, such as thinking of how the factors in conformity have happened in your life, or considering real-world implications of topics – what would happen if we stopped using psychiatric drugs and everyone was treated using CBT? Linking topics together and making links with other subjects such as Biology and Modern Studies is also great elaborative learning.

The **Cornell note-taking** system involves dividing your page into three sections, using a large margin at the side to write the key questions and essential terms, with your more detailed class notes alongside. A section is left blank at the foot of the page to write an overview later and make links to other topics (see image). This is a good way of making connections:

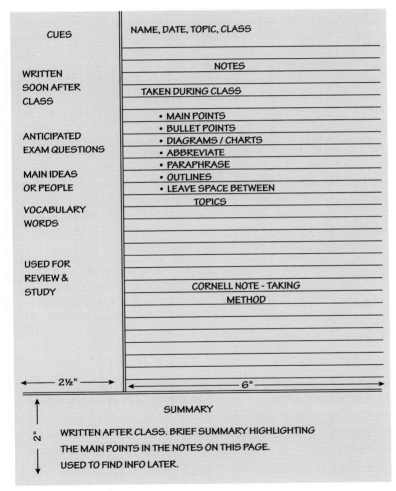

The Cornell note-taking system

Elaboration will also help to practice the skill of applying information to real-world situations – a key part of the course.

Spacing

Many studies of memory have shown that a pattern of spacing out learning over time can make a big difference to retention (e.g. Cepeda *et al.*, 2008). This **spacing effect** could include:

- Revising something soon after studying it (e.g. later the same day).
- Looking at the material again a week or two later (e.g. one weekend later in the month).
- Revising it again a couple of months later (e.g. at prelim time).

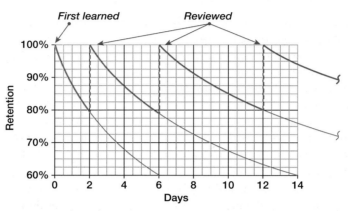

Typical forgetting curve for newly-learned information

This gradually increasing schedule is thought to be the most effective way of encoding information. For example, Kapler *et al.*, (2015) found that with lecture-type material, an eight-day gap before revision resulted in better long-term recall than a gap of just one day before revision. In both cases, students were tested five weeks later.

If you have used index cards as suggested, then by the end of the course you should have established a stack of cards summarising different theories, studies and applications. Study them, then set them aside, and come back to them again after a few days. The key is to leave a gap of time before reviewing the information.

Testing

Perhaps most importantly of all, testing yourself is highly effective in improving recall (McDaniel *et al.*, 2007). This is known as the **testing effect**. One reason for this is by making the revision harder, it has a larger effect on LTM. Unfortunately, it may have to be difficult in order to be effective!

Again, index cards make it easy to test yourself – just look at one side and try to remember what's on the other side. For example if you have facts about a theory on one side, you could test yourself on the evaluation points written on the other.

Testing yourself is highly effective in improving recall

🔍 **Top tip**

Promote the testing effect by trying to remember items rather than just looking over them. Just highlighting your notes is not an effective study strategy!

Added value

Added value means the extent to which you have gone beyond simply learning facts and skills. The main things that it refers to are:

- How broad is your learning – knowing more theories/explanations for a particular concept or a broader range of relevant research.
- How deep is your learning – learning about a single concept in more detail.
- Can you apply your learning to real situations.

Added value is assessed in the exam by your ability to demonstrate these three aspects and it is important if you want to get an A grade. The best preparation is to develop good study habits and find opportunities throughout the course to broaden and deepen your learning. Every section in this textbook includes an 'applied' section (e.g. sleep disorders), but it is a good learning habit to always look for ways in which new information is relevant to real life. As mentioned earlier, application is a skill, and it can be developed by using elaborative memory strategies rather than simply reading over notes.

It is not necessary to achieve the same level of breadth and depth in your learning in every area of the course. Ideally, it will derive from having an interest in particular areas. The main message is that finding out more about a particular theory or area is always beneficial and you should not try to do just the bare minimum to pass!

Activities such as project work and additional reading on a topic help to promote breadth and depth of learning. Relevant activities are suggested in each section of the topics after the review questions.

Practice questions on research (Higher only)

For research questions in the Higher exam, you are presented with a series of questions totalling 20 marks. There is usually a research scenario on which some of the questions are based. Once you have worked through chapter 8 and completed your Assignment (see chapter 9), your understanding of the research process should be at a good level. However, it really helps to practice exam-style questions. The following section presents three example research sections, followed by suggested answers.

Added value means the extent to which you have gone beyond simply learning facts and skills

🔑 Key concepts

- Index cards
- Analysis
- Forgetting
- Short-term memory (STM)
- Long-term memory (LTM)
- Cue
- Mnemonic
- Acrostic
- Visualisation
- Elaboration
- Cornell note-taking
- Spacing effect
- Testing effect

Practice exam section 1

✓ Section 1: Research

Answer **all** questions from this section.

		Marks
a.	Explain what is meant by an independent variable and a dependent variable.	2
b.	Explain what is meant by an extraneous variable, and give an example.	3
c.	Explain why the following ethical considerations are important in research:	
	i. Informed consent	2
	ii. Confidentiality	2
d.	Name and explain one stage of the research process in psychology.	3
e.	Explain the different types of sampling that are used in psychology, including their strengths and weaknesses.	8

(20)

Practice exam section 2

✓ Section 1: Research

Answer **all** questions from this section.

		Marks
a.	Briefly explain one stage of the research process.	2

Read the following research scenario and answer the questions below:

> A team of psychologists conducted a naturalistic observation study into multitasking – doing more than one task at the same time. They observed workers in a large office building over a period of one week. They wanted to find out about the role of multitasking in the workplace. The researchers used an observation schedule to record how many occasions more than one task was done at the same time and they wrote a brief description of the tasks done, including how successfully the tasks were completed. The office workers knew they were being observed.
>
> The results showed that multi-tasking was quite common. However, when people tried to do two or more complex tasks, the researchers observed a lot of mistakes being made.

b.	Explain the features of an observation study.	4
c.	Explain two ethical concerns that the researchers should consider in this study.	4
d.	Explain the strengths and weaknesses of observations, giving examples of extraneous variables that could affect the results in this study.	10

(20)

Practice exam section 3

✔ Section 1: Research

Answer **all** questions from this section.   *Marks*

    a. What are the key features of the case study method of research?   **3**

    b. What are the strengths and weaknesses of case studies?   **4**

Read the following research scenario and answer the questions below:

A psychology researcher studied the case of Peter, a man who has had considerable memory problems since suffering a brain injury. Peter was in a car accident, and although he fully recovered from his injuries, he lost all memory of the time leading up to the accident. His ability to learn new facts and events is normal but his short-term memory is very poor.

In a longitudinal study, the psychologist studied Peter over the 12 months following his accident using memory tests, and found that his memory improved slightly during this time. The study also used unstructured interviews with open questions, to find out more about Peter's experiences.

    c. Explain one extraneous variable that could affect Peter's score on the memory tests.   **3**

    d. Briefly explain one type of interview.   **2**

    e. Discuss the ethical concerns that might arise in the study.   **8**

    (20)

Answer guide to practice exam section 1

Explain what is meant by an independent variable and a dependent variable. (2)

IV is the variable that a researcher controls and manipulates. DV is the variable that is measured, and therefore, forms the results of the study.

Explain what is meant by an extraneous variable and give an example. (3)

This is an uncontrolled variable that causes error in the results. One example is a participant variable such as a participant's intelligence.

Explain why the following ethical considerations are important in research:

    i.   **Informed consent (2)**

    ii. **Confidentiality (2)**

Informed consent is important because people must be willing to take part and not forced, and they must understand what they are consenting to, otherwise they may be upset or harmed. Confidentiality is important to protect participants from embarrassment or harm if their data were released.

Name and explain one stage of the research process in psychology. (3)

Theory/hypothesis/research/data analysis. For example, one stage in the process is developing a theory. This is where researchers gather the data from a number of experiments and use it to make a general statement about how a psychological process works.

Explain the different types of sampling that are used in psychology, including their strengths and weaknesses. (8)

Could explain two in detail or more in lesser detail. Random sampling: every participant has the same chance of being selected. Results in a representative sample and eliminates researcher bias. Opportunity sampling – obtaining participants who are conveniently available, tends to result in a biased sample depending on how/where obtained. Volunteer sample – participants come forward, for example, in response to an advert. Reduces researcher bias, but participants are still not representative as not everyone will see the advert. Stratified sampling – attempt to create a sample with the same proportions of groups as the target population, for example, 50% female, 20% ethnic minority etc. Ensures representative sample but only in identified areas; other areas, for example personality, may not be representative.

Answer guide to practice exam section 2

Briefly explain one stage of the research process. (2)

For example – hypothesis: this is when a researcher uses theories to generate a prediction that can then be tested in research.

Explain the features of an observation study. (4)

Observation is a non-experimental method that involves watching people's behaviour as it happens. Naturalistic – observes in their natural environment, the researcher does not set up a task or give instructions and simply observes real behaviour as it happens. Structured – a task is given and the researcher observes behaviour on that task, often in a laboratory. Observation often uses an observation schedule – a sheet of anticipated behaviours that an observer uses during an observation. It aims to help the observer focus on the behaviours in which the research is interested. It may take the form of a checklist and it may have a time allocation.

Explain two ethical concerns that the researchers should consider in this study. (4)

Ensuring that participants have given informed consent/ensuring that participants are aware of their right to withdraw during or after the study/ensuring confidentiality of all data gathered, especially not sharing the info with the company's managers/ensuring no harm comes to participants, including not unduly distracting them from their work as this may get them into trouble, etc.

Explain the strengths and weaknesses of observations, giving examples of extraneous variables that could affect the results in this study. (10)

Naturalistic observations such as this are a good method to use to study real life behaviour as it happens. They have high ecological validity being in a real setting, and as they use real world tasks, they have high mundane realism too. They are superior to lab experiments on both of these issues.

However, naturalistic observations are not controlled, meaning that it is not possible to determine cause and effect. People may not do the same task twice, making it hard to make valid comparisons. The sample is opportunistic, unlike in an experiment where people could be randomly sampled and then matched and allocated to different groups. Participant variables will play a role in the results. In this specific example, everyone is an office worker, making it hard to generalise the findings to students, children, or other types of worker.

The tasks they are doing have not been chosen by the researchers. It would be easier to draw conclusions from a task that had been designed to measure multi-tasking, which could be done using a structured observation. There is no control of how good the participants are at the various tasks – practice could play a role. In addition, there is no control over how much time they spend on the tasks. In an experiment, they could all be given the same time limit.

Another limitation is that the presence of the observer may have affected the results, for example by making the participants nervous. This is called the observer effect.

However, overall, observation is one of the best research methods because it records real data as it happens, and with a naturalistic observation, the setting is not at all artificial.

Answer guide to practice exam section 3

What are the key features of the case study method of research? (3)

Three from: study of one individual or a small group/usually longitudinal/involves a variety of tests and techniques including interviews and brain scans/tends to generate mainly qualitative data/ in-depth study/ideal for unusual cases, for example, brain injury, exceptional abilities or rare psychological disorders.

What are the strengths and weaknesses of case studies? (4)

Possible advantages: allows researcher to focus on a specific instance/ in-depth and identify complex processes/insights from participant(s) may reveal an unusual and highly relevant perspective. Possible disadvantages: results are specific to the individual and can't always be generalised/often impossible to replicate/time consuming and expensive to carry out (two in-depth or four more briefly)

Explain one extraneous variable that could affect Peter's score on the memory tests. (3)

Should demonstrate understanding of EV and give one suitable example, for example, fatigue/practice/distractions.

An extraneous variable causes random error in the results. In this case, Peter is doing the tests repeatedly and he would get better due to practice.

Briefly explain one type of interview. (2)

For example, unstructured – the researcher doesn't carefully plan the questions asked during an interview, and asks questions spontaneously, following up on responses – interview develops like a natural conversation.

Discuss the ethical concerns that might arise in the study. (8)

Peter is a vulnerable individual and it is possible that he is not fully competent to give informed consent, and consent from next of kin should be obtained. Peter's wellbeing is the top priority and research mustn't harm him/interfere with his recovery. They shouldn't deceive him into thinking that the research will fix his memory. Peter must be told he can withdraw from the study at any time, including retrospectively. His data must be kept confidential, as with all research data in psychology.

Answers

Answers

Chapter 2: The biological approach (page p. 18)

1. *A neuron.*
2. *The central nervous system.*
3. *Broca's area.*
4. *Emotions.*
5. *Oxytocin.*
6. *Depression and eating disorders.*
7. *A gland.*
8. *A gene.*
9. *Environmental factors stop the gene from having an effect on the individual, i.e. it does not do anything.*
10. *Et al. means 'and others'.*

Chapter 2: The psychoanalytic approach (page p. 26)

1. *The id.*
2. *An iceberg.*
3. *The anal stage.*
4. *A fear of horses.*
5. *Oedipus complex.*
6. *Denial.*
7. *Reaction formation.*
8. *Projection.*
9. *Free association.*
10. *One patient/longitudinal/lots of in-depth data/several techniques used/ideal for unusual cases.*

Chapter 2: The cognitive approach (page p. 32)

1. *A cognitive process - something that occurs between a stimulus and the behavioural response.*
2. *Computer.*
3. *He said that cognition is a meaningful process, and computers do not try to make sense of stimuli.*
4. *A schema is a set of ideas or a pattern of thought about a particular concept or situation.*
5. *A script is similar to a schema, but it concerns how to act in social situations.*
6. *Jean Piaget.*

7. *A child focusing on one aspect of a problem and ignoring other important aspects, such as the height or width of a water glass when judging volume.*
8. *Personalisation.*
9. *A distortion in thinking, where the person focuses on a small negative detail.*
10. *Cognitive behavioural therapy (CBT).*

Chapter 2: The behaviourist approach (page p. 40)

1. *False. It shows classical conditioning.*
2. *Classical conditioning.*
3. *Reinforcement.*
4. *Punishment. Negative reinforcement strengthens a behaviour.*
5. *Classical conditioning.*
6. *False.*
7. *True.*
8. *The Skinner box.*
9. *Systematic desensitisation.*
10. *Something that represents part of a reward – several can be saved up and then exchanged for the reward, for example a star on a star chart.*

Chapter 2: The evolutionary approach (page p. 48)

1. *Charles Darwin.*
2. *Modern humans have existed for around 200,000 years but various other species of the genus 'Homo' for around 2 million years.*
3. *Yes, humans are classified as apes.*
4. *No, apes (like us) are generally larger and have certain key physical differences including no tail, opposable thumbs and brachiating arms (able to swing beneath branches).*
5. *Our ancestors probably lived in rainforests up to around 5 million years ago, but for the key period of human evolution – when we started walking, using language, using fire and making complex tools – we lived in an open savannah environment.*
6. *Approximately 12,000 years.*
7. *The environment of evolutionary adaptiveness.*

8. A person who lives by foraging and hunting rather than farming.
9. 150 individuals.
10. Fossil evidence is often incomplete, meaning we cannot know everything that happened during human evolution/sometimes evolution is used to justify sexism or immoral behaviour, but this is a case of the naturalistic fallacy/ humans are very different from other species, making comparisons with apes very limited.

Chapter 3: The nature of sleep (page p. 62)

1. REM sleep.
2. Circadian rhythms.
3. The brain's electrical activity/brain waves.
4. Five sleep stages, four to five times per night, therefore, 20-25 stages in total.
5. Yes.
6. Drugs, zeitgebers, stress.
7. 'Time giver'.
8. Caffeine/amphetamine/alcohol/ anti-depressants.
9. Money/work/relationships/family.
10. Hallucinations and an inability to concentrate on simple tasks.

Chapter 3: Approaches to sleep and dreams (page p.69)

1. The hypothalamus.
2. Melatonin.
3. Adenosine.
4. Activation-synthesis.
5. Latent content.
6. Giraffes.
7. Condensation.
8. Memory.
9. A lot of dream content is very different to our waking experiences.
10. The mind's dreams are seen as drawing on the same concepts and knowledge, i.e. schemas, and scripts as we use during the day.

Chapter 3: Theories of sleep and dreams (page p.77)

1. To repair their bodies.
2. Repairing injuries/removal of waste chemicals/replenishing neurotransmitters.
3. Because it is physically inactive and therefore energy is not being used for other jobs.
4. Non-REM sleep.

5. A longer period of non-REM sleep.
6. No, there are large variations, for example, carnivores sleeping more.
7. Cause it to be forgotten/deleted.
8. In order to improve organisation and make space.
9. Neural network computer models of learning, in which reverse learning was shown to be useful.
10. No. Sleep is generally thought to be beneficial to memory, while a lack of sleep harms cognitive functioning.

Chapter 3: Real-world application: sleep disorders (page p. 81)

1. Making it unsafe to drive/mental health problems/loss of alertness/physical health problems such as CHD.
2. Breathing.
3. Lack of light as a zeitgeber.
4. Difficulty sleeping due to air travel to a different time zone.
5. Age 3–8.
6. No. They may appear to be fully awake but they are not.
7. Six days of 'nightshifts'.
8. Use of bright light as a zeitgeber to change circadian rhythms, combined with total darkness when sleeping.
9. No. Sighted individuals can also have these disorders.
10. For example, circadian rhythm disorders can be treated via melatonin supplements that promote sleepiness on a regular 24-hour schedule.

Chapter 4: What is psychopathology? (page p.87)

1. Abnormal psychology/atypical behaviour.
2. A typical way to behave in a culture or group.
3. They are seen as weird/people want to distance themselves.
4. Inability to lead a normal life.
5. Harm/maladaptiveness and statistical infrequency.
6. The World Health Organisation's 'WHODAS'.
7. Professionals cannot tell sane from insane/ patients treated in depersonalised way/ psychiatric labels tend to stick/all behaviour.
8. What symptoms are shown and for how long they are shown.

9. Mood disorder/eating disorders/anxiety disorders/disorders of childhood/etc.
10. Lack of validity/removed useful categories, for example, Asperger's/other categories too broad/accused of boosting drug companies' profits.

Chapter 4: Common psychological disorders (page p. 94)

1. An anxiety disorder.
2. Hallucinations/delusions/disordered speech.
3. Lack of affect/mutism/cataleptic state.
4. Weight loss, distorted body image, aversion to being overweight, and cessation of menstruation.
5. Depressed mood, loss of interest/pleasure.
6. A lifetime prevalence of 10%, which means that 10% of the population will be diagnosed with depression at some point during their life.
7. Generalised anxiety disorder.
8. Social phobias are more common.
9. Addictions/gambling/falling in love.
10. The individual cannot stop thinking about the thing that causes anxiety.

Chapter 4: Approaches to psychopathology (page p. 99)

1. The psychoanalytic approach.
2. Neurotransmitter imbalance theory.
3. Serotonin.
4. Dopamine.
5. 177.
6. Fails to take account of social processes/leads to missed opportunities to intervene in social processes.
7. The biological approach.
8. Self, world and future.
9. Classical conditioning.
10. I must do well and win approval or else I am a bad person/other people must behave well or else they deserve to be punished/my life must be easy, without any discomfort or danger or else I cannot enjoy life.

Chapter 4: Theories of psychopathology (page p. 106)

1. The diathesis-stress model.
2. A predisposition in someone's biology or thought processes that makes them more vulnerable to illness.
3. Genetics/personality/thought processes/lack of support.

4. Life events involving suffering, injury or trauma that make a disorder more likely to develop.
5. Zubin and Spring (1977).
6. Something that is invented by society or culture.
7. Thomas Szasz.
8. The anti-psychiatry movement.
9. R.D. Laing.
10. The Mental Health Act of 2007.

Chapter 4: Real-world application: therapies (page p. 110)

1. Treatment based on chemicals, that is, drugs.
2. Anxiety disorders/bulimia nervosa.
3. Risperidone.
4. Sexual dysfunction/nausea/headaches/ suicidal thoughts.
5. Cognitive-behavioural therapy.
6. Both CBT and anti-depressants were better than a placebo; drugs worked faster but CBT caught up and did not have negative side effects. A combination was best overall.
7. No.
8. CBT or combination of drugs/CBT.
9. For example, focus on underlying causes versus current symptoms.
10. Therapy using a mixture of techniques drawn from more than one approach.

Chapter 5: The nature of memory (page p. 118)

1. Short-term memory (STM)/working memory
2. Retrieved.
3. Long-term memory (LTM).
4. Working memory.
5. Prospective memory.
6. Recognition.
7. Encoding, storage and retrieval.
8. Retrieval.
9. Recognition involves comparing a stimulus to a memory, free recall is retrieval of information when the stimulus is absent.
10. Semantic encoding.

Chapter 5: Approaches to memory (page p. 124)

1. The frontal lobe of the neocortex.
2. Long-term potentiation.
3. Declarative LTM.
4. Brewer and Treyens (1981).
5. Eyewitness testimony.
6. Pezdek et al. (1989).

7. The id.

8. A deliberate form of repression.

9. The tasks are not similar to the childhood emotions that Freud thought most likely to be repressed.

10. False.

Chapter 5: Theories of memory (page p. 131)

1. Sensory memory.

2. Time spent in STM, that is, how long maintenance rehearsal lasts for.

3. Attention being paid to the stimulus.

4. Serial position effect (or primacy/recency effect).

5. Because they demonstrate that LTM and STM are processed in different parts of the brain.

6. The word length effect.

7. Multi-tasking.

8. The phonological loop.

9. The episodic buffer.

10. The central executive.

Chapter 5: Real-world application: eyewitness testimony (page p. 139)

1. Münsterberg and Bartlett.

2. To find out if misleading questions could distort the memory of a witness.

3. One had only three conditions, and questioning occurred one week later.

4. 16/50 participants.

5. Three from: misinformation effect, social pressure, emotion/anxiety, change blindness, violence, expectations.

6. Wright et al. (2000).

7. Failure to notice changes in our surroundings, for example, the appearance of another person.

8. The witness focuses on the weapon ('weapons focus') and fails to take in other information such as the appearance of the suspect.

9. Any from: cognitive interview, witness line-ups one at a time, treating memory like a crime scene, not relying on EWT alone.

10. Lack of emotional involvement, more attention paid to stimuli, (often) watching events on a screen, student participants who are not typical adults, etc.

Chapter 6: What is stress? (page p. 147)

1. Short-term/immediate stress.

2. Sweating/tense muscles/increased blood clotting/glucose released/slowed digestion/ heightened vision and awareness.

3. Adrenaline and cortisol.

4. Stress.

5. Social.

6. Both showed a hierarchy in stress outcomes, with lower-ranked individuals more stressed and unhealthy.

7. Workload/exams/deadlines/meetings/ interaction with colleagues/low pay/ being fired.

8. Time urgency, competitiveness, do several things at once, general tension, hostility, etc.

9. Teenagers feel the effects of stressors more and display the symptoms more openly.

10. Males have a greater and more sustained release of adrenaline/women benefit more from a release of oxytocin during social support.

Chapter 6: Approaches to stress (page p. 155)

1. The nervous system and the endocrine system.

2. Triggers the adrenal cortex to increase production of cortisol.

3. It does not explain which stimuli cause stress/ it does not explain individual differences/a lot of the research has been conducted on animals.

4. Because in that environment it was necessary for survival, while modern stressors often do not involve running or fighting.

5. The tend-or-befriend response.

6. Because there are no historical records and the fossil evidence is very limited.

7. The tendency to underestimate task times.

8. They stopped following instructions and used a heuristic that resulted in getting the task wrong.

9. Panic disorder.

10. CBT.

Chapter 6: Theories of stress (page p. 161)

1. After 6–48 hours.

2. Resistance.

3. A general term for illnesses that occur due to changes in the exhaustion stage of GAS and could include ulcers, CHD and hypertension.

4. That all stressors have the same effect/ everyone reacts the same to stressors.

5. Lazarus and Folkman.

6. *A person assesses their own ability to cope with stressors.*
7. *Primary appraisal.*
8. *Emotion-focused.*
9. *Best: problem-focused; middle: emotion-focused; worst: avoidance.*
10. *Because it proposes that changing our thought processes can result in less stress and better health.*

Chapter 6: Real-world application: stress management (page p. 166)

1. *Chronic stress.*
2. *Anger and irritability/emotional outbursts/difficulty concentrating.*
3. *Coronary heart disease.*
4. *Depression and eating disorders (could also mention panic disorder, schizophrenia, etc.).*
5. *Fleshner (2000).*
6. *Deep breathing and visualisation.*
7. *Conceptualisation.*
8. *Using the techniques in real-life stressful situations e.g. in the workplace.*
9. *'A'.*
10. *Benzodiazepines.*

Chapter 7: Defining intelligence (page p. 173)

1. *A talent or skill – something that people are good or bad at.*
2. *IQ is only a score on a test.*
3. *Sir Charles Spearman (Spearman, 1904).*
4. *Crystallised.*
5. *General intelligence.*
6. *'Interpersonal' is the ability to interact sensitively with others, while 'intrapersonal' is the ability to self-reflect and understand your own feelings and motivations.*
7. *Later born children, on average, have lower IQ scores.*
8. *Verbal intelligence.*
9. *The Flynn effect.*
10. *Interactionist view.*

Chapter 7: Approaches to intelligence (page p. 180)

1. *Positron emission tomography (PET) scans.*
2. *The frontal lobe.*
3. *0.77*
4. *Adverts*
5. *Assimilation means changing the schema to include new information, while*

accommodation means splitting it into different schemas.
6. *Sensorimotor/pre-operational/concrete operational/formal operational.*
7. *Artificial intelligence.*
8. *Testing whether people think that they are communicating with a human, when it is actually a computer.*
9. *Washoe.*
10. *The social group.*

Chapter 7: Theories of intelligence (page p.187)

1. *Sternberg.*
2. *More.*
3. *Creative intelligence.*
4. *Practical intelligence.*
5. *Defining problems/planning what to do/carrying out plans/monitoring processes during problem solving/evaluating solutions/acquisition of knowledge/learning new strategies.*
6. *Growth mindset.*
7. *No.*
8. *False.*
9. *373 middle school pupils in New York.*
10. *Two years.*

Chapter 7: Testing intelligence (page p. 194)

1. *Binet and Simon.*
2. *Dividing mental age by chronological age and multiplying by 100.*
3. *The Stanford Binet test/Raven's progressive matrices/11-plus/SAT test.*
4. *It can be used on participants who have poor reading or English language skills.*
5. *Creative, practical, etc.*
6. *Mathematical/verbal/logic.*
7. *Entry tests/streaming/recruitment.*
8. *Eight months/one school year.*
9. *Cultural bias.*
10. *Reliability.*

Chapter 8: The scientific method and the research process (page p.202)

1. *They can disprove but not prove a theory.*
2. *An explanation of the available facts.*
3. *Because the scientific method requires all ideas to be supported by reliable research evidence.*

4. *Karl Popper.*
5. *Yes, though the criticism should be based on evidence.*
6. *Experiments, observations, surveys, interviews, case studies.*
7. *Gathering data.*
8. *Each study provides a single piece of evidence and our overall understanding builds up over time.*
9. *Yes, because it is important to check/confirm results.*
10. *There is no final stage, because it is a continual, cyclical process!*

Chapter 8: Populations and samples (page p. 206)

1. *The group of participants who are studied.*
2. *The target population.*
3. *There is no perfect size but the larger the better.*
4. *Findings from unrepresentative samples cannot always be generalised to the target population.*
5. *Random or systematic.*
6. *No, not always. It could be unrepresentative due to chance factors.*
7. *It should be unbiased, representative and large.*
8. *It is not susceptible to systematic bias.*
9. *Because it needs to be combined with another method of sampling, for example, opportunity.*
10. *Stratified.*

Chapter 8: Experimental methods (page p. 211)

1. *Lab experiments.*
2. *IV and DV.*
3. *Repeated measures.*
4. *Control over variables.*
5. *Cause and effect.*
6. *Artificiality/demand characteristics.*
7. *A field experiment is a true, controlled experiment whereas a natural experiment is not controlled by the researcher.*
8. *A quasi-experiment is controlled in most ways except that allocation to conditions/groups is non-random, while a natural experiment is uncontrolled.*
9. *5.*
10. *Noise, personality, ability.*

Chapter 8: Non-experimental methods (page p. 221)

1. *One with a fixed selection of answers.*
2. *Leading questions/loaded questions/jargon/ ambiguity/bias.*
3. *Semi-structured.*
4. *It might be important to be able to explain the questions face-to-face.*
5. *Naturalistic.*
6. *Observer effect.*
7. *Obtains data on real behaviour as it happens.*
8. *Longitudinal, in-depth, individual case/small group.*
9. *Interviews, observations, brain scans, tests.*
10. *False. Studies often use a mixture of different methods.*

Chapter 8: General research issues (page p. 231)

1. *A prediction of expected results.*
2. *Yes. Variables in a hypothesis must be operationalised.*
3. *Internal validity.*
4. *Whether the findings of a study can be related to everyday situations.*
5. *No. Nobody would do that in everyday life.*
6. *Population validity.*
7. *No. A lab experiment involving a realistic, everyday task such as memorising a shopping list would have high mundane realism.*
8. *A set of ethical research standards published by an official research body or professional science organisation such as the British Psychological Society (BPS).*
9. *Confidentiality.*
10. *Yes, but parental consent is also needed.*

Chapter 8: Data and graphs (page p. 238)

1. *Mean, mode, median.*
2. *Bar graph, histogram, pie chart (or scattergram).*
3. *The median.*
4. *When there are extreme high or low scores.*
5. *The range.*
6. *The average amount by which the data deviate from the mean.*
7. *Often there is no mode – no score appears more than once – or more than one are equally common (multi-modal).*

8. *It includes every score in the calculation.*
9. *The bars of a histogram are continuous/joined together.*
10. *It standardises scores making them easier to compare.*

Chapter 10: The nature of conformity (page p. 278)

1. *Normative.*
2. *Identification.*
3. *Dissent.*
4. *Beans.*
5. *75%.*
6. *Compliance.*
7. *Internalisation.*
8. *Minority influence.*
9. *Lab.*
10. *Engineering students.*

Chapter 10: Explanations of conformity (page p. 283)

1. *The rise from two to three.*
2. *False.*
3. *True.*
4. *Three from: age, sex, personality, thought processes, culture.*
5. *Santee and Maslach (1982).*
6. *Becoming more different from the majority rather than more similar.*
7. *Collectivist cultures.*
8. *They used filter sunglasses that resulted in people seeing different lengths of lines.*
9. *Male participants did not conform; having an 'ally' made very little difference.*
10. *104 Japanese university students.*

Chapter 10: Obedience (page p.289)

1. *False.*
2. *Charismatic.*
3. *A hierarchy.*
4. *40.*
5. *26 of the participants (i.e. 65%).*
6. *Deception and stress to participants.*
7. *A hospital.*
8. *Peer (confederate teacher) giving the shock.*
9. *Agentic and autonomous state.*
10. *False. Authoritarian parenting does so, while democratic parenting encourages negotiation of reasonable boundaries.*

Chapter 10: Resisting social pressure (page p. 296)

1. *Behaviours and beliefs.*
2. *Lying politician/abusive partner, etc.*
3. *Behaviour control, information control, thought control, emotional control.*
4. *Jonestown.*
5. *One from: view of normality distorted; guilt and self-blame used; kindness and cruelty are alternated; victims are isolated; fear and intimidation are used.*
6. *Moral reasoning, questioning motives, disobedient models.*
7. *Because awareness of the cult makes people less likely to join.*
8. *Possible answers include raised awareness, confidence, assertiveness, democratic parenting.*
9. *Rank and Jacobson (1977).*
10. *Hornsey et al. (2003).*

Chapter 10: Activity 2 (page p. 303)

(Parentheses indicate that it is relevant but not the best answer)

Education: (a), (f), j.
Role models/group support: c, g.
Moral reasoning/confidence in own beliefs: a, d, f, i.
Questioning motives of advertisers/politicians/cults: b, h, k.
Responsibility for own actions: e, (j).

Chapter 11: Prejudice, stereotypes and discrimination (page p. 305)

1. *In-group and out-group.*
2. *An emotional reaction to a type of person, object or situation.*
3. *Stereotypes.*
4. *They are learned from society/from our early childhood/from the media.*
5. *Confirmation bias causes us to be poorer at remembering information that contradicts the stereotype.*
6. *96 students.*
7. *To 'pre-judge'.*
8. *Racism/sexism/ageism/heterosexism.*
9. *The Equality Act of 2010.*
10. *When a rule, for example, in an organisation, is unfair to a particular group.*

Chapter 11: Theories of stereotypes and prejudice (page p. 313)

1. Because cognitive resources, such as attention, are limited.
2. He stated that group categories are meaningful/useful/accurate.
3. Psychoanalytic approach.
4. Upbringing.
5. Previous comments made by research participants.
6. Authoritarian aggression/authoritarian submission/conventionalism.
7. Social categorisation/social identification/social comparison.
8. Schoolboys aged 14–15.
9. Population validity – difficulty in generalising the results to older ages or to other groups in society.
10. They said that discrimination does not boost self-esteem.

Chapter 11: Reducing prejudice (page p. 321)

1. An educational technique of promoting knowledge and understanding of an issue, for example, prejudice, and its effects.
2. Eye colour.
3. Self-esteem, liking for other children and academic performance.
4. Support from authorities, personal acquaintance, introduction to non-stereotypical individuals, cooperation between groups and equal status.
5. Majorities.
6. The two groups were kept apart and each developed an in-group identity.
7. Broken water supply/broken-down truck.
8. This avoided pre-existing stereotypes playing a role in later attitudes.
9. Possible harm and distress, deception of both participants and their parents, etc.
10. Conflict over resources.

Chapter 12: Aspects of NVC (page p. 328)

1. Posture and gesture.
2. Gesture.
3. Posture.
4. As a sign that you are interested and paying attention.

5. A tribe in Papua New Guinea that had very little contact with the outside world before Ekman and Friesen's (1971) study.
6. 189 adults and 130 children.
7. It includes both positive and negatives/sounds and words/some indicate the speaker should continue and others that the listener would like a turn.
8. 'Uh huh', 'mmm', 'yeah', etc.
9. Anger/disgust/contempt/surprise/fear/sadness.
10. Paralanguage, because the tone and volume of the speech are being used to communicate, as well as the words.

Chapter 12: Theories and debates in NVC: nature and nurture (page p. 334)

1. The nature-nurture debate.
2. The amygdala.
3. Smiling age six to eight weeks/preferring to look at faces by 4 months.
4. That activating individual/social schemas affected people's chosen proximity.
5. False.
6. 'Begging' gesture, stroking hands, body language, hugging.
7. Facial movements are involved in regulating blood flow to the brain/unintentionally communicating emotions would not have been an advantage to our ancestors.
8. That they were due to innate racial differences.
9. For example, Tibet: seen as friendly/Maori: seen as angry/defiant.
10. Matsumoto and Kudoh (1993).

Chapter 12: Uses of NVC research (page p. 340)

1. A smaller number of longer gazes.
2. A photo identification task.
3. They were completely unaware of it.
4. They were poor (only slightly above chance level) but could improve through training.
5. False. It is possible to get much better than 50:50, especially after training. However, it is not possible to be perfect.
6. Yes.
7. Kismet.
8. A sad face.
9. Efficient way to get information across/very challenging to design/more engaging for users/may be culture-specific.

10. *Not really – they would probably notice and find it creepy. The chameleon effect happens by itself without your being aware of it. If you are going to mimic someone then do it subtly and mimic the general movement as suggested by Sparenberg et al. (2012).*

Chapter 13: The nature of relationships (page p. 347)

1. *No, not necessarily.*
2. *Affiliation*
3. *Maslow/Baumeister and Leary.*
4. *Using caregiver as a base, social releasers, develops schema for relationships, monotropy.*
5. *Less emphasis on parents/peers have a strong influence on personality development/loneliness is more common.*
6. *The nucleus accumbens.*
7. *Insecure-resistant.*
8. *Rather than opposites, people who are similar tend to be attracted to each other.*
9. *Internet dating sites, social networking sites, discussion forums.*
10. *Secure attachment.*

Chapter 13: Theories of relationships (page p. 357)

1. *Money, time, etc.*
2. *Childcare, company, etc.*
3. *Sampling, bargaining, commitment, institutionalisation.*
4. *To an extent – it implies a rational choice, but social exchange theory would predict that higher risk would lead to people choosing less attractive partners, which is not what was found by Berscheid et al. (1971).*
5. *A schema for relationships, which people use to judge current/potential new relationships.*
6. *Aim for different numbers of offspring or males aim for youthful partner/females aim for partner who can support them.*
7. *150*
8. *It is seen as an innate response to signs of health and fertility.*
9. *Investment is the amount of costs incurred in looking after offspring. 'Differential' means that this is often unequal between the mother and father.*
10. *Due to an innate need for comfort.*

Chapter 13: Relationship conflict (page p. 364)

1. *For example, behaviour: slamming doors/procrastinating. Saying 'whatever/it's fine/I'm not annoyed' etc.*
2. *Those who have cheated before/people with a '9' at the end of their age/wealthier males/poorer females.*
3. *'If it weren't for you'/'Ain't it awful'.*
4. *Parent, adult and child.*
5. *Fear, obligation and guilt ('F.O.G').*
6. *A temporary breaking apart of two people who have an attachment bond.*
7. *Intrapsychic, dyadic.*
8. *Age/length/substitute attachment figures.*
9. *Nine days.*
10. *Psychoanalysis/CBT/person-centred.*

Feedback

Feedback for Discussion on page p. 15

The points listed are the key ideas behind the approaches you will study during this chapter. You probably found some easier than others to use as an explanation. This could be partly because you are used to this kind of explanation – some approaches are more prevalent in our media and in everyday conversation. There is a worked example for you to look at (see Rob's case on page p. 15).

Feedback for Discussion point on page p. 23

This is short for 'et alli' which is Latin for 'and others'.

Feedback for Activity 1 on page p. 53

Australopithecus	*2–4 million years ago*
Homo erectus	*150,000–2 million years ago*
Start of agriculture	*12,000 years ago*
The first cities appeared	*5,000 years ago*
First modern humans	*200,000 years ago*
'Missing link' ancestor between humans and chimpanzees	*6–7 million years ago*
Beginning of the current ice age	*2.5 million years ago*
Neanderthals died out	*40,000 years ago.*

Feedback for Discussion point on page p. 135

Attention from the CE is limited, so you can only carry out several tasks if those tasks combined do not exceed the total attention available. If one task starts to take up most of your attention then it becomes much harder to do anything else and performance on that task (e.g. conversation while driving) may slow down or stop altogether. Tasks that are novel or complex require more attention, while routine tasks such as washing the dishes do not require much. If a task is automatic then it requires hardly any attention at all and it can be done without thinking about it.

Feedback for Discussion point on page p. 137

A model is simply a more detailed version of a theory. It sets out a possible structure for a process (e.g. memory) that can then be tested and changed.

Feedback for the mindset questions on page p. 190

Agreeing with items 1, 4 and 5 indicates a fixed mindset. Agreeing with items 2, 3 and 6 indicates a growth mindset.

Feedback for Discussion point on page p. 216

If the experimenter were to choose which participant went into which condition, this choice could be biased.

Feedback for Discussion point on page p. 323

A superordinate goal is a particular type of shared goal. You and your friend might both want to pass an exam. That is a shared goal, but it is not a superordinate goal, because you don't need to work together to achieve it. However, if both of you want to lift a sofa up a flight of stairs and it is a two-person job, then it is a superordinate goal.

References

Abel, T., Havekes, R., Saletin, J.M. and Walker, M.P. (2013). Sleep, plasticity and memory from molecules review to whole-brain networks. *Current Biology, 23*, R774–R788.

Aboud, F.E. (2003). The formation of in-group favoritism and out-group prejudice in young children: Are they distinct attitudes? *Developmental Psychology, 39*, 48–60.

Abrams, D. and Houston, D. M. (2006). Equality, diversity and prejudice in Britain: results from the 2005 national survey. *Report for the Cabinet Office Equalities Review.* Kent: University of Kent Centre for the Study of Group Processes.

Abrams, D., Wetherell, M., Cochrane, S., Hogg, M.A. and Turner, J.C. (1990). Knowing what to think by knowing who you are: self-categorisation and the nature of norm formation. *British Journal of Social Psychology, 29*, 97–119.

Adolphs, R., Tranel, D. and Damasio, A.R. (1998). The human amygdala in social judgment. *Nature, 393*, 470–474.

Adorno, T.W., Frenkel-Brunswik, E., Levinson, D.J. and Sanford, R.N. (1950). *The Authoritarian Personality.* New York: Harper.

Ainsworth, M.D.S. and Bell, S.M. (1970). Attachment, exploration, and separation: Individual differences in strange-situation behavior of one-year-olds. *Child Development, 41*, 49–67.

Ainsworth, M.D.S., Bell, S.M. and Stayton, D.J. (1971). Individual differences in the strange-situation behaviour of one-year-olds. In H.R. Schaffer (Ed.), *The Origins of Human Social Relations.* New York: Academic Press, 17–52.

Allport, G. (1954). *The Nature of Prejudice.* New York: Double-Day Anchor.

Almendros, C., Carrobles, J.A. and Rodríguez-Carballeira, Á. (2007). Former members' perceptions of cult involvement. *Cultic Studies Review, 6*, 1–18.

Altemeyer, B. (1981). *Right-wing Authoritarianism.* Manitoba: University of Manitoba Press.

Altemeyer, B. (2006). *The Authoritarians.* Retrieved 28 July 2010 from http://home.cc.umanitoba.ca/~altemey/.

Ambady, N. and Rosenthal, R. (1992). Thin slices of expressive behavior as predictors of interpersonal consequences: a meta-analysis. *Psychological bulletin, 111*, 256–274.

Ambady, N., Shih, M., Kim, A. and Pittinsky, T.L. (2001). Stereotype susceptibility in children: Effects of identity activation on quantitive performance. *Psychological Science, 12*, 385–390.

American Psychiatric Association (2013). *DSM-5.* Washington, D.C.: American Psychiatric Press.

Andersen, S.M. and Zimbardo, P.G. (1984). On resisting social influence. *Cultic Studies Journal, 1*, 196–219.

Anderson, D.A. and Hamilton, M. (2005). Gender role stereotyping of parents in children's picture books: The invisible father. *Sex Roles, 52*, 145–151.

Anderson, J.R., Gillies, A. and Lock, L.C. (2010). Pan thanatology. *Current Biology, 20*, R349–R351.

Anderson, M.C. and Green, C. (2001). Suppressing unwanted memories by executive control. *Nature, 410*, 366–369.

Ando, J., Ono, Y. and Wright, M. J. (2001). Genetic structure of spatial and verbal working memory. *Behavior genetics, 31*, 615–624.

Andrews, C. and Brewin, C.R. (2000). What did Freud get right? *The Psychologist, 13*, 605–607.

Angold, A., Costello, E.J., Erkanli, A. and Worthman, C.M. (1999). Pubertal changes in hormone levels and depression in girls. *Psychological Medicine, 29*, 1043–1053.

Anthony, A. (2009). Jane Elliott, the American schoolmarm who would rid us of our racism. *The Guardian.* Retrieved 26 January 2015 from http://www.theguardian.com/culture/2009/oct/18/racism-psychology-jane-elliott-4.

Argyle, M. and Cook, M. (1976). *Gaze and Mutual Gaze.* Cambridge: Cambridge University Press.

Aronson, E. and Bridgeman, D. (1979). Jigsaw groups and the desegregated classroom: in pursuit of common goals. In E. Aronson (Ed.), *Readings About the Social Animal* (6th edn). New York: W.H. Freeman.

Asch, S.E. (1951). Effects of group pressure upon the modification and distortion of judgment. In H. Guetzkow (Ed.), *Groups, Leadership and Men.* Pittsburgh, PA: Carnegie Press.

Asch, S.E. (1955). Opinions and social pressure. *Scientific American, 193*, 31–35.

Atkinson, R.C. and Shiffrin, R.M. (1968). Human memory: a proposed system and its control processes. In K.W. Spence and J.T. Spence (Eds.), *The Psychology of Learning and Motivation*: Vol. 2. London: Academic Press.

Avigdor, R. (1951). *The Development of Stereotypes as a Result of Group Interaction, on file in the Library,* New York University. Cited by Sherif *et al.* (1954).

Baddeley, A.D. (1966). Short term memory for word sequences as a function of acoustic, semantic and formal similarity. *Quarterly Journal of Experimental Psychology, 18*, 362–365.

Baddeley, A.D. (2000). The episodic buffer: a new component of working memory? *Trends in Cognitive Sciences, 4*, 417–423.

Baddeley, A.D. (2012). Working memory: theories, models, and controversies. *Annual Review of Psychology, 63*, 1–29.

Baddeley, A.D., Grant, S., Wight, E. and Thomson, N. (1973). Imagery and visual working, In P.M.A. Rabbitt and S. Darnit (Eds.), *Attention and Performance: V.* London: Academic Press.

Baddeley, A.D. and Hitch, G. (1974). Working memory. In G.H. Bower (Ed.), *The Psychology of Learning and Motivation*: Vol. 8. London: Academic Press.

Baddeley, A.D., Thomson, N. and Buchanan, M. (1975). Word length and the structure of short-term memory. *Journal of Verbal Learning and Verbal Behaviour, 14*, 575–589.

Bandura, A. (1965). Influence of models' reinforcement contingencies on the acquisition of imitative responses. *Journal of Personality and Social Psychology, 1*, 589–595.

Bartlett, F.C. (1932). *Remembering: A Study in Experimental and Social Psychology*. Cambridge: Cambridge University Press.

Bailenson, J.N. and Yee, N. (2005). Digital chameleons automatic assimilation of nonverbal gestures in immersive virtual environments. *Psychological Science, 16*, 814–819.

Bailly, G., Raidt, S. and Elisei, F. (2010). Gaze, conversational agents and face-to-face communication. *Speech Communication, 52*, 598–612.

Barco, T. (1999). We're all copycats: The chameleon effect happens naturally and frequently, because we feel a rapport with people who mimic our moves. *Psychology Today.* Retrieved 15 January 2015 from https://www.psychologytoday.com/articles/199911/were-all-copycats.

Bargh, J.A. and Chartrand, T.L. (1999). The unbearable automaticity of being. *American Psychologist, 54*, 462.

Baron, R.A. and Byrne, D. (1997). *Social Psychology* (8th edn). London: Allyn and Bacon.

Baron-Cohen, S., Leslie, A.M. and Frith, U. (1985). Does the autistic child have a 'theory of mind'? *Cognition, 21*, 37–46.

Bass, B.M. (1955). Authoritarianism or acquiescence? *Journal of Abnormal and Social Psychology, 51*, 616–623.

Baumeister, R.F. and Leary, M.R. (1995). The need to belong: Desire for interpersonal attachments as a fundamental human motivation. *Psychological Bulletin, 117*, 497–529.

Beck, A. (1976). *Cognitive therapy and the emotional disorders*. New York: International Universities Press.

Bell, V. (2014). The concept of stress, sponsored by Big Tobacco. *Mindhacks Blog.* Retrieved 1 December 2014 from http://mindhacks.com/2014/07/14/the-concept-of-stress-sponsored-by-big-tobacco/.

Benington, J.H. and Heller, H.C. (1995). Restoration of brain energy metabolism as the function of sleep. *Progress in Neurobiology, 45*, 347–360.

Berndt, T.J. (1982). The features and effects of friendship in early adolescence. *Child Development, 53*, 1447–1460.

Berne, E. (1968). *Games People Play: The Psychology of Human Relationships*. London: Penguin.

Berne, E. (1975). *What Do You Do After You Say Hello*. [Kindle DX version]. Retrieved from Amazon.com.

Berscheid, E., Dion, K., Walster, E. and Walster, G.W. (1971). Physical attractiveness and dating choice: A test of the matching hypothesis. *Journal of Experimental Social Psychology, 7*, 173–189.

Bertamini, M., Byrne, C. and Bennett, K.M. (2013). Attractiveness is influenced by the relationship between postures of the viewer and the viewed person. *i-Perception, 4*, 170.

Bezrukova, K., Jehn, K. A. and Spell, C. S. (2012). Reviewing diversity training: where we have been and where we should go. *Academy of Management Learning and Education, 11*, 207–227.

Bickman, L. (1974). Clothes make the person. *Psychology Today, 8*, 48–51.

Binder, J., Brown, R., Zagefka, H., Funke, F., Kessler, T., Mummendey, A., Schiller, F., Maquil, A., Demoulin, S. and Leyens, J.P. (2009). Does contact reduce prejudice or does prejudice reduce contact? A longitudinal test of the contact hypothesis among majority and minority groups in three European countries. *Journal of Personality and Social Psychology, 96*, 843–856.

Binet, A. and Simon, T. (1916). *The Development of Intelligence in Children*. Baltimore: Williams and Wilkins. (Original work published 1905).

Blackwell, L.S., Trzesniewski, K.H. and Dweck, C.S. (2007). Implicit theories of intelligence predict achievement across an adolescent transition: a longitudinal study and an intervention. *Child Development, 78*, 246–263.

Boese, A. (2007). *Elephants on Acid: and Other Bizarre Experiments*. Orlando: Harvest Books.

Bohm, J. and Alison, L. (2001). An exploratory study in methods of distinguishing destructive cults. *Psychology, Crime and Law, 7*, 133–165.

Bouchard, T. and McGue, M. (1981). Familial studies of intelligence: a review. *Science, 212*, 1055–1059.

Boulette, T.R. and Andersen, S.M. (1985). 'Mind control' and the battering of women. *Community Mental Health Journal, 21,* 109–118.

Bower, G.H. (1972). Mental imagery and associative learning. In L.W. Gregg and G.H. Bower (Eds.), *Cognition in Learning and Memory.* New York: Wiley, 51–88.

Bowlby, J. (1953). *Child Care and the Growth of Love.* Harmondsworth: Penguin Books.

Bowlby, J. (1958). The nature of the child's tie to his mother. *International Journal of Psychoanalysis, 39,* 350–373.

Breazeal, C. and Scassellati, B. (2002). Robots that imitate humans. *Trends in Cognitive Sciences, 6,* 481–487.

Breus, M.J. (2012). Nighttime worries worst in middle age: basic steps to reduce our nighttime worrying and improve our sleep. *Psychology Today.* Retrieved 20 December 2014 from http://www.psychologytoday. c o m / b l o g / s l e e p - n e w z z z / 2 0 1 2 1 2 / nighttime-worries-worst-in-middle-age.

Brewer, W.F. and Treyens, J.C. (1981). Role of schemata in memory for places. *Cognitive Psychology, 13,* 207–230.

British Psychological Society (2009). Code of ethics and conduct. Retrieved 22 April 2015 from http://www. bps.org.uk/system/files/documents/code_of_ethics_ and_conduct.pdf.

British Psychological Society (2011). Response to the American Psychiatric Association: DSM-5 development. Retrieved 3 February 2015 from http:// apps.bps.org.uk/_publicationfiles/consultation-responses/DSM-5%202011%20-%20BPS%20 response.pdf.

Brooks, A.G. and Arkin, R. C. (2007). Behavioral overlays for non-verbal communication expression on a humanoid robot. *Autonomous Robots, 22,* 55–74.

Brown, G.W. and Harris, T.O. (1978). *Social Origins of Depression: A Study of Psychiatric Disorder in Women.* London: Tavistock Publications.

Brown, R. and McNeill, D. (1966). The 'tip-of-the-tongue' phenomenon. *Journal of Verbal Learning and Verbal Behaviour, 5,* 325–337.

Brown, R.J. and Turner, J.C. (1981). Interpersonal and intergroup behaviour. In J.C. Turner and H. Giles (Eds.), *Intergroup Behaviour.* Oxford: Basil Blackwell, 33–65.

Bruch, H. (1979). *The Golden Cage.* New York: Vintage Books.

Bruner, J. (1992). *Acts of Meaning.* Boston, MA: Harvard University Press.

Buehler, R., Griffin, D. and Ross, M. (1994). Exploring the 'planning fallacy': why people underestimate their task completion times. *Journal of Personality and Social Psychology, 67,* 366–381.

Bulevich, J.B., Roediger, H.L., Balota, D.A. and Butler, A.C. (2006). Failures to find suppression of episodic memories in the think/no-think paradigm. *Memory and Cognition, 34,* 1569–1577.

Bulkeley, K. (2014). Why sleep deprivation is torture: prolonged sleep deprivation is a cruel and useless method of interrogation. *Psychology Today.* Retrieved 15 December 2014 from http://www.psychologytoday. com/blog/dreaming-in-the-digital-age/201412/ why-sleep-deprivation-is-torture.

Burger, J.M. (1992). *Desire for Control: Personality, Social and Clinical Perspectives.* New York: Plenum.

Burt, C. (1911). Experimental tests of higher mental processes and their relation to general intelligence. *Journal of Experimental Pedagogy and Training, 1,* 93–112.

Buss, D. (1989). Sex differences in human mate preferences: evolutionary hypotheses tested in 37 cultures. *Behavioural and Brain Sciences, 12,* 1–14.

Buss, D.M. (2000). *The Dangerous Passion: Why Jealousy is as Necessary as Love and Sex.* New York: Simon and Schuster.

Byrne, R.W. and Corp, N. (2004). Neocortex size predicts deception rate in primates. *Proceedings of the Royal Society of London B, 271,* 1693–1699.

Cacioppo, J.T. and Hawkley, L.C. (2009). Perceived social isolation and cognition. *Trends in Cognitive Science, 13,* 447–454.

Calhoun, J. B. (1962). Population density and social pathology. *Scientific American, 206,* 139–148.

Caldera, Y.M., Huston, A.C. and O'Brien, M. (1989). Social interactions and play patterns of parents and toddlers with feminine, masculine, and neutral toys. *Child Development, 60,* 70–76.

Cannon, W.B. (1927). The James-Lange theory of emotions: a critical examination and an alternative theory. *American Journal of Psychology, 39,* 106–124.

Carlson, N. (1998). *Physiology of Behaviour* (5th edn). Boston: Allyn and Bacon.

Catania, A.C. (1992). *Learning* (3rd edn). Englewood Cliffs: Prentice Hall.

Cattell, R.B. (1971). *Abilities: Their Structure, Growth, and Action.* New York: Houghton Mifflin.

Cepeda, N.J., Vul, E., Rohrer, D., Wixted, J.T. and Pashler, H. (2008). Spacing effects in learning: a temporal ridgeline of optimal retention. *Psychological Science, 19,* 1095–1102.

Chartrand, T.L. and Bargh, J. (1999). The chameleon effect: The perception-behaviour link and social interaction. *Journal of Personality and Social Psychology, 76,* 893–910.

Chomsky, A.N. (1959). A review of Skinner's verbal behavior. *Language, 35,* 26–58.

Clayton, R.B. (2014). The third wheel: The impact of twitter use on relationship infidelity and divorce. *Cyberpsychology, Behavior, and Social Networking, 17,* 425–430.

Cohen, C.E. (1981). Person categories and social perception: testing some boundaries of the processing effects of prior knowledge. *Journal of Personality and Social Psychology, 40*, 441–452.

Cohen, F., Tyrrell, D.A.J. and Smith, A.P. (1991). Psychological stress and susceptibility to the common cold. *New England Journal of Medicine, 325*, 606–612.

Cohen, S., Evans, G.W., Krantz, D.S. and Stokols, D. (1980). Physiological, motivational, and cognitive effects of aircraft noise on children: moving from the laboratory to the field. *American Psychologist, 35*, 231.

Cohen, S., Janicki-Deverts, D., Turner, R.B. and Doyle, W.J. (2015). Does hugging provide stress-buffering social support? A study of susceptibility to upper respiratory infection and illness. *Psychological Science, 26*, 135–147.

Colman, A.M. (1987). *Facts, Fallacies and Frauds in Psychology*. London: Routledge.

Colten, M.E. and Gore, S. (1991). *Adolescent Stress: Causes and Consequences*. Piscataway: Transaction Publishing.

Cook, M. (1978). *Perceiving Others*. London: Routledge.

Corbett Burris, C. and Garrity, D.T. (2008). *Detracking for Excellence and Equity*. Alexandria: Association for Supervision and Curriculum Development.

Coren, S. (1998). Sleep deprivation, psychosis and mental efficiency. *Psychiatric Times, 15*, 1–3.

Cox, T. (1978). *Stress*. Macmillan: London.

Cutrona, C.E. (1996). *Social Support in Couples: Marriage as a Resource in Times of Stress*. Thousand Oaks: Sage Publications.

Craik, F.I.M. and Watkins, M.J. (1973). The role of rehearsal in short-term memory. *Journal of Verbal Learning and Verbal Behavior, 12*, 599–607.

Craik, F.I.M. and Tulving, E. (1975). Depth of processing and the retention of words in episodic memory. *Journal of Experimental Psychology: General, 104*, 268–294.

Crick, F. and Mitchison, G. (1983). The function of dream sleep. *Nature, 304*, 111–114.

Crystal, D. (1997). *The Cambridge Encyclopedia of Language*. Cambridge: Cambridge University Press.

Czeisler, C., Johnson, M.P., Duffy, J.F., Brown, E.N., Ronda, J.M. and Kronauer, R.E. (1990). Exposure to bright light and darkness to treat physiologic maladaption to night work. *The New England Journal of Medicine, 322*, 1253–1259.

Dalal, P.K. and Sivakumar, T. (2009). Moving towards ICD-11 and DSM-V: concept and evolution of psychiatric classification. *Indian Journal of Psychiatry, 51*, 310.

Dartnell, L. (2014). *The Knowledge*. London: Bodley Head.

Davies, G. and Hine, S. (2007). Change blindness and eyewitness testimony. *The Journal of Psychology, 141*, 423–434.

De Gelder, B. (2006). Towards the neurobiology of emotional body language. *Nature Reviews Neuroscience, 7*, 242–249.

De Geus, E.J.C. and Van Doornen, L.J.P. (1993). The effects of fitness training on the physiological stress response. *Work and Stress, 7*, 141–159.

DeLongis, A., Coyne, J.C., Dakof, G., Folkman, S. and Lazarus, R.S. (1982). The impact of daily hassles, uplifts and major life events to health status. *Health Psychology, 1*, 119–136.

Dement, W. and Kleitman, N. (1957). The relation of eye movements during sleep to dream activity: an objective method for the study of dreaming. *Journal of Experimental Psychology, 53*, 339–346.

De Ruiter, J., Weston, G. and Lyon, S.M. (2011). Dunbar's number: group size and brain physiology in humans reexamined. *American Anthropologist, 113*, 557–568.

DeScioli, P. and Kurzban, R. (2009). The alliance hypothesis for human friendship. *PloS One, 4*, e5802.

DeSteno, D., Breazeal, C., Frank, R.H, Pizarro, D., Baumann, J., Dickens, L. and Lee, J.J. (2012). Detecting the trustworthiness of novel partners in economic exchange. *Psychological Science, 23*, 1549–1556.

Deutsch, M. and Gerrard, H.B. (1955). A study of normative and informational influence upon individual judgement. *Journal of Abnormal and Social Psychology, 51*, 629–636.

Devlin, Rt. Hon. Lord Patrick (Chair) (1976). *Report to the Secretary of State for the Home Department of the Departmental Committee on evidence of identification in criminal cases. PP.XIX. No. 338.* London: Her Majesty's Stationery Office.

Diamond, L.M., Hicks, A.M. and Otter-Henderson, K.D. (2008). Every time you go away: changes in affect, behavior, and physiology associated with travel-related separations from romantic partners. *Journal of Personality and Social Psychology, 95*, 385.

Doidge, N. (2007). *The Brain That Changes Itself*. New York: Viking.

Dollard, J. and Miller, N.E. (1950). *Personality and Psychotherapy*. New York: McGraw-Hill.

Domhoff, G.W. (2005). The content of dreams: methodologic and theoretical implications. In M.H. Kryger, T. Roth and W.C. Dement (Eds.), *Principles and Practices of Sleep Medicine* (4th edn). Philadelphia: W.B. Saunders, 522–534.

Domhoff, G.W. (2011). Dreams are embodied simulations that dramatize conception and concerns: the continuity hypothesis in empirical, theoretical, and historical context. *International Journal of Dream Research, 4*, 50–62.

Domhoff, G.W., Meyer-Gomez, K. and Schredl, M. (2006). Dreams as the expression of conceptions and concerns: a comparison of German and American college students. *Imagination, Cognition and Personality, 25*, 269–282.

Duck, S. (1998). *Human Relationships* (3rd edn). London: Sage Publications.

Duggan, F., Lee, A.S. and Murray, R.M. (1990). Does personality predict long-term outcome in depression? *British Journal of Psychiatry, 157*, 19–24.

Dunbar, R.I.M. (1992). Neocortex size as a constraint on group size in primates. *Journal of Human Evolution, 22*, 469–493.

Dunbar, R.I.M. (1993). Coevolution of neocortical size, group size and language in humans. *Behavioural and Brain Sciences, 16*, 681–735.

Dunbar, R.I.M. (1996). *Grooming, Gossip and the Evolution of Language.* Cambridge: Harvard University Press.

Dunbar, R.I.M. (1998). The social brain hypothesis. *Brain, 9*, 178–190.

Duncan, J., Seitz., R.J., Kolodny, J., Bor, D., Herzog, H., Ahmed, A., Newell, F.N. and Emslie, H. (2000). A neural basis for general intelligence. *Science, 289*, 457–459.

Dutton, D.G. and Aron, A.P. (1974). Some evidence for heightened sexual attraction under conditions of high anxiety. *Journal of Personality and Social Psychology, 30*, 510–517.

Dweck, C.S. (2006). *Mindset: How You Can Fulfil Your Potential.* London: Robinson Books.

Dweck, C.S. (2007). The perils and promises of praise. *Early Intervention at Every Age, 65*, 34–39.

Eagly, A.H. (1987). *Sex Differences in Social Behaviour: A Social-Role Interpretation.* Hillsdale: Lawrence Erlbaum.

Efron, D. (1941). *Gesture, Race and Culture: A Tentative Study of the Spatio-temporal and 'Linguistic' Aspects of the Gestural Behavior of Eastern Jews and Southern Italians in New York City, Living under Similar as well as Different Environmental Conditions.* The Hague: Mouton.

Ekirch, A.R. (2006). *At Day's Close: Night in Times Past.* New York: Norton.

Ekman, P. (1999). Basic Emotions. In T. Dalgleish and M. Power (Eds.), *Handbook of Cognition and Emotion.* Sussex: Wiley.

Ekman, P. (2009a). Lie catching and microexpressions. In C.W. Martin (Ed.), *The Philosophy of Deception.* New York: OUP USA, 118–133.

Ekman, P. (2009b). Darwin's contributions to our understanding of emotional expressions. *Philosophical Transactions of the Royal Society of London B - Biological Sciences, 364*, 3449–3451.

Ekman, P. and Friesen, W.V. (1971). Constants across cultures in the face and emotion. *Journal of Personality and Social Psychology, 17*, 124–129.

Elliott, J. (1977). The power and pathology of prejudice. In P.G. Zimbardo and F.L. Ruch (Eds.), *Psychology and Life* (9th edn). Glenview: Scott, Foresman.

Ellis, A. and Grieger, R. (1977). *Handbook of Rational-Emotive Therapy.* New York: Springer.

Ellis, A. (2003). Early theories and practices of rational emotive behavior therapy and how they have been augmented and revised during the last three decades. *Journal of Rational-Emotive and Cognitive-Behavior Therapy, 21*, 219–243.

Ellis, N.C. and Hennelly, R.A. (1980). A bilingual word-length effect: Implications for intelligence testing and the relative ease of mental calculation in Welsh and English. *British Journal of Psychology, 71*, 43–51.

Eriksson, P.S., Perfilieva, E., Björk-Eriksson, T., Alborn, A., Nordborg, C., Peterson, D.A. and Gage, F.H. (1998). Neurogenesis in the adult human hippocampus. *Nature Medicine, 4*, 1313–1317.

Evans, G. and Johnson, D. (2000). Stress and open-office noise. *Journal of Applied Psychology, 85*, 779–783.

Evans, G.W., Lercher, P., Meis, M., Ising, H. and Kofler, W.W. (2001). Community noise exposure and stress in children. *Journal of the Acoustical Society of America, 109*, 1023.

Eysenck, M.W. (1986). Working memory. In G. Cohen, M.W. Eysenck and M.A. Le Voi (Eds.), *Memory: A Cognitive Approach.* Milton Keynes: Open University Press.

Fagan, J.F. (1976). Infants' recognition of invariant features of faces. *Child Development, 47*, 627–638.

Fayol, M. and Monteil, J. (1988). The notion of script: from general to developmental and social psychology. *Cahiers de Psychologie Cognitive/Current Psychology of Cognition, 8*, 335–361.

Felipe, N.J. and Sommer, R. (1966). Invasions of personal space. *Social problems, 14*, 206–214.

Fisher, S. and Greenberg, R.P. (1996). *Freud Scientifically Reappraised: Testing the Theories and the Therapy.* New York: Wiley.

Fiske, S.T. and Linville, P.W. (1980). What does the schema concept buy us? *Personality and Social Psychology Bulletin, 6*, 543–557.

Fiske, S.T., Cuddy, A.J. and Glick, P. (2007). Universal dimensions of social cognition: warmth and competence. *Trends in Cognitive Sciences, 11*, 77–83.

Fiske, S.T. and Taylor, S.E. (1991). *Social Cognition.* New York: McGraw-Hill.

Fleshner, M. (2000). Exercise and neuroendocrine regulation of antibody production: protective effect of physical activity on stress-induced suppression of the specific antibody response. *International Journal of Sports Medicine, 21*, 14–15.

Flynn, J.R. (1984). The mean IQ of Americans: massive gains 1932 to 1978. *Psychological Bulletin, 95*, 29–51.

Folkman, S., Lazarus, R.S., Dunkel-Schetter, C., DeLongis, A. and Gruen, R.J. (1986). Dynamics of a stressful encounter: cognitive appraisal, coping, and encounter outcomes. *Journal of Personality and Social Psychology, 50*, 992–1003.

Forward, S. (1997). *Emotional Blackmail: When the People in Your Life Use Fear, Obligation and Guilt to Manipulate You*. London: Transworld.

Frankenhauser, M., Dunne, E. and Lundberg, U. (1976). Sex-differences in sympathetic-adrenal medullary reactions induced by different stressors. *Psychopharmacology, 47*, 1–5.

Freedman, J. L. (1975). *Crowding and Behavior*. San Francisco: Freeman.

Freud, S. (1900/1991). *The Interpretation of Dreams*. In *The Complete Psychological Works of Sigmund Freud*, Vol. 4. London: Penguin Books.

Freud, S. (1909/2002). Analysis of a phobia in a five year old boy. In *The 'Wolfman' and Other Cases* (Penguin Modern Classics). London: Penguin Books.

Freud, S. (1910). The origin and development of psychoanalysis. *American Journal of Psychology, 21*, 181–218.

Freud, S. (1933/1965*). New Introductory Lectures on Psychoanalysis*. Standard Edition. New York: Norton.

Friedman, M. and Rosenman, R.H. (1974). *Type A Behaviour and Your Heart*. New York: Harper Row.

Fujimoto, D.T. (2007). Listener responses in interaction: A case for abandoning the term, backchannel. *Journal of Osaka Jogakuin College, 37*, 35–54.

Furley, P. and Schweizer, G. (2014). The expression of victory and loss: estimating who's leading or trailing from nonverbal cues in sports. *Journal of Nonverbal Behavior, 38*, 13–29.

Fyock, J. and Stangor, C. (1994). The role of memory biases in stereotype maintenance. *British Journal of Social Psychology, 33*, 331–343.

Gaab, J., Rohleder, N., Nater, U.M. and Ehlert, U. (2005). Psychological determinants of the cortisol stress response: the role of anticipatory cognitive appraisal. *Psychoneuroendocrinology, 30*, 599–610.

Gardner, H. (1983). *Frames of Mind: The Theory of Multiple Intelligences*. New York: Basic Books.

Gardner, H. (2006). On failing to grasp the core of MI theory: A response to Visser *et al*. *Intelligence, 34*, 503–505.

Gathercole, S.E. and Baddeley, A.D. (1990) Phonological memory deficits in language disordered children: is there a causal connection? *Journal of Memory and Language, 29*, 336–360.

Geiselman, R., Fisher, R., Mackinnon, D. and Holland, H.L. (1985). Enhancement of eyewitness testimony with the cognitive interview. *American Journal of Psychology, 99*, 385–401.

Gladwell, M. (2010). *What the Dog Saw*. London: Penguin.

Glanzer, M. and Cunitz, A.R. (1966). Two storage mechanisms in free recall. *Journal of Verbal Learning and Verbal Behaviour, 5*, 351–360.

Glass, D.C., Singer, J.E. and Friedman, L.N. (1969). Psychic cost of adaptation to an environmental stressor. *Journal of Personality and Social Psychology, 12*, 200–210.

Glassman, W.E. (2000). *Approaches to Psychology* (3rd edn). Buckingham: Open University Press.

Glick, P. and Fiske, S.T. (2001). An ambivalent alliance: Hostile and benevolent sexism as complementary justifications for gender inequality. *American Psychologist, 56*, 109–118.

Goldacre, B. (2012). *Bad Pharma*. London: Fourth Estate.

Goldfarb, W. (1953). Emotional and intellectual consequences of psychologic deprivation in infancy: a revaluation. In *Proceedings of the Annual Meeting of the American Psychopathological Association*, 105–119.

Goldstein, D.S. and Kopin, I.J. (2007). Evolution of concepts of stress. *Stress, 10*, 109–120.

Gonçalves, B., Perra, N. and Vespignani, A. (2011). Modeling users' activity on twitter networks: validation of Dunbar's number. *PLoS One, 6*: e22656.

Good, C., Aronson, J. and Inzlicht, M. (2003). Improving adolescents' standardized test performance: An intervention to reduce the effects of stereotype threat. *Applied Developmental Psychology, 24*, 645–662.

Goodwin, R. (1999). *Personal Relationships Across Cultures*. London: Routledge.

Gordon, G. and Breazeal, C. (2014). *Learning to Maintain Engagement: No One Leaves a Sad DragonBot*. In Arlington: 2014 AAAI Fall Symposium Series.

Gordon, I., Zagoory-Sharon, O., Leckman, J.F. and Feldman, R. (2010). Oxytocin and the development of parenting in humans. *Biological Psychiatry, 68*, 377–382.

Gottfredson, L.S. (1998). The general intelligence factor. *Scientific American Presents, 9*, 24–29.

Gottfredson, L.S. (2003). Dissecting practical intelligence theory: Its claims and evidence. *Intelligence, 31*: 343–397.

Gould, S.J. (1982). A nation of morons. *New Scientist, 6*, 349–352.

Grant, D. and Williams, D. (2011). The importance of perceiving social contexts when predicting crime and antisocial behaviour in CCTV images. *Legal and Criminological Psychology, 16*, 307–322.

Griffin, A. (2015). Artificial intelligence will become strong and threaten us, says Bill Gates, as he details new AI-driven personal assistant. *The Independent*. Retrieved 29 January 2015 from http://www.independent.co.uk/life-style/gadgets-and-tech/news/artificial-intelligence-will-become-strong-and-threaten-us-says-bill-gates-10010988.html.

Gueguen, N. (2009). Mimicry and seduction: An evaluation in a courtship context. *Social Influence, 4*, 249–255.

Guilford, J.P. (1967). *The Nature of Human Intelligence.* New York: McGraw-Hill.

Gujar, N., McDonald, S., Nishida, M. and Walker, M. (2010). A role for REM sleep in recalibrating the sensitivity of the human brain to specific emotions. *Cerebral Cortex, 21*, 115–123.

Halasz *et al.*, 1985, cited by Carlson, N. (1998). *Physiology of Behaviour* (5th edn). Boston: Allyn and Bacon.

Hammen, C. and Goodman-Brown, T. (1990). Self-schemas and vulnerability to specific life stress in children at risk for depression. *Cognitive Therapy and Research, 14*, 215–227.

Harlow, H. F. (1959). Love in infant monkeys. *Scientific American, 200*, 688–674.

Hart, B. and Risely, T. (1995) *Meaningful Differences in Everyday Parenting and Intellectual Development in Young American Children*. Baltimore: Brookes.

Haslam, S.A., Jetten, J., Postmes, T. and Haslam, C. (2009). Social identity, health and well-being: an emerging agenda for applied psychology. *Applied Psychology: An International Review, 58*, 1–23.

Hassan, S. (2012). *Freedom of Mind: Helping Loved Ones Leave Controlling People, Cults, and Beliefs* [Kindle DX version]. Retrieved from Amazon.com.

Hazan, C. and Shaver, P.R. (1987). Romantic love conceptualised as an attachment process. *Journal of Personality and Social Psychology, 52*, 511–524.

Hazan, C. and Zeifman, D. (1999). Pair bonds as attachments: evaluating the evidence. In J. Cassidy and P.R. Shaver (Eds.), *Handbook of Attachment: Theory, Research and Clinical Applications*, 336–354.

Hebb, D.O. (1949). *The Organization of Behavior.* New York: John Wiley and Sons.

Heider, F. (1958). *The Psychology of Interpersonal Relations* (1st edn). New York: John Wiley and Sons.

Henn, B.M., Gignoux, C.R., Jobin, M., Granka, J.M., Macpherson, J.M., Kidd, J.M., Rodríguez-Botigué, L., Ramachandran, S., Honf, L., Brisbin, A., Lin, A.A., Underhill, P.A., Comas, D., Kidd, K.K., Norman, P.J., Parham, P., Bustamante, C.D., Mountain, J.L. and Feldman, M.W. (2011). Hunter-gatherer genomic diversity suggests a southern African origin for modern humans. *Proceedings of the National Academy of Sciences, 108*, 5154–5162.

Herculano-Houzel, S. (2012). The remarkable, yet not extraordinary, human brain as a scaled-up primate brain and its associated cost. *Proceedings of the National Academy of Sciences, 109(Suppl. 1)*, 10661–10668.

Hewstone, M., Rubin, M. and Willis, H. (2002). Intergroup bias. *Annual Review of Psychology, 53*, 575–604.

Hill, R.A. and Dunbar, R.I. (2003). Social network size in humans. *Human Nature, 14*, 53–72.

Hobson, J.A. (2005). Sleep is of the brain, by the brain and for the brain. *Nature, 437*, 1254–1256.

Hobson, J.A. and McCarley, R.W. (1977). The brain as a dream state generator: an activation-synthesis hypothesis of the dream process. *The American Journal of Psychiatry, 134*, 1335–1348.

Hodgman, C. (2010). The rise and fall of the workhouse. *BBC History Extra*. Retrieved 21 February 2015 from http://www.historyextra.com/workhouse.

Hofling, C.K., Brotzman, E., Dalrymple, S., Graves, N. and Pierce, C.M. (1966). An experimental study in nurse-physician relationships. *Journal of Nervous and Mental Disease, 143*, 171–180.

Hogg, M.A. and Abrams, D. (1988). *Social Identifications: A Social Psychology of Intergroup Relations and Group Processes*. London: Routledge.

Holland, R.W., Roeder, U., van Baaren, R.B., Brandt, A.C. and Hannover, B. (2004). Don't stand so close to me: the effects of self-construal on interpersonal closeness. *Psychological Science, 15*, 237–242.

Holt-Lunstad, J., Smith, T.B. and Layton, J.B. (2010). Social relationships and mortality risk: a meta-analytic review. *PLoS Med, 7*: e1000316.

Holz, J., Piosczyk, H., Landmann, N., Feige, B., Spiegelhalder, K., Riemann, D., Nissen, C. and Voderholzer, U. (2012). The timing of learning before night-time sleep differentially affects declarative and procedural long-term memory consolidation in adolescents. *PLoS One, 7*, e40963.

Horn, J.M. (1983). The Texas Adoption Project: adopted children and their intellectual resemblance to biological and adoptive parents. *Child Development, 54*, 266–275.

Horne, J.A. (1978). A review of the biological effects of total sleep deprivation in man. *Biological Psychology, 7*, 55–102.

Horne, J.A. and Harley, L.J. (1988). Human SWS following selective head heating during wakefulness. In: J.A. Horne (Ed.), *Sleep '88*. Stuttgart: Fischer Verlag, 188–190.

Hornsey, M.J., Spears, R., Cremers, I. and Hogg, M.A. (2003). Relations between high and low power groups: the importance of legitimacy. *Personality and Social Psychology Bulletin, 29*, 216–227.

Horwitz, A. (2007). Transforming normality into pathology: the DSM and the outcomes of stressful social arrangements. *Journal of Health and Social Behavior, 48*, 211a222.

Howitt, D., Billig, M., Cramer, D. and Edwards, D. (1989). *Social Psychology: Conflicts and Continuities*. New York: McGraw-Hill International.

Humphrey, L.L. (1989). Observed family interactions among subtypes of eating disorders using structural analysis of social behavior. *Journal of Consulting and Clinical Psychology, 57*, 206–214.

James, O. (2002). *They F*** You Up: How to Survive Family Life*. London: Bloomsbury.

Janis, I.L. (1972). *Victims of Groupthink: A Psychological Study of Foreign-Policy Decisions and Fiascoes*. Oxford: Houghton Mifflin.

Jenness, A. (1932). The role of discussion in changing opinion regarding matter of fact. *Journal of Abnormal and Social Psychology, 27*, 279–296.

Jewkes, R. (2002). Intimate partner violence: causes and prevention. *The Lancet, 359*, 1423–1429.

Johansson, G., Aronsson, G. and Lindstrom, B.O. (1978). Social psychological and neuroendocrine stress reactions in highly mechanised work. *Ergonomics, 21*, 583–99.

Jones, F. and Bright, J. (2001). *Stress: Myth, Theory and Research*. Harlow: Pearson.

Jones, H.E. and Bayley, N. (1941). The Berkeley Growth Study. *Child Development, 12*, 167–173.

Jones, S.S. (2009). The development of imitation in infancy. *Philosophical Transactions of the Royal Society B: Biological Sciences, 364*, 2325–2335.

Joseph, J. (2001) Separated twins and the genetics of personality differences: a critique. *American Journal of Psychology, 114*, 1–30.

Joseph, J. (2012). The 'missing heritability' of psychiatric disorders: elusive genes or non-existent genes? *Applied Developmental Science, 16*, 65–83.

Jourard, S.M. (1966). An exploratory study of body – accessibility. *British Journal of Social and Clinical Psychology, 5*, 221–231.

Judd, C.M. and Park, B. (1988). Out-group homogeneity: judgments of variability at the individual and group levels. *Journal of Personality and Social Psychology, 54*, 778–788.

Jung, C.G. (1910). The association method. *American Journal of Psychology, 31*, 219–269.

Jung, C.G. (1961). *Freud and Psychoanalysis. Collected Works*, Vol. 4. New York: Pantheon.

Jung, C.G. (1964). *Man and his Symbols*. New York: Dell.

Kandel, E.R. and Hawkins, R.D. (1992). The biological basis of learning and individuality. *Scientific American 267*, 78–86.

Kapler, I.V., Weston, T. and Wiseheart, M. (2015). Spacing in a simulated undergraduate classroom: Long-term benefits for factual and higher-level learning. *Learning and Instruction, 36*, 38–45.

Karlins, M., Coffman, T.L. and Walters, G. (1969). On the fading of social stereotypes: Studies in three generations of college students. *Journal of Personality and Social Psychology, 13*, 1–16.

Kayaoglu, A., Batur, S. and Aslitürk, E. (2014). The unknown Muzafer Sherif. *The Psychologist, 27*, 830–833.

Kelman, H. (1958). Compliance, internalisation and identification: three processes of attitude change. *Journal of Conflict Resolution, 2*, 51–60.

Kempermann, G., Kuhn H.G. and Gage, F.H. (1997). More hippocampal neurons in adult mice living in an enriched environment. *Nature, 386*, 493–495.

Kendon, A. and Cook, M. (1969). The consistency of gaze patterns in social interaction. *British Journal of Psychology, 60*, 481–494.

Kiecolt-Glaser, J.K., Garner, W., Speicher, C.E., Penn, G.M., Holliday, J. and Glaser, R. (1984). Psychosocial modifiers of immunocompetence in medical students. *Psychosomatic Medicine, 46*, 7–14.

Kiecolt-Glaser, J.K., Marucha, P.T., Malarkey, W.B., Mercado, A.M. and Glaser, R. (1995). Slowing of wound healing by psychological stress. *The Lancet, 346*, 1194–1196.

Kilham, W. and Mann, L. (1974). Level of destructive obedience as a function of transmitter and executant roles in the Milgram obedience paradigm. *Journal of Personality and Social Psychology, 29(5)*, 696-702.

Kim, J. (2015). Who is most likely to cheat? Five types of people who tend to be unfaithful. *Psychology Today*. Retrieved 22 February 2015 from https://www.psychologytoday.com/blog/valley-girl-brain/201502/who-is-most-likely-cheat.

Kohlberg, L. (1969). *Stages in the Development of Moral Thought and Action*. New York: Holt.

Krauss Whitbourne, S. (2011). The essential guide to defense mechanisms: can you spot your favorite form of self-deception? Retrieved 12 November 2014 from http://www.psychologytoday.com/blog/fulfillment-any-age/201110/the-essential-guide-defense-mechanisms.

Krauss Whitbourne, S. (2012). The ultimate guide to body language. *Psychology Today*. Retrieved 22 January 2015 from http://www.psychologytoday.com/blog/fulfillment-any-age/201206/the-ultimate-guide-body-language.

Kris, A.O. (1997). *Free Association: Methods and Process: Method and Process*. London: Routledge.

Kruijshaar, M.E., Barendregt, J., Vos, T., de Graaf, R., Spijker, J. and Andrews, G. (2005). Lifetime prevalence estimates of major depression: an indirect estimation method and a quantification of recall bias. *European Journal of Epidemiology, 20*, 103–111.

Kulik, J.A. and Kulik, C.C. (1992). Meta-analytic findings on grouping programs. *Gifted Children Quarterly, 36*, 73–77.

Laar, C.V., Levin, S., Sinclair, S. and Sidanius, J. (2005). The effect of university roommate contact on ethnic attitudes and behaviour. *Journal of Experimental and Social Psychology, 41*, 329–345.

Laing, R.D. (1967). *The Politics of Experience and the Bird of Paradise*. London: Penguin Books.

Lamb, M.E. (1981). The development of father-infant relationships. In M.E. Lamb (Ed.), *The Role of the Father in Child Development*. New York: Wiley.

Lang, P.J. and Lazovik, A.D. (1963). Experimental desensitisation of a phobia. *Journal of Abnormal and Social Psychology, 66*, 519–525.

Langlois, J.H. and Roggman, L.A. (1990). Attractive faces are only average. *Psychological Science, 1*, 115–121.

LaPiere, R.T. (1934). Attitudes versus actions. *Social Forces, 13*, 230–237.

Lazarus, R.S. (1990). Theory-based stress measurement. *Psychological Inquiry, 1*, 3–13.

Lazarus, R.S. (1995). Psychological stress in the workplace. In R. Crandall and P.L. Perrewe (Eds.), *Occupational Stress: A Handbook* (Series in Health Psychology and Behavioral Medicine). London: Taylor and Francis.

Lazarus, R.S. and Folkman, S. (1984). *Stress, Appraisal and Coping*. New York: Springer.

Leathers, J. (2005). Separation from siblings: Associations with placement adaptation and outcomes among adolescents in long-term foster care. *Children and Youth Services Review, 27*, 793–819.

Lehner, P., Seyed-Solorforough, M., Nallappa, B., O'Conner, M., Sak, S. and Mullin, T. (1992). Cognitive biases and time stress in team decision making. *IEEE Transactions on Systems, Man and Cybernetics, Part A: Systems and Humans, 27*, 698–703.

Lesku, J.A., Robb, T.C., Rattenborg, N.C., Amlaner, C.J. and Lima, S.L (2008). Phylogenetics and the correlates of mammalian sleep: a reappraisal. *Sleep Medicine Reviews, 12*, 229–244.

Levinger, G. and Clark, J. (1961). Emotional factors in the forgetting of word associations. *Journal of Abnormal and Social Psychology, 62*, 99–105.

Lindzey, G., Hall, C.S. and Thompson, R.F. (1978). *Psychology* (2nd edn). New York: Worth Publishers.

Liu, W.C., Wang, C.K.J. and Parkins, E.J. (2005). A longitudinal study of students' academic self-concept in a streamed setting: the Singapore context. *British Journal of Educational Psychology, 75*, 567–586.

Loftus, E.F., Loftus, G.R. and Messo, J. (1987). Some facts about 'weapon focus'. *Law and Human Behavior, 11*, 55–62.

Loftus, E.F. and Palmer, J.C. (1974). Reconstruction of automobile destruction: an example of the interaction between language and memory. *Journal of Verbal Learning and Verbal Behaviour, 13*, 585–589.

Lømo, T. (2003). The discovery of long-term potentiation. *Philosophical Transactions of the Royal Society of London. Series B: Biological Sciences, 358*, 617–620.

Long, B.C. and Flood, K.R. (1993). Coping with work stress: psychological benefits of exercise. *Work and Stress, 1*, 109–119.

McDaniel, M.A., Roediger, H.L. and McDermott, K.B. (2007). Generalizing test-enhanced learning from the laboratory to the classroom. *Psychonomic Bulletin and Review, 14*, 200–206.

McEwen, B.S. and Sapolsky, R.M. (1995). Stress and cognitive function. *Current Opinion in Neurobiology, 5*, 205–216.

McGuffin, P., Katz, R., Rutherford, J. and Watkins, S. (1996). The heritability of DSM-IV unipolar depression: a hospital based twin register study. *Archives of General Psychiatry, 53*, 129–136.

McNamara, P. (2012). The fatal lure of the continuity hypothesis: dreams do not merely reflect waking life. *Psychology Today*. Retrieved 4 March 2015 from https://www.psychologytoday.com/blog/dream-catcher/201212/the-fatal-lure-the-continuity-hypothesis.

McNeill, D. (1992). *Hand and Mind: What Gestures Reveal About Thought*. Chicago: University of Chicago Press.

Maguire, E.A., Gadian, D.G., Johnsrude, I.S., Good, C.D., Ashburner, J., Frackowiak, R.S.J. and Frith, C.D. (2000) Navigation-related structural change in the hippocampi of taxi drivers. *Proceedings of the National Academy of Sciences of the United States of America, 97*, 4398–4403.

Mann, J.H. (1959). The relationship between cognitive, affective, and behavioral aspects of racial prejudice. *The Journal of Social Psychology, 49*, 223–228.

Marazziti, D. and Canale, D. (2004). Hormonal changes when falling in love. *Psychoneuroendocrinology, 29*, 931 936.

March, J.S., Silva, S., Petrycki, S., Curry, J., Wells, K., Fairbank, J., Burns, B., Domino, M., McNulty, S., Vitiello, B. and Severe, J. (2007). The treatment for adolescents with depression study (TADS): long-term effectiveness and safety outcomes. *Archives of General Psychiatry, 64*, 1132e1143.

Marmot, M. G., Bosma, H., Hemingway, H., Brunner, E. and Stansfeld, S. (1997). Contribution of job control and other risk factors to social variations in coronary heart disease incidence. *The Lancet, 350*, 235–239.

Marsh, R.L., Hicks, J.L. and Cook, G.I. (2005). On the relationship between effort toward an ongoing task and cue detection in event-based prospective memory. *Journal of Experimental Psychology: Learning, Memory, and Cognition, 31*, 68–75.

Marsh, R.L., Hicks, J.L. and Landau, J.D. (1998). An investigation of everyday prospective memory. *Memory and Cognition, 26*, 633–643.

Maslow, A.H. (1943). A theory of human motivation. *Psychological Review, 50*, 370–396.

Matsumoto, D. (1989). Cultural differences of the perception of emotion. *Journal of Cross-Cultural Psychology, 20*, 92–105.

Matsumoto, D. and Kudoh, T. (1993). American-Japanese cultural differences in attributions of personality based on smiles. *Journal of Nonverbal Behavior, 17*, 231–243.

Mednick, S., Nakayama, K. and Stickgold, R. (2003). Sleep-dependent learning: a nap is as good as a night. *Nature Neuroscience, 6*, 697–698.

Meichenbaum, D. (2007). Stress inoculation training: a preventative and treatment approach. In P.M. Lehrer, R.L. Woolfolk and W.E. Sime (Eds.), *Principles and Practice of Stress Management* (3rd edn). New York: Guilford Press.

Meloen, J.D. (1993). The F scale as a predictor of fascism: an overview of 40 years of authoritarianism research. In W.F. Stone, G. Lederer and R. Christie (Eds.), *Strength and Weakness: The Authoritarian Personality Today*. New York: Springer-Verlag, 47–69.

Meltzoff, A.N. and Moore, M.K. (1977). Imitation of facial and manual gestures by human neonates. *Science, 198*, 75–78.

Messinger, D.S., Fogel, A. and Dickson, K. (2001). All smiles are positive, but some smiles are more positive than others. *Developmental Psychology, 37*, 642–653.

Middlemist, R.D., Knowles, E.S. and Matter, C.F. (1976). Personal space invasions in the lavatory: suggestive evidence for arousal. *Journal of Personality and Social Psychology, 33*, 541–546.

Milgram, S. (1963). Behavioural study of obedience. *Journal of Abnormal and Social Psychology, 67*, 371–378.

Milgram, S. (1974). *Obedience to Authority*. New York: Harper and Row.

Miller, G. A. (1956). The magical number seven, plus or minus two: Some limits on our capacity for processing information. *Psychological Review, 63*, 343–355.

Miller, K. (2005). *Communication Theories*. New York: McGraw Hill.

Milner, B. (1970). Memory and the medial temporal regions of the brain. *Biology of Memory, 23*, 31–59.

Mischel, W., Ebbeson, E.B. and Raskoff Zeiss, A. (1972). Cognitive and attentional mechanisms in delay of gratification. *Journal of Personality and Social Psychology, 21*, 204–218.

Mori, K. and Arai, M. (2010). No need to fake it: reproduction of the Asch experiment without confederates. *International Journal of Psychology, 45*, 390–397.

Morris, D. (1967). *The Naked Ape*. London: Jonathan Cape.

Morris, P.E., Tweedy, M. and Gruneberg, M.M. (1985). Interest, knowledge, and the memorising of soccer scores. *British Journal of Psychology, 76*, 415–425.

Moscovici, S. (1981). On social representations. In J.P. Forgas (Ed.), *Social Cognition: Perspectives in Everyday Understanding*. London: Academic Press.

Moscovici, S., Lage, E. and Naffrechoux, M. (1969). Influence of a consistent minority on the responses of a majority in a color perception task. *Sociometry, 32*, 365–380.

Mowrer, O.H. (1939). A stimulus-response analysis of anxiety and its role as a reinforcing agent. *Psychological Review, 46*, 553–565.

Mumford, D.B., Whitehouse, A.M. and Plattes, M. (1991). Sociocultural correlates of eating disorders among Asian schoolgirls in Bradford. *British Journal of Psychiatry, 158*, 222–228.

Münsterberg, H. (1908). *On the Witness Stand: Essays on Psychology and Crime*. New York: Doubleday.

Murray, C.J. and Lopez, A.D. (1997). Alternative projections of mortality and disability by cause 1990–2020: Global burden of disease study. *The Lancet, 349*, 1498–1504.

Murray, D.J. (1968). Articulation and acoustic confusability in short-term memory. *Journal of Experimental Psychology, 78*, 679–684.

Murstein, B.I. (1972). Physical attractiveness and marital choice. *Journal of Personality and Social Psychology, 22*, 8–12.

Navarro, J. (2014). 9 Truths exposing a myth about body language: don't judge too quickly; crossing one's arms can signal many different things. *Psychology Today*. Retrieved 21 January 2015 from https://www.psychologytoday.com/blog/spycatcher/201410/9-truths-exposing-myth-about-body-language.

Neisser, U., Boodoo, G., Bouchard, T.J., Boykin, A.W., Brody, N., Ceci, S.J., Halpern, D.F., Loehlin, J.C., Perloff, R., Sternberg, R.J. and Urbina, S. (1996). Intelligence: knowns and unknowns. *American Psychologist, 51*, 77–101.

Nelson-Jones, R. (2000). *Six Key Approaches to Counselling and Therapy*. London: Continuum International.

NHS (2014a). Sleeping pills and the alternatives. *NHS Choices*. Retrieved 10 April 2015 from http://www.nhs.uk/Livewell/insomnia/Pages/treatment.aspx.

NHS (2014b). Beta blockers. *NHS Choices*. Retrieved 4 March 2015 from http://www.nhs.uk/Conditions/Beta-blockers/Pages/Introduction.aspx.

Norman, R.M., Sorrentino, R.M., Gawronski, B., Szeto, A.C., Ye, Y. and Windell, D. (2010). Attitudes and physical distance to an individual with schizophrenia: the moderating effect of self-transcendent values. *Social Psychiatry and Psychiatric Epidemiology, 45*, 751–758.

Nuckolls, K.B., Cassel, J. and Kaplan, B.H. (1972). Psychological Assets, life crisis and the prognosis of pregnancy. *American Journal of Epidemiology, 95*, 431–441.

Nutt, D. (2009). Equasy: an overlooked addiction. *Journal of Psychopharmacology, 23*, 3–5.

O'Keefe, M. (1997). Predictors of dating violence among high school students. *Journal of Interpersonal Violence, 12*, 546–568.

Orne, M.T. (1962). On the social psychology of the psychological experiment: With particular reference to demand characteristics and their implications. *American Psychologist, 17*, 776–783.

Orr-Andrawes, A. (1987). The case of Anna O.: a neuropsychiatric perspective. *Journal of the American Psychoanalytic Association, 35*, 387–419.

Oswald, I. (1966). *Sleep*. London: Penguin.

Paivio, A. (1969). Mental imagery in associative learning and memory. *Psychological Review, 76*, 241–263.

Parkin, A.J., Lewinsohn, J. and Folkard, S. (1982). The influence of emotion on immediate and delayed retention: Levinger & Clark reconsidered. *British Journal of Psychology, 73*, 389–393.

Patel, V. (2001). Cultural factors and international epidemiology: depression and public health. *British Medical Bulletin, 57*, 33–45.

Percy, J. (2014). David Elleray should face FA action for racist remarks to another official, says Lord Ouseley. *The Telegraph*. Retrieved 26 January 2015 from http://www.telegraph.co.uk/sport/football/news/10946451/David-Elleray-should-face-FA-action-for-racist-remarks-to-another-official-says-Lord-Ouseley.html.

Perrett, D.I., May, K.A. and Yoshikawa, S. (1994). Facial shape and judgments of female attractiveness. *Nature, 368*, 239–242.

Perrett, D.I., Lee, K.J., Penton-Voak, I., Rowland, D., Yoshikawa, S., Burt, D.M., Henzi, S.P., Castles, D.L. and Akamatsu, S. (1998). Effects of sexual dimorphism on facial attractiveness. *Nature, 394*, 884–887.

Perrin, S. and Spencer, C. (1981). Independence or conformity in the Asch experiment as a reflection of cultural and situational factors. *British Journal of Social Psychology, 20*, 205–209.

Perry, G. (2014). The view from the boys. *The Psychologist, 27*, 834–5.

Peterson, L.R. and Peterson, M.J. (1959). Short-term retention of individual verbal items. *Journal of Experimental Psychology, 58*, 193–198.

Pettigrew, T.F. (1998). Intergroup contact theory. *Annual Review of Psychology, 49*, 65–85.

Pezdek, K., Whetstone, T., Reynolds, K., Askari, N. and Dougherty, T. (1989). Memory for real-world scenes: the role of consistency with schema expectation. *Journal of Experimental Psychology: Learning, Memory, and Cognition, 15*, 587–595.

Phillips, M. L. (2009). Circadian rhythms: of owls, larks and alarm clocks. *Nature, 458*, 142–144.

Pickel, K. (1998). Unusualness and threat as possible causes of 'weapon focus'. *Memory, 6*, 277–295.

Piliavin, I.M., Rodin, J. and Piliavin, J.A. (1969). Good Samaritanism: an underground phenomenon? *Journal of Personality and Social Psychology, 13*, 289–299.

Pines, M. (1976). A psychoanalytic view of sleep. *Postgraduate Medical Journal, 52*, 26–31.

Pinker, S. (1994). *The Language Instinct*. London: Penguin Books.

Polikovsky, S., Kameda, Y. and Ohta, Y. (2009). Facial micro-expressions recognition using high speed camera and 3D-gradient descriptor. In *Imaging for Crime Detection and Prevention, Proceedings of 3rd International Conference*, 16, doi: 10.1049/ic.2009.0244.

Poulsen, S., Lunn, S., Daniel, S.I., Folke, S., Mathiesen, B.B., Katznelson, H. and Fairburn, C.G. (2014). A randomized controlled trial of psychoanalytic psychotherapy or cognitive-behavioral therapy for bulimia nervosa. *American Journal of Psychiatry, 171*, 109–116.

Preckel, F., Lipnevich, A., Boehme, K., Brandner, L., Georgi, K., Könen, T., Mursin, K. and Roberts, R. (2013). Morningness-eveningness and educational outcomes: the lark has an advantage over the owl at high school. *British Journal of Educational Psychology, 83*, 114–134.

Premack, D. (1971). Language in chimpanzees. *Science, 172*, 808–822.

Premack, D. and Premack, A.J. (1983). *The Mind of an Ape*. New York: Norton.

Quinlan, R.J. (2008). Human pair-bonds: Evolutionary functions, ecological variation, and adaptive development. *Evolutionary Anthropology, 17*, 227–238.

Rachman, S. (2004). Fear of contamination. *Behaviour Research and Therapy, 42*, 1227–1255.

Rahe, R.H., Mahan, J. and Arthur, R. (1970). Predictions of near-future health-change from subjects' preceding life changes. *Journal of Psychosomatic Research, 14*, 401–406.

Raine, A., Buchsbaum, M. and LaCasse, L. (1997). Brain abnormalities in murderers indicated by positron emission tomography. *Biological Psychiatry, 42*, 495–508.

Raj, A. and van Oudenaarden, A. (2008). Nature, nurture, or chance: stochastic gene expression and its consequences. *Cell, 135*, 216–226.

Rank, S.G. and Jacobson, C.K. (1977). Hospital nurses' compliance with medication overdose orders: a failure to replicate. *Journal of Health and Social Behavior, 18*, 188–193.

Rasch, B. and Born, J. (2013). About sleep's role in memory. *Physiological Review, 93*, 681–766.

Raven, J. (2011). Spearman on intelligence. *WebPsychEmpiricist*. Retrieved 16 February 2015 from http://wpe.info/vault/raven11a/raven11a.html.

Reicher, S. and Haslam, S.A. (2014). Camps, conflict and collectivism. *The Psychologist, 27*, 826–828.

Reynolds, K.J., Subašić, E. and Tindall, K. (2015). The problem of behaviour change: from social norms to an ingroup focus. *Social and Personality Psychology Compass, 9*, 45–56.

Rich, C., Ponsler, B., Holroyd, A. and Sidner, C.L. (2010). Recognizing engagement in human-robot interaction. In *Human-Robot Interaction (HRI), Proceedings of 5th ACM/IEEE International Conference*, 375–382.

Robertson, J. and Robertson, J. (1967–73). *Film Series, Young Children in Brief Separation, No.3* (1969). *John, 17 months, 9 days in a residential nursery.* London: Tavistock.

Robinson, K. (2001). *Out of our Minds: Learning to be Creative.* Chichester: Capstone Publishing.

Roediger, H. L. and Karpicke, J.D. (2010). Intricacies of spaced retrieval: a resolution. In A.S. Benjamin (Ed.), *Successful Remembering and Successful Forgetting: A Festschrift in Honor of Robert A. Bjork.* New York: Psychology Press, 23–47.

Roehrs, T. and Roth, T. (2001). Sleep, sleepiness, and alcohol use. *Alcohol Research and Health, 25,* 101–109.

Rosenhan, D.L. (1973). On being sane in insane places. *Science, 179,* 250–258.

Rosenthal, R. and Jacobson, L. (1968). *Pygmalion in the Classroom: Teacher Expectation and Pupils' Intellectual Development.* New York: Holt, Rinehart and Winston.

Rotter, J.B. (1966). Generalised expectancies for internal versus external control of reinforcement. *Psychological Monographs, 80,* 1–28.

Rowley-Conwy, P. (2001). Time, change and the archaeology of hunter-gatherers: how original is the 'original affluent society'? In C. Panter-Brick, R.H. Layton and P. Rowley-Conwy (Eds.), *Hunter-gatherers: An Interdisciplinary Perspective.* Cambridge: Cambridge University Press, 39–72.

Royal College of Psychiatrists (2013). Benzodiazepines. Retrieved 5 January 2015 from http://www.rcpsych. ac.uk/healthadvice/treatmentswellbeing/ benzodiazepines.aspx.

Rubenstein, C., Shaver, P. and Peplau, L.A. (1979). Loneliness. *Human Nature, 2,* 58–65.

Rubin, M. and Hewstone, M. (1998). Social identity theory's self-esteem hypothesis: a review and some suggestions for clarification. *Personality and Social Psychology Review, 2,* 40–62.

Rubin, Z. (1973). *Liking and Loving: An Invitation to Social Psychology.* New York: Holt, Rinehart and Winston.

Rutland, A. (1999). The development of national prejudice, in-group favouritism and self-stereotypes in British children. *British Journal of Social Psychology, 38,* 55–70.

Rutter, M., Beckett, C., Castle, J., Colvert, E., Kreppner, J., Mehta, M., Stevens, S. and Sonuga-Barke, E. (2007). Effects of profound early institutional deprivation: An overview of findings from a UK longitudinal study of Romanian adoptees. *European Journal of Developmental Psychology, 4,* 332–350.

Sackeim, H.A., Prudic, J., Fuller, R., Keil, J., Lavor, P.W. and Olfson, M. (2007). The cognitive effects of electroconvulsive therapy in community settings. *Neuropsychopharmacology, 32,* 244–254.

Sacks, O. (1998). *The Man who Mistook his Wife for a Hat and Other Clinical Tales.* London: Picador.

Samuel, J. and Bryant, P. (1984). Asking only one question in the conservation experiment. *Journal of Child Psychology and Psychiatry, 25,* 315–318.

Santee, R.T. and Maslach, C. (1982). To agree or not to agree: personal dissent amid social pressure to conform. *Journal of Personality and Social Psychology, 42,* 690–700.

Santhi, N., Thorne, H. C., van der Veen, D. R., Johnsen, S., Mills, S. L., Hommes, V., Schlangen, L.J., Archer, S.N. and Dijk, D.J. (2012). The spectral composition of evening light and individual differences in the suppression of melatonin and delay of sleep in humans. *Journal of Pineal Research, 53,* 47–59.

Sapolsky, R.M. (1995). Social subordinance as a marker of hypercortisolism: Some unexpected subtleties. *Annals of the New York Academy of Sciences, 771,* 626–639.

Saunders, T., Driskell, J.E., Johnston, J.H. and Salas, E. (1996). The effect of stress inoculation training on anxiety and performance. *Journal of Occupational Health Psychology, 1,* 170–186.

Schachter, S. and Singer, J.E. (1962). Cognitive, social and physiological determinants of emotional state. *Psychological Review, 69,* 379–399.

Schaffer, H.R. and Emerson, P.E. (1964). The development of social attachments in infancy. *Monographs of the Society for Research in Child Development, 29,* serial no. 94.

Schaffer, H.R. (1996). *Social Development.* Oxford: Blackwell.

Scheele, D., Striepens, N., Güntürkün, O., Deutschländer, S., Maier, W., Kendrick, K.M. and Hurlemann, R. (2012). Oxytocin modulates social distance between males and females. *Journal of Neuroscience, 32,* 16074–16079.

Schmidt, F.L. (1992). What do data really mean? Research findings, meta-analysis, and cumulative knowledge in psychology. *American Psychologist, 47,* 1173–1181.

Scoville, W.B. and Milner, B. (1957). Loss of recent memory after bilateral hippocampal lesions. *Journal of Neurology, Neurosurgery and Psychiatry, 20,* 11–21.

Sears, D.O. (1986). College sophomores in the laboratory: influences of a narrow data base on psychology's view of human nature. *Journal of Personality and Social Psychology, 51,* 513–530.

Seehagen, S., Konrad, C., Herbert, J. S. and Schneider, S. (2015). Timely sleep facilitates declarative memory consolidation in infants. *Proceedings of the National Academy of Sciences, 112,* 1625–1629.

Seligman, M.E.P. (1975). *Helplessness: On Depression, Development and Death*. London: W.H. Freeman.

Selye, H. (1936). A syndrome produced by diverse nocuous agents. *Nature, 138*, 32.

Selye, H. (1956). *The Stress of Life*. New York: McGraw-Hill.

Shapiro, C.M., Bortz, R., Mitchell, D., Bartel, P. and Jooste, P. (1981) Slow-wave sleep: a recovery period after exercise. *Science, 214*, 1253–1254.

Sheffield, M.E.J. and Dombeck, D.A. (2015). Calcium transient prevalence across the dendritic arbour predicts place field properties. *Nature, 517*, 200–204.

Sherif, M. (1935). A study of some factors in perception. *Archives of Psychology, 27*, 1–60.

Sherif, M. (1977). Crisis in social psychology: some remarks towards breaking through the crisis. *Personality and Social Psychology Bulletin, 3*, 368–382.

Sherif, M., Harvey, O.J., White, B.J., Hood, W.R. and Sherif, C.W. (1954). *Experimental Study of Positive and Negative Intergroup Attitudes between Experimentally Produced Groups*. Oklahoma: University of Oklahoma Press.

Shields, J. (1962). *Monozygotic Twins: Brought up Apart and Brought up Together*. Oxford: Oxford University Press.

Shimamura, A.P. (2000). Toward a cognitive neuroscience of metacognition. *Consciousness and Cognition, 9*, 313–323.

Siegel, J.M. (2005). Clues to the functions of mammalian sleep. *Nature, 437*, 1264–1271.

Singer, M.T. (1979). Coming out of the cults. *Psychology Today, 12*, 72–82.

Skeels, H.M. and Dye, H.B. (1939). A study of the effects of differential stimulation on mentally retarded children. *Proceedings and Addresses, American Association for Mental Defectiveness, 44*, 114–115.

Skinner, B.F. (1938). *The Behavior of Organisms: An Experimental Analysis*. New York: Appleton-Century.

Skinner, B.F. (1957). *Verbal Behavior*. Acton: Copley Publishing.

Slagter, H.A., Lutz, A., Greischar, L.L., Francis, A.D., Nieuwenhuis, S., Davis, J.M. and Davidson, R.J. (2007). Mental training affects distribution of limited brain resources. *PLoS Biology*, 5, e138.

Sloane, R.B. (1975). *Psychotherapy versus Behavior Therapy*. Cambridge: Harvard University Press.

Smith, P.B. and Bond, M.H. (1993). *Social Psychology Across Cultures: Analysis and perspectives*. Hemel Hempstead: Harvester Wheatsheaf.

Smithsonian National Museum of Natural History (2015). Homo erectus. *Human Origins*. Retrieved 5 March 2015 from http://humanorigins.si.edu/evidence/human-fossils/species/homo-erectus.

Sparenberg, P., Topolinski, S., Springer, A. and Prinz, W. (2012). Minimal mimicry: Mere effector matching induces preference. *Brain and Cognition, 80*, 291–300.

Spearman, C. (1927). *The Abilities of Man*. New York: Macmillan.

Spearman, C. (1904). 'General intelligence' objectively determined and measured. *American Journal of Psychology*, 15, 201–293.

Spencer, S.J., Steele, C.M. and Quinn, D.M. (1999). Stereotype threat and women's math performance. *Journal of Experimental Social Psychology, 35*, 4–28.

Sperling, G. (1960). The information available in brief visual presentations. *Psychological Monographs, 74*, 1–29.

Squire, L.R. (2004). Minireview - memory systems of the brain: a brief history and current perspective. *Neurobiology of Learning and Memory, 82*, 171–177.

Statland, B.E. and Demas, T.J. (1980). Serum caffeine half-lives: Healthy subjects vs. patients having alcoholic hepatic disease. *American Journal of Clinical Pathology, 73*, 390–393.

Stein, M.B., Walker, J.R. and Forde, D.R. (1994). Setting diagnostic thresholds for social phobia: considerations from a community survey of social anxiety. *American Journal of Psychiatry, 151,* 408–412.

Steinberg, L. and Monahan, K.C. (2007). Age differences in resistance to peer influence. *Developmental Psychology, 43*, 1531p1543.

Stemler, S.E., Grigorenko, E.L., Jarvin, L. and Sternberg, R.J. (2006). Using the theory of successful intelligence as a basis for augmenting AP exams in psychology and statistics. *Educational Psychology, 31*, 344–376.

Sternberg, R.J. (1985). *Beyond IQ: A Triarchic Theory of Human Intelligence*. New York: Cambridge University Press.

Sternberg, R.J. (1988). *The Triarchic Mind: A New Theory of Human Intelligence*. New York: Viking–Penguin.

Sternberg, R.J. (1997). What does it mean to be smart? *How Children Learn, 54*, 20–4.

Sternberg, R.J. (1999). Intelligence as developing expertise. *Contemporary Educational Psychology, 24*, 359–375.

Sternberg, R.J. (2001). Why schools should teach for wisdom: the balance theory of wisdom in educational settings. *Educational Psychologist, 36*, 227t245.

Sternberg, R.J. (2003). A broad view of intelligence: the theory of successful intelligence. *Consulting Psychology Journal: Practice and Research, 55*, 139l154.

Sternberg, R.J. (2005). The theory of successful intelligence. *Interamerican Journal of Psychology*, 39, 189–202.

Sternberg, R.J. (2008). Assessing what matters. *Educational Leadership, 65*, 20–26

Sternberg, R.J. and Grigorenko, E.L. (2004). Successful intelligence in the classroom. *Theory Into Practice, 43*, 274–280.

Stickgold, R. (2009). How do I remember? Let me count the ways. *Sleep Medicine Reviews, 13*: 305 308.

Stoet, G., O'Connor, D.B., Conner, M. and Laws, K.R. (2013). Are women better than men at multi-tasking? *BioMed Central Psychology, 1*, 18.

Stroop, J.R. (1935). Studies of interference in serial verbal reactions. *Journal of Experimental Psychology, 18*, 643.

Szasz, T. (1962). *The Myth of Mental Illness*. New York: Harper and Row.

Szasz, T. (2004). Remarks at the 35th Anniversary and Human Rights Award Dinner Citizens Commission on Human Rights, International Beverly Hilton Hotel, California. Retrieved 5 February 2015 at http://www.szasz.com/cchr.html.

Tajfel, H. (1970). Experiments in intergroup discrimination. *Scientific American, 223*, 96–105.

Tajfel, H. (1982). Social psychology of intergroup relations. *Annual Review of Psychology, 33*, 1–39.

Tajfel, H. and Turner, J.C. (1979). An integrative theory of intergroup conflict. In: W.G. Austin and S. Worchel (Eds.), *The Social Psychology of Intergroup Relations*. Monterey: Brooks/Cole.

Taylor, S.E., Klein, L.C., Lewis, B.P., Gruenewald, T.L., Gurung, R.A.R. and Updegraff, J.A. (2000). Biobehavioural responses to stress in females: tend-and-befriend, not fight-or-flight. *Psychological Review, 107*, 411–429.

Tellegen, A., Lykken, D.T., Bouchard, T.J., Wilcox, K.J., Segal, N.L. and Rich, S. (1988). Personality similarity in twins reared apart and together. *Journal of Personality and Social Psychology, 54*, 1031–1039.

Thibaut, J.W. and Kelley, H.H. (1959). *The Social Psychology of Groups*. New York: Wiley.

Thigpen, C. and Cleckley, H. (1954). A case of multiple personality disorder. *Journal of Abnormal and Social Psychology, 49*, 135–151.

Trivers, R.L. (1972). Parental investment and sexual selection. In B. Campbell (Ed.), *Sexual Selection and the Descent of Man*. Chicago: Adeline, 136–179.

Tucker-Ladd, C. (2010). Building Assertiveness in 4 Steps. *Psych Central*. Retrieved December 17 2014 from http://psychcentral.com/blog/archives/2010/02/25/building-assertiveness-in-4-steps/.

Tulving, E. and Schacter, D.L. (1990). Priming and human memory systems. *Science, 247*, 301–306.

Tulving, E. and Thomson, D.M. (1973). Encoding specificity and retrieval processes in episodic memory. *Psychological Review, 80*, 352–373.

Turing, A.M. (1950). Computing machinery and intelligence. *Mind, 59*, 433–460.

Tversky, A. and Kahneman, D. (1974). Judgment under uncertainty: heuristics and biases. *Science, 185*, 1124–1131.

Van Dongen, H.P.A., Vitellaro, K.M. and Dinges, D.F. (2005). Individual differences in adult human sleep and wakefulness: Leitmotif for a research agenda. *Sleep, 28*, 479–496.

van Ijzendoorn, M.H. (1989). Moral judgment, authoritarianism, and ethnocentrism. *Journal of Social Psychology, 129*, 37–45.

van Ijzendoorn, M.H. and Kroonenberg, P.M. (1988). Cross-cultural patterns of attachment: a meta-analysis of the strange situation. *Child Development, 59*, 147–156.

Wagner, D.R. (1999). Circadian rhythm sleep disorders. *Current Treatment Options in Neurology, 1*, 299–308.

Walker, M.P., Brakefield, T, Hobson, J.A. and Stickgold, R. (2003). Dissociable stages of human memory consolidation and reconsolidation. *Nature, 425*, 616–620.

Walker, M.T. (2006). The social construction of mental illness and its implications for the recovery model. *International Journal of Psychosocial Rehabilitation, 10*, 71–87.

Walker, R.S., Hill, K.R., Flinn, M.V. and Ellsworth, R.M. (2011). Evolutionary history of hunter-gatherer marriage practices. *PLoS One, 6*, e19066.

Walster, E., Aronson, V., Abrahams, D. and Rottman, L. (1966). Importance of physical attractiveness in dating behavior. *Journal of Personality and Social Psychology, 4*, 508–516.

Ward, N. (1996). Using prosodic clues to decide when to produce back-channel utterances. In *Spoken Language, Proceedings of 5th International Conference*, 1728–1731.

Watson, J.B. (1913). Psychology as the behaviourist views it. *Psychological Review, 20*, 158–177.

Watson, J.B. and Rayner, R. (1920). Conditioned emotional reactions. *Journal of Experimental Psychology, 3*, 1–14.

Waugh, N.C. and Norman, D.A. (1965). Primary memory. *Psychological Review, 72*, 89–104.

Wedekind, C., Seebeck, T., Bettens, F. and Paepke, A.J. (1995). MHC-dependent mate preferences in humans. *Proceedings of the Royal Society of London. Series B: Biological Sciences, 260*, 245–249.

Wegner, S. and Macrae, N. (2007). Wandering minds: the default network and stimulus-independent thought. *Science, 315*, 393–395.

Wehr, T.A. (1992). In short photoperiods, human sleep is biphasic. *Journal of Sleep Research, 1*, 103–107.

Weissman, A.N. and Beck, A.T. (1978). *Development and validation of the dysfunctional attitude scale: a preliminary investigation*. Paper presented at the annual meeting of the American Educational Research Association, Toronto.

Wells, G.L. and Loftus, E.F. (2012). Eyewitness memory for people and events. *Handbook of Psychology* (2nd edn), *11*, V, 25.

Wells, R.E., Yeh, G.Y., Kerr, C.E., Wolkin, J., Davis, R.B., Tan, Y., Spaeth, R., Wall, R.B., Walsh, J., Kaptchuk, T.J., Press, D. Phillips, R.S. and Kong, J. (2013). Meditation's impact on default mode network and hippocampus in mild cognitive impairment: a pilot study. *Neuroscience letters, 556*, 15–19.

Whitaker, R. (2011). *Anatomy of an Epidemic: Magic Bullets, Psychiatric Drugs, and the Astonishing Rise of Mental Illness in America.* New York: Broadway Books.

Whitson, S. (2010). 10 things passive aggressive people say: your early-warning system for hidden hostility. *Psychology Today.* Retrieved 21 February 2015 from https://www.psychologytoday.com/blog/passive-aggressive-diaries/201011/10-things-passive-aggressive-people-say.

Williams, R.W. and Herrup, K. (1988). The control of neuron number. *Annual Review of Neuroscience, 11*, 423–453.

Wilson, S. and Nutt, D.J. (2013). *Sleep Disorders.* Oxford: Oxford University Press.

Wiseman, R. (2014). *Night School: The Life-Changing Science of Sleep.* London: Macmillan.

Wittchen, H.U., Stein, M.B. and Kessler, R.C. (1999). Social fears and social phobia in a community sample of adolescents and young adults: prevalence, risk factors and co-morbidity. *Psychological Medicine, 29*, 309–323.

Wolfson, A.R. and Carskadon, M.A. (1998). Sleep schedules and daytime functioning in adolescents. *Child Development, 69*, 875–887.

World Health Organization (2010*). Measuring health and disability: manual for WHO disability assessment schedule. WHODAS 2.0.* Geneva: WHO Press.

Wright, A. (2014). Limbic sytem: amygdala. *Neurocience Online: An Electronic Textbook for the Neurosciences.* Retrieved 22 January 2015 from http://neuroscience.uth.tmc.edu/s4/chapter06.html.

Wright, D.B., Self, G. and Justice, C. (2000). Memory conformity: exploring misinformation effects when presented by another person. *British Journal of Psychology, 91*, 189–202.

Yuille, J.C. and Cutshall, J.L. (1986). A case study of eyewitness testimony of a crime. *Journal of Applied Psychology, 71*, 291–301.

Zajonc, R.B. (1968). Attitudinal effects of mere exposure. *Journal of Personality and Social Psychology, 9*: 1–27.

Zajonc, R.B. (1980). Feeling and thinking: preferences need no inferences. *American Psychologist, 35*, 151–175.

Zajonc, R.B. (1985). Emotion and facial efference: A theory reclaimed. *Science, 228*, 15–21.

Zajonc, R.B., Adelmann, P.K., Murphy, S.T. and Niedenthal, P.M. (1987). Convergence in the physical appearance of spouses. *Motivation and Emotion, 11*, 335–346.

Zajonc, R.B., Markus, H. and Markus, G.B. (1979). The birth order puzzle. *Journal of Personality and Social Psychology, 37*, 1325–1341.

Zimbardo, P.G., Banks, P.G., Haney, C. and Jaffe, D. (1973). Pirandellian prison: the mind is a formidable jailor. *New York Times Magazine*, 38–60.

Zubin, J. and Spring, B. (1977). Vulnerability: a new view of schizophrenia. *Journal of Abnormal Psychology, 86*, 103–126.

Index

11-plus 195

A
ABC analysis 169
ABC model 102
ability 173
abnormality 88–90, 93
abstract thought 183
abusive behaviour 299, 358, 362, 365
accommodation 35
acoustic encoding 121, 122
acquiescence bias 223
acrostics 388
ACTH see adrenocorticotrophic hormone
activation-synthesis hypothesis 70, 71
added value 391
adenosine 69
ADHD see attention deficit hyperactivity disorder
Adorno, T.W. 259, 315, 316
adrenal gland 155–6, 162
adrenalin 148, 153, 156, 170, 268
adrenocorticotrophic hormone (ACTH) 156
advanced sleep phase 82
affective intergroup bias 306
affiliation 347–8
    strategic 348
age effects
    and conformity 285
    and stress 153
    see also mental age
ageism 310, 311
agency theory 293
agentic states 293–4, 301
aggression 18, 43, 306, 314
agriculture 51
Ainsworth, Mary 349, 355
Ainsworth, M.D.S. 350
alcohol 22, 67
alliances 348
allocortex 19
Allport, G. 305, 322
Altemeyer, B. 259, 316
alternative hypothesis 233, 254, 265

amnesia 124–5, 393
amphetamine 67
amygdala 312, 334–5
anal stage 27, 72, 103
analysis 204, 263, 375, 382–3, 384–6
analytic intelligence 187, 188, 189
anger 15
Anna O 28
anorexia nervosa 23, 96, 103
anti-depressants 110, 112
anti-histamines 67
anti-intraception 315
anti-psychiatry movement 108
anti-psychotics 110
antisocial behaviour 150
antisocial personality disorder 89
anxiety 67–8, 96
    behaviourist approach to 104–5
    and eyewitness testimony 142
    separation anxiety 366–7
    therapies for 111, 113
    see also obsessive-compulsive disorder; phobias
ape sign language 185
appendices 264, 267, 272–3, 275
applications
    eyewitness testimony 139–45
    intelligence theory in education 191
    non-verbal communication 342–4
    prejudice reduction 321–6
    relationship theories 360
    resisting social pressure 296–303
    sleep disorders 81–5
    stress management 166–71
    therapies 110–15
approaches 12–59
    behaviourist 39–47, 53, 104–5, 338, 382
    definition 14
    humanist 53–5, 57
    sociocultural 53, 56–7
    see also biological approach;

cognitive approach; evolutionary approach; psychoanalytic approach
Arai, M. 287, 383, 384, 385–6
arousal 155
articulatory process 136
artificial intelligence 182, 183
artificiality 221, 233
Asch, Solomon 280–1, 283–5, 286, 287, 377, 383, 385–6
assertiveness training 300
assignments 245–67
    aims 253, 255, 263, 265, 268–9
    appendices 264, 267, 272–3, 275
    background reading 247–8, 263
    backing up/saving work 274
    conclusions 267
    contents page 253, 265
    data analysis 263
    data gathering 262–3
    deadlines 247
    design 264, 266, 269
    discussion 264, 266–7, 271–2
    drafts 247
    ethics 250, 252, 254, 256
    evidence 246–7
    example 267–73
    final checks 274–5
    hypotheses 253–4, 256, 263, 265, 269–71
    introduction/background 252–3, 263, 265, 267–9
    key skills 374
    marking scheme 263–4
    materials 252, 254, 261–2, 264, 266, 269
    methodology 252, 254, 256, 263, 266, 269–70
    overall style 264
    participants 264, 266, 269
    place in the course 246
    plagiarism 146–7
    planning the assignment 249–73
    presentation 264
    procedure 252, 254, 256, 264, 266, 270

references 248–9, 252, 254–5, 264, 267, 272
research plan 252, 254, 255–6
results 264, 266, 270–1
skills for 247–9, 257
spot checks 246–7
statistics 266, 270–1
suggested studies 250–2, 258–61
supporting information 264
terminology 253
titles 253, 265
working as a group 247
write-up sections 252–5
writing the assignment 249–74
writing style 249
assimilation 35
association 40
Atkinson, R.C. 131
atrocities 289
attachment 348–52, 359
    innate nature 361–3
    insecure 349
    insecure-avoidant 349, 350, 352, 355
    insecure-resistant 349, 350, 352, 355, 366
    parental 349
    secure 349–50, 352, 355
attention 132, 135, 137, 174, 387
attention deficit hyperactivity disorder (ADHD) 24
attentional-blink deficit 168
attitudes 305–6, 309–10, 311, 316
attraction 351–2, 358, 361
attractiveness 352–4, 362–3
Australopithecus 49, 185
authoritarian aggression 314
authoritarian parenting 294
authoritarian personality theory 314–16
authoritarian submission 314
authority 292
    legal 290
    legitimate 289–90, 292
authority figures 289, 291, 293–4
auto-kinetic effect 279–80
automaticity 261, 312, 313, 314, 316, 318, 331, 340
autonomic nervous system (ANS) 18, 155–6

parasympathetic branch 18, 155
sympathetic branch 18, 155–6, 170
autonomous states 293
availability heuristic 36
averages 239
    see also mean; median; mode
avoidance behaviours 164
awareness raising 300, 321

B
babies 335–6
backchannel 332–3, 338
Baddeley, Alan 118, 121, 122, 133–6, 255, 384
Bandura, Albert 43, 338
bar graphs 241, 271
bargaining 358
Bargh, J. 340, 341
Bartlett, F.C. 34–5, 139
Beck, A. 101–2, 103, 111, 160
behaviour 4, 12, 13, 19
    see also individual behaviour; social behaviour
behaviour control 297
behavioural experiments 369
behavioural tasks 37
behavioural therapy 44
behaviourist approach 39–47, 53, 104–5, 338, 382
beliefs 102–3
    core 102
    irrational 36, 37, 102–3, 111, 159–60
Bell, S.M. 350
belongingness 348
benzodiazepines 170
Berne, E. 365
Berscheid, E. 353–4, 358
beta-blockers 170
bias 36, 314
    acquiescence bias 223
    cultural bias 57, 197
    intergroup bias 306, 310, 318, 319
    and interviews/questionnaires 221, 223
    researcher bias 209, 228
    sample bias 206–9
    social desirability bias 223
Binet, Alfred 194, 195
bio-medical approach 100
biological approach 16–25, 39, 48, 53, 268

to intelligence 180–2
to memory 124–6
to non-verbal communication 334–6, 339
to psychopathology 99–101
to sleep 69–71, 380
to stress 155–6
bipolar mood disorder 95
birth order 177
Blackwell, L.S. 192–3
`blue eyes/brown eyes' exercise 321
body clock (circadian clock) 62, 84
body image, distorted 96
body language 328–30, 335–7, 340, 342
bonding 23
bonobos (pygmy chimps) 51, 185, 186
`bottle of beans' study 279–80
Bower, G.H. 260
Bowlby, John 349, 359, 361, 367
brain 4, 15, 16, 18, 19
    abnormalities 17, 21, 384
    areas 18–20, 24, 69–71, 124, 155, 180, 182
    electrical stimulation 20
    evolution 51
    and intelligence 180, 182, 185–6
    lobes 19
    localisation of function 19, 24, 126
    and memory 124
    and non-verbal communication 334–5
    size 360
    and sleep 64, 69–71, 78, 79
    social brain hypothesis 360
    and stress 155
brain cells 21–2, 24
brain damage 20, 393
    and memory loss 124–5, 126, 133, 134, 136
brain scans 20
brain waves 20
brainwashing 299
breadth 7, 391
breathing techniques 167
Breazeal, Cynthia 343–4
Brewer, W.F. 127, 143
briefing 235, 257–61
British Psychological Society (BPS) 234–5, 235, 249, 255

BPS research digest 248
Broca, Paul 19
Broca's area 19
'broken record' technique 300
buffers 293
bulimia nervosa 113

C
caffeine 67, 69, 212, 379–80
Cannon, Walter 148
capacity 121, 135, 386, 387
caregivers 349
case history 227
case study method 26–8, 30,
    72–3, 204, 227–9, 396
    in-depth case studies 30,
        227, 388
catalepsy 95
Cattell, R.B. 174–5
cause and effect 21, 123, 193,
    211, 229, 233, 241, 323,
    342, 363
CBT see cognitive behavioural
    therapy
cell body 24
central executive (CE) 134, 136,
    137
central nervous system (CNS)
    18–19
    see also brain; spinal cord
centration 35–6
cerebral cortex 19, 20
chameleon effect 340–2, 343
change blindness 142
charisma 290
Chartrand, T.L. 340, 341
CHD see coronary heart disease
chemotherapy (drug therapy)
    67, 110–11, 112, 114, 170
child development 183–4
child research, ethical issues
    235–6
childhood attachment 349–51,
    352, 355, 359, 361–2, 366–7
childhood experience 129, 228,
    352
    see also upbringing
childrearing 359
    see also parenting
chimpanzees 49, 51, 52, 158–
    9, 185, 337
Chomsky, Noam 45
chromosomes 23
circadian clock (body clock)
    62, 84
circadian rhythm sleep disorder
    (CRSD) 82–3, 380

circadian rhythms 62–3, 67, 69,
    83–4, 380
Civil Service 150
CL see comparison level
classical conditioning 40–1, 44,
    45, 104–5, 119, 382
client-centred practice 54–5
CNS see central nervous system
co-variables 240–1
code of ethics 234, 235
cognition, and emotion 311–12
cognitive approach 16–17,
    32–9, 53, 268
    and case studies 227
    and intelligence 182–4
    and memory 126–8
    and psychopathology 101–3
    and sleep 74–6
    and stress 159–60
cognitive behavioural therapy
    (CBT) 37, 111–14, 369, 380
    see also stress inoculation
cognitive development 35–6
cognitive interviews 143
cognitive miser theory 313–14
cognitive neuroscience 75
cognitive primacy 37
cognitive restructuring 111
cognitive therapy 102–3
Cohen, C.E. 308–9
coin-tossing 36, 37
collectivist cultures 56, 57, 286
commitment 358
common sense 4
communication see non-verbal
    communication
comparison level (CL) 358
compliance 278, 279, 283
compulsions 97
computer analogy 32–3, 74,
    126, 128, 182–3
concentration 66, 128, 267–73
concepts 7
concrete operational stage 183
condensation 72
conditioned response (CR) 41
conditioned stimulus (CS) 41
conditioning 40–5
    classical 40–1, 44, 45, 104–
        5, 119, 382
    operant 42, 43, 44, 45, 105
conditions 212–18
confederates 281–2, 283–4,
    291, 293, 340–1, 385
confidentiality 236, 394, 395
confirmation bias 308–9
conflict 27, 364–70

conformity 6, 56, 2[...]
    250–1, 278–304,
    384–6
    definition 278
    explanations of 2[...]
    and individual differences
        283, 285–7
    and minority influence
        281–2
    motivation to conform 279
    and obedience 289–96
    resisting social pressure
        296–303
    and situational factors 283–5
    types of 278–9
congruence 55
conscious decision making/
    information processing 15,
    16, 17, 26–8
consent 234–6
    informed 234, 235–6, 394,
        395
    parental 235–6
consent forms 262, 275
'conservation' 183, 184
consolidation 118–19
contact comfort 362
contact hypothesis 321, 322–3
contents page 253, 265
context 121
continuity hypothesis of dreams
    75
control
    lack of 160
    locus of 153
control conditions 212
conventionalism 314
coping behaviours 164, 166–71
    avoidance as 164
    emotion-focused coping
        164, 170
    problem-focused coping 164
Cornell note-taking system 389
coronary heart disease (CHD)
    153
corpus callosum 21
correlation 240–1
cortisol 148, 149, 153, 156,
    162, 165, 387
costs and benefits 357–8
counselling 368–9
counselling psychologists 369
counter-conformity 286
counterbalance 213–14
course structure 5
CR see conditioned response
Craik, F.I.M. 133

creative intelligence 187, 188, 189
Crick, F. 79
crime 21, 139–45, 342
CRSD see circadian rhythm sleep disorder
crystallised intelligence 174, 175
CS see conditioned stimulus
cues 120–1, 387
cults 296–9
  benign 297
  BITE model 297–8
  destructive 297
  how they exert control 299
  recognition 297–8
  resisting pressure from 299–302
cultural bias 57, 197
cultural relativism 88
cultural universals 330, 331–2, 337, 338, 339, 355
cultural values 88
cultural variation 354–6
culture 15, 16, 17, 24
  and attractiveness 362–3
  collectivist cultures 56, 57, 286
  and conformity 286, 385
  definition 56
  individualist cultures 56, 57, 286
  and memory 126–7
  and non-verbal communication 338–9
  and relationships 354–6
cumulative knowledge 204
Czeisler, Charles 83–4, 383

D
Darwin, Charles 337
Darwinian theory 48–9, 50, 185, 337, 359
Darwin's finches 49
data 238–43
  analysis 204, 263
  and descriptive statistics 239–40
  gathering 204, 262–3
  qualitative 238–9
  quantitative 238–9
dating 340
  Internet 355
debriefing 235, 262
decay theory 121
deception 234–5, 256, 338, 342, 365, 385–6

defence mechanisms 28–9, 31, 104, 129
defining psychology 4–5
delayed sleep phase 82
delirium 66
delta waves 64
delusions 95
demand characteristics 214, 215, 309
Dement, W. 65–6, 383
democracy 316
democratic parenting 294, 300
dendrites 24
denial 29, 104
deoxyribonucleic acid (DNA) 23
dependent variable (DV) 211–13, 218, 228, 232–3, 254, 256, 269, 394
depression 23, 24, 95, 99–101, 103
  major depressive disorder 95
  and stress 160
  therapies for 110–13
deprivation 177, 228
depth 7, 391
descriptive statistics 239–40
destructiveness 315
determinism 105
development 183–4
  psychosexual 27–8, 29, 72, 103
developmental psychology 228
Devlin Report (1976) 143
Diagnostic and Statistical Manual of Mental Disorders, Fifth Edition (DSM-5) 90–4
diathesis-stress model 107
differential investment 359
disclosure (observation) 225–6
discrimination 305, 306, 310–11
  combatting 322
  direct 311
  indirect 311
  minimal conditions for 317–19
discussion 264, 266–7, 271–2
diseases of adaptation 163, 166
disorders 94–8
dispersion 239–40
displacement (psychoanalysis) 29, 121
dissociative identity disorder 228
distress 88–9, 90
diversity training 322

DNA see deoxyribonucleic acid
Domhoff, G.W. 75
dopamine 99, 110
dream analysis 30, 104
dream interpretation 72–3
dreams 6, 65, 75
  biological approach to 70
  cognitive approach to 75
  continuity hypothesis of 75
  latent content 72
  manifest content 72
  psychoanalytic approach to 71–2, 375–6
  reorganisational theory of 79–80
  theories of 77–81
drug therapies 110–12, 114
  side effects 67, 110, 111, 170
drugs
  prescription 67, 81, 110, 111, 170
  psychoactive 22, 67
  sleeping pills 81
  stimulants 67, 69, 379–80
  for stress 170
DSM-5 see Diagnostic and Statistical Manual of Mental Disorders, Fifth Edition
dual-task studies 134
Duchenne smile 330, 339
Duck, S. 368
Dunbar, Robin 51, 186, 360
Dunbar's number 360, 363
DV see dependent variable
Dweck, Carol 190–2, 251

E
eating disorders 23, 37, 96, 103, 166
eclectic approaches 114
ecological validity 217, 225, 233, 234, 292, 325, 395
economic theories 357–8
education 178
  and cults 300, 301
  and intelligence 191, 192–3, 195–7
  and prejudice 321–2
  and the stereotype threat 307
EEA see environment of evolutionary adaptiveness
EEG see electroencephalogram
effect, lack of 95
effort 191
ego 26–30, 36, 71, 113, 128
ego states 365

egocentrism 183
Ekman, Paul 330–2, 338, 342
elaboration 388–9
Electra complex 28, 103
electrical stimulation 20
electroencephalogram (EEG) 20, 64
Elliott, Jane 321
Ellis, Albert 36, 102, 103, 111
emoticons 343
emotion 102–3
    and cognition 311–12
    and eyewitness testimony 142
    and facial expression 330–2, 337
    hidden 15, 16, 17
    and the limbic system 19
emotion-focused coping 164, 170
emotional blackmail 365
emotional control 298
empathy 55, 340
encoding 118, 119, 121–2, 132, 308–9, 387, 390
    acoustic 121, 122
    semantic 121, 122
endorphins 170
engagement 343
environment
    enriched 177
    and intelligence 177
environment of evolutionary adaptiveness (EEA) 49–50, 157
epigenetics 24
epilepsy 20, 124–5
episodes 89
episodic buffer 136
episodic long-term memory 119, 136
equal status contact 322
Equality Act 2010 311
errors, random 212
essays 377–80
ethics 234–6, 250, 252, 254, 291, 325, 383, 394–6
evaluation 7, 375, 383–4
Evans, G. 268
Eve 228
evolution 14, 15, 16, 48–50, 185
evolutionary approach 39, 48–53
    and intelligence 184–6
    and non-verbal communication 337–40

and relationships 359–63
and sleep 77–8
and stress 157–9
EWT see eyewitness testimony
exams 5–6
    effect on health 150–1, 166
    essays 377–80
    extended answers 376–7
    memory strategies 386–90
    practice questions 391–6
    short answer questions 375–6
    tackling questions 375–80
exercise (physical) 169–70
exhaustion 163
expectations 143, 196–7
experimental design 213–16
    independent groups 213, 214, 215, 269
    matched participants 214–16
    repeated measures 213–14, 215, 216
experimental hypotheses 232, 254, 256, 265, 269
experiments 13, 37, 45, 204, 228
    conditions 212–18
    definition 211
    experimental methods 211–20
    field experiments 217
    laboratory experiments 217
    natural experiments 218, 384
    and random allocation 216–17
    see also experimental design
expertise, developing 177
expression (of genes) 24
external validity 233–4, 384
extraneous variables 212–15, 233, 394–6
extremity 89–90
eye contact 330, 340
eyewitness testimony (EWT) 139–45
    and changes to the legal process 143
    unreliability 139–44

F
F Scale 259, 260, 315–16
facial expression 330–2, 335–43
facial symmetry 353, 355, 361
facts 203
familiarity 353
fantasies 75

fascism 314, 315–16
favouritism 306
fear 16, 41, 104–5, 298
    see also phobias
'fear hierarchies' 44
fear, obligation and guilt (F.O.G.) 365
field experiments 217
fight-or-flight response 147–8, 153, 157–8, 162–3, 166, 169–70, 348
fixation 27
fixed entity 177, 190
fixed mindsets 190–3
flooding (exposure therapy) 44
Flynn effect 176
fMRI see functional magnetic resonance imaging
F.O.G. (fear, obligation and guilt) 365
Folkman, Susan 160, 163–4, 268
Fore people 331–2
forgetting 121, 386
formal operational stage 184
fossil studies 52, 159, 185
free association 30, 104
free recall 120–1, 135
free will 105
'freeze' response 148
Freud, Anna 28, 29
Freud, Sigmund 26–30, 36, 71–4, 75, 103–4, 113, 129, 227, 352
friendship 351, 360
Friesen, W.V. 331–2
frontal lobe 19, 124, 180
functional magnetic resonance imaging (fMRI) 20

G
'g' factor see general intelligence
GAD see generalised anxiety disorder
Galapagos Islands 49
galvanic skin response (GSR) 129
games 365–5
gamma-aminobutyric acid (GABA) 170
Gardner, Allen 185
Gardner, Beatrix 185
gaze 330, 340
general adaptation syndrome (GAS) 161–3, 166

general intelligence (`g' factor) 174–5, 176, 178, 180–1, 189, 194, 197
generalisability 207, 233, 384
generalised anxiety disorder (GAD) 96
genes 15, 16, 17, 18, 23, 48
    expression 24
    and intelligence 176, 181, 182
    and psychopathology 100–1
    switching on and off 24
gestures 329, 336, 337, 338
Glass, D.C. 268
glycogen 69
God 50
`Good Samaritan' study 236
Google Scholar 248
grammar 45, 185
graphs 238, 241–2
    bar graphs 241, 271
    histograms 241
    pie charts 241
grief 337, 349
group support 300
groups
    conformity to 278–81, 283–5
    and prejudice 309
    similarity of 285
    size 51–2, 283–4
    social 51–2
    and social identity theory 316–19
    see also in-groups; out-groups
growth mindset 190, 191–3, 251
GSR see galvanic skin response

H
habits 16, 102
hallucinations 95
halo effect 251
happiness 260
Harlow, H.F. 361–2
harm 88–9, 91
    avoidance 235
    see also self-harm
Hassan, S. 297–8, 299
health 150–1, 164
Hebb, Donald 22
Hebbian learning 24
heterosexism 310, 311
heuristics 36, 184
hierarchy 150, 289, 293
    fear hierarchies 44
hierarchy of needs 54, 57

hippocampus 124–5, 387
histograms 241
Hitch, Graham 133–4, 136
Hitler, Adolf 314, 315
HLA see human leukocyte antigen
`H.M.' (Henry Molaison) 124–5, 133, 236, 258
Hofling, C.K. 292, 294, 300
Holocaust 316–17
homeostasis 62–3, 69, 148
hominins 49, 52
Homo erectus 49, 50, 52
Homo sapiens 49, 50
hormones 18, 22–3
    sleep 23, 67, 70–1, 82, 83
    stress 23, 148, 149, 150, 153, 155–6, 162, 165, 268, 387
hospital stays 367
HPA see hypothalamic-pituitary-adrenal axis
hugging 335
human leukocyte antigen (HLA) 361
human nature 15–16, 17
human rights 316
humanist therapy 54–5, 57
hunter-gatherers 49, 51, 157–9, 169–70, 338, 360, 363
hypersomnia 81, 82, 83
hypnosis 104
hypothalamic-pituitary-adrenal axis (HPA) 155, 156
hypothalamus 69, 148, 155–6
hypotheses 204, 231–2, 253–4, 394
    alternative hypotheses 233, 254, 265
    assignments 253–4, 256, 263, 265, 269–71
    correlational hypotheses 241, 254, 265
    directional (one-tailed) hypotheses 232
    experimental hypotheses 232, 254, 256, 265, 269
    non-directional (two-tailed) hypotheses 232
    null hypotheses 232, 233, 269, 270
hysteria 26

I
ICD see International Statistical Classification of Diseases
id 26–7, 29, 71, 103–4, 128–9

identification 278–9
    social 318
identity, social 318, 348
illusions 32, 259, 279–80
imitation 335–6, 340–2, 343
immune system 162, 166
implicit memory 119–20
in-depth 30, 227, 388, 396
in-groups 305, 306, 319
    in-group favouritism 314
in-line citations 248
incremental intelligence 177, 187–93
independent groups design 213, 214, 215, 269
independent variable (IV) 211–14, 218, 228, 232–3, 235, 254, 256, 269, 394
index cards 381, 390
individual behaviour 7, 14, 61–199
    intelligence 173–99
    memory 118–46
    psychopathology 87–117
    sleep 62–86
    stress 147–72
individual difference 153
individualist cultures 56, 57, 286
inferential statistics 239
infidelity 364
information control 297
information processing 32–3, 74, 126
informational influence 279–80
informed consent 234, 235–6, 394, 395
insomnia 67, 68, 81, 82, 83, 379–80
institutionalisation 358
instructions 235, 262, 270
intelligence 173–99, 251
    analytic intelligence 187, 188, 189
    approaches to 180–7
    creative intelligence 187, 188, 189
    crystallised intelligence 174, 175
    definition 173–4
    as developing expertise 177
    as fixed entity 177, 190
    fluid intelligence 174, 181, 194, 197
    general intelligence (`g' factor) 174–5, 176, 178, 180–1, 189, 194, 197

as incremental 177, 187–93
as innate/genetic elements 176, 178, 181, 182
interactionist view 178
metacomponents (executive processes) 188
mindsets 189–93
as multiple ability set 173, 175, 175–6
nurture arguments 177–8
practical intelligence 188, 189
as single ability 173, 174–5, 176
stereotypes about 190
successful intelligence 187–9
theories of 187–93
verbal intelligence 177
WICS model 189
intelligence quotient (IQ) 174, 176, 194–7
and analytic intelligence 187
and birth order 177
and education 178
Flynn effect 176
genetic 181
standard IQ scores 195
intelligence tests 194–9
inter-observer reliability 226
interactionist view 178
intergroup bias 306, 310, 318, 319
affective 306
aggressive 306
behavioural 306
cognitive 306
internal validity 233
internalisation 279
International Statistical Classification of Diseases (ICD) 90
Internet dating 355
interquartile range 240
interviews 204, 221–5, 228, 396
cognitive interviews 143
semi-structured interviews 224
strengths and weaknesses 229
structured interviews 224
unstructured interviews 224–5, 396
intimacy 365–6
introduction (assignments) 252–3, 263, 265, 267–9

IQ see intelligence quotient
irrational beliefs 36, 37, 102–3, 111, 159–60
IV see independent variable

J
Jackson, L. 196–7
jargon 222
jealousy 364
Jenness, A. 250–1, 279–80, 286, 385
jet lag 83
Jews 316–17
jigsaw technique 323, 325
Johnson, D. 268
Jones, Jim 298
Jonestown 298
Jung, C.G. 28, 72, 74, 104

K
Kahneman, D. 36, 38
Kelley, H.H. 357–8
key skills 373–96
added value 391
analysis 375, 382–3, 384–6
applying 375
evaluating 375, 383–4
literacy 374
mnemonics 386–90
numeracy 374
practice questions 391–6
tackling exam questions 375–80
understanding 374
understanding research 381–6
Kiecolt-Glaser, J.K. 150–1, 166
King, Martin Luther 321
`Kismet' (social robot) 343
kissing 352
Kleitman, N. 65–6, 383
knowledge, cumulative 204

L
labelling 108
laboratory experiments 38, 40–1, 45, 65, 105, 122, 129, 144, 170, 184, 217, 256, 270, 336, 350, 384, 395
Laing, R.D. 108
Lang, P.J. 44
language acquisition 45, 137, 186
LaPiere, R.T. 311
larks 63
latent content 72
lateral prefrontal cortex 180

Lazarus, Richard 160, 163–4, 268
Lazovik, A.D. 44
learned helplessness 105
learning 15, 16, 17
Hebbian learning 24
language learning 45
neurons and 22
reverse learning 79
social learning 43, 338
see also conditioning
Leeper's Lady illusion 32
legal authority 290
legal process 143
`length of lines' study 280–1, 283–5, 287, 377, 385
libido 26, 27
life, origins of 50
life events 151–2, 160, 165
light, as zeitgeber 67, 69, 70, 82, 83
light therapy 83–4, 380
likeability 340, 341, 343
Likert scale 223
limbic system 19, 124, 312, 334–5
literacy 374
`Little Albert' 41, 105, 235
Little Hans 27, 29, 30, 72–3, 103–4
localisation of function 19, 24, 126
locus of control 153
Loftus, Elizabeth 139–41, 143, 144
loneliness 347, 351
long-term memory (LTM) 118, 119, 121–2, 386–8
biological approach to 124–6
cognitive approach to 128
encoding 121–2, 132
episodic LTM 119, 136
multi-store model 131–3
psychoanalytic approach to 128
semantic LTM 119
long-term potentiation (LTP) 125
longitudinal studies 30, 112, 149–50, 153, 160, 177, 192–3, 227, 323, 350, 396
love 97, 153, 348, 351–2, 355
mother 349
romantic 97, 153, 351–2, 355
love bombing 298

LTM see long-term memory
lying 342

M
McGuffin, P. 100, 101
maintenance rehearsal 132, 133
major depressive disorder 95
maladaptive behaviours 89
manic states 95
manifest content 72
manipulators 296, 298, 299–301
`marshmallow test' 259
Maslow, Abraham 54, 57, 348
matched participants design 214–16
matching hypothesis 353–4, 358
mean 239, 270–1, 272, 376
meaning
    effort after 35
    and memory 387, 388–9
media pressure 278
median 239, 270, 272
mediators 32
medical students 150–1
meditation 167–8
    guided 167
melatonin 23, 67, 70–1, 83, 380
    supplements 82, 83
Meltzoff, A.N. 336
memory 32, 34, 118–46, 251, 260
    adaptive memory 79
    approaches to 124–30
    consolidation 118–19
    declarative memory 119, 124
    distortion 35
    elaboration 388–9
    encoding 118, 119, 121–2, 132, 308–9, 387, 390
    eyewitness testimony 139–45
    failure 124–5, 386–7
    free recall 120–1, 135
    implicit memory 119–20
    mnemonics 386–90
    multi-store model 126, 131–3, 135
    parasitic memories 79
    procedural (non-declarative) memory 119, 258
    prospective memory 120, 137
    recall 120–1, 135, 251
    recognition 120–1

repression 28–9, 103–4, 129
retrieval 118, 308–9, 387
retrospective memory 120
sensory memory (SM) 131–2
and sleep 74, 79–80
spacing 390
and stereotypes 308–9
storage 118
and stress 387
testing effect 390
theories of 131–8
working memory model 126, 128, 131, 133–7, 255–6
see also long-term memory; short-term memory
memory problems 124–5, 386–7, 393
mental age 195
mental agility 66
mental energy 174
Mental Health Act 2007 108
mental illness 4, 87–8, 160
    see also psychopathology
metacognition 180
metacomponents (executive processes) 188
method 13, 202–3, 383–4
    assignments 252, 254, 256, 263, 266, 269–70
    experimental 211–20
    non-experimental 221–31
microexpressions 330–1, 342
Milgram, Stanley 208, 214, 235, 290–4, 296, 301
Miller's magic number 255
Milner, B. 124–5
mimicry 340–2, 343
mind 4, 13
    see also unconscious mind
mindsets 102, 189–93, 251
    fixed 190–3
    growth 190, 191–3, 251
minimal groups experiment 317–19
minorities 314–15
    minority influence 281–2
mirror drawing 258
misinformation effect 140–1
Mitchison, G. 79
mnemonics 386–90
mode 239
modelling 43
monkeys 361–2
monotropy 349
mood boosters 170
Moore, M.K. 336
moral development 295

moral reasoning 295, 300–1
    conventional 295
    post-conventional 295, 301
    pre-conventional 295
Mori, K. 287, 383, 384, 385–6
Moscovici, S. 281–2
mother love 349
mother-child relationship 23, 349–50
motives, questioning 301
motor cortex 335
multi-store model (MSM) 131–3
multi-tasking 134, 258, 392
mundane realism 233–4, 385, 395
Münsterberg, Hugo 139
murderers, brain abnormalities 21, 384
Mussolini, Benito 315
mutism 95

N
napping 63, 74
National Institute of Mental Health 112
Native American tradition 34–5
natural experiments 218, 384
natural killer cells 150–1
natural selection 15, 48, 49, 185, 337, 359, 362
naturalistic fallacy 52
nature-nurture debate 14, 176–7, 334–40
Nazis 290, 292, 314, 315, 338
needs 348, 359
    hierarchy of needs 54, 57
negative cognitive triad 101–2
negative reinforcement 42
negative symptoms 95
neocortex 19, 51
    and body language 335
    and cognition 312
    and intelligence 180
    and memory 124
    and sleep 70
    and the social brain hypothesis 650
nerves 155
nervous system 18–20
    autonomic nervous system 18, 155–6, 170
    central nervous system 18–19
    and intelligence 180
    and memory 124
    parasympathetic branch 18, 155

peripheral nervous system 18
and sleep 69–71
somatic nervous system 18
and stress 155–6, 170
sympathetic branch 18,
155–6, 170
neural networks 79
neurons 18, 21–2, 24
and memory 124, 125–6
and psychopathology 99
and sleep 69
neurotics 26
neurotransmitter imbalance
theory 99, 100, 110
neurotransmitters 18, 21–2
and memory 125
and psychopathology 99,
100
and stress 170
night terrors 84
nightmares 74, 84
noise 67–8, 149, 267–73
non-rapid eye movement
(nREM) sleep 64, 67, 78
non-verbal communication
(NVC) 328–46
body language 328–30,
335–7, 340, 342
cultural explanations 338–9
evolutionary theory 337–40
facial expression 330–2,
335–43
nature-nurture debate
334–40
paralanguage 332–3
social applications 340–2
and technology 342–4
work applications 340–2
noradrenaline 352
normal distribution 89–90
normality, definition 88
normative influence 279, 280–1
norms
statistical norms 89–90
see also social norms
nREM (non-rapid eye
movement) sleep 64, 67, 78
nucleus accumbens 351–2
null hypothesis 232, 233, 269,
270
numeracy 374
NVC see non-verbal
communication

O

obedience 6, 208, 214, 235,
289–96, 296
definition 289
and situational effects 292–4
and society 293–4
objectivity 88, 239
observation 204, 225, 228,
394–5
data 238
disclosed observation 225–6
naturalistic observation 225,
394–5
non-participant observation
226
participant observation 92,
226
strengths and weaknesses
229, 395
structured observation 225,
395
undisclosed observation
225–6
observation schedules 226–7,
395
observer effect 225–6, 395
obsessive-compulsive disorder
(OCD) 97, 104, 352
occipital lobe 19
Oedipus complex 27–8, 73,
103
oestrogen 1453
one-tailed (directional)
hypotheses 232
operant conditioning 42, 43,
44, 45, 105
operants 42
operationalisation 232
opportunity sampling 207–8,
212, 256, 262, 269, 394, 395
oral stage 27, 72, 103
order effects 213–14, 215
out-groups 305, 306, 309, 319,
322
overcrowding 149–50
overgeneralisation 36, 102,
309
owls 63
Oxford Happiness Inventory
260
oxytocin 23, 153, 329, 352

P

Palmer, J.C. 140–1
panic disorder 160
paralanguage 332–3
parasitic memories 79
parasomnia 81
parasympathetic branch 18,
155

parent-child relationship 23,
26, 349–50
parental attachment 349
parental consent 235–6
parental investment 359
parenting 355
democratic 294, 300
and intelligence 177
and obedience 294
see also childrearing
parietal lobe 19
participant observation 92, 226
participant variables 212, 214,
215, 217, 218, 394
participants 264, 266, 269
passive voice 249
passive-aggressive behaviour
365
past tense 249
Pavlov, Ivan 40–1, 104
peer groups 279
peer pressure 278, 293
peers 278, 293, 296, 300
Penfield, Wilder 20
Peoples Temple cult 298
percentages 242
perception 32
peripheral nervous system
(PNS) 18
Perrin, S. 385
person-centred therapy 114,
369
personal identity 318
personal space 329
personalisation 36
personality 153, 285
personality disorder, antisocial
89
PET (Positron Emission
Tomography) scans 180
phallic stage 27, 72, 103
pharmaceutical industry 92,
111
pheromones 361
phobias 27, 44, 73, 97, 103,
104
social 97
specific simple 97
phonological loop 134, 135,
136, 137
phonological store 136, 137
physical exercise 169–70
Piaget, Jean 35–6, 183–4
pie charts 241
pigeon holing 91
Piliavin, Irving 236
pilot studies 262

planning fallacy 159–60, 169
'play dead' strategy 148
PNS see peripheral nervous system
police 143, 342
politics, right-wing 315–16
polysomography 63–4, 65
pons 70
Popper, Karl 205
population validity 233–4
populations 206–11
    target 206
positive distinctiveness 318
positive reinforcement 42
positive stereotypes 307
positive stress 161
positive symptoms 95
Positron Emission Tomography (PET) scans 180
post mortem 19
posture 329, 337, 340
power 150, 315
practical intelligence 188, 189
praise 191
pre-operational stage 183
preconscious 27, 71, 128
predators 77, 78
prefrontal cortex 21
    lateral 180
prejudice 251, 259, 305–27
    as attitude 305–6, 309–10, 311
    contact hypothesis 321, 322–3
    definition 305
    and education 321–2
    inconsistency of 311–12
    reduction 321–6
    superordinate goals 321, 323–6
    theories of 313–20
primacy effect 132
primary appraisal 163–4
primates 49, 51, 52, 185, 337, 360
priming 119
problem-focused coping 164
problem-solving 35–6
procedural (non-declarative) memory 119, 258
procedure 252, 254, 256, 264, 266, 270
projection 29
projectivity 315
prospective memory 120, 137
protected characteristics 311
proximity 293, 329, 335, 337

Psyblog 248
psychoanalysis 26, 30, 113–14, 369
psychoanalytic approach 16–17, 26–31, 39, 53
    to dreams 375–6
    to memory 128–9
    to psychopathology 103–5
    to sleep 71–4
psychoanalytic therapy 30–1, 113–14
psychological literacy 7–8
psychopathology 87–117, 160
    approaches to 99–106
    common psychological disorders 94–8
    definition 87–91
    DSM-5 90–4
    theories of 106–9
    therapies 110–15
psychopathy 89
psychosexual development 27–8, 29, 72, 103
psychotherapy 110–14
    see also cognitive behavioural therapy; psychoanalysis; psychoanalytic therapy
puberty 23
punishment 42, 43, 44

Q
qualitative data 238–9
quantitative data 238–9
quasi-experiments 21, 218
questioning motives 301
questionnaires 37, 221–5, 228–9
questions 224–5
    closed questions 222–3, 224
    for interviews/questionnaires 222
    leading questions 140–1, 143, 222
    loaded questions 222
    open questions 222, 225
quotas 209–10

R
racial difference 182
racism 310, 311, 321, 322–3
Rahe, R.H. 151–2, 165
Raine, A. 21, 384
raising awareness 300, 321
random allocation 216–17, 218
random error 212
random number software 208

random sample 208, 394
range 240, 270–1, 272, 376
rapid eye movement (REM) sleep 64–5, 67, 78–9, 84, 119
rarity 89–90
rationality 36
Raven's Progressive Matrices 194, 197
Rayner, R. 41, 105, 235
reaction formation 29
recall 120–1, 135, 251
recency effect 132
recognition 120–1
redintegration 143
references 248–9, 252, 254–5, 264, 267, 272
regression 29
rehearsal 121, 132, 133
reinforcement 42, 362
    negative 42
    positive 42
relationship counselling 368, 369
relationships 347–71
    abusive 299, 358, 362, 365
    affiliation 347–8
    attachments 348–52
    break-ups 368
    conflict 364–70
    definition 347
    same-sex 362
    stages 358
    theories 357–64
    universals 354–6
    variations 354–6
relaxation techniques 167, 387
reliability 90, 197, 226
    inter-observer 226
religion 50
REM (rapid eye movement) sleep 64–5, 67, 78–9, 84, 119
reorganisation 79–80
repeated measures design 213–14, 215, 216
replication 203
repression 28–9, 103–4, 129
reproductive success 359
research 6, 7, 13, 201–43, 392–5
    cycle 204, 205
    data 238–43
    ethics 234–6, 250, 252, 254, 291, 325, 383, 394–6
    general issues 231–4
    graphs 238, 241–2
    populations 206–11
    process 203, 204, 205

samples 206–11
theory revision 204, 205
research brief 235, 257–61
research files 381–2
research methods
    experimental methods
        211–20
    non-experimental methods
        221–31
    overlap between methods
        228
    scientific method 202–3
research plans 252, 254, 255–6
researcher bias 209, 228
responsibility taking 301
response 13, 40–1
responsiveness 353
'rest and digest' state 155
restoration 77–8
results 264, 266, 270–1
retrieval 118, 308–9, 387
reverse learning 79
rewards 42, 43, 44, 357
right to withdraw 236, 395
right-wing authoritarianism 316
right-wing politics 315–16
'Robbers Cave' study 323–5
Robertson, J. 367
Robertson, J. 367
robots 343–4
Rogers, Carl 55, 57
role models 17, 300
romantic love 97, 153, 351–2,
    355
romantic relationships 23, 329,
    340, 347, 351–3, 355, 357–8,
    368–9
Rorschach test 104
Rosenhan, D.L. 92
Rosenthal, R. 196–7
RWA Scale 259

S
SAM see sympathetic-adrenal
    medulla axis
same-sex relationships 362
samples 206–11, 384
    definition 206
    generalisation from 207
    opportunity samples 207–8,
        212, 256, 262, 269, 394,
        395
    quota samples 209–10
    random samples 208, 394
    representative 206, 208–9
    selection 207–10
    self-selecting samples 208

size 206–7
stratified samples 209, 394
systematic samples 208–9
unbiased samples 206–7
volunteer samples 394
sampling (relationship stage)
    358
sampling (research methods)
    206–9, 252, 254, 256, 262,
    394
San people 51
SAT test 195
scattergrams 241
schemas 33–6, 387
    and dreams 75
    and intelligence 183
    and memory 126–7, 128,
        139, 143
    and psychopathology 101–3
    and relationships 358
    and stereotypes 306
    and stress 160
schizophrenia 23, 94–5, 99,
    110–11
scientific explanations 13
scientific method 13, 202–3
scientific standards 203
SCN see suprachiasmatic
    nucleus
Scoville, W.B. 124–5
Scoville, William 124
scripts 33, 75
SD see standard deviation
Sears, D.O. 57
secondary appraisal 164
secondary elaboration 72
secrecy of response 284
secure base 349
sedatives 81, 170
selective abstraction 36
self-actualisation 54, 57
self-esteem 319
self-fulfilling prophecy 196–7
self-harm 88, 92
self-help 369
self-image 318
self-selecting sample 208
Seligman, M.E.P. 105
Selye, Hans 161, 166, 268
semantic encoding 121, 122
semantic LTM 119
sensorimotor stage 184
sensory memory (SM) 131–2
separation 366–7
serial position effect 132–3
serotonin 99, 110
sex differences

and childrearing 359
and conformity 286, 287
and obedience 294
and stress 153, 158
sexism 310, 311, 365
sexual obsession 315
sexual orientation 310, 311
Sherif, Muzafer 279–80, 323–6
Shiffrin, R.M. 131
shift work 82, 83–4, 379–80
short-term memory (STM) 118–
    19, 121–2, 255, 386–7
    biological approach to 124,
        126
    and caffeine 212
    capacity 121, 135, 386, 387
    encoding 121–2
    limitations 121–2, 386, 387
    multi-store model 131–3
    working memory model
        133–7
shyness 348
SI see successful intelligence
side effects 67, 110, 111
siestas 63
sign language, ape 185
similarity 353
Simon, Théodor 194, 195
Skinner, B. F. 42, 45
Skinner box 42
Slagter, H.A. 167, 168
slave systems 134, 135, 136,
    137
sleep 6, 62–86, 251
    biological approach to
        69–71
    and circadian rhythms 62–3
    cognitive approach to 74–6
    definition 62
    evolutionary approach to
        77–8
    factors that affect 66–8
    and homeostasis 62–3
    hormones of 23, 67, 70–1,
        82, 83
    and memory 119
    monitoring 63–5
    polyphasic sleep 63
    psychoanalytic approach to
        71–4
    reorganisational theory of
        79–80
    restoration theory of 77–8
    slow-wave 64
    stages of 64–5
    theories of 77–81
sleep apnoea 81–2

sleep debt 63
sleep deprivation 66, 78, 81, 380
sleep disorders 68, 81–5, 379–80
sleep spindles 64
sleep/wake cycle 62, 380
sleeping pills 81
sleepwalking 84
slow-wave sleep 64, 119
SM see sensory memory
smiling 330, 335, 341
    Duchenne smile 330, 339
social acceptability 88
social behaviour 6, 7, 277–371
    conformity 278–304
    non-verbal communication 328–46
    prejudice 305–27
    relationships 347–71
social brain hypothesis 360
social categorisation 318
social comparisons 318
social construct 108
social desirability bias 223
social distance 309
social exchange theory 357–8
social groups 51–2
social identification 318
social identity 318, 348
social identity theory 316–19
social learning 43, 338
social networking sites 343, 355
social norms 88, 89, 91, 93, 108
    conformity to 279
    and non-verbal communication 329, 338
    and obedience 294
social pressure 141, 377
    resisting 296–303
Social Readjustment Rating Scale (SRRS) 152
social releasers 349, 361
social robots 343
social support 151, 153, 218, 284, 347, 348
social values 88
socialisation 294, 301
society 15, 16, 24, 56
sociocultural approach 53, 56–7
sociology 56
somatic nervous system (SoNS) 18
spacing effect 390

Spearman, Sir Charles 174, 176, 178, 181
speech
    disordered 95
    production 19
Spencer, C. 385
spinal cord 18, 19, 155
Spring, B. 107
SRRS see Social Readjustment Rating Scale
standard deviation (SD) 240, 270
Stanford Binet test 194
Stanford Prison Experiment 288, 294
statistical norms 89–90
statistics 266, 270–1
    assignments 266, 270–1
    descriptive statistics 239–40
    inferential statistics 239
stereotype threat 307
stereotypes 305, 306–9
    combatting 321, 322
    and confirmation bias 308–9
    effects of 307
    origins 307–8
    positive stereotypes 307
    raising awareness about 321
    regarding intelligence 190
    theories of 313–20
Sternberg, Robert 177, 180, 187–90, 197
Stickgold, R. 74, 75
stigma 100, 108, 196, 197
stimulants 67, 69, 379–80
stimulus 12–13, 40–2, 44, 97, 105
    stressful 149, 162, 163–4
STM see short-term memory
Stockholm syndrome 362
storage 118
strange situation test 349–50
strategic affiliation 348
stratified samples 209, 394
streaming 196
stress 89, 147–72, 267–8
    acute stress 147–8, 166
    approaches to 155–61
    causes of 148–52
    chronic stress 149, 166, 170
    definition 147
    diathesis-stress model 107
    environmental causes 149–50
    general adaptation syndrome 161–3

and health 150–1, 156, 162, 164–6
individual differences in 153
measuring the body's response to 260
and memory 387
and mental health 166
occupational causes 149, 150–1
positive stress 161
and relationships 347
social causes 149, 151–2
theories of 161–6
transactional model of 160, 163–5
stress dots 260
stress hormones 23, 148, 149, 150, 153, 155–6, 162, 165, 268, 387
stress inoculation 168–9
stress management 165, 166–71
stressors 149, 151–3, 160, 162–3, 166, 268
Stroop test 261
subcultures 56, 286
subheadings 266
subjectivity 88, 89, 239
successful intelligence (SI) 187–9
suicide, mass 298
summarising 382
superego 26–7, 30, 71, 113, 128
superordinate goals 321, 323–6
superstition 315
suppression 129
suprachiasmatic nucleus (SCN) 69–71, 83, 380
surveys 204, 221–5, 229
symbolic thought 183
symbols 72
sympathetic branch 18, 155–6, 170
sympathetic-adrenal medulla axis (SAM) 155–6
symptom substitution 103
symptoms 90
    negative 95
    positive 95
synapses 22, 24, 125
syndrome 94
systematic desensitisation 44
systematic samples 208–9
Szasz, T. 108

T

TADS (Treatment of Adolescents with Depression Study) 112
Tajfel, Henri 316–19
target populations 206
technology, and non-verbal communication 342–4
temporal lobe 19
tend-and-befriend response 158
testing effect 390
theory 203, 204, 394
    revision 204, 205
    see also specific theories
therapies 110–15
    behavioural 44
    cognitive 102–3
    cognitive behavioural 37, 111–14, 369, 380
    drug 67, 110–12, 114, 170
    humanist 54–5, 57
    person-centred 114, 369
    psychoanalytic 30–1, 113–14
    psychotherapy 110–14
therapists 4
Thibaut, J.W. 357–8
thin slicing 330, 335
thinking style 153
thought control 297
thought processes 13, 286
threats 23, 147, 148, 155, 162
    appraisal 163–4, 268
time management 159–60, 169
tip-of-the-tongue phenomenon 120
to-do lists 169
toilet training 27
toughness 315
tradition 290
tranquillisers 170
transaction 163–4
transactional model of stress 160, 163–5
Treatment of Adolescents with Depression Study (TADS) 112
Treyens, J.C. 127, 143
Trier social stress test 165
trigrams 121
Tripp, Peter 66, 81
Tulving, E. 133
Turin, Alan 183, 184
Turing test 183, 184, 343
turn-taking 332–3
Turner, John 318

Tversky, A. 36, 38
twin studies 18, 23
    fraternal twins 23, 101
    identical twins 23, 101, 176, 181
    and intelligence 176, 181
    and psychopathology 100–1
Twitter 355, 360, 363
two-tailed (non-directional) hypotheses 232
type A personality 153
type B personality 153

U

unconditional positive regard 55
unconditioned response (UR) 41
unconditioned stimulus (US) 40, 41
unconscious mind 15, 16, 17, 26–8, 36
    and defence mechanisms 104
    and dreams 30, 71–2
    and memory 128, 129
    and phobias 103, 104
    and psychopathology 103, 104, 113
understanding (key skill) 374, 381–6
undisclosed observation 225–6
universals
    cultural 330, 331–2, 337, 338, 339, 355
    relationship 354–6
upbringing 15, 17
    see also childhood experience
UR see unconditioned response
US see unconditioned stimulus

V

validity 197, 207
    ecological 217, 225, 233, 234, 292, 325, 395
    external 233–4, 384
    internal 233
    population 233–4
values 88, 300–1
variables 211–18, 221
    in assignments 252, 254, 256
    confounding variables 213, 218, 233
    dependent variables (DVs) 211–13, 218, 228, 232–3, 254, 256, 269, 394

environmental variables 212
extraneous variables 212–13, 214, 215, 233, 394, 395, 396
independent variables (IVs) 211–14, 218, 228, 232–3, 235, 254, 256, 269, 394
participant variables 212, 214, 215, 217, 218, 394
verbal intelligence 177
video cameras 226
violence 143
visualisation 167, 388
visuospatial sketchpad 134, 136

W

`War of the Ghosts' story 34–5
warmth 284, 298, 309
`Washoe' (chimp) 185
Watson, J.B. 41, 105, 235
Watson, John 40, 41, 45
weapons focus 142, 143
Weber, Max 290
Wechsler Memory Scale 124–5
WHODAS see World Health Organisation's Disability Assessment Schedule
WICS model (wisdom, intelligence, and creativity, synthesised) 189
willpower 259
wisdom 189
wish fulfilment 71
witness line-ups 141, 143, 144
word association 104, 129
word length effect 135, 137, 255–6, 384
working memory model (WMM) 126, 128, 131, 133–7, 255–6
World Health Organisation's Disability Assessment Schedule (WHODAS) 91

X

xenophobia 310

Y

Yerkes-Dodson law 142

Z

Zajonc, R.B. 312, 337
zeitgebers 67, 69, 71, 82, 83, 379
Zimbardo, P.G. 285, 294
Zubin, J. 107

001/29102015

10 9 8 7 6 5 4 3 2 1

ISBN 9780008113513

Published byLeckie & Leckie Ltd
An imprint of HarperCollinsPublishers
Westerhill Road, Bishopbriggs, Glasgow, G64 2QT
T: 0844 576 8126   F: 0844 576 8131
leckieandleckie@harpercollins.co.uk
www.leckieandleckie.co.uk

Commissioning Editor: Katherine Wilkinson
Project manager: Craig Balfour and Keren McGill

Special thanks to
David Christie (copy edit)
Louise Robb (proofread)
Keren McGill (proofread)
Lauren Reid (image research and editorial)
Jouve (layout and illustration)

Printed in Italy by Lego, S.P.A.

A CIP Catalogue record for this book is available from the British Library.

Acknowledgements

P19 (bottom) © Apic/Hulton Archive/Getty Images; P20 (top) © rook76 / Shutterstock.com;P21 © Paul Harris/Hulton Archive/Getty Images; P26 © ullstein bild/Getty Images; P28 (top) © De Agostini Picture Library/De Agostini/Getty Images; P28 (bottom) © magno/Hulton Archive/Getty Images; P34 (top left) Hans-Werner / licensed under the Creative Commons Attribution-Share Alike 3.0 Unported license; P34 (top right) © Reg Burkett/Hulton Archive/Getty Images; P35 © AFP/Getty Images; P40 © Hulton Archive/Archive Photos/Getty Images; P41 (top) © Sovfoto/Universal Images Group/Getty Images; P41 (bottom) "Little-albert" by John B Watson - Akron psychology archives. Licensed under Public Domain via Wikimedia Commons - https://commons.wikimedia.org/wiki/File:Little-albert.jpg#/media/File:Little-albert.jpg; P42 © Nina Leen/The LIFE Picture Collection/Getty Images; P43 (top) © Jon Brenneis/The LIFE Images Collection/Getty Images; P44 (bottom) © Boston Globe/Getty Images; P45 (bottom) © ullstein bild/Getty Images; P47 © ullstein bild/Getty Images; P49 (bottom) Reconstruction by John Gurche; photographed by Tim Evanson. Licensed under the Creative Commons Attribution-Share Alike 2.0 Generic license; P51 (bottom) © Gil.K / Shutterstock.com; P52 © Kenneth Garrett/National Geographic/Getty Images; P54 Albert Einstein 1947 by Photograph by Oren Jack Turner, Princeton, N.J. - The Library of Congress. Licensed under Public Domain via Wikimedia Commons - https://commons.wikimedia.org/wiki/File:Albert_Einstein_1947.jpg#/media/File:Albert_Einstein_1947.jpg; P57 (top) © Iakov Filimonov / Shutterstock.com; P64 © BSIP/Universal Images Group/Getty Images; P66 © Ted Russell/The LIFE Images Collection/Getty Images; P72 © Central Press/Hulton Archive/Getty Images; P79 (top) © AFP/Getty Images; P82 (top) © Roberto Machado Noa/LightRocket/Getty Images; P83 (bottom) © Boston Globe/Getty Images; P89 (bottom) © Christophe Michot / Shutterstock.com; P92 (bottom) Center building at Saint Elizabeths, August 23, 2006 by User:Tomf688 - User:Tomf688. Licensed under CC BY-SA 2.5 via Wikimedia Commons - https://commons.wikimedia.org/wiki/File:Center_building_at_Saint_Elizabeths,_August_23,_2006.jpg#/media/File:Center_building_at_Saint_Elizabeths,_August_23,_2006.jpg; P96 © BSIP/Universal Images Group/Getty Images; P101 © National Public Radio; P102 (bottom) © Martin Good / Shutterstock.com; P107 © Leonard Zhukovsky / Shutterstock.com; P108 © David Montgomery/Getty Images; P122 "Alan Baddeley" by from Alan Baddeley - from Alan Baddeley. Licensed under CC BY-SA 3.0 via Wikimedia Commons - https://commons.wikimedia.org/wiki/File:Alan_Baddeley.jpg#/media/File:Alan_Baddeley.jpg; P124 Photograph of Henry Molaison by Jenni Ogden, author of Trouble In Mind: Stories from a neuropsychologist's casebook. OUP, New York, 2012. Reproduced with permission from Jenni Ogden; P127 Photograph of lab from Brewer, W.F. and Treyens, J.C. (1981). Role of schemata in memory for places. Cognitive Psychology, 13, 207–230. Reprinted with permission from AAAS. P128 (bottom) © The Washington Post/Getty Images; P140 (top) "Elizabeth Loftus-TAM 9-July 201,1" by BDEngler - Own work. Licensed under CC BY-SA 3.0 via Wikimedia Commons - https://commons.wikimedia.org/wiki/File:Elizabeth_Loftus-TAM_9-July_2011.JPG#/media/File:Elizabeth_Loftus-TAM_9-July_2011.JPG; P141 © Weegee(Arthur Fellig)/International Center of Photography/Getty Images; P144 © Pool/Getty Images News; P149 (bottom) © EQRoy / Shutterstock.com; P157 © erichon / Shutterstock.com; P162 (top) © Toronto Star Archives/Toronto Star/Getty Images; P183 (top) © Science & Society Picture Library/SSPL/Getty Images; P186 © Nina Leen/The LIFE Picture Collection/Getty Images; P194 (bottom) © Science & Society Picture Library/SSPL/Getty Images; P195 (bottom) © Evening Standard/Hulton Archive/Getty Images; P228 © Archive Photos/Moviepix/Getty Images; P259 (middle) Mond-vergleich. Licensed under Public Domain via Wikimedia Commons - https://commons.wikimedia.org/wiki/File:Mond-vergleich.svg#/media/File:Mond-vergleich.svg; P280 (middle) Asch conformity 1955 by Source (WP:NFCC#4). Licensed under Fair use via Wikipedia - https://en.wikipedia.org/wiki/File:Asch_conformity_1955.jpg#/media/File:Asch_conformity_1955.jpg; P281 Asch experiment by Fred the Oyster. Licensed under GFDL via Wikimedia Commons - https://commons.wikimedia.org/wiki/File:Asch_experiment.svg#/media/File:Asch_experiment.svg; P286 (top) © Lisa Maree Williams/Getty Images News; P297 (top) © Photofusion/Universal Images Group/Getty Images; P297 (middle) © Sahm Doherty/The LIFE Images Collection/Getty Images; P297 (bottom) Thugs Blinding and Mutilating Traveller by Unknown artist, 1829–1840. - Scanned from plate between pages 80 and 81 of Peers, Douglas M. (2006). India under colonial rule: 1700-1885. Pearson Education. ISBN 978-0-582-31738-3. Retrieved 31 August 2011.. From the British Library, Add 41300, c5575-05. Licensed under Public Domain via Wikipedia - https://en.wikipedia.org/wiki/File:Thugs_Blinding_and_Mutilating_Traveller.JPG/media/File:Thugs_Blinding_and_Mutilating_Traveller.JPG; P298 © The Washington Post/Getty Images; P299 © Tony Linck/The LIFE Picture Collection/Getty Images; P306 (bottom) Terrence Spencer/The LIFE Picture Collection/Getty Images; P307 (top) FOX/FOX Image Collection/Getty Images; P310 (top) © David M. Benett/Getty Images Entertainment/Getty Images; P310 (middle) © NICHOLAS KAMM/AFP/Getty Images; P310 (bottom) © Christian Marquardt/Getty Images News; P311 (bottom) © Matt Cardy/Getty Images News; P315 (middle) © Becker/Hulton Archive/Getty Images; P315 (bottom) © Photo 12/Universal Images Group/Getty Images; P317 (top) "Henri Tajfel" by European Association of Social Psychologie - www.easp.eu/_img/pics/persons/tajfel.jpg. Licensed under CC BY 3.0 via Wikimedia Commons - https://commons.wikimedia.org/wiki/File:Henri_Tajfel.jpg#/media/File:Henri_Tajfel.jpg; P317 (middle) © DEA / G. NIMATALLAH/De Agostini/Getty Images; P317 (bottom) © DEA / E. LESSING/De Agostini/Getty Images; P318 (top) © Matt Cardy/Getty Images; P318 (bottom) © Aspen Photo / Shutterstock.com; P321 (top) © Paul Schutzer/The LIFE Premium Collection/Getty Images; P324 © ullstein bild/Getty Images; P329 © Clive Brunskill/Getty Images Sport; P332 Photographs from key study reproduced with permission from Paul Ekman, Ph.D./ Paul Ekman Group, LLC ; P336 Photographs from key study from Meltzoff, A.N. and Moore, M.K. (1977). Imitation of facial and manual gestures by human neonates. Science, 198, 75–78. Reprinted with permission from AAAS; P339 © Apic/Getty Images; P342 (top) © Stefano Tinti / Shutterstock.com; P343 (middle) "Kismet robot 20051016". Licensed under CC BY-SA 2.5 via Wikimedia Commons - https://commons.wikimedia.org/wiki/File:Kismet_robot_20051016.jpg#/media/File:Kismet_robot_20051016.jpg; P343 (bottom) YOSHIKAZU TSUNO/AFP/Getty Images; P362 © Nina Leen/The LIFE Picture Collection/Getty Images; P365 (bottom) Expect Respect tookit cover reproduced with permission from Women's Aid; P367 Photograph of John reproduced with permission from Robertson Film.

All other images © Shutterstock.com or public domain.

Whilst every effort has been made to trace the copyright holders, in cases where this has been unsuccessful, or if any have inadvertently been overlooked, the Publishers would gladly receive any information enabling them to rectify any error or omission at the first opportunity.